A History of Cape Elizabeth Maine

William B. Jordan, Jr.

HERITAGE BOOKS
2014

HERITAGE BOOKS
AN IMPRINT OF HERITAGE BOOKS, INC.

Books, CDs, and more—Worldwide

For our listing of thousands of titles see our website
at
www.HeritageBooks.com

Published 2014 by
HERITAGE BOOKS, INC.
Publishing Division
5810 Ruatan Street
Berwyn Heights, Md. 20740

Copyright © 1965 William B. Jordan, Jr.

Heritage Books by the author:
Burial Records, 1717–1962, of the Eastern Cemetery, Portland, Maine
Burial Records, 1811–1980 of the Western Cemetery in Portland, Maine
A History of Cape Elizabeth, Maine
Index to Portland Newspapers, 1785–1835
CD: *Maine: A History*

All rights reserved. No part of this book may be reproduced or transmitted in any form or by any means, electronic or mechanical, including photocopying, recording or by any information storage and retrieval system without written permission from the author, except for the inclusion of brief quotations in a review.

International Standard Book Numbers
Paperbound: 978-1-55613-043-4
Clothbound: 978-0-7884-9089-7

To Susan

For her limitless encouragement

and understanding

INTRODUCTION

Local history is the warp and woof of state and national history and deserves the hand of the master craftsman. Only a small number of Maine towns have received modern and adequate treatment at the hands of competent historians. Now among them is Cape Elizabeth which this year is observing its bicentennial.

William B. Jordan, Jr., a native son, first attracted my attention as an undergraduate at the University of Maine where he excelled in the techniques of historical research and particularly as they applied to the history of Maine. As a graduate student he was my advisee and wrote his master's thesis on Cape Elizabeth's early history. I regard this thesis as one of the finest of over sixty which were written under my direction and I urged him to extend his research to other facets of Cape history with the view to ultimate publication. This he has done and now Cape Elizabeth boosts one of the most comprehensive Maine town histories.

Mr. Jordan has made superb use of official records of the town and its various organizations, the Portland newspapers and the manuscript collections of the Maine Historical Society and other libraries. Particular mention should be made of the Willis papers and the Benjamin Woodbury collection. He has also uncovered many hitherto unpublished illustrations.

The coverage is all encompassing, from the *Cabo de muchas islas* of the 1500's to the present-day Portland suburb, dealing with political, economic, religious, social, and cultural facets of the community's life. It takes the reader from Walter Bagnall's days on Richmond's Island, through the harrowing experiences of John Winter and the Reverend Robert Jordan in their struggle for control of the Casco Bay area with George Cleaves, through the terrible Indian Wars (1675-1763), the Revolutionary War, the War of 1812, and the Civil War, the early beginnings and growth (and sometimes death) of churches, schools, and many fraternal and social organizations. It deals with fishing, shipbuilding, lumbering, fortifications and military companies, farming, ferries and bridges, breweries, brickyards, kerosene works, the rolling mill, the water company, and other local businesses. Of special interest and significance are those chapters dealing with shipbuilding and shipwrecks and Cape Elizabeth as a watering place and summer resort.

It is a work of which Cape Elizabeth and Mr. Jordan should both be very proud and it will serve as a model for those who seek to redeem their town's history from oblivion or misrepresentation. I am proud to commend it to the general public and the history profession.

Dr. Robert M. York
State Historian and
Dean of Gorham State
College.

Gorham, Maine.
14 July 1965.

PREFACE

It has often been said that preoccupation with local history is an infectious, and generally incurable, disease. As the author of this work, I will gladly and enthusiastically testify to the truthfulness of this assertion. In my own case I can identify with ease, as the sources of this affliction, three men who have had a deep and profound influence in making the study of Maine's local history so much a part of my life.

When I was very young my maternal grandfather, George H. Weeks, provided the first exposure by relating to me the adventures of my colonial ancestors who helped to settle what is now the Greater Portland area. In addition he introduced me to the writings of two highly articulate local historians, William Willis and William Goold.

As my interest in the Portland area broadened, I came in contact with the dean of antiquarian bookmen in Maine, Francis M. O'Brien. Utilizing his extraordinary knowledge of local history source material, he encouraged and directed my exploratory studies. With his unique assistance, I was able to accumulate many of the standard works so necessary to an understanding of Maine history.

The infection became absolutely incurable, when, as a graduate student at the University of Maine, I had the honor to study under the guidance of Dr. Robert M. York. In his official capacity as a professor of American history he provided me with a new viewpoint that put state and nation in proper perspective. At his urging I decided to capitalize upon my interest in Cape Elizabeth and prepare a history of the town as a thesis for the degree of Master of Arts in History. The results were four chapters that are now incorporated in the first three chapters of this book.

In writing this history of Cape Elizabeth I made a few discoveries that may be of some small benefit to a prospective local historian. Although the secondary sources listed in the bibliography were of immense value in providing a general background, the most fruitful fund of information were the newspapers of Portland. Here was social and political history that could not be obtained, in most cases, from any other source, material that was quite literally the life blood of local history. Second only to the newspapers were the official records of the town that are fortunately complete and well preserved.

A great disappointment, and the cause of considerable disillusionment, were many of the local histories written in the late years of the nineteenth century and the early years of this century. Unfortunatly, a great many of the more popular works are studies in historical inaccuracy. With a grand disregard for the validity of their sources, many of these pseudo-historians perpetuated myths, traditions, and distortions of fact that pass for local history. A case in point is that nebulous relic of the colonial era, the King's Highway. From the records that survive, these Great Roads, as they were called, were required by law but seldom existed in areas as wild as that north of Wells. As late as 1673, there was no road whatsoever between Wells and Falmouth. If any common "highway" existed, it could have been nothing more than a crude trace, negotiable only on foot or horseback. The absence of any official map showing a clearly defined road has not prevented various individuals from plotting a "King's Highway" where none existed, and embellishing it with suitable folklore.

Typical of these compilers of fact and fancy was Stephen P. Mayberry who spent most of his adult life in the Knightville section of what is now the city of South Portland. A frequent contributor of historical articles to the local newspapers, he became something of an "authority" on the early days of Cape Elizabeth. Much of his material is unverifiable conjecture, identifiable as the product of a lively imagination. When he died 25 May 1907 at the age of seventy-five, most of his papers were deposited in the Maine Historical Society. In the years that followed, several local historians utilized Mayberry's jottings as an unimpeachable source, thereby compromising the value of their work. He was a specialist in untrustworthy traditions of doubtful events.

Another subject of considerable interest to the undiscerning local historian is the aura of refinement and affluence that they attach to the seventeenth and eighteenth century settlers in such rural areas as Cape Elizabeth. With extraordinarily few exceptions they were crude and untutored products of a harsh environment. In reality, the life of these early days was plebian and prosiac, filled with danger, hardship, and slavish toil. The dry and unpoetic character of such an existence is often glossed over by the romanticist. Essentially, the history of these early years is a history of work with very meager returns. In speaking of New England in general, James Russell Lowell could have been speaking specifically of Cape Elizabeth when he said, "so much downright work was perhaps never wrought on the earth's surface in the same space of time . . . ." This struggle for a bare existence produced very little that could be called tangible wealth. Under the circumstances it is not a subject of amazement that very little has survived. The absence of any substantial homes dating from these centuries, to say nothing of the total lack of fine heirloom furnishings, is therefore easy to understand and appreciate. The early Cape Elizabeth yankees left a legacy of temperament rather than a legacy of personal wealth.

Hoping to profit from the mistakes of earlier historians, I have tried to be as accurate and precise as possible. However, I fully realize that mistakes will undoubtedly be found. In such an instance I would consider it a great favor if they could be brought to my attention with corroborating evidence. I have tried to view the history of Cape Elizabeth impartially, tracing its development without rancor or bias. If this narrative occasionally appears to the contrary, and I am sure there must be instances, it is not intentional.

In collecting and collating material for this history, I have received courteous treatment and generous aid from nearly all to whom I have applied, and with pleasure acknowledge the valuable assistance given by many. While I cannot mention them all, I feel under special obligation to Marion B. Rowe and E. Marie Estes of the Maine Historical Society Library; to Dr. Robert M. York, indefatigable historian of the state of Maine; to my friend and critic of many years, Francis M. O'Brien; and to George S. Jackson, Professor of English at the University of Maine, for his invaluable advice and technical assistance.

> WILLIAM B. JORDAN, JR.
> Portland, Maine

14 April, 1965.

CONTENTS

	Page
EXPLORATION AND EARLY SETTLERS	1
INDIAN WARS, INCORPORATION, AND THE REVOLUTION	27
EARLY DEVELOPMENTS	56
PAINS OF URBANIZATION	87
WATERING PLACES	129
SHIPS AND THE SEA	165
PERILOUS SHORES	223
MIND AND SOUL	256
SUBURBIA-BY-THE-SEA	347
APPENDIXES	359

CHAPTER I

EXPLORATION AND EARLY SETTLERS

Geographical Cape Elizabeth in its configuration, elevation, and appearance, is in many respects one of the most remarkable points on the coast of Maine. It juts out several miles beyond the general line of the coast and marks a distinct change in the direction of the coast line. As far as the Cape the coast runs northerly and beyond it, turns more to the eastward. It also marks a distinct change in the general nature of the coast. To the south of of Cape Elizabeth, long, low, sandy beaches are often found among the rocky necks and spits; however, to the northeast, these sandy beaches generally disappear, and it becomes predominantly rocky cliffs, necks and islands. Due to this geographical phenomena, it has been ascertained that Cape Elizabeth is the headland that the Spaniards called *Cabo de muchas islas,* "cape of the many islands."

The sixteenth century Spanish map-maker, Diego Ribero, compiled a map in 1529 on which he placed *Cabo de muchas islas.* This is the earliest existing map on which it appears. It was also included on the map compiled by the Spaniard Alonso de Chaves in 1536. A description of this map, written in 1556, places *Cabo de muchas islas* about twenty leagues from what is now Penobscot Bay and at the entrance to a bay filled with many islands, hence the name. Therefore, it can readily be seen that so prominent a landmark as Cape Elizabeth could not be left blank on a navigational chart and through necessity a name was affixed from its geographical location.

The earliest detailed description that we have of the area was written by Samuel de Champlain during a voyage of exploration in 1604 with Sieur de Monts. They passed Casco Bay, which Champlain described as full of islands, without entering it, and came upon the headland of Cape Elizabeth on the 8th of July. The next day they proceeded along the coast and anchored inside of what is now Stratton Island, just off Pine Point. Here they held a friendly conference with a large group of Indians, and from this point they made a visit to an island ". . . which is very beautiful in view of what it produces; for it has fine oaks and nut-trees, the soil cleared up, and many vineyards bearing beautiful grapes in their season, which were the first we had seen on all these coasts from the Cap de la Heve. We named it Isle de Bacchus." One can, without too much difficulty, recognize by this description the Richmond's Island of today. The fine oaks, nut-trees and luxuriant vines have vanished but its location and size proves beyond the shadow of a doubt that this is Champlain's "Isle de Bacchus." Champlain revisited the island late in September of the same year and ". . . saw at the island of Bacchus some grapes which were ripe and very good and some others not yet ripe, as fine as those in France; and I am sure that, if they were cultivated, they could produce good wine."

On August 28th of the year 1607 Captain Raleigh Gilbert of the Sagadahoc Colony sailed with fourteen others on a voyage of discovery to the westward. That day they sailed "by many gallant islands" and that night anchored

. . . under the headland Semeamis whear we found the Land to be most fertill the trees growinge thear doeth exceed for goodnesse & Length being the most part of them ocke and wallnutt growing a greatt space assoonder one from the other as in our parks in England and no thickett growinge under them. Hear wee also found a gallant place to fortefye whom Nattuer her Selffe hath already framed without the hand of man with a runynge stream of water hard adjoyninge under the foot it.

From Gilbert's description it is evident that he bypassed Casco Bay and encountered Cape Elizabeth, not far from the present Portland Head Light. His anchorage was in all probability Ship Cove which lies less than a mile north of the light. Semeamis, the name Gilbert applied to the headland of Cape Elizabeth was undoubtedly of Indian origin, the meaning of which is uncertain.

The following day they "rowed to the westward" against an adverse wind which blew so hard that they were forced to "remain under an island 2 Leags from the place we remayned the night before." This island was of course Richmond's Island which is approximately six miles, or the two leagues of their estimate, from Ship Cove. From here they sailed westward another day and then returned to the Sagadahoc Colony.

In 1614 there arrived on the coast the intrepid explorer Captain John Smith. Although he did not venture ashore in the vicinity of Cape Elizabeth he recorded this prominent headland on his charts. When he returned to England, Smith presented his map to Charles, Prince of Wales, and later King

Charles I. This map of 1614 contained for the first time the geographical location of Cape Elizabeth. It is not known whether Prince Charles or Captain Smith bestowed the name but it is fairly certain that was in honor of Charles' sister, Elizabeth, later Queen of Bohemia.

Richmond's Island and Cape Elizabeth probably received other visitors in these early years but the accounts of their voyages have so far escaped detection. However, it was about this time that Dutch navigators referred to Richmond's Island as "Wingardes Eylant" along with the Italians who referred to its as "Wingert" Island. These names were apparently derived from the German word "Weingut" meaning "vineyard." If Champlain's account can be taken as valid these names were anything but misnomers.

The next observer to appear on the scene was Christopher Levett who arrived late in the summer of 1623. He found Richmond's Island to be uninhabited by Europeans, but he described the locality as an ideal resort for fishermen. His statement was that "There hath been more fish taken within two leagues of this place this year than in any other in the land."

Fishing vessels must have made periodic trips to the island. This is borne out by the fact that on April 11, 1627, a John Burgess, master of the fishing vessel *Annes*, hailing from Westleigh, England, made his will while lying sick "in Richmond's Island In New England." The will was probated May 24, 1628, and disposed of considerable marine equipment.

Sometime during the year 1627 the island's first permanent settler appeared in the person of one Walter Bagnall. It has been suggested that he was one of Thomas Morton's "merry men" and later banished from Mount Wollaston, now Braintree, Massachusetts. The death of Bagnall on October 3, 1631, was described by Governor Winthrop as a murder committed by an ". . . Indian sagamore called Squidrayset, and his company, upon one Walter Bagnall, called Great Walt, and one John P—, who kept with him. They, having killed them, burnt the house over them and carried away their guns and whatelse they liked." His violent end was apparently not unwarranted for Winthrop further states that "This Bagnall was sometimes servant to one in the bay, and these three years had dwelt alone in the said isle, and had gotten about 400 p. most in goods. He was a wicked fellow, and had much wronged the Indians." The Indian sagamore Squidrayset, according to Levett, was living at the first fall on the Presumpscot River in 1624.

Thomas Morton, in alluding to Bagnall's demise, remarked "a servant of mine in 5 yeares was thought to have 1000 p. in ready gold gotten by beaver when hee dyed; whatsover became of it . . ." This perhaps bears out the conjecture that Bagnall was a member of Morton's company at Merry Mount.

The companion of Bagnall referred to by Governor Winthrop was without a doubt John Peverly, whose name is preserved in a list of indentured servants sent to New England by Captain John Mason between 1622 and 1635. The first of these colonists settled in Massachusetts.

On October 22nd Governor Winthrop received the news of this massacre from Captain Thomas Wiggin of Piscataqua, "who persuaded the Governor to send twenty men presently to take revenge; but the Governor, advising with some of the council, thought best to sit still awile, partly because he heard that Capt. (Walter) Neale, etc., were gone after them, and partly because of the season, it being then frost and snow, and want of boats fit for that expedition."

Bagnall's death was finally investigated some fifteen months later. At that time, pirates under the leadership of one Dixie Bull, were ravaging the fishing and trading stations about Pemaquid and the Penobscot, and Captain Walter Neale had dispatched a few vessels and men to assist the colonists. Governor Winthrop says of the expedition that ". . . about the beginning of this month of January (1633) the pinances which went after the pirates returned, the cold being so great as they could not pursue them, but, in their return they hanged up at Richmond's Isle an Indian, one Black Will, one of those who had there murdered Walter Bagnall." It so appears that by this summary procedure, the guilty Squidrayset got away unharmed, while one of his followers was hanged as an atonement for the crime. A bit of irony flavors the untimely end of "Great Walt" in that on the 2nd of December 1631, he was granted a patent to Richmond's Island.

There has always been some conjecture as to what became of the gold that Bagnall had accumulated during his residency of three years. It has been asserted that the Indians took what they wanted, but the distribution of the money by them was never detected by the English traders. Morton assumed that it was confiscated by the Massachusetts authorities, but disposed of the mystery with the expression, "what-soever became of it." In 1855, however, an earthen jug, containing a signet ring, with the initials "G. V." engraved upon it, and assorted coins, was uncovered on a northerly slope of the island during the spring plowing. The historian, William Willis, attributes the treasure trove to Bagnall as part of his illgotten gains.

Before taking up the various grants of this early period a general description of the grantors is in order. Influenced largely by the enthusiastic reports by Captain George Weymouth of his voyage to the New England Coast in 1605, a joint stock company was formed at Plymouth, England, on application of Sir Ferdinando Gorges and others, for the express purpose of establishing colonies in America. This had two distinct branches; one made its headquarters in London and the other at Plymouth, the official home of Gorges. The Virginia or London Company, controlled the area from Cape Fear to the mouth of the Potomac, and the North Virginia or Plymouth Company, later called the New England Company after Captain John Smith reported on his exploration, had jurisdiction over the section from Long Island to Nova Scotia. The strip in between from the Potomac to the Hudson was available to both companies. In the renewal of the charter in 1609 control was extended from ocean to ocean.

The most active promoter of the Plymouth Company was Sir Ferdinando Gorges, and associated with him were such men as John Popham and Raleigh Gilbert. Gorges was commander of the harbor defenses at Plymouth, where, amid the pressure of official duties both public and private, he never faltered in his plans for the settlement of New England. In 1620 a controversy broke out between the London and Plymouth Companies over their respective limits of authority that soon involved Sir Ferdinando in the bitter struggle for power between King James I and Parliament. Before the disagreement was settled King James dissolved Parliament and by "royal order continued" the Plymouth Council for New England with all its powers. Gorges was the victor but he had also become identified with the insolent tyranny of James I.

On the 3rd of December 1620, pursuant to an order by the King in Council, a charter was issued to the company. It was named "The Council Established in Plymouth, in the County of Devon, for the Planting, Ruling, Ordering, and Governing of New England in America" and constituted a complete monopoly. Among other things it could establish all forms and regulations of government, not only within its precincts, but upon ocean travel to and from the colony. New England commerce of every kind was controlled by their managers with rights transferrable. Even the fisheries could not be operated without their consent. Gorges was now the most active and influential member of the Council for New England, or as it was more commonly called, the Plymouth Council.

The first grant with reference to the present town of Cape Elizabeth was issued on the 10th of August, 1622, and was the second grant made by the Plymouth Council. The Grantees were Sir Ferdinando Gorges and Captain John Mason, both members of the Plymouth Council. They received "all that part of the mainland in New England lying upon the sea coast betwixt the rivers of Merrimach and Sagadahock and to the furtherest heads of the said rivers and so forward up into the new land westward until three score miles be finished from the first entrance of the afoersaid rivers and half way over, that is to say to the midst of the said two rivers . . . said portions of lands with the appurtenances the said Sir Ferdinando Gorges and Captain John Mason, with the consent of the president and council intend to name the Province of Maine." It is interesting to note that the name "Province of Maine" is first used in this document. The grantees were authorized to "established such government in the said portions of lands and island . . . as shall be agreeable as near as may be to the laws and customs of the realm of England.

Seven years later, on the 7th of November, 1629, by mutual agreement Gorges and Mason divided the Province of Maine. Mason received "all that part of the main land in New England, lying upon the sea coast, beginning from the middle part of Merrimack river and from thence to proceed northwards along the sea coast to Piscataqua river, and so forwards up within the said river, and to the furthest head therof, and from thence to proceed northwards along the sea coast to Piscataqua river, and so forwards up within the said river, and to the furthest head therof, and from thence northwestwards until three score miles be finished from the first entrance to Piscataqua river, and also from Merrimack through the said river, and to the furthest head therof, and so forwards up into the land westwards until three score miles be finished; and from thence to cross over all islands and islets within five leagues distance from the premises, and abutting upon the same or any part of parcel thereof." With the consent of the Plymouth Council, Mason bestowed upon this tract of land the name, New Hampshire. The remaining section of the original grant, specifically the territory between the Piscataqua and the Sagadahoc, extending from the sea coast inland as far as is stated in Mason's grant, remained in Gorges possession and retained the name Province of Maine.

The movement towards the coast of Maine was rapidly increasing as is shown by the number of grants issued by the Plymouth Council. Six separate patents were granted in 1630 and one in particular, the Lygonia or Plough Patent, had a direct bearing upon Cape Elizabeth. It was issued the 26th of June, 1630, but the original document, so far as is known, has not been preserved. Governor Winthrop mentioned this particular patent in his journal under the date 6 July, 1631: "A small ship of sixty tons arrived at Natascott (Nantasket), Mr. Graves, Master. She brought ten passengers from London. They came with a patent for Sagadahoc, but not liking the place came hither . . . These were the company called the Husbandmen and their ship called the Plough. Most of them proved Familists and vanished away."

With a singular disregard for the fact that in 1629 Gorges had been granted the territory between the Piscataqua and the Sagadahoc the Plymouth Council now took from the Gorges grant a tract of land forty miles square and bestowed it upon this company of Husbandmen. However, this action could not have been without his knowledge as he was still an influential member of the Plymouth Council.

Late in 1630 there appeared at Spurwink River, two men who were to play leading roles in the early history of that area. They were Richard Tucker and George Cleaves. Of Tucker's place of origin we know very little other than that he probably came from Devon, England. Not much more is known about Cleaves except that he made his way to the Maine coast from Plymouth, England, bringing with him his wife and daughter.

The next pertinent grant made by the Plymouth Council was dated the 4th of November, 1631, with one Richard Bradshaw, the grantee. It consisted of fifteen hundred acres "above the head of Pashippscot (Pejepscot) on the north side thereof . . . The consideration for and in respect of the charge he had been at in his liveing there some yeares before . . . he purposed to settle himselfe there with othr his frinds & srvants . . ." This extract is the only evidence there is that Bradshaw ever lived at Pejepscot. It is known that after his arrival upon the Maine coast he spent some time in seeking a favorable location for settlement. This he found on the southern shore of Cape Elizabeth just east of the Spurwink river. Bradshaw lost no time in obtaining from Captain Walter Neale, Governor of the Province of Maine, a "delivery" of this tract of land giving him the right to claim it by pre-emption and occupation.

Without a doubt it was this tract at Spurwink that he sought to obtain from the Plymouth Council and that an error was made by carelessly inserting "Pashippscot" for Spurwink in the recording of the grant. As far as this area is concerned Bradshaw's efforts were a failure. Richard Tucker purchased the pre-emption right and allied himself with George Cleaves who was under the delusion that he had a valid claim to the same territory by virtue of a promise made to him by Sir Ferdinando Gorges before he left England concerning a grand of land. Their collective plans were doomed however, from the beginning, as this much coveted area had already been granted to others.

This very important patent was issued on the 1st of December, 1631 to Robert Trelawny and Moses Goodyear, prominent merchants of Plymouth, England. Neither of the two men ever visited the New England coast, but they were acquainted with men who had, especially Thomas Cammock of Black Point. When he was in England securing his grant, in 1631, he visited Robert Trelawny. Apparently his description of Cape Elizabeth and Richmond's Island were vivid enough to convince the two merchants that here was the fishing and trading station they had been seeking.

The grant to Trelawny and Goodyear included all the territory between the grant made to Cammock and ". . . the Bay and River of Casco, extending and to be extended Northwards into the Maine land so far as the limits and bounds of the lands granted to the said Captaine Thomas Cammock . . . with liberty to erect and maintain stages and places for preserving fish . . . in, upon and neere the Ilsland comonly called Richmonds Ileland, and all other Ilelands within or neere the limits and bounds aforesaid which are not formerly granted to the said Captaine Thomas Camock . . ."

It is to be noted that only the use of Richmond's Island was granted to Trelawny and Goodyear in the patent. The reason for this is probably that they had already committed themselves as to the disposition of Richmond's Island. On the 2nd of December 1631, the day following the Trelawny and Goodyear patent, the Plymouth Council granted to Walter Bagnall Richmond's Island and fifteen hundred acres on the mainland. His title, of course, soon lapsed leaving the two Plymouth merchants in undisputed possession. An interesting legend has flourished for many years concerning the original patent document granted to Trelawny and Goodyear. The traditional story is that the wife of Robert Jordan, Jr., needing some paper to keep her pastry from burning, took this document from a chest of papers and used it for that purpose, thus destroying it. Fortunately, this intriguing bit of history is quite erroneous, as the document in question is now a treasured possession of the Maine Historical Society.

John Winter, factor for Trelawny and Goodyear, arrived at Richmond's Island the 17th of April, 1632. Equipped with the power of attorney he set to work to consolidate the holdings of his employers and immediately secured the services of Richard Vines to establish possession of the territory. However, it was not until the 21st of July that formal proceedings were consumated. Almost at once, Winter served an eviction notice on George Cleaves and Richard Tucker, thereby ordering them off the land they had occupied in 1630. He obdurately denied the legality of Neale's delivery to Tucker. As to Cleaves' assertion of a pre-emption right, because of a promise made by Gorges, he simply refused to consider it, maintaining that it was without foundation as Cleaves could show neither where nor when the promise was made.

According to Trelawny permission was granted to Cleaves and Tucker "to injoye a first & second crop" before departing. Winter also informed Cleaves that he was welcome to "become a tenant to . . . Robert Trelawny . . . in some other parte of his land" . . . under such conditions as Trelawny might offer. To this Cleaves replied "that he would be tenant to never a man in New England."

With the preliminary work at Richmond's Island accomplished Winter prepared to return to England. Trelawny and Goodyear were now in possession of their lands and had gained valuable information as to the men and materials needed for the enterprise they had in mind. He sailed for Plymouth early in the fall apparently satisfied with his accomplishments.

On the 2nd of March 1633 Winter reappeared at Richmond's Island and made immediate preparations for the removal elsewhere of Cleaves and Tucker. He lent them a boat to carry their household goods and they embarked posthaste. The group consisted of Tucker, Cleaves, Cleaves' wife and daughter and a colored servant Oliver Weeks. Winter lost the boat when Cleaves wrecked it losing all his effects in the process. It was due to carelessness on the part of Cleaves in not unloading his goods at once after he selected a location on Falmouth Neck. This was the beginning of a life-long feud between the two men that grew in bitterness as the years passed.

During the first year at Richmond's Island, Winter was able

to send back to England in the ship *Welcome* 13 hogshead of fish oil and about 61,000 dried and salted fish. In June of 1634 he reported that he had built the July previous a substantial two-story house 40 feet long by 18 feet wide. It was equipped with a large fireplace spacious enough to carry on brewing, baking and boiling operations all at the same time. In an adjoining house was a kitchen, sieves, mill and mortar for the processing of corn meal. The second story consisted of two chambers, one containing sleeping accommodations for his men, the other sails and dry goods. The sleeping chambers must have been very spacious as each man had his own close-boarded bunk and at one time there were forty-seven men living there. He also built a store-house capable of storing 18 to 20 tons of goods in casks, with a combination kitchen and dining hall for his men. On the mainland he settled a man in Cleaves' old house, added a shelter for pigs, and fenced in 4 or 5 acres for corn and pumpkins. The fence must have been a stockade as it consisted of six foot poles set upright in the ground. Also situated on the mainland were his pigs numbering about seventy. They apparently ran wild rooting for clams and feeding on acorns in season. No mention is made of any other live stock at this early date. Winter quickly made use of the fertile soil. He soon had extensive gardens under cultivation and wrote to Trelawny that "there is nothing that we set or sow but doth prove very well. We have proved divers sorts as barley, peas, pumpkins, carrots, parsnips, onions, garlic, radishes, turnip, cabbage, lettuce, parsley, melongs, and I think so will other sorts of herbs if they be set or sown." This revealing letter was written in the fall of 1634 and certainly displays unusual forethought on Winter's part.

The Indian trade did not turn out to be very profitable. In the year that he had been at Richmond's Island he had received only three skins and that was in trade for some liquor. He did, however, do a little better by sending a man inland. At first he tried using various articles of clothing, but as it did not prove profitable enough he changed to beads by which he realized six and a half pounds of beaver.

As he manufactured much of his own strong drink his trade in this item was particularly remunerative. Not only did he sell it to the Indians but visiting fishermen spent a large part of their earnings on it, thus making its manufacture a very profitable venture.

The ship *Hunter* brought in a tremendous amount of supplies and equipment from England that first year. Included were many and varied food stuffs, clothing, naval supplies, weapons, candles, wine, and a myriad of incidentals. By the end of the year 1634 the trading station was more than a going concern, but Winter added the cautious note that ". . . the most parts of the dwellers heare ar good byers by bad payers."

Late in 1634 the inhabitants constructed a 15 foot palisade around the buildings and mounted what ordnance they had on platforms within the walls. As the year closed the ship *James* arrived with more stores and the crops were harvested. The fishing had not been very good but the beaver trade with the Indians was picking up despite the large number of persons engaged in it. The supply of fish was large enough, however, to send a cargo out in the *James*.

The ship *Speedwell* arrived in the summer of 1635 bringing with it, among other things, some live sheep, the beginning of a badly-needed flock. Also in the ship was Narius Hawkins and a new company of men to replace the old one that was returning to England. When the *Speedwell* sailed for England, Winter was aboard, along with a substantial cargo of fish. Hawkins was left in charge of the station.

An interesting commentary on the Richmond's Island settlement was written during August of this year. The Reverend Richard Mather, an ancestor of the famous Mather family, called at the island on his way westward and recorded in his famous journal the following account for the 10th of August.

> Monday morning, the wind still continuing against us, we came to anchor at Richmond's Island, in the east part of New England; the Bay of Massachusetts, whither we were bound partly because of necessity they must come to anchor to take in a pilot somewhere before we came to the Bay, by reason that our pilot knew the harbours no further but to the Isle of Shoals. When we came within sight of the island, the planters there (or rather fishers, for their chief employment was fishing) being but two families, and about forty persons, were sore afraid of us, doubting lest we had been French, came to pillage the island, as Penobscots had been served by them about ten days before. When we were come to anchor, and their fear was past, they came some of them aboard to us in their schallops, and we went some of us ashore into the island, to look for fresh water and grass for our cattle; and the planters bade us welcome, and gave some of us courteous entertainment in their houses.

On the 12th they sailed from the island for Massachusetts Bay. As Winter was on his way to England at the time they were undoubtedly greeted by his second in command, Narias Hawkins.

Another visitor during Winter's absence was Edward Trelawny, brother of Robert, who appears to have held some position of authority in regard to the plantation at Richmond's Island. The letters he sent back to his brother deal rather largely with business matters. He did, however, recommend that Robert obtain the services of "... a religious, able minister for the plantation." This appeal probably resulted in the sending of the Reverend Richard Gibson in 1636. Edward departed from Richmond's Island some time previous to the return of John Winter.

The year 1635 proved to be an important one in England. The direct control of New England now come under the despotic guidance of the new King Charles I. Few of the Plymouth Council members still attended its meetings, but these few drew up a plan to surrender their charter with the understanding that the territory under their collective control should be divided among themselves respectively, a scheme suggestive of colossal self-interest. Consequently on the 7th of June 1635 the Plymouth Council or the Council for New England, as it is sometimes called, surrendered its charter to the King. The Commissioners of American Plantations were appointed to take charge of colonial affairs and New England was divided into royal provinces. Sir Ferdinando's region between the Piscataqua and the Kennebec was named New Somersetshire. Captain William Gorges was sent over in 1636 as Deputy Governor to replace Richard Vines who had been acting in the capacity of Steward General since 1634. Captain Gorges, with six commissioners, held the first provincial court at Saco in 1636. One of its first acts was to bestow upon Narias Hawkins the power and authority to execute any Indians against whom it was proven that they had killed a pig or pigs belonging to the English.

In this early period the inhabitants of Black Point were loyal to the established Church of England and signs of any dissension among the factions represented in the western colonies were matters of general interest to these eastern settlers. In Massachusetts politics and religion masqueraded under the same banner. The Wheelwright controversy was one in which Massachusetts authorities were fearful of criticism in those neighboring eastern communities where political sentiment was favorable to the Gorges administration. As an illustration, on the 17th of April, 1637, one Edward Winslow reported to Governor John Winthrop that "... the last news is this wherat I am most grieved that all the late differences between Mr. Wheelwright & yorselves in Church & Court are in writing at Richmond's Isle where Turlany showed him (Myles Standish) six sheets of pap full writetn about them ..." The sequel to this dispute was a bloodless one, in which the Wheelwright adherents were deprived of their arms and ammunition and left helpless in case of Indian assault. Fortunately the natives were then at peace with the settlers.

John Winter arrived at Richmond's Island the 24th of May, 1636. Accompanying him was the Anglican clergyman, Richard Gibson, the first of the established church to hold services at Richmond's Island. The ship's cargo included among other things a valuable addition in the form of cattle. One particularly important item that Winter returned with was an additional grant of two thousand acres, from Gorges, as an enlargement of the Trelawny grant towards the Casco River. He was also designated by Gorges as "Governor of Mr. Trelawny's People." These proceedings were too much for George Cleaves, who was living at Machigonne, so he sailed for England to obtain a legal status for his grant from Gorges.

The trade at Richmond's Island had now expanded somewhat and its principal exports were clapboards, pipe-staves, dried or salted fish, fish oil and beaver skins. The major imports, other than the plantation's yearly supplies, consisted chiefly of wine, fruits and other products of Spain and Portugal. These two countries took in trade most of the fish and fish products of the plantation.

The year 1637 saw the return of George Cleaves with a patent from Gorges verifying the title to ". . . a neck of land called by the Indians Machigonne," that he held jointly with Richard Tucker. Despite this patent Winter still considered Cleaves as occupying land that rightfully belonged to Robert Trelawny. This same year, Moses Goodyear, Trelawny's relatively inactive partner, died quietly in Plymouth, England. This left Trelawny as the sole beneficiary of the Richmond's Island Plantation. Winter's wife, and daughter Sarah, arrived in the supply ship *Hercules* sometime in the spring for in his letter dated the 10th of July Mrs. Winter sends her regards to Mrs. Trelawny.

Winter now had six boats in his fishing fleet which he kept at sea as much as possible. His only difficulty was in finding men to handle them. Narias Hawkins had left with his company to fish elsewhere for themselves. The population of the island was about forty-seven persons. The pigs now numbered approximately 100 despite the inroads made by marauding wolves. The cattle and newly arrived goats were doing very well on the island and were increasing fairly rapidly.

On the 10th of June, Winter launched the bark *Richmond,*

of about 30 tons, the first vessel he built at Richmond's Island. Despite the fact that she was completed that year it was impossible for her to sail due to the lack of a suitable master and crew. Consequently, Winter was forced to keep her on an inactive status throughout the following winter. It was not until the 26th of July, 1638, that she sailed on a coasting voyage with a cargo of wine, fish oil and earthenware. Winter had been able, early in that year, to engage Narias Hawkins as master with some of his company making up the crew.

The ship *Fortune* arrived in May of 1638 bearing a cargo of supplies and returned laden with dried fish, three hogsheads of oil and ten hogsheads of peas. This last item seems to indicate that Winter had built up a flourishing money crop of peas.

The other industries of the plantation were yielding substantial returns. The fishing trade was quite extensive consisting of nine boats constantly at sea. Winter hired of Narias Hawkins his two boats, with crews, to augment his own fleet of seven boats. The live stock was also doing well, the only difficulty being in curbing the increasing loss of pigs on the mainland due to large numbers of wolves and bears. Still another sign of prosperity was the laying of a keel for a new ship to have a length (keel) of 50 feet, a beam of 18½ feet, with 4½ feet between the two decks, a forecastle, a quarterdeck, and a 9 foot hold. It can be safely stated that this was the peak year of the Richmond's Island trade and that in the years leading up to Winter's death in 1645 a gradual decline set in that eventually resulted in the collapse of the plantation.

In a letter Winter wrote to Trelawny, dated the 27th of August, 1638, he speaks of purchasing a quantity of goods from one George Richmond of Bandonbridge, Ireland. This gentleman seems to have been the leader of some colonial enterprise which was situated at or near Richmond's Island and employed fishermen and shipbuilders. They departed in a ship of their own construction. This is the only record we have of the man and his colony, but from this brief reference it seems quite plausible that the island bears his name as there is no other Richmond prominent in the history of the area, with the possible exception of the Duke of Richmond. He received a grant of Richmond's Island and some territory on the mainland, the 24th of July, 1622. However, nothing ever materialized and the patent eventually lapsed.

This same year the island was visited by John Josselyn, brother to Henry of Black Point, who recorded in a journal some very interesting observations of the region. He spoke briefly of the topography of Richmond's Island, concluding with the remark that on the sandbar that connects it with the mainland ". . . are found excellent whetstones, and . . . stages for fishermen." However, he is more revealing in his statements regarding the inhabitants. He divided the people into ". . . Magistrates, Husbandmen, or Planters, and fishermen . . ." adding the description that some of the ". . . Magistrates . . be Royalists, the rest perverse Spirits, the like are the planters and fisher, of which some be planters and fishers both, other meer fishers." Of their habits he painted the following picture, "They have a custom of taking tobacco, sleeping at noon, sitting long at meals sometimes four times a day, and now and then drinking a dram of the bottle extraordinarily . . ." Josselyn also wrote extensively on the trade, merchants and various occupations native to the area including much that was of a derogatory nature.

The ship *Hercules* appeared on the 30th of January, 1639, with its usual cargo of supplies for the plantation. She was reloaded with approximately 150,000 dried fish, 19 hogsheads of fish peas, and 5 hogsheads of fish oil. The bark *Richmond* was also in the process of loading, the cargo consisting of pipe-staves. The *Hercules* sailed for Bilbao, Spain on the 17th of July and the *Richmond* departed on the 20th for Plymouth.

Trade was still fairly good at the island. Large amounts of ardent spirits were arriving in practically every vessel and traffic in it continued to be brisk. As money was a great rarity beaver was substituted for currency, providing a stable basis for the existing colonial economic system. However, Winter became dissatisfied with the current price of beaver and instituted a depreciation of its value. This proved to be a serious matter and precipitated a panic, incurring at the same time the wrath of the settlers. He did not escape the ensuing difficulties and was prosecuted the following year for various offenses, the sum of which, to use a modern phrase, was profiteering.

The plantation's livestock was still increasing, despite wolves on the mainland, and the goats were now so numerous that the flock was too large for the island. A small addition was made in the form of three asses. The crops were doing well, consisting largely of English corn, Indian corn, grain, wheat, barley, rye, oats, and peas. Winter had approximately six acres under cultivation, all situated at Spurwink. However, the fishing industry had decreased to the extent that now only six boats were kept at sea. Lastly, work was progressing slowly on the ship.

During this year the Reverend Richard Gibson terminated his services at Richmond's Island as his three-year contract with Robert Trelawny was expiring. His relations with Winter had become somewhat strained due to the fact that the inhabitants had not consulted him about a projected raise in Gibson's wages. Conseqently, he departed for Piscataqua to minister to the needs of the fishing settlement at the Isle of Shoals, late in the summer of 1639.

An inventory that Winter sent to Trelawny during the year yields up some interesting items as to the armament of the plantation. He listed two small cannons with a bore of three and a half inches, one large cannon with a four-inch bore, all three mounted on carriages, one small bore swivel-gun, two salute cannons, a large musket that fired from a worked rest, eight regular muskets, three halberds, four swords, twenty-four cannon balls, eight barshort, musket balls, and a barrel of powder. It was certainly quite a formidable array for a plantation of this size. However, the turbulent nature of the period certainly warranted their presence.

Affairs in England had taken an auspicious turn, for, on the 3rd of April, 1639, Charles I, after four years of evasion and delay granted to Sir Ferdinando Gorges the celebrated charter of the Province or Palatinate of "Mayne." It had arrived almost too late for Gorges was now an old man, but he still had the zeal of youth, and so, side by side with Puritan Massachusetts, he set up the Episcopal Palatinate of Maine. The boundaries were the same as those of the 1635 division.

Under the new powers granted to this independent colony, Gorges proceeded to establish his idea of a model government, the Saxon Palatinate. The Province of Maine was divided into eight bailiwicks, which in turn were subdivided into hundreds, parishes, and tithings. Gorges could personally appoint the clergy and could consecrate any new churches with all their prerogatives according to the ecclesiastical laws of England. He could also pardon offenders, proclaim martial law, and maintain a standing army. A Board of Councillors was soon established, and the freeholders were allowed the privilege of electing eight deputies to sit with them. There was also a Keeper of the Provincial Seal, a Chancellor, a Treasurer, a Marshall of Militia, an Admiral, a Master of Ordnance, and a Secretary. No transfers of land could be made without the express permission of the Council, therefore all holdings were subservient to Gorges as Lord Palatine, and he could grant leasehold estates to be occupied by tenantry.

The old colony New Somersetshire had now become the Province of Maine and William Gorges ceased to be Governor. Sir Ferdinando was still unable to leave England, so he appointed his cousin, Thomas Gorges, Deputy Governor and Keeper of the Provincial Seal. The Deputy Governor arrived early in 1640 and the new government was soon in full operation.

The Massachusetts settlers viewed these proceedings in Gorges' Province of Maine with alarm, and well they might, for behind it was the despotic Charles I, determined to assert his royal authority. They were resolved not to submit without a struggle and immediately began to arm themselves. However, assistance came from an unexpected quarter in the form of a governmental upheavel in England. The Long Parliament began its famous period of opposition to the King in November of 1640. It was soon followed by Oliver Cromwell's Great Rebellion and the establishment of the Commonwealth. This spelt disaster for the Palatinate of Maine, and the independence of Massachusetts was assured. In the civil war that now began, between the King and Parliament, Sir Ferdinando gallantly espoused the cause of his royal master.

At Richmond's Island the situation remained comparatively unchanged. In June of 1640 Winter was tried on a profiteering charge brought against him by Cleaves and others but was acquitted. The court decided that it was in no way proper to attempt to regulate a man's profits in trade. This trial was immediately followed by another suit brought against Winter by Cleaves for damages sustained when he was forced to move from Spurwink. In this case the verdict rendered was in Cleaves' favor. Winter was required to pay damages amounting to eighty pounds sterling. Cleaves was also awarded approximately four acres of land at Spurwink and the house that he had constructed there. Winter promptly requested a stay of judgment but was denied it. These court proceedings were held at Saco and presided over by Gorges' Board of Councillors.

When the marshall proceeded to Richmond's Island to levy execution against Winter, in accordance with the judgment of the Court, he discovered that Winter was not at home. The marshall was forceably ejected from the island by Winter's men and subsequently departed empty-handed.

In relation to trade carried on at Richmond's Island a status quo was maintained throughout 1640 and 1641. Winter, however, made the observation that money was practically non-existant throughout the surrounding area and that he was unable to dispose of any livestock. The crops continued to do quite well as did the livestock with the exception of the pigs on the mainland that were still plagued by the wolves.

On the 1st of April, 1641, Winter delivered to the Board of Councillors goods to the value of eighty pounds to cover the court's decision of September, 1640. This consiliatory move was made to diplomatically prepare the way for further legal action in regard to his old opponent Georges Cleaves.

Winter began his legal offensive by petitioning the Board of Councillors in June for a reversal of the decision of September 1640. He maintained that he sustained a great injury and hardship due to the court's action and that his ignorance of the laws, plus a lack of trained legal assistance had been one cause of his poor showing. His real grievance was, however, that the jurors were moved by personal feelings toward him in rendering their decision and that they were swayed by the derogatory utterances of Thomas Cammock regarding a witness presented in his behalf. Winter also hinted that he would carry it to England where the rich and powerful Robert Trelawny could bring his skillful lawyers into play. One can imagine the consternation that was engendered as the full significance of Winter's words became evident. Finally it was agreed to submit the dispute to four arbitrators, with both Winter and Cleaves swearing to abide by the decision. At the last minute Winter included another suit against Cleaves for defaming the character of Mrs. Winter.

The arbitrators found the jury correct in awarding damages to Cleaves for the loss of his house and land at Spurwink, but they reduced the amount from eighty pounds to sixty pounds. They also decided, in reference to Cleaves' defamation of Winter's wife, that he should acknowledge to the court and to Mrs. Winter "his failing therein." Lastly, they confirmed Cleaves' title to Machigonne.

By rights this should have ended the controversy, but neither Winter nor Trelawny were satified with the decision. In a letter dated the 29th of June, 1641, Trelawny instructed Winter to pay Cleaves twenty pounds for his house and land at Spurwink, but he also directed him to begin a new suit for land at Machigonne, with the expectation that Cleaves would be declared a trespasser there. He closed his letter with the statement that "In case Jusice be not donn you . . . I shall send a warrent hence from Parliament to bringe them all over here to answer itt, where I believe they will not justifie there doeings . . ." These carefully laid plans, however, came to naught due to the violent political upheaval taking place in England.

This same year, there appeared at Richmond's Island a gentleman destined to play a leading role in the affairs of this area. He was the Reverend Robert Jordan, an Anglican clergyman, and a graduate of Oxford University, who had previously resided for two years at Pejepscot with Thomas Purchase, a relative. His first public appearance was at the court proceedings held at Saco in 1640. Winter's earliest mention of him was made in a letter to Trelawny dated the 2nd of August 1641. In it he states that "Heare is one Robert Jordan, a minister which hath bin with us this three months, which is a very honest, religious man by any thing as yett I can find in him. I have not yett agreed with him for stayings heare, but did refer it till I did heare some word from you . . ." The Reverend Mr. Jordan settled at Richmond's Island and soon married Winter's daughter Sarah. He early allied himself with Winter in the difficulties with Cleaves who described him as "well nigh able to deceave the wiset braine." This was truly the judgment of an expect in such matters.

Winter finally launched on the 15th of June, his second vessel, the ship *Richmond*. As soon as the upper deck was caulked, he commenced loading the cargo of dried fish, fish oil, peas, and wood. In July under the command of a Stephen Sargent she sailed for Bilbao, Spain, taking with her many of the men whose length of service was up. Of her subsequent history nothing is known.

The plantation was now experiencing a rapid decline. Despite the fact that Winter still represented the power of wealth and influence the decrease in trade was alarming. The crops and livestock were still doing well despite the constant depredations of wolves. Winter found it increasingly hard to keep fishing boats at sea as he had virtually no crews to man them. The severity of the winter of 1641-2 added to the complications until in 1642 he found it impossible to keep any fishing craft at sea. The lack of remunerative trade finally prompted Trelawny to notify Winter that if he could sell the plantation for a fair profit to do so. However, the inhabitants did not even have the means to purchase livestock to say nothing of the whole plantation. Whenever Winter did sell anything he was forced to accept produce in lieu of cash. Over and over again he reiterated the degree of poverty that had settled upon the colony, leaving him with large stocks of unsaleable goods.

The *Hercules* arrived in June of 1642 and sailed in July with a cargo of 13,000 dried cod and three hogsheads of fish peas for Bilboa, Spain. The letters that Winter wrote to Trelawny in 1642 were the last ones to pass between the two men. The reason behind this sudden stop in correspondence was that Robert Trelawny was now languishing in Winchester House prison accused of Royalist dealings. Winter's last inventory made at Richmond's Island was dated the 27th of June, 1643, and displayed very little change from previous accounts. However, Winter was still a force to be reckoned with especially so now that Reverend Robert Jordan was ably assisting him. This is amply borne out by the fact that he was still pressing for the ejection of Cleaves from Machigonne.

George Cleaves, whose perception was just as keen as his opponents on Richmond's Island, was desperately seeking some new method of permanently establishing his Machigonne claim. He found the weapon he was seeking in the old Lygonia or Plough Patent of 1630. This patent covered territory forty miles square from Cape Porpoise to the Sagadahoc River, and not only included but antedated the Trelawny patent. The possibilities that this presented, if the grantees could be induced to part with the patent, prompted Cleaves to depart immediately for England. Upon reaching London he started negotiations and at the same time acquainted Colonel Alexander Rigby, a member of Parliament, with his plans. Apparently Cleaves encountered no difficulty in arousing Rigby's interest in colonial undertakings and induced him to make the small outlay required to purchase the Lygonia Patent. The transfer was consumated the 7th of April, 1643. In due course Colonel Rigby gave Cleaves a commission as Deputy President of the Province, retaining only nominal leadership. While in London, Cleaves learned that Robert Trelawny was in prison. This removed most of the opposition that might form in England when he exerted his authority. Late in 1643, he returned to New England. Landing in Boston, he immediately sought the aid of Governor Winthrop who prudently remained neutral.

One can imagine the excitement that followed Cleaves' return to Machigonne. He encountered at once the wrath of Richard Vines, the official representative of Gorges' Province, since the departure of Thomas Gorges. To gain control Cleaves had to remove Vines, so with this in mind, he convened his first court the 25th of March, 1644, at Saco, in an attempt to set up his authority. He also sent his agent Richard Tucker to Vines with the suggestion that they submit to arbitration by the Magistrates of Massachusetts Bay. Vines' answer to this was Tucker's arrest on

Brass baptismal basin reputedly used by Rev. Robert Jordan and now in the possession of the Maine Historical Society.

North Congregational Church on Meeting House Hill before it was moved from Mount Pleasant Cemetery. Circa 1870.

Portland Head Light as it appeared in 1883.

Portland Head Light with the frigate *U.S.S. Constitution* being towed to sea after its visit to Portland, 24 July 1931.

a charge of "preemptory and abusive language." The only concession that Vines made was that if an order came from either King or Parliament, for the establishment of Rigby's patent, he would submit to that authority.

The years 1644 and 1645 saw in England the collapse of the Royalist forces under Charles I. Robert Trelawny, still in prison, died early in 1644, and was succeeded by his ten-year old son John. At Richmond's Island, Winter still endeavored to carry on for Trelawny's son but his efforts were unsuccessful. Partly the minority of John Trelawny and principally the want of funds accelerated the collapse of the plantation as a commercial enterprise. John Winter died in 1645, and shortly afterwards trouble with the Indians broke out. All this finally produced the complete failure of the Trelawny adventure. The trade once so flourishing sought other channels, leaving the mouth of the Spurwink and Richmond's Island practically deserted.

In 1646 Massachusetts attempted to settle the issue by trying the jurisdictional case with Cleaves and Tucker representing the Rigby claims and with Henry Josselyn of Black Point and Francis Robinson of Saco representing the Gorges' interests. The court's find was inconclusive as the perplexed jury ruled that evidence was not clear enough for a definite decision. The Massachusetts magistrates also added the suggestion that the contending parties await the pleasure of English authority. Just previous to the court action, Richard Vines, weary and disheartened, sold his holdings and sailed for Barbadoes, where he found a new home for his family under more peaceful conditions. His immediate successor as Deputy Governor was Henry Josselyn of Black Point.

The decision of Parliament was not long in coming. When the case came before the Earl of Warwick and the commissioner for foreign plantations, Colonel Rigby appeared in his own interest and John Gorges, eldest son of Sir Ferdinando, represented the Gorges interests. A decision was rendered the 27th of March, 1647 in favor of Rigby, who was declared the rightful owner and proprietor of the Province of Lygonia, embodying the territory from the Kennebunk River to the Sagadahoc, leaving to Gorges and his heirs only the small tract of land between the Kennebunk and Piscataqua River. Sir Ferdinando died shortly after the decision was made, and with this gallant old knight, the Palatinate of Maine ceased to live. To the last he stoutly insisted upon his rights and left the Province of Maine to his son John. Probably the fact that he was an avowed Royalist contributed largely to his loss of governmental power and influence.

Cleaves, with his commission as Deputy Governor, now proceeded to organize the Province of Lygonia. In this he had the able assistance of a commission appointed by Parliament and consisting of such prominent Massachusetts officials as John Winthrop, Thomas Dudley, and Richard Bellingham. In the selection of assistants necessary for the proper administration of the affairs of the Province, Cleaves did not overlook his most outspoken opponents. Among the early records is one of a court held at Black Point, the last of May, 1648, and signed by three judges of the Province of Lygonia, George Cleaves, Henry Josselyn, and Robert Jordan. Here, obviously, is an illustration of the new order that followed the establishment of Rigby's claim.

In September of the same year, the Reverend Robert Jordan petitioned the General Assembly of Lygonia for reimbursement in his settling of his father-in-law's legacies. As executor of the estate he attempted to open communication with Robert Trelawny's executors but received no reply. Unfortunately they adopted an attitude of silence, and Winter's estate remained unsettled, much to the dissatisfaction of all concerned. The Court of Lygonia appointed a committee to examine the plantation's accounts and to make a report of their condition. This committee pursued unusually minute investigations, and submitted a detailed report. With this account before them the Court authorized Jordan to retain all goods, lands, cattle, and chattels belonging to Robert Trelawny, within the Province, from that day forward and forever, unless the executors of Robert Trelawny should redeem and release them, with the consent and allowance of Robert Jordan, his heirs, etc.

From an examination of the proceedings it does not appear that the executors of Robert Trelawny were allowed much time to make an appeal. They had ample funds to cover their extensive debts to John Winter, but they never got the chance to use them. Under this hasty decision the Trelawny heirs lost everything that their venerated ancestor had labored so hard, and spent so much, to construct. The efforts made to recover the estate by Trelawny's son John in 1676, and 1696, and 1700, by his grandson Samuel in 1719, and by his great grandson Samuel Pollefen Trelawny in 1758, were all in vain. Under the Statute of Limitation their posterity became debarred from all further attempts at recovery.

The Court's order granting possession of Trelawny's lands to Jordan was signed by George Cleaves as deputy president of the Province of Lygonia. In placing the Reverend Mr. Jordan in such a position of power and influence Cleaves certainly exhibited a great repression of personal feeling. Under the existing circumstances he doubtless considered it an act for the general good and peace of the area. However, he had innumerable occasions throughout the remainder of his troubled life to regret this magnanimous act. Reference has already been made to Winter's claim that Trelawny's patent embraced Machigonne and how the claim was finally settled in court in Cleaves' favor. However, Jordan almost immediately exhibited evidence that he had not forgotten this former claim in which he had supported Winter. After obtaining permission to erect a sawmill on the Presumpscot River he began proceedings by asserting a prior claim based on his possession of Trelawny's patent. This was the opening of a legal battle equalled by few.

The list of wrongs that Cleaves suffered because of Jordan's efforts to sustain his claim to Machigonne is a lengthy one, and involves a labyrinth of legal manipulations. Cleaves sought to obtain a redress for his wrongs, but was deprived of needed support by the death of Colonel Rigby in 1650. During the Commonwealth and the Protectorate in England, Massachusetts, with pressing interests of her own, was not inclined to listen to the quarrels of rival claimants within her newly acquired county of Yorkshire. After the restoration of Charles II Cleaves' added efforts were useless. The King's commissioners, invited by native royalists, to advance their own interests, declared the grants of territory made by Cleaves on authority derived from Rigby, to be null and void. Not long after this, in 1667, Cleaves died with all hope of redress extinguished and found in the grave the peace of which he had known so little in his long and troubled life. The magistrates of Massachusetts Bay had always regarded Gorges' aristocratic Province of Maine as hostile to their independence. The success of Parliamentary forces in England presented them with new possibilities in this area. With this in mind they re-read their charter and "discovered" that it included Maine, and that they had rights there superior to those of either Gorges or Rigby. In 1652 they took possession and extended their jurisdiction over the closest of the Maine settlements renaming the area the county of Yorkshire. The Massachusetts commissioners soon set out to obtain the submission of the inhabitants to Massachusetts control. In the territory beyond Saco they encountered considerable opposition from Henry Josselyn, Robert Jordan, and Arthur Mackworth of Machigonne, with George Cleaves also joining in. The first three gentlemen based their opposition on religious and political grounds, whereas Cleaves was endeavoring to retain his place in connection with the Rigby interest which otherwise would be blotted out.

Despite the continued opposition Massachusetts held firmly to her purpose and finally in 1658 the recalcitrant inhabitants north of Saco were forced to submit. On the 26th of May, Henry Josselyn, Robert Jordan, George Cleaves, and twenty-six others, all inhabitants of Black Point, Spurwink and Casco Bay, met at Robert Jordan's house on the east bank of the Spurwink River mouth, and signed the articles of submission. Included also in the document was the provision that from that time on those places formally called Spurwink and Casco Bay or the area from the Spurwink River to Clapboard Island in Casco Bay, and running eight miles inland was to be known as the town of Falmouth. In this new county of Yorkshire the inhabitants could send two delegates to the Massachusetts General Court. Also they were allowed to vote without becoming members of the Puritan church, but complete freedom of worship was not allowed them. Within the county the town of Falmouth could maintain commissioners to try cases, involving sums up to fifty pounds or not requiring a jury. The first commissioners were Henry Josselyn, Robert Jordan, George Cleaves, Henry Watts, and Francis Neale, with judicial authority covering Scarborough and Falmouth. In England the Puritans were in full control of the government and there is little doubt but that Massachusetts' claim to Maine territory was promoted if not suggested there. During Oliver Cromwell's time they asserted their authority with a strong hand and the triumph of the republican ideal of Massachusetts over the aristocratic ideal in Maine was for a time complete.

In 1660 young Ferdinando Gorges, the impecunious heir of old Sir Ferdinando, by the court's decision, owned all the Gorges' grant. The Reverend Jordan, having yielded unwilling obedience to the Massachusetts Bay colony, was one of those who, on restoration of Charles II in England, sought the king's assistance in establishing a new provincial government, and with Henry Josselyn and others of the royalist party was indicted in 1663 by the Massachusetts grand jury for renouncing the authority of the Bay colony. The arrival of the King's commissioners in 1665 revived the hopes of Jordan and his royalist associates; but it was only temporary. By prudent management in her relations with the Province of Maine, and also with the governmental party in England, Massachusetts succeeded in maintaining her authority. When, in 1686, the commissioners were recalled, Massachusetts resumed full control of provincial affairs. However, in 1677, young Ferdinando Gorges again revived his claims to the Province of Maine. The men of Massachusetts met this new threat with thrifty promptness. Commissioners from Governor John Leverett hastened to England and quietly purchased from Gorges the entire Province of Maine for twelve hundred and fifty pounds. Massachusetts statutes were immediately put in force throughout the province. The charter of the capital Gorgeana was annulled and its name changed to York. Under the new regime every trace of the old Palatinate was obliterated.

In 1680, Massachusetts reorganized the administration of Maine providing for a provincial president and deputy president to be chosen annually. The legislature was composed of a standing council of eight members with a lower house of deputies chosen from the towns. However, in 1684, Charles II annulled the charter of Massachusetts and for seven years Maine, as well as Massachusetts, was governed directly by the crown. On the 17th of May, 1686, Joseph Dudley became president of New England by royal commission. He held office until the 19th of December when he was replaced by Sir Edmund Andros, who became Governor, Captain General and Vice Admiral of New England, New York and the Jerseys. Andros formed a council of twenty-five members, five of whom constituted a quorum. All legislative, judicial and executive functions were vested in this department, thus creating a despotic government without constitutional limits. Sir Edmund was deposed by a popular revolution in April of 1689 and a "Council for the Safety of the People and the Conservation of the Peace" was formed. Delegates from the towns were chosen and at a meeting of the revived General Court in May, it was decided to restore the government, according to charter rights. Thomas Danforth, the first president of the Province of Maine, resumed office.

Massachusetts received from King William III, in 1691, her second charter. The Province of Massachusetts Bay was created, embracing the old colonies of Massachusetts and Plymouth, plus the Province of Maine as far north as the St. Croix River. The governor, lieutenant governor and the secretary of state were appointed and commissioned by the crown to hold office, with the governor retaining supreme executive authority within the province. The legislature or general court, consisted of two branches, an upper, called the council or board of assistants, and a lower, the house of representatives. According to the charter, three members of the council were always to be from the Province of Maine.

It was also stipulated that there be eight representatives elected by the Maine towns. As an added restraint, all laws promulgated by the General Court had to be approved by the King. This was the system created by the charter of 1691 that remained in force until General Thomas Gage dissolved the General Court in 1774 just prior to the outbreak of the American Revolution.

CHAPTER II

INDIAN WARS, INCORPORATION, AND THE REVOLUTION

At the beginning of the first Indian War in 1675, called King Philip's War, Falmouth, of which Cape Elizabeth was then an integral part, was enjoying a thrifty trade in fish, masts, spars, timber, and sawed lumber. In Cape Elizabeth, just prior to the outbreak of hostilities, the settlements were few and far between. The largest grouping was at Purpooduck, the area later called Spring Point, and consisted largely of the families of John Wallis, Joseph Phippen, Thomas Stanford, Robert Stanford, John Skillings, Joel Madiver, Isaac Davis, Ralph Turner, Nicholas White, and Sampson Penley. The name, Purpooduck, is of Indian origin, meaning a place that conspicuously juts out into the water and is little frequented. Unfortunately there is no basis for the traditional meanings of "often frozen over" and "burying place."

Further out on the Cape, at Spurwink, resided the Reverend Robert Jordan and his family. Walter Gendall, Jordan's tenant, and John Guy. It is not to be wondered at that Jordan was about the only inhabitant of Spurwink, as he retained possession of practically the entire area for his own family, granting largely those lands lying on the southern shores of Fore River. Here he made grants to numerous parties including Joseph Phippen, Sampson Penley, Thomas and Robert Stanford and Ralph Turner.

In the beginning of the year 1675, the prosperity of Falmouth stood at a high point, with the population steadily increasing. King Philip's War broke out in June but hostilities did not commence in this area until September. By attempting to disarm the neighboring Indians some clashes took place in which the inhabitants of Falmouth had a leading part. The first attack was in the region of Pejepscot and was closely followed by skirmishes on the borders of Casco Bay. The Wakely family that settled just below the falls on the Presumpscot River were the first to be massacred. After this slaughter the blows fell thick and fast. The houses at Capisic, in north-western Falmouth were burned, and Robert Jordan's home at Spurwink also went up in flames.

The Jordan family had just departed by boat when the torch was applied to their home. They moved to Great Island, now Newcastle, in the Piscataqua River and there Reverend Jordan lived under the watchful eye of Massachusetts until his death in 1679. Through his will, we get a glimpse of his extensive land holdings. To his wife Sarah he left the old plantation at Spurwink, consisting of one thousand acres plus a two thousand acre farm in Scarborough. His sons also received large amounts of land, viz., Dominicus, two thousand acres at Spurwink; Samuel, eleven hundred acres at Spurwink; John, three hundred acres at Long Sands, (Bowery Beach), plus Richmond's Island; and Robert one thousand acres at Spurwink. His youngest son Jeremiah to receive Sarah Jordan's lands when she died.

Early in 1676 the inhabitants began to evacuate the Falmouth area; many moved to Scarborough and the itinerant minister, Reverend George Burroughs, led his Purpooduck flock, plus a large group from the Neck, to the safety of Bang's now Cushing's Island.

The only fatality in the vicinity of Spurwink was Ambrose Bowden, who resided in Scarborough directly across the Spurwink River from Robert Jordan's residence. He arrived in the area about 1646 and maintained a ferry across the river for the convenience of those travelling the King's Highway. The landing on the Spurwink side was close by Jordan's home and many travelers enjoyed a night's lodging with him. Apparently the Jordan home served also as a tavern and a public meeting place, through necessity, as it was the only substantial dwelling in the area.

In October of 1676 Henry Josselyn was forced to surrender his garrison at Black Point. Just previous to this a vessel had anchored at Richmond's Island and after Josselyn surrendered, the Indians succeeded in taking it. Walter Gendall of Spurwink, one of the prisoners, joined the raiding Indians as interpreter and messenger. This affair at Richmond's Island was the last engagement fought in the area during the war. Early in 1678 a treaty was signed at Falmouth, under the "Smoking Tree" on the bank of Long Creek, bringing to the region an uneasy peace lasting approximately ten years.

This period between the first and second Indian War saw the return of many settlers to Falmouth. As soon as the inhabitants were quietly settled again, it became a matter of deep concern to provide for the security of the settlement. Consequently Fort Loyal was built on the Neck to coincide with garrisons constructed at Spurwink and Purpooduck. Despite these warlike preparations the settlement began to grow. A saw-mill was constructed on Long Creek by Samuel Webber in 1681 and a year later George Ingersoll built a grist-mill on Barberry Creek. Land was cleared on the Cape for farming and many fishermen set up operations there. Communications also improved and were not confined to the water routes as they formally had been. The King's Highway that ran along the shore from Spurwink around to Purpooduck became increasingly active and the ferry across the Spurwink was reestablished. A ferry also made irregular trips from Purpooduck to the Neck. This route was, however, circuitous and long, and it was soon found expedient to lay out shorter routes. Consequently in 1686 the Court of Sessions at York granted a ferry to Silvanus Davis at Nonecusk Point for the transporting of man and beast over Casco or Fore River. This point was on the southern side of Long Creek nearly opposite the landing on the Neck which must have been a little below the present Veterans' Bridge. Lastly, the once flourishing trade conducted at Richmond's Island was now nonexistent with no prospects of revival. This then was the scene that greeted the outbreak of hostilities in August, 1688, when King William's War or the first inter-colonial war opened the "decade of sorrows."

The first Indian depredations took the form of cattle killing, but soon became more violent, resulting finally in a bloody battle at North Yarmouth. In June, 1689, Anthony Brackett, Robert Lawrence, and George Ingersoll wrote to the government urging immediate assistance. They succeeded in obtaining the services of Major Benjamin Church of the Plymouth colony. He arrived in September with a substantial force of volunteers and friendly Indians. Almost immediately, Major Church set to work improving the fortifications, a precaution that proved to be very timely indeed, as the Indians soon put in an appearance. The attack began on the 12th in the vicinity of Anthony Brackett's farm at Back Cove. The battle that followed was fought with equal vigor by both sides. By late afternoon the attacking Indians were forced to retreat and as the English forces were low on ammunition they withdrew to the Neck. Little is known of the Indian losses that, by appearances, must have been quite heavy. The English lost eleven killed and wounded. At daybreak the Cape Elizabeth men returned to their respective garrisons to wait out further developments. Just before his departure in November, Church succeeded in persuading the inhabitants to remain on their farms, assuring them of governmental protection. The garrison commanded by

Dominicus Jordan at Spurwink however suffered a brief attack after the Major left but succeeded in beating the assailants off. During the engagement an Indian trying to intimidate the besieged called out "we are ten hundred" to which Dominicus reputedly replied "I don't care if you're ten thousand." Several houses were also burned by the savages in this visitation at Spurwink.

Early in the following year the Indians, with their French allies, renewed their depredations. The inhabitants of Falmouth were soon aware of the approaching enemy. Madockawando, leader of the eastern Indians, and ably assisted by the French, began the attack on the 15th of May. The settlers took refuge in Fort Loyal and the seige began in earnest on the 16th. Due to a great loss in men they commenced negotiations with the French on the 29th and surrendered the same day under the impression that they would be conducted to the nearest English settlement. However, they were badly mistaken in their trust, for when they marched out of the fort, many were murdered and the others carried off to Canada as captives. When the news of this defeat reached the garrisons at Purpooduck and Spurwink they were immediately abandoned. These surviving inhabitants retreated to Wells, thus leaving the entire region eastward completely deserted until 1698.

To cover the retreat to Wells ships from the Portsmouth area reconnoitered the Richmond's Island, Spurwink, and Black Point area. They arrived just as the Indians were burning the deserted buildings left by the fleeing settlers. Before they departed for Portsmouth every dwelling was either in flames or had already been reduced to ashes. These conflagrations probably removed all that was left of Winter's old plantation on Richmond's Island and the early homes at Spurwink. In September Major Benjamin Church returning from his second expedition to the eastward anchored in Casco River close to Purpooduck Point. As the ships were very crowded some of the troops disembarked to spend the night ashore among the ruins on the Point. During the night some of the enemy were detected and early the following morning they launched an attack. Major Church and the remaining troops hurried ashore to assist the besieged. He immediately organized the troops and friendly Indians for a frontal assault. At a given signal they rushed the attacking Indians and succeeded in completely routing them, inflicting heavy losses. Some prisoners were taken in the charge and were quickly killed by the Major's Indian allies. His losses amounted to twenty-four killed and twenty wounded.

This engagement ended the fighting in the area for the duration. After the peace of 1698, very few of the approximately fifty prewar families returned to the vicinity of Purpooduck and Spurwink. The Jordan family, whose property lay in the latter region, returned to their old holdings and began anew, being probably the first to return. By spring of 1703 an indeterminate number of settlers had returned to Purpooduck Point and erected new homes there. The prominent families were those of Michael Webber, Benjamin, Joseph, James, and Josiah Wallis, Joseph Morgan, Thomas Loveitt, Nathaniel White, and Joel Madiver. Their hopes were soon to be shattered for during the previous year England and France had renewed their conflict. An attempt was made to keep the war from spreading to the colonies but the Indians were too friendly with the French for this to become a reality. Consequently Queen Anne's or Governor Dudley's War soon broke forth in all its fury. The month of August, 1703, saw the French and Indian forces descend upon the settlements in a surprise attack. Early in the morning of the 10th they struck at Purpooduck killing twenty-five and capturing eight. The victims were mostly women and children as the men had departed for the fields. Among those killed were Thomas Loveitt and family, Joel Madiver and the wives of Josiah and Benjamin Wallis. Mrs. Michael Webber, being great with child, was slaughtered in an especially horrible manner. Josiah Wallis carrying his son, John, escaped across country to Black Point.

At Spurwink the assault was just as sudden. Dominicus Jordan, greatly feared by the Indians due to his unusual strength, and called by them the "Indian Killer," was plowing with his flintlock strapped to his back. As the Indians often visited him in times of peace he did not suspect their intentions. They made signs to trade and as he turned to go to the garrison they felled him with a hatchet. The Indian that struck him down is supposed to have exclaimed, "There Dominicus, now kill'em ten thousand Indians." With this the Indians launched their attack and immediately killed or took prisoner twenty-two persons, all bearing the name Jordan. Among the captives taken to Canada were Dominicus' wife Hannah, his six children and his brother, Jeremiah. They all eventually returned except one daughter, Mary Ann. Jeremiah remained many years in Canada, and in France; so many in fact that when he returned he was dubbed "French Jeremy." After the melancholy events of 1703, Falmouth was again entirely deserted of inhabitants, and did not become the scene of further fighting during the war. A treaty of peace was eventually signed in 1713.

The first notice that we have of the return of any of the former inhabitants is early in 1715 when Dominicus Jordan, son of the Dominicus killed in the late war, reoccupied the paternal estate at Spurwink. At Purpooduck, Dr. Gilbert Winslow built the first house in 1716 or 1717, and the same year he was joined by Samuel Cobb, a shipcarpenter, who built the second house there, moving the next year to the Neck. When he moved in 1718 there were thirteen families, besides his own, living at Purpooduck Point.

The unsettled nature of the period is amply demonstrated by an event that occurred in 1717. In May of that year, a pirate sloop of eight guns and manned by approximately ninety men, anchored in Richmond's Island Roads. Almost immediately they descended upon the Jordan family at Spurwink. However, their movements had apparently been observed for the Jordans fled in ample time to avoid the pirates. As they departed the marauders stole a sloop and a shallop belonging to Dominicus Jordan. This was probably Captain Paul Williams, consort of the pirate, Samuel Bellamy, who was active in the area about this time.

The General Court had in 1714 appointed a committee of five persons to settle the eastern frontier by laying out the towns in a regular and defensible manner. They established the boundaries of Falmouth in July, 1718, and the General Court incorporated it as a town the same year. The boundary lines correspond almost exactly to those of the 1658 survey.

During the winter of 1718 a vessel carrying Scotch-Irish immigrants anchored for some weeks close under Clarks Point. The passengers resided on Purpooduck Point until they sailed the following spring for Londonderry, N.H. Several families remained, however, becoming valuable citizens.

The first meeting of the inhabitants to organize the town, after the incorporation, was held the 10th of March, 1719. Now that the inhabitants had provided a municipal government for the town they turned their attention to the means of securing their possessions. Most of the settlers squatted upon land to which they had no title, trusting to the future arrangements of the town for protection and a suitable title. Much of the land was claimed by persons who had been inhabitants of the former settlement, or their heirs or assigns, and called themselves the "Old Proprietors," whereas the new citizens comprising a majority of the inhabitants who settled without title were known as the "New Proprietors." The town, in order to comply with the requirements of the General Court, immediately proceeded to admit seventy-four new settlers, thus augmenting the ranks of the "New Proprietors." During the years 1727 and 1728 one hundred and thirty-eight new arrivals were allowed to settle. Finally, in May of 1731 the Supreme Court at Boston upheld the "Old Proprietors" and made provisions for an amicable settlement between the contesting groups.

While the land squabbles were in progress the business of settlement proceeded unabated. As the ever increasing number of travelers continued to use the old King's Highway from Spurwink to Purpooduck it became necessary to place the ferry running between Clay Cove on the Neck and Purpooduck Point under suitable regulation. Therefore, in May of 1719, John Pritchard, living on the Neck, received the privilege of keeping the ferry for the ensuing seven years. In addition, due to the difficulty of calling across the river from Purpooduck, John Sawyer received the privilege of keeping a canoe for the accommodation of passengers at that location. When Pritchard's term ended he was succeeded by Benjamin Wright. He in turn relinquished it to John Phinney in 1729.

Early in 1722 Indian troubles began anew, heralding the outbreak of Governor Dummer's or the Three Years' War. By September of the following year two garrisons at Purpooduck were collectively manned by twelve men. At Spurwink nine men under the command of Lieutenant Dominicus Jordan occupied a garrison. A sustained attack could not be beaten off, however, due to the scarcity of powder, ball, and flints. Fortunately there were no disturbances until the spring of 1724. In April of that year the Indians renewed their desultory attacks, killing one man and capturing two others at Spurwink. The Purpooduck garrisons had one man killed and another wounded in May. A second raid was made at Spurwink in July. On the 17th the Indians mortally wounded Solomon Jordan. A pursuit was organized the next day and the Indians were surprised a short distance from the garrison. In the ensuing fight the leader was slain, whereupon they fled leaving twenty-five packs, twelve blankets, and several other items behind. The sachem was scalped for which the province paid a bounty of one hundred pounds. Some sporadic sniping continued to occur until the war ended in 1725.

By 1727 the number of emigrants had considerably increased. Among them was Joshua Woodbury, the first of the name to settle here, who established himself at Purpooduck. About the same time approximately eight families settled in the Pond Cove area. They built a garrison near Zeb Cove, constructed a saw-mill on Pond Cove Brook, and agreed to assist each other in peace or war.

The meeting house that the Purpooduck inhabitants constructed in 1722 was fitted with seats and glass windows in 1728. This log house, built for the common purpose of a garrison and a church, was the earliest public structure built on the Point. It stood on the high ground, now within the limits of Fort Preble, with a burying ground extending from it in a southerly direction to the shore of Simonton's Cove. The new minister, Reverend Thomas Smith preached here every third Sunday and in 1733 the school teacher Robert Bayley used it for teaching school three months of the year.

Despite the Indian wars the town continued to grow. A grant of land on Lawrence's Creek, sometimes referred to as Sawyer's Brook, Meadow Brook, Trout Brook, or Mill Creek, was bestowed upon a group of men as an encouragement to construct a mill. The project was slow in developing but by 1738 a combination grist and saw mill was operating successfully. Two other mill privileges were granted in 1728. One was for a saw mill on Long Creek to be constructed by Samuel Cobb, William Rogers, Francis Hull, and John Owen. The other, to be used for the same purpose, was to be built on Barberry Creek by Joshua Moody and John Brown. Both mills were immediately established. Other signs of growth were the thriving enterprises of John White and Thomas Delano. The former built up an extensive tannery at Purpooduck about 1725 and the latter opened a blacksmith shop on the bank of Delano Brook somewhat later. Here he burned his own charcoal and did a thriving business in calked horse and ox shoes.

By 1725 the total number of families at Spurwink and Purpooduck amounted to approximately seventeen. New settlers were arriving every day. The town of Falmouth, despite its large extent of territory and the remote situation of many of its inhabitants, continued united in one parish until 1733. This year saw Spurwink and Purpooduck set off as the Second Parish of Falmouth. The church was formed by the dismissal of five persons from the First Parish for that express purpose. They were John Armstrong, William Jamison, Robert Means, Robert Thorndike, and Jonathan Cobb. On the 24th of August the Massachusetts General Court ruled that "all the Lands with the Inhabitants thereon lying on the South Side of Fore River in the Town of Falmouth, were erected into a separate Precinct or Parish, and were discharged from being rated for the Support of the Ministry in the other part of the Town provided that the Petitioners shall constantly support the Ministry from this time and within two years shall build a sufficient House for the public Worship of God and shall also settle a learned and Orthodox Minister among them of good and sober conversation."

The inhabitants began at once to carry out the terms of their contract with the General Court. The first parish meeting, under the act, was held the 18th of September, 1733. At that meeting they voted to build a meeting house and to invite the Reverend Benjamin Allen to settle as pastor. The erection of the meetinghouse was soon started and was ready for occupancy the following year. It was framed of white oak cut from the immediate vicinity and stood in the southwestern corner of the present Mount Pleasant Cemetery. During the period that the Parish was synonomous with Falmouth, the parish records were a part of the towns records, but after the separation, the records of the first and second parishes were kept by each and the inhabitants were taxed for the support of the ministry in the parishes in which they resided. The installation of Reverend Allen occurred the 10th of November, 1734.

This was a fairly prosperous period for the town of Falmouth. So much time was spent in lumbering operations that the cultivation of land was sadly neglected. Lumber was in constant demand, and afforded a quick remuneration for labor; but the consequence was frequent suffering for lack of the staple food stuffs. The year 1737 was a particularly distressing one. Throat distemper assumed the proportions of an epidemic killing off a total of twenty-six people in Purpooduck. It continued throughout the year and proved to be particularly fatal among children.

Indian troubles again flared up in 1744 resulting in a declaration of war. In the vicinity of Falmouth occasional shots were exchanged. To the inhabitants the hostilities were identified as the Old French and Indian War, Governor Shirley's War or the Five Years' War; abroad it was called King George's War. There was sporadic sniping along the banks of Long Creek, and in 1745 a son of Colonel Ezekiel Cushing of Purpooduck was killed. However, the town was so well covered by other settlements, that it enjoyed a compartive degree of quiet. In June of the same year the Wescott family on Long Creek was attacked. Here two men were killed and scalped, their clothes were taken, and three guns were stolen. As the war progressed the inhabitants were kept in a state of constant agitation by repeated depredations.

The latter part of September the inhabitants were in a state of fearful apprehension due to an expected invasion from France. On the 10th of September, a French fleet, consisting of eleven ships of the line, with frigates, transports and fire-ships, under the command of the Duc d'Anville and containing over three thousand troops, arrived in Nova Scotia. They did not attempt to disguise the fact that they were here with the avowed purpose of wreaking destruction upon the New England coast. The town books were shipped to Newburg and many people sent their valuables inland. Two large guns were hired of one Moses Pearson and placed on Spring Point. Along with this, four barrels of powder, plus a quantity of balls and flints, were hastily collected. A small fort was also constructed on Fort Point at Seal Cove, further out on the Cape. Fortunately the invasion did not materialize, due to the outbreak of an epidemic within the French fleet, which, incidentally also struck down the Duc d'Anville. The force that weathered the scourge was widely dispersed and partially destroyed by a violent storm. This was indeed a singular deliverance.

The spring of 1747 witnessed the renewal of Indian raids and alarms. They were literally everywhere, sniping at people, killing cattle, and causing widespread destruction. Long Creek was again the scene of sporadic fighting. Throughout the whole war and especially during this period, Captain Dominicus Jordan's Snowshoe Company did yeomen duty in the defense of the town. In October of this year peace was concluded in Europe, but it was not until September of 1748 that a treaty was arranged with the Indians.

Although hostilities were constantly in progress, trade was still increasing. In addition to the timber and lumber trade, a few vessels were engaged in the West India business, bringing home rum, sugar, and molasses, in exchange for lumber and fish. A number of vessels were also employed in the fishery. There was a considerable amount of shipping tonnage owned by residents of the second parish. As early as 1745 five schooners and five sloops hailed the settlement as their home port. Colonel Ezekiel Cushing, who settled at Purpooduck about 1743, and William Simonton, one of the Scotch-Irish who arrived in 1718, carried on an extensive West Indian trade. Colonel Cushing was one of the wealthiest men in the town and lived in style somewhat above his neighbors. His home, located at the tip of Purpooduck Point, was the first two-story dwelling to be erected in the Second Parish. The extremity of land on which he lived, and where his wharf, warehouse, etc. once stood, was known until recent years as Cushing's Point. Besides being a prosperous merchant, he was a colonel in the Massachusetts militia and a selectman of Falmouth for nine years.

Cushing's competitor in the West Indian trade, William Simonton, maintained a large wharf and warehouse in the cove that bears his name. The wharf was constructed of cribwork and extended out into the cove from what is now Wharf Point. In all probability the first cargoes of rum and molasses ever brought here from the West Indies were landed at this wharf. More commercial business was carried on in the Second Parish previous to 1760 than on the Neck. Simonton's Cove was frequently thronged with vessels, and many inhabitants of Falmouth sought employment here. This extensive trade, however, was annihilated during the revolution, and the fishing industry soon replaced it.

The population of the Second Parish had, by 1749, increased to approximately 900 including 150 families. Lumber, wood, and fishing still provided the principal business pursuits. Those engaged in the lumber trade specialized in the procurement of masts, spars, timber, and deal for the British Navy. The farming interests remained much neglected, so much so, that the people were almost entirely dependent upon importations from the South. The houses were all constructed of wood, generally unpainted and of but one story. As to the style of living, it was, in most cases, very plain and simple. However, good imported wines and liquor were more universally used than at the present time due to their direct importation and the low cost. The most common drinks were punch and flip, especially on public occasions that called the people together, notably town meetings, militia musters, ordinations, weddings, and funerals. These gatherings were quite likely to involve copious libations of these two beverages. Considerable importance was given to one's clothing on all such occasions, and provided a brief respite from the ordinary duties of ekeing out an existance. Those in the upper ranks of society took great care to display their superiority by careful attention to this matter of dress.

The mode of communication was primarily unchanged. There was no regular mail east of Portsmouth until 1760, and then but once a week. Previous to that time letters were kept until a sufficient number accumulated to warrant their being forwarded either by horseback or on foot to Falmouth. These two forms of transportation, other than by ship, provided the only means by which the inhabitants were able to travel. The old King's Highway through the Second Parish was still extensively used despite the road from Scarborough to the bridge at Stroudwater. Such then was the condition of the Second Parish when the last French and Indian War was declared in 1756.

This war, also called the Seven Years War, commenced one year earlier in the colonies. The town of Falmouth was spared the alarms and dangers to which it had formerly been exposed. However, the condition of fortifications was not overlooked and some of the more important ones were repaired. With the signing of the peace treaty in 1763, the defeated French ceded their North American holdings to Great Britain and Spain. The settlements in New England at last became forever free from the fear of future French and Indian depredations. The Penobscot, Passamaquoddy, St. John and Nova Scotia Indians had earlier entered into treaties with the English that remain unbroken to this day.

The first settled minister in the Second Parish, the Reverend Benjamin Allen, died the 6th of May, 1754. Almost immediately a bitter controversy broke out between the Presbyterian and Congregational elements over a successor. The first choice was the Reverend Eleazer Holyoke of Harvard College who, due to the controversy, declined the call. Soon after, the Reverend Ephraim Clark began to preach in the second Parish and accepted the call to settle there. Whereas a majority of the inhabitants were in favor of Mr. Clark, the vociferous Presbyterian minority, led by Colonel Ezekiel Cushing, railed against him. Their machinations were in vain, however, for he was subsequently installed and served the people for a total of forty-one years. The ill feeling continued for some time, but by 1765 the errant parishioners were back in the fold participating in the establishment of the District of Cape Elizabeth. That same year Colonel Cushing died at his residence on Cushing Point after a long and fruitful life.

The inhabitants of the Second Parish had been agitating for some time to be set off as a separate entity from the town of Falmouth. As early as 1742 they petitioned the General Court for an act of separation. The petitioners stressed the fact that poor roads, faulty ferry service and a lack of sufficient boats prevented the attendance of the inhabitants at the town meetings on the Neck. Due to this inability to attend to their particular interests they were not properly represented at the meetings. They also objected to supporting a school that their children were unable to attend for want of suitable transportation. The General Court stipulated that the petition be presented to the town meeting in May, 1743, and for all objections to it to be heard at that time.

Apparently the petition of 1742 was rejected at the town meeting for in 1749 the inhabitants again petitioned the General Court, elaborating on the original grievances. They were again instructed to present the petition to the next town meeting. This time the town of Falmouth drafted a reply to this petition and sent it to the General Court. In it they claimed that the inhabitants of the Second Parish were unjustly trying to rid themselves of their duty in maintaining the bridge at Stroudwater. The inhabitants of the Neck also declared that if the Second Parish was willing to support a school of their own that the town of Falmouth would release them from the support of any other. In conclusion they added that there was no objection to the Second Parish being set off if the matter of the bridge was attended to by either making it a county bridge or by stipulating that the proposed town assist in its maintainance. Nothing further was accomplished, however, until seven years later.

The Second Parish officially became the district of Cape Elizabeth on the 1st of November, 1765. The governmental affairs of the parish had been limited to church matters and the levying of taxes for ecclesiastical purposes. Under its new designation as a district it could perform all the functions of a town except the sending of a representative to the General Court. In the election of a representative the inhabitants of the District of Cape Elizabeth joined with the town of Falmouth.

Colonel Samuel Waldo, representative to the General Court from Falmouth, forwarded a warrant for the first meeting late in November. The first district meeting was held in the combination church and meeting house on the 2nd of December. A slate of officers was elected to manage the district affairs until the regular March meeting. The officers chosen were: James Maxwell, Captain Samuel Skillings, and Jonathan Loveitt, Selectmen; Thomas Simonton, District Clerk; Peter Woodbury, Constable; and Joseph Mariner, Clement Jordan, and Jos. Winslow, Assessors.

The March meeting of 1766 really established the district of Cape Elizabeth as a going concern. Elections were held and the Selectmen were re-elected. Also in accordance with the proper management of the district the other necessary officers were now elected. Besides the Selectmen, Assessors, District Clerk, Constable, District Treasurer, and Tax Collector, there was chosen a Clerk of the Market, a Sealer of Weights and Measures, four Fence Viewers and Field Drivers, nine Surveyors of the Highways, Six Hog Reeves, four Sealers of Wood and Surveyors of Lumber, three Cullers of Fish, two Sealers of Leather, two Deer Reeves, two

Wardens, three Tithing Men, two Cullers of Hoops and Staves, one Measurer of Corn, one Pound Keeper and a caretaker for the meeting house. There was also appropriated £40 for the support of a grammar school and £80 for Reverend Ephraim Clark's salary. A pound for stray livestock was ordered constructed in the southern part of the district and it was voted that the hogs be allowed to go at large if they were properly yoked and ringed. Apparently no attempt was made to confine the livestock to a district commons despite the fact that one had been previously designated and laid out in the northern part of the town.

Three other meetings were held during the year. In October Loring Cushing was hired as schoolmaster for the district and in December thirty men were dispatched to repair vital Long Creek Bridge. At this December meeting the district went on record as being in favor of quietly settling the recent disputes over enforcement of the Stamp Act of 1765 in Falmouth.

The district of Cape Elizabeth was rapidly acquiring the vestiges of an established town. Just prior to the incorporation a new grist mill had been established on Alewive Brook at the shore road. Further out on the tip of the Cape, at High Head, another new grist mill was also in operation. Both mills, however, have long since vanished. One stone from the Alewive Brook mill rested for some years atop the small hill at the Pond Cove intersection.

The mill at High Head was wind driven and similar in construction to those on Cape Cod. The windmill's pivot shaft rested in a socket cut into an outcropping of ledge. This socket can still be seen as the ledge is located in the front yard of the house occupied by the keeper at Two Lights State Park. Apparently the mill survived to the end of the century for in Blunt's *American Coast Pilot* of 1798 it is given as a land mark for mariners. When it was dismantled the upper millstone was used as a mooring anchor at Seal Cove. The lower stone now rests on the front lawn of the Alonzo Murray summer cottage at Peabble's Cove.

Another industry that was proving to be quite profitable, and had also been instituted shortly before incorporation, was the manufacturing of salt. General Samuel Waldo's farm at Long Creek was the scene of an extensive salt works and the product found a ready market in this area. Much of it was shipped from Waldo's Wharf at Long Creek Point. Simonton's Cove also figured prominently in the production of salt. Here was situated a small salt-boiling establishment, not quite as large as that on Waldo's farm, but ample enough to satisfy the local requirements.

The area under cultivation was increasing as was the population. In these years prior to the revolution the business of running the district went placidly on. The usual matters were brought before the voters with occasional items that shed some light on conditions of the period. At the March meeting in 1767 wolves were so numerous that the district added a bounty of five pounds per head over and above that granted by the Province. This same year the constable found it necessary to encourage the departure of undesirable settlers and the district for the first time had to support several persons in distressed circumstances. The year 1768 saw an expenditure of twenty shillings for the building of stocks and a choir granted the use of the rear pews in the men's section of the church.

The inhabitants joined with Falmouth in September of 1768 in sending General Jedidiah Preble as their delegate to the "convention for governmental reform" held in Faneuil Hall, Boston. As this was the first protest of its kind the representatives calmly recorded their grievances, declared their loyalty and advised the people to refrain from riotous gatherings, at the same time obeying civil authority. Evidently they were apprehensive of the step they had taken and sought to avoid unpleasant repercussions by recommending moderate measures. They were doomed to disappointment as George III soon dispatched troops to Boston producing disastrous results. It was to be two years, however, before any organized rebellion would occur.

In the interim the district continued to be preoccupied with its own municipal affairs. The wolf bounty was maintained at forty shillings per head, the care of the poor was farmed out to various inhabitants, the Reverend Mr. Clark received his salary of eighty pounds, Loring Cushing, the teacher, was presented with twenty pounds, and the choir was granted the privilege of constructing a pew, at their own expense, in the back of the church. The citizens were not, however, oblivious of colonial affairs for in 1770 six pounds was appropriated to purchase a town stock of ammunition.

It was not until 1772 that the course of events took on an ominous note. Late in that year the district received a "Letter of Correspondence" from the committee appointed at Boston's town meeting. This missive listed the violations of their colonial rights by acts of Parliament, and the minutes of their protest meeting. The district met on the 22nd of December, and chose a committee of eleven men to take the matter into consideration. This committee consisted of Peter Woodbury, Daniel Strout, Thomas Simonton, John Armstrong, Samuel Dunn, James Maxwell, Samuel Skillin, Joseph Weston, Clement Jordan, Henry Dyer, and Joseph Mariner. Another meeting was called on the 24th and the committee presented five resolves for the district to act upon. The report stipulated in essence that Cape Elizabeth could and should protest against the "manifest violations" of their "charter rights and privileges," and seek a redress of these grievances by constitutional methods. They also recommend that the district unite with Boston, or any other town, to accomplish this end, that a Committee of Correspondence be appointed "to correspond with the town of Boston and any other district . . . who have spirit enough to stand up in defense of their charter rights and privileges . . ." and that the district extend "their thanks to the town of Boston for their early and indefatigable zeal in endeavoring to preserve the constitutional rights of this Province." The resolves were passed in the affirmative and a copy thereof forwarded to Boston. A Committee of Correspondence was immediately formed, consisting of five men, viz., Henry Dyer, Joseph Mariner, Dr. Nathaniel Jones, Dr. Clement Jordan, and Daniel Strout. With this protestation on the record the district waited out the next developments. The inhabitants of Cape Elizabeth were apparently a little more zealous in these matters than their Falmouth brethren for it was not until early in 1774 that a Committee of Correspondence was formed in that town. This lack of activity in Falmouth was largely due to the adoption of an extremely cautious attitude.

The following year, 1773, six men were added to the Committee of Correspondence, viz., Patrick Maxwell, David Strout, Captain Samuel Skillin, George Strout, Jr., Captain Jonathan Loveitt and Noah Jordan. But it was not until 1774 that the District again displayed its revolutionary leanings. At the meeting held on the 23rd of February a new set of resolves were drawn up and immediately approved by the citizens. It was resolved that

> At such an alarming and critical time of our publick affairs as this when our enemies in Great Britain are using every stratagen in their power to wrest from us that best of blessings Liberty, we think ourselves and all the Sons of Freedom loudly called upon to express our abhorance of such measures, and our willingness at all times to join our brethren upon this Continent in preventing their deep laid schemes taking effect by all lawful Constitution methods. . .

With this as their salutation, they proceeded to proclaim that they were in complete accord with the resolves recently passed in

Philadelphia, i.e., that the method of taxation was unjust, had a tendency to introduce arbitrary government and slavery, and must be opposed if even the shadow of liberty was to be preserved. They also reiterated that this opposition was a duty that every free man in America owed to his country, to himself, and to posterity. They further declared that the duty on tea was an attack upon the liberties of America, that anyone who aided or abeted the use of this tea was an enemy of the people, and that they would not use it in their homes or associate with people who did. The meeting was closed with the vote that the district exend its heartfelt thanks "to the town of Boston for their vigilance and care in the Publick cause, and also to all other towns who have exerted themselves in the glorious cause of Liberty."

The meeting on the 21st of March disposed of the usual business of the district and provided for a new Committee of Correspondence, viz., Joseph Mariner, David Strout, Clement Jordan, Nathaniel Jones, Daniel Strout, Samuel Skillin and Henry Dyer. Later in the year on the 6th of September the citizens again met in reference to the distressing state of affairs. They sent Doctor Clement Jordan, Doctor Nathaniel Jones, and Samuel Dunn to the Convention at Falmouth that met on the 21st to effect a plan of action in relation to a nonimportation agreement. Peter Woodbury, George Strout, and Captain Judah Dyer were added to the Cape Elizabeth delegation on the 8th. This convention met at Alice Greely's tavern and presented a definite warlike appearance, as half the delegates were armed. As General Thomas Gage had dissolved the General Court in May, the convention summoned his representative, Sheriff William Tyng, and instructed him not to enforce the late act of Parliament in reference to regulating civil government in the province.

The district, at the meeting on the 6th, also voted unanimously that it would abide by the Charter, granted by King William and Queen Mary in 1691, and the laws of the province with reference to the holding of town and district meetings. At the same time seventeen pounds was appropriated to purchase a district supply of powder and balls.

Three other meetings were held in this decisive year of 1774. On the 23rd of September nine shillings were voted to purchase of Samuel Freeman a copy of the resolves formulated at the late convention. At the next meeting, the 21st of October, two volunteer companies of Minute Men were formed. Captain Nathaniel Jordan, Jr., and Lieutenant Clement Jordan were elected to form the Spurwink Company, with Captain Daniel Strout and Lieutenant Samuel Dunn forming the Purpooduck Company. Officers of each company were to choose their own subalterns and the district clerk was authorized to draw up the commissions. The last meeting, held the 21st of December, certainly left no doubt as to the district's position. The first Continental Congress had convened the 5th of September at Philadelphia and the first Provincial Congress met at Salem, Massachusetts, October 7th. In reference thereto, the citizens of Cape Elizabeth passed the following resolutions whereby they

> . . . highly approved and sincerely accede to the just state of the rights & grievances of the British Colonies in American & of all the Measures adopted & recommended by the American Continental congress for the restoration & reestablishing of our former rights & privileges . . . that we think if the association is strictly adhered to, it will be the most probable means under God to procure a repeal of the late grievances & oppressive Acts of Parliament & thereby restore harmony between the Mother Country and the Colonies . . . that we fully approve of the recommendations of the Provincial Congress, and that our conduct shall be regulated accordingly . . . that our most Hearty Thanks are due to those Patriotic Gentlemen who composed the Continental & Provincial Congresses & we shall always esteem them the Barriers of our Libertys.

As a token of their concern for the poor of Boston they sent a donation of forty-four and a half cords of wood to alleviate a shortage thereof. Accompanying the donation of fire wood was the following letter dated Cape Elizabeth, 18 January 1775:

> To the Committee of Correspondence.
> Gentlemen: This you will receive by Capt. Judah Dyer, by whom district have sent about forty-eight cords of wood, as a small present to the poor sufferers of Boston. We shall assist in relieving their wants as far as our ability will admit until that detestable Act for blocking up the harbor of Boston is repealed.
> We are, Gentlemen, your hearty friends in the cause of liberty.
> By the order of the Committee of Correspondence,
> David Strout, Clerk

To this the Boston Committee of Correspondence replied 1 February 1775:

> Mr. David Strout at Cape Elizabeth.
> Sir: The kind relief you have afforded our industrious poor in your generous donation of forty-four and a half cords of wood, merit our acknowlegement. Though grievously oppressed, and suffering the most severe trials by a most cruel and arbitrary ministry, yet we are determined to stand firm and hope that we shall be favored with a continuance of your friendship, which we shall ever esteem ourselves

happy in maintaining by a steady and uniform conduct. Being in haste, we only wish the Parent of the Universe may shower down the greatest blessings on our benevolent friends, and am with much esteem.

Jno. Avery,
Per order Committee

The year 1775 opened on a solemn note with the Provincial Congress urging the people to prepare for resistance and the district of Cape Elizabeth restated its position by again voting acceptance of the Philadelphia resolves of 1774 at its meeting on the 23rd of February. The news of the battle of Lexington arrived on the 21st of April and three days later on the 24th the citizens of Cape Elizabeth assembled to prepare for war. A night watch of eight men was immediately instituted to forestall an attack by water. At five o'clock p.m. each day two men were to proceed to Falmouth, four to positions between Spring Point and the ferry, and two more to the outer Cape. The district voted to supply the Minute Men with provisions for a fortnight, muskets, bayonets, and a dollar per man, if it became necessary that they be called to arms. The district's supply of powder and balls was also carefully checked. The same day Captain Samuel Dunn mustered his company into the Continental service for active duty. This company was made up largely of Cape Elizabeth men and was at first billeted within the town. Three district meetings were held in May. On the 4th one hundred pounds was raised to purchase food stuffs for the use of the district and to be under the supervision of the Committee of Inspection. An additional stock of powder was procured on the 20th and distributed among the citizens. The most drastic steps were taken on the 30th when it was voted:

> ... that if any dispute arise between any persons in this District we advise them not to go to law but to choose three or more persons to decide their disputes, and if any persons who shall refuse & will go to law he or they shall be judged Enemies to this District & we will withdraw all connections with them & post them in said District at the Meeting House by the Committee of Inspection.

Cape Elizabeth was now irrevocably committed to the pursuance of open revolt against the British Crown.

The company of Cape Elizabeth men, under Captain Samuel Dunn, remained billeted in the district until the 11th of July. On this day, they left to join Colonel Edmund Phinney's 31st Regiment of Foot at Cambridge after being supplied with provisions by the district. The regiment remained on active duty until the 31st of December, when it was disbanded to form the 18th Continental Regiment. Some of the men reenlisted in this new regiment, also commanded by Colonel Phinney, and some returned home. During their stay at Cambridge Parson Ephraim Clark visited the regiment late in August and remained about a month serving as temporary chaplain.

A new company was formed under Captain David Strout in June, 1775, just prior to the departure of Captain Dunn's company. It was designated a Sea Coast Company and remained on active duty until the 1st of November. Like its predecessors it was billeted in the district, but differed in that it remained throughout its term of service.

The district of Cape Elizabeth became a town by resolve of the Provincial Congress on the 23rd of August. Henceforth it could elect its own representatives to the Massachusetts General Court or Provincial Congress as it was now designated. At its first meeting as a town on the 6th of September the citizens restated their pledge to abide by King William's Charter of 1691. They met again on the 19th and formed a new twelve man Committee of Correspondence and Inspection, viz., David Strout, Doctor Nathaniel Jones, Daniel Strout, Deacon Henry Dyer, Joseph Cobb, Peter Woodbury, John Armstrong, Jr., Jonathan Emery, Captain Samuel Skillin, James Leach, Doctor Clement Jordan, and Jonathan Fickett. This Committee was equal in authority to the newly formed five man Committee of Safety, viz., Willian Simonton, Doctor Nathaniel Jones, Deacon Henry Dyer, Captain Joseph Mariner, and Major Thrasher. Needless to say there was some duplication of authority.

This year was not without its anxious moments however, for on the 18th of October Captain Henry Mowatt of the Royal Navy, with a fleet of five vessels bombarded the town of Falmouth for approximately nine hours. When evening fell a large part of the town was in ashes, but fortunately the inhabitants suffered no fatalities. During the bombardment Captain David Strout and his Sea Coast Company took defensive measures at Cape Elizabeth to prevent the removal of any livestock by the British.

The town was now continually occupied with matters pertaining to the conflict with England. The year 1776 saw James Leach sent as their first representative to the General Court and the usual items of business relative to the running of the town attended to. A new Committee of Correspondence was voted and fifty pounds was appropriated for a town stock of powder. Their revolutionary zeal continued as before and they voted in May to comply with the Continental Congress with reference to independence. When the Declaration of Independence was promulgated in July, the town clerk copied this momentous document into the town records in full. Early in the year Captain Briant Morton's company of volunteers replaced the Sea Coast Company under Captain David Strout. Almost immediately they set to work constructing a fort on Peter Woodbury's land at Spring Point to be named Fort Hancock. This point recently occupied by Fort Preble, received its name from an excellent spring located at its extremity, that was famous for many years due to the purity of its water.

In May 1776 Captain Morton received an order from Colonel Jonathan Mitchell, his regimental commander, to place a guard of eight men at Portland Head as a lookout for enemy vessels. To give the alarm he was to fire one gun for a single ship and two guns for any number above that. He was also ordered to keep at least forty-eight men continually employed each day at Fort Hancock until it was completed. The men were not to leave the area of the fort and were to reside in barracks to be built immediately. This fort, named for Governor John Hancock, was finished in June and the Massachusetts General Court dispatched four cannon, i.e., two twelve pounders and two nine pounders, forty pounds of shot, and four barrels of powder for its armament. However, the cannon they designated had one or both trunnions missing. Captain Morton's Company served until late November when it was replaced by a company under Captain James Leach. By this time the fort was serving as the protector of an ever increasing number of privateers that used Falmouth harbor as a base of operations.

The town began to really feel the privations incident to the rebellion the following year. The new paper money was rapidly depreciating and in the month of February the town posted an extensive list fixing the prices of food stuffs, wages, dry goods, etc. pursuant to an order of the General Court. Practically everything that involved the expenditure of money was included in this listing. At the July meeting Lieutenant John Armstrong was appointed to ferret out any Tories in the town and to provide the General Court with evidence thereof. The enforcement of price control was not overlooked and four men were given authority to see that it was not neglected. Later in the year, the town voted to provide for the familes of men serving in the Continental Army and a committee of five were elected to attend to it.

The force at Fort Hancock continued with Captain John Wentworth's company of forty men replacing Captain Leach's in May of 1777. Its armament was reinforced by the addition of more powder and other necessities. Further out on the Cape, at Portland Head, two poles were erected for signaling purposes. One flag denoted enemy ships to the westward and two flags, enemy ships to the eastward. When Captain Wentworth's company finished its tour of duty late in 1777 it was replaced by a force under the command of Sergeant George Deake and henceforth the garrison at Fort Hancock was to be a part of the combined defenses of Falmouth. The total number of men at the fort varied considerably depending upon the season with fewer men being stationed there during the winter months.

The town found it necessary in 1778 to petition the General Court for a reduction of its quota of men. In April it supplied eight men for the Continental Army, but only after sixteen hundred dollars had been raised as a bounty. Despite the fact that the country as a whole was suffering acutely from inflation, this was quite a sum to raise for such purposes. In the petition dated the 26th of May, the citizens declared that so many men were serving in the army that it was affecting the ability of the town to raise sufficient crops to supply its own needs. Also that in providing sufficient men to repel an attack on Fort Hancock the number of available men was considerably reduced. Unfortunately the General Court did not grant the reduction and the situation was to grow a great deal worse before they changed their minds. Despite these difficulties the town voted that they ". . . fully & cheerfully agree to the Articles of Confederation & Perpetual Union agreed on by the Honorable Congress of the United States of America."

Late in this same year an epidemic of small pox broke out in the town and in order to enforce isolation a fine of fifty pounds was imposed upon those persons who visited the afflicted other than those granted permission by the Selectmen. The town authorities also decreed that any person that went to Falmouth and was vaccinated could not reenter the town for a period of thirty-five days. Coupled with this epidemic was the scarcity of food. The crop yield was reduced to one-half by a severe drought sending the cost of provisions even higher than before and causing further depreciation of the Continental currency. These were indeed distressing times.

This then was the situation that greeted the new year, 1779.

People were moving from the town, the number of soldiers' families to be cared for was increasing, and the price of food stuffs was prohibitive. In addition to these domestic difficulties there appeared in June a request for more troops to be enlisted for an undisclosed project. The town appointed a committee at the 28th of June meeting viz., Captain Daniel Strout, Jonathan Fickett and Lieutenant George Deake, to enlist men for a "secret expedition." This was the ill-fated Bagaduce Expedition against the British base at Castine. It was primarily a Massachusetts undertaking for which they appropriated fifty thousand pounds. The newly formed District of Maine was requested to supply approximately one thousand men.

Cumberland County's contribution was a regiment of foot under the able command of Colonel Jonathan Mitchell of North Yarmouth. Despite the fact that able bodied men were at a premium Cape Elizabeth did manage to enlist one company of fifty-three men with Captain Joshua Jordan in command. The town also supplied the regiment's second in command and surgeon; they were Lieutenant Colonel Nathaniel Jordan and Doctor Nathaniel Jones respectively. Possibly to ensure secrecy the citizens at this same June meeting, voted to forbid the departure of any boat or ship from the town without permission of the Committee of Safety.

The regiment sailed on the 16th of July and rendezvoused at Boothbay Harbor. The combined forces arrived at Castine the 24th and a landing was effected the 28th at Trask's Rock. If the whole operation had been as successful as this landing of four hundred green militia-men and marines the final outcome of the expedition would have been far different. On August 14th the British succeeded in destroying the entire fleet engaged in the expedition thus ending Massachusetts' separate naval force. As no military success had been or could be obtained the troops commenced their disastrous withdrawal. Colonel Mitchell's regiment arrived in Falmouth about the middle of September after a long and laborious journey through the woods. In this arduous retreat one of Cape Elizabeth's leading citizens, Doctor Nathaniel Jones, died of exposure on the 4th of September. Captain Joshua Jordan's company was officially discharged the 24th of September thus ending the participation of Cape Elizabeth in the Bagaduce imbroglio.

The condition of the town grew worse in the next two years as it bravely carried on in support of the revolution. To raise its quota of men in 1780 it was again necessary to provide a bounty. As an incentive to enlist the town promised each man a gratuity of forty shillings per month for the time spent in the Continental service beyond the limits of the town. This same year it compensated the men of Captain Joshua Jordan's company by paying them forty shillings in silver or produce for each month they spent on active duty. To meet assessments made on the town by the General Court to help support the Continental Army, it sent produce in lieu of cash and also forwarded its quota of shirts, shoes, stockings, blankets, etc. In order to fill the beef levy the sum of nine thousand pounds was raised by the town to purchase it, as their own supply was practically nonexistent. Added to the inherent discomforts of the war was the severe winter of 1779-80. The cold was so intense that the harbor froze over as far as Simonton's Cove. In addition the snow was unusually deep, and blown by fierce winds, accumulated in tremendous drifts making travel impossible. There was great suffering throughout the area due to a lack of wood and water. The meeting house was apparently untenantable as the meetings were held in Mrs. Jane Woodbury's tavern during the early months of 1780.

There occurred in February of this year an incident that produced great excitement both in the town of Cape Elizabeth and in Falmouth. On the 12th the schooner *Nancy* ran ashore and bilged near the tip of the Cape. This vessel proved to be a cartel from Halifax, Nova Scotia, carrying between fifty and sixty prisoners, bound for Boston. Aboard was her owner, Mr. Prescott, and the government's representative, Commander Patrick Valence. There was apparently some disagreement between the two as to whether or not the schooner could be saved. Commander Valence, however, took charge and arranged with the Committee of Safety in Cape Elizabeth to sell the vessel while Prescott was away obtaining assistance to save her. Within forty-eight hours the vessel had been stripped and auctioned off, and hull burnt for the metal it contained. Commander Valence realized about seventeen hundred dollars from the sale. Prescott, meanwhile, notified Colonel Peter Noyes of Falmouth of this action and he in turn contacted the Massachusetts General Court.

The following March the General Court commissioned Colonel Noyes to seize the various articles, etc. saved from the *Nancy* and to return the names of those who refused to comply with his demands. Unfortunately his endeavors were not crowned with success as he was forced to turn in a list of the offenders who readily admitted receiving articles from the wreck but who also refused to deliver them up. In this list were such prominent men as Stephen Hall, Joseph, William, and Arthur McLellan, Benjamin Titcomb, Daniel Ilsley, John Fox, Nathaniel Deering, and Joseph Ingraham. The General Court ordered their respective arrests but the final outcome is unknown. Commander Valence, however, was cashiered for his part in the sale of the schooner and was deported to Halifax.

The garrison was continued at Fort Hancock by various companies drawn from Colonel Joseph Prime's regiment, stationed at Falmouth. In relation to the fort the town of Cape Elizabeth petitioned the General Court to supply it with colors, guard boats, and more troops. This was accomplished in 1780 much to the satisfaction of the inhabitants, despite the fact that it brought a request that more troops be recruited from the town the following year.

This new quota of men for the Continental service in 1781, required the raising of a new bounty of one hundred and sixty "hard dollars" plus the added incentive of ten "hard dollars" per month before enlistments could be started. A committee of three members, viz., Captain Daniel Strout, Joshua Jordan and Benjamin Fickett, was chosen to sign the men up and was given an ample supply of rum with which to treat the enlistees. Closely following the call for men was another demand for supplies. Once again it became necessary to purchase the required number of shirts, stockings, blankets, etc. in order to satisfy the levy. Of the money appropriated, two hundred and fifty seven pounds were set aside to also purchase the beef quota, amounting to 19,205 pounds.

The winters continued to be severe and added much to the general misery of the inhabitants. The heavy accumulations of snow isolated many and in some cases caused protracted sufferings. When it was necessary for a meeting to be held during the colder months, the citizens adjourned to Mrs. Woodbury's tavern, to warm themselves internally as well as externally. Without a doubt these gatherings became quite social after the business was attended to and occasioned the frequent imbibing of stimulants sufficient to withstand the rigors of a Maine winter.

Perhaps the most heartrending document that this town ever drafted in any war was the petition it forwarded to the General Court in January of 1782. In it the town gave evidence of why its quota of men for the Continental service should be reduced. They stated that the town had furnished more than their quota in former times, with few of the men ever returning, which, coupled with their extraordinary losses at sea, had produced a large number of widows and orphans. Additional to this was their loss in the shipping and fishing trades. To verify their statements, the petitioners, i.e. the selectmen, enumerated in detail their losses since 1776. The heaviest casualty list was that involving operations at sea. Lost in the privateer *Cumberland,* Captain Collins commander, were Joseph Parker, Richard Langley, Robert Stanford, Jr., Thomas Stanford, James Dyer, Samuel Jordan, John Curate, David Strout, Jr., Thomas Cushing, Samuel Small, Isaac Jordan, Thomas Webster, Thomas Jordan, and Nathaniel Wheeler; in the privateer *Stilflen,* Captain Day commander, Reuben Dyer; in a Newbury ship of eighteen guns, Simon Jordan; in the privateer *General Wadsworth,* Andrew Jordan; in the guardship at New York, Josiah Walles, Benjamin Dyer, and Christopher Strout; in the privateer *Civil Usage,* Peter Dyer, Barney Sawyer, Thomas York, and John Gammon; with Captain George Mitchell, William Jones, Stephen Cash, James Webber, Samuel Robinson, and Samuel Gammon; with Captain Stone, Joseph Maxwell, Thomas Maxwell, and Francis Cash; with Captain Hinkley, Joseph Stanford, Jeremiah Jordan, Ebenezer Jordan, and Israel Jordan; with Captain Arthur McCallen, William McCallen, and Mathew Simonton; and in a prize brigantine at Piscatiqua Harbor, Ebenezer Robinson, Walter Simonton, Ebenezer Sawyer, and Richard Stanford. Those who died in the Continental Army numbered nineteen with an additional six missing in action. Lastly was a list of forty-six men who moved away in the same period which included, incidentally, two "refuges" or torys, viz. Stileman Jordan and Jacob Webb. This petition had been preceded by a petition of like purpose but gave in greater detail the maritime troubles. By the end of the year 1781, the town did not have a single vessel capable of carrying on foreign or coastal trade and retained only a few fishing boats. These remaining vessels were unable to leave the harbor due to the large number of British ships, heavily armed, that were operating from the Penobscot area. Even the vessels at anchor in the harbor were not entirely safe, as the British occasionally carried on successful cutting-out activities. Supplemental to this doleful state of affairs, was the fact that the town had been plagued for several years by a protracted drought, practically negating agricultural pursuits. The General Court, after carefully weighing all the factors in the case, plus a mistake as to the number of taxable polls, granted the town an abatement in future quotas.

The war was now drawing to a close but still the burdens

Spurwink Church as rebuilt in 1835.

Octagonal stone pyramid built in 1811 on the site of the current Cape Elizabeth Light and demolished in 1828.

Eastern tower of Cape Elizabeth Lights showing iron towers erected in 1874. Circa 1878.

Western tower of Cape Elizabeth Lights. Circa 1920.

were many and exacting. One particularly galling problem was the clandestine trade carried on with the British. A committee of twenty-two men was appointed by the town late in 1782 to obliterate it and prosecute the offenders. This same year the citizens, acting on a circular from Boston, gave their support to insure a united expression on the fisheries protection issue with reference to the proposed peace treaty. The Committee of Safety and Correspondence was chosen for the last time at the 18th of March meeting in 1783. On the 31st news arrived that hostilities had at last ended and on the 4th of April it was officially confirmed. There was widespread rejoicing throughout the day punctuated by sporadic artillery saluates. The garrison at Fort Hancock was disbanded and the town took charge of its cannon, powder, etc. The 1st of May witnessed another celebration when it was learned that the preliminary articles of peace had been ratified. It occasioned extensive festivities, and artillery salutes, thirteen at a time, were fired during the day.

Cape Elizabeth, at the end of the war, contained 175 houses valued at twenty-five pounds each, 131 barns valued at fifteen pounds each, and 4 mills valued at forty-five pounds each. There were 24 tons of vessel property, 111 horses, 236 oxen, 600 cows, 1164 sheep, and 178 swine. There was also 1034 acres of English mowing land, 858 acres of salt marsh, 4023 acres of pasturage, and 4588 acres of woodland. That the citizens were not particularly wealthy is borne out by the fact that there was not a carriage in the town and but 100 ounces of silver plate scattered among the inhabitants. These figures are probably an approximation due to the unsettled nature of the times.

Almost immediately the town became engrossed in its own municipal affairs. A settlement was reached with the Reverend Ephraim Clark over his back salary, construction was started on a workhouse for the poor, the alewive fishery at Alewive Brook was closely regulated, and the ferry across the harbor at Spring Point was brought under the surveillance of a citizens committee. As in earlier times some livestock, viz., oxen, rams, sheep, and swine, were allowed to run at large under certain laws promulgated by the town. These animals had distinctive ear markings that denoted ownership and were recorded by the town clerk. Each inhabitant had his own special mark, i.e. Jonathan Loveitt's had a hole in each ear; Henry Dyer's had a swallow-tall cut in each ear; the Reverend Ephriam Clark's had a swallow-tail cut in each ear and a half penny on the underside of the left ear; etc. A pound was maintained for those animals that strayed or were loose during a closed period. Despite the fact that funds were frequently appropriated for the building of a town pound it is doubtful if one was ever constructed. The Pound Keeper usually impounded the recalcitrant creatures in his barn until claimed by the owner or otherwise disposed of.

The neighboring town of Falmouth also experienced a rapid return to more normal conditions. On the 4th of July, 1786, the Massachusetts General Court set off that portion of the town known as the "Neck" and incorporated it as the town of Portland. The name was chosen for its euphonious qualities and its early connections with the area. Cushing's Island was first called by this name. The point of land opposite in Cape Elizabeth was known as Portland Head and the body of water between the two was designated as Portland Sound. It is of interest to note here that the citizens of Cape Elizabeth once considered giving this name to their community but when it was set off as a district in 1765 the General Court decided otherwise.

The postal service had improved to the extent that the mails arrived from Boston three times a week in summer and twice a week in the winter. A post office had been established at Falmouth in 1775, and in 1787 the Mail Stage between Portland and Portsmouth was inaugurated. The stage required three days to cover the distance between these two towns. The residents of Cape Elizabeth in order to receive their mail had to journey to the Portland Post Office. This was facilitated somewhat by the posting of lists containing the names of persons who had letters awaiting them.

One very important event of these post-war years was the incorporation of Portland Bridge, later called Vaughan's Bridge, the 25th of February 1794. The proprietors, twenty in number, were headed by William Vaughan. This gentleman settled on Bramhall's Hill at Portland late in 1787. He envisioned a great real estate development at this western terminus of the Neck and the bridge was to be the beginning. Work on the new bridge was not begun, however, until 1800 when the act of incorporation was extended and the name of the structure changed to Vaughan's Bridge.

The bridge spanned Fore River at Bramhall's Point and was located approximately where Davis plied his ferry about 1686. Its total span was twenty-six hundred feet and was built of cobbwork with archs across the gaps between cobbs. A lift draw was constructed in the bridge over the river's east channel pursuant to the act of incorporation. It was quite naturally a toll bridge and when it was opened late in 1800 a detailed list of rates were posted. To cross one way on foot cost two cents, on horseback six cents, with a chaise, sulkey or sleigh drawn by two horses twelve cents and a half, with a coach, chariot, phaeton or curricle twenty-five cents and on up until most combinations of man and beast were covered. The new bridge considerably shortened the trip to Portland from Saco and beyond. Previously, travelers had to journey to Stroudwater and use the bridge built by Colonel Thomas Westbrook. Almost immediately Vaughan's Bridge became one of the busiest thoroughfares in the area despite the toll exactions. The need for the bridge had been great and the town of Cape Elizabeth lent its support to the project as early as 1791. A year prior to the incorporation of the bridge the town had reconstructed Long Creek Bridge after a freshet had carried it away. Here they constructed four cobb-work piers to support the structure and provide a substantial bridge. When William Vaughan and his associates began their crossing of Fore River, Cape Elizabeth had a large amount of valuable experience to donate to the project.

As the century drew to a close the town of Cape Elizabeth still exhibited signs of the recent war. Abandoned farms and fallow fields were much in evidence for the town had experienced a severe drop in the number of its inhabitants in the period 1776 to 1800. The war with its inherent privations and Cape Elizabeth's particularly heavy losses quite possibly account for the decrease from 1469 in 1776 to 1355 in 1790. This exodus of its inhabitants must have continued after the war for the population had dwindled to 1275 by 1800. This was, however, the lowest point for as the new century progressed the town was to grow both in population and prosperity.

CHAPTER III

EARLY DEVELOPMENTS

The opening years of the nineteenth century found the town actively employed in the running of its own governmental affairs. As usual the regular town officers were elected at the March meeting, with such matters as the care of the poor, the regulation of the alewive fishery, the collection of taxes, the maintenance of roads, and establishment of a crow bounty of twelve and a half cents a head, rigorously pursued. Occasionally a note of military preparedness was injected into the meetings. A powder magazine was constructed in 1808 for the towns' stock of powder with additional sums appropriated from time to time to keep up the supply and its repository in repair.

Spring Point once again became the scene of martial activity. In view of the existing difficulties with England, Congress made provision for coast defense and ordered the construction of a fort at the Point. Massachusetts ceded the land to the government in March, along with land on House Island, for fortification purposes, and work was immediately begun.

This new brick and granite fort was constructed upon the site of Fort Hancock thus obliterating all traces of the revolutionary defenses. Its channel front was semi-circular in plan, and on its flanks and rear it had the lines of a star fort. The length of the superior slope from the interior to the exterior crest was ten feet, six inches, and on the land side, near the sally-port, four feet and two inches. Inside the enclosure were two double buildings for officer's quarters, a shot furnace, magazine, barracks, and a well. Its armament consisted of seven thirty-two pounders, five eight-inch howitzers, and one twelve pounder, all mounted in barbette.

Dedication services were held on Saturday the 26th of November, 1808 and the fort was named in honor of Commodore Edward Preble, hero of the Barbary Wars and a native of Portland. The fort was immediately garrisoned by a company of the United States Light Infantry.

Under the date of January 6, 1809, President Thomas Jefferson, in a message to Congress on the subject of seacoast defense, reported that "Fort Preble, a new enclosed work of stone and brick masonry with a brick barrack quarters and magazines, is completed. This work is erected on Spring Point, and commands the entrance of the harbor through the main channel." Later this same year on the 4th of March its sister work Fort Scammel, located on House Island, was dedicated.

Previous to this time, a storm had been gathering in Europe, which threatened to involve the United States in a war with England. In May, 1806, Great Britain declared the continent of Europe, from the Elbe to Brest, to be under blockade. On the 21st of November, Napoleon issued his famous "Berlin Decree," placing the British Isles under a blockade, whereby the vessels of neutral countries, in visiting English ports, were liable to seizure. By way of retaliation, the British government, issued an "order in council," forbidding neutral nations to visit French ports or countries from which British vessels were barred. This was followed by another "order in council" on the 11th of November, 1807, prohibiting all neutrals from trading with France or her allies unless they paid tribute to Great Britain. These acts, coupled with the impressment of American merchant seamen, and unwarranted attacks on American naval vessels, prompted the United States Congress to pass, on the 21st of December, 1807, an Embargo Act forbidding American vessels to sail for any foreign ports.

The enforcement of the Embargo Act was so ruinous to local interests that it was violated. Cargoes were gathered, and when the auspicious moment arrived, loaded aboard a vessel in the dead of night. By morning the vessel was usually far beyond the reach of governmental officials. In a few particularly flagrant cases, vessels were quickly loaded and sailed away in broad daylight so rapidly, that they left the federal officials with their gunboats and forts powerless to interfere. The two harbor entrance forts, Preble and Scammel, were dubbed "Embargo Forts," designed more to keep American shipping in than to prevent the entrance of British naval vessels.

When War was finally declared against Great Britain on the 19th of June, 1812 Portland Harbor presented a doleful appearance. Both the Cape Elizabeth and Portland shores were crowded with dismantled ships and lesser craft, some ashore in the several coves, some swinging at anchor, with still others lining the wharves, all in the same state of inactivity. The officers and men who had sailed these vessels were idle and ready for any adventure that would offer remunerative employment. Encouraged by the government, the owners of many a small, fast vessel in the District of

Maine began to think of making her a private cruiser. Early in the war men were not wanting to ship for wages or a share in the profits. On the 26th of June, 1812, Congress authorized the issuance of letters of marque and reprisal. Within a week Isaac Ilsley, collector of the port of Portland, issued several to local men. It brought a welcome relief from the distress and inactivity of the embargo days. All along the coast keels were laid and vessels rapidly assembled often of green lumber, with their prime requisite being high speed and maneuverability.

Early in the war Cape Elizabeth appointed Anthony Strout, Charles Staples, and John Sawyer a committee of safety, Zebulon Trickey keeper of the town's replenished stock of powder and ball, and voted to pay militia men on active duty fifteen dollars per month. It was not until 1814, however, that the town was actually threatened by the enemy. A state of blockade on the New England coast had been proclaimed by the British in April with three seventy-fours, two frigates, one schooner, a tender and ten transports dispatched to the Maine coast. The flag-ship of this detachmen, the *Bulwark,* a seventy-four, had been putting in daily appearances just beyond Portland Head when the news arrived the first of September that the British were preparing an invasion force at Castine. At this time they occupied inland Maine as far as Hampden. As Portland was considered the destination of this projected invasion the town of Cape Elizabeth was greatly alarmed. A large number of families fled inland with their household effects and valuable stocks of goods were removed to places of safety.

Two companies of militia were put on active duty in the town the 8th of September to supplement Captain Watson Rand's company of Cape Elizabeth men that had been activated the 5th of August. These two companies were commanded by Captain Ezekiel Dyer, and Lieutenant Henry Dyer. All three companies were stationed at the Cape or saw service in Portland.

Captain Rand's company bivouaced for a while near the old Dyer house at High Head. It was probably during their encampment that a British vessel carried out a sheep stealing raid at Richmond's Island. From the meager evidence available it appears that the British fired a few six-pounder balls in the direction of the militia encampment to discourage interference. Two of these balls have since been turned up by the plow in the vicinity of the old Dyer place and both are six-pounder shot.

Fort Preble was reinforced by various militia companies during this anxious period. Some of them were billeted with the inhabitants living nearby. Captain Samuel Robinson's company from Hebron is an excellent example of this. Some of his men resided at the old Ebenezer Thrasher house, leaving the "Widow" Thrasher only one room, with still other militiamen messing there. When the company arrived the "widow" had a flock of over seventy chickens, but as their period of residence lengthened the number of chickens decreased until only the old rooster remained. He vanished the night before the company departed for home. They may not have had to face British fire but they certainly braved the sniping of irate farmers during potato foraging expeditions at night.

Most of the militia companies had been discharged by the 1st of November. The two companies under Captain and Lieutenant Dyer were both discharged the 20th of September closely followed by Captain Rand's on the 5th of November. Fortunately the British invasion force never materalized despite the fact that they were ordered to "destroy the coast towns and shipping, and ravage the country." The companies at Portland and vicinity were also discharged at about the same time as those in Cape Elizabeth.

News of the Treaty of Ghent and the ensuing peace arrived the 13th of February, 1815. It was celebrated by the ringing of bells, illuminations, cannon salutes, and across the river in Portland, dazzling balls and festive dinners, complimented by copious potations of punch, flip and other potent beverages. At the March meeting the town of Cape Elizabeth disposed of its camp utensils and military impedimenta but continued to maintain its powder stock until 1828 when it too was sold at a public vendue.

With the second war for independence at last over Cape Elizabeth returned quickly to the ways of peace and town affairs. It was not long, however, before the question of separation from Massachusetts became the topic of the day. The citizens of Cape Elizabeth had discussed the move in years previous and entered in the town records their own particular views. Agitation had appeared in Falmouth late in 1785 and a test vote was run by the town of Cape Elizabeth in 1786 at the 18th of October meeting. The anti-separationists carried the day with a majority of sixty votes, the final tally being 21 for and 81 against. Separation was again put to a vote in April of 1795 and the town reversed its previous stand by casting 26 votes for separation with only 3 negative votes. A third vote was taken the 10th of May 1797 when the question of whether or not to apply to the Massachusetts legislature for separation was raised. Like the second voting it too was in the affirmative, i.e. 22 yeas and 10 nays. The overall results were the same as those in 1786 and 1795 in that the attempts at separation were unsuccessful. This ended the agitation for a time as it was decided by those spearheading the movement that the people were not ready to sever the ties binding them to Massachusetts.

Soon after the conclusion of peace in 1815 the topic was again revived with an intensive campaign organized to accomplish complete and irrevocable separation. Pursuant to the public's demand Cape Elizabeth once again placed the subject before the voters. The citizens voted ". . . unanimously for an immediate separation of the destrick of Main from old Massachusetts . . ." In view of the sentiment expressed by the inhabitants of Maine, Massachusetts authorized the various towns in the District of Maine to send delegates to a convention to be held at Brunswick for the express purpose of forming a constitution if a majority of five to four of the votes returned from the towns were in favor of separation. The Cape Elizabeth citizenry were not so sure this time as to the relative merits of separation, for they cast 80 votes yea and 44 votes no. At this same meeting, held the 2nd of September, 1816, Captain Silvanus Higgins was appointed Cape Elizabeth's delegate to the Brunswick Convention. When the votes were all in Massachusetts decided that the majority favoring separation was too small and dissolved the Convention thus terminating that attempt.

Nothing more was attempted until early in 1819 when a meeting was held in Boston by persons friendly to separation to make preparatory arrangements. The Massachusetts legislature passed an act providing for the taking of another vote, and, if there was a majority of fifteen hundred affirmative votes, for the calling of a convention to be held at Portland the second Monday in October. Pursuant to the Massachusetts act the citizens of Cape Elizabeth voted at the July meeting on this question of separation. Once again the town expressed an affirmative opinion with 79 yeas to 17 nays. At the town meeting held on the 20th of September, Ebenezer Thrasher was chosen the delegate from Cape Elizabeth to the Portland Convention. As a majority of 9,959 votes was cast in favor of separation the Convention met on the 11th of October and soon formed the present state constitution. The State was then admitted as an independent member of the Union by Act of Congress on the 4th of March, 1820, and became an independent state the 16th of the same month.

Closely following the birth of the State of Maine was the birth of a period of prosperity and expansion in the town of Cape Elizabeth. The first signs of the movement for municipal improvement became evident in March of 1821. On the 15th the legislature of the State of Maine constituted a group of seventeen Cape Elizabeth and Scarborough men a corporation for the purpose of improving a certain section of the Spurwink salt marshes. Their plan was to turn the marsh into pasturage by erecting a dam to keep the tidal waters out. An earthwork dam was constructed but the project was apparently unsuccessful for the area still remains a salt marsh. The Cape Elizabeth and Scarborough Diking Corporation, as it was then called was incorporated the same day as the Cumberland and Oxford Canal.

One improvement that the people of Cape Elizabeth had been seeking for some time was the establishment of a second bridge across Fore River, from Malems Neck to a point southwesterly of Robinsons' Wharf in Portland. The first mention we have of this particular bridge is in June of 1792 when Thomas Robinson, Nathaniel F. Fosdick, John Waite, James Leach, Nathaniel Coffin, James Fosdick, Thomas Motley, Samuel Freeman, Barzillai Delano, George Deake, Stephen Codman and John Armstrong petitioned the Massachusetts General Court for incorporation. For some unknown reason their plea was turned down thereby preventing construction. Somewhat later, in May of 1806, the town of Cape Elizabeth appointed the Reverend William Gregg its agent to "ade and assest a Mr. Ebenezer Libby and his associates" in making this Bridge a reality. Others were aware of the desirability to erecting another bridge across Fore River. On the 28th of January, 1809, Robert Ilsley of Portland wrote to Senator William King, Maine's political factotum of the period, asking for governmental assistance. In this letter he stressed the obvious advantages of shortening the distance to the Scarborough turnpike thereby eliminating long and tedious hills, and also making Cape Elizabeth more accessable to say nothing of increasing its land values. The closing argument was its great importance as a military installation. When General Henry Dearborn visited Portland in the summer of 1808 he conferred with Ilsley and recommended constructing a bridge and locating a six or eight gun fort at its center in the river. This structure, with an additional battery at the Portland terminus of the bridge plus the existing " embargo forts," would insure perfect security for any vessels in Portland Harbor. Unfortunately Mr. Ilsley's appeal went unheeded and governmental aid was not forthcoming.

The citizens of Cape Elizabeth continued to support the project and on the 1st of May, 1809, voted unanimously that they had no objection to the construction of a toll bridge by John Thrasher and others. Despite this display of enthusiasm nothing more was accomplished until 1823. At the town meeting of the 23rd of January, Cape Elizabeth again lent its assistance by backing a petition to the state legislature. This attempt was successful and on the 10th of February, 1823, the third legislature of the State of Maine incorporated Silvanus Higgins, Richworth Jordan, William Gregg, Lemuel Cobb, John Emery, Greely Hannaford, Elisha Jordan, James Neal, Thomas Robinson, Robert Ilsley, Isaac Ilsley, Abiel W. Tinkham, Henry Ilsley and John Mussy, Jr., as the Proprietors of Portland Bridge. It was designated a toll bridge with rates the same as those charged at Vaughan's Bridge, i.e. for each foot passenger two cents; each person and horse, six cents; each chaise or sulkey, twelve and one half cents; etc. Additional to this was the proviso that persons on military duty were to pass free of charge, the bridge was to be left open for free passage if the toll gatherer was absent, and that after ten years the rates were subject to revision by the state. A draw was also to be an integral part of the bridge with an opening of thirty-two feet. Two docks were to be provided, one on each side to accommodate vessels passing through. No toll was to be charged against any vessel except those used for pleasure. Work was immediately begun and the town of Cape Elizabeth simultaneously laid out a road connecting the Cape Elizabeth end with the road leading to Meeting House Hill and Vaughan's Bridge. Incidental to the laying out of this highway was the building of still another bridge. This one was across Mill Creek just above the tidal grist mill and cost the town two hundred dollars.

The new bridge was finished late in 1823 and was opened to public travel the same year. It was a flat, wooden bridge built on piling, with an overall width of about twenty-five feet, and length of approximately a quarter of a mile. Incorporated within its length was a toll gate, toll house, a lift-draw, and a large, conspicuous sign displaying the toll charges. The entire structure cost the proprietors the sum total of $7,000. At the Portland end access to the bridge was gained by a ramp that extended downward to York Street and passed over Canal Street, now Commerical Street. On its opening day Portland Bridge became the chief artery to and the most traveled thoroughfare from Cape Elizabeth. Its commercial importance was at once recognized and the town soon profited thereby. Unfortunately travel over the bridge was all too frequently interrupted by storms, freshets, and by ship collision. Typical was the damage inflicted by a northeast gale in September of 1838. On this occasion a ship, a barque, and a brig were all driven violently against the bridge injuring it so badly that travel thereon was suspended for several days.

The United States experienced throughout the twenties and thirties a canal-building craze of herculean proportions. Cape Elizabeth also felt the surge of this new "harbinger of prosperity." On the 27th of February, 1826, the state legislature constituted Joshua Mitchell, Samuel Waterhouse, Charles Peabbles, Richard Jordan, and Elliot Jordan a corporation to be known as the Proprietors of the Cape Elizabeth Canal. They were authorized to dig a canal from Great Pond, in a northerly direction, to the salt marsh about a half a mile away. The waters of Great Pond were to be used to feed the canal and to run the mills constructed upon its banks. A dam was to be built at the junction of the canal and Great Pond to retain the pond's normal level. The act further stipulated that the canal was not to interfere with the alewive fishery as the regular outlet of the pond was close to the proposed canal-dam. Despite these auspicious beginnings the canal was never finished. A start was made and a short length of canal dug, but the enterprise petered out in a very short time. Most of the ditch that was dug has since been absorbed but signs may still be seen of a scheme that was to bring prosperity to the town of Cape Elizabeth.

Another interesting project that was formulated in the year 1826 was the establishment of a town hearse. Mrs. Mary C. Stanwood of Cushing's Point became greatly incensed over the rough treatment accorded to the coffin of a departed associate as it bounced along to the cemetery in an old farm wagon. Without further adieu she drew up a subscription paper and canvassed the town to raise funds for a municipal hearse. She covered the town quite thoroughly and almost everyone solicited contributed something. One prominent citizen refused to give and termed the movement a foolish expense. Had he known that his end was near he might have thought differently for he was the first to ride in the new hearse. After the money had been raised and a suitable hearse purchased, a small building was built, in what is now Mount Pleasant Cemetery, just east of the old North Congregational Church. The hearse was an elaborate affair and built to last for many years. Its upkeep was regulated by the newly formed Union Hearse Company.

One of its early drivers was a Mr. Hinds of Dutch descent who lived on what is now Turkey Hill. He was rather striking in appearance, for he wore his blond hair very long and capped it with a large earlapped cap that never left his head winter or summer. Besides his job as hearse driver he filled in as mortician. When the town was divided in 1895 the old hearse remained at Mount Pleasant Cemetery and Cape Elizabeth purchased a new green one of simpler design. A little leanto was built to house it close to the South Congregational Church at Spurwink.

Eventually Mr. Hinds died and new methods of burial were employed. Consequently the little green hearse fell into disuse and finally ceased to be employed. The officers of Union Hearse Company sold it to a Mr. Paquette, a fisherman, who lived near the present site of Sprague Hall. This gentleman promptly equipped the old hearse with a fine assortment of fresh fish and made the rounds of the town. He so shocked the citizenry, and so loud were the protests, that he subsequently moved down east taking the old hearse with him.

The Union Hearse Company eventually dissolved and its last legal existance was an unclaimed disposit at the Portland Savings Bank. Through the efforts of a few Cape citizens its assets amounting to $250.73, were transferred to the Seaside Cemetery Corporation on the 3rd of August, 1949.

As usual the routine matters inherent to the running of the town government were closely attended to. With the establishment of Portland Bridge, travel over Cape roads quite naturally increased and the necessity of repairs grew proportionately. In general the mode of financing these repairs involved a direct tax on the inhabitants. However, if one was so inclined the tax could be paid by working on the roads. A fixed rate was determind by the selectmen, and passed on at the town meeting, whereby a man was allowed one dollar per day for road-work. If he employed his oxen he was allowed seventy-five cents a day per yoke, if he used his plow that was an additional seventy-five cents per day. A man, his implements, or his animals could be used either collectively or separately to satisfy the highway assessment. Despite the work thus accomplished the roads were still liable to be choked with dust in the summer, seas of mud in spring and fall, and frozen ruts in the winter.

The town's bridges were also constantly in need of repairs. In 1824 a freshet carried away Long Creek Bridge and the expenditure of one hundred dollars was necessary to replace it. These occasional freshets had an unpleasant habit of periodically dislodging the town's bridges. The Spurwink Bridge had achieved a singular state of dilapidation by 1832 and it was found expedient to rebuild it. At first a bridge on piling was decided upon but the vote was rescinded and stone was used for the foundation instead. The bridge at Barberry Creek also received annual refurbishing appropriations. Although it did not officially involve the town, Vaughan's Bridge was badly in need of repair at this time. The owners were not able to accomplish this so it was sold at auction on the 18th of May, 1830, to Stephen Little of Portland for $3830. Under new ownership repairs were forthcoming, but not, unfortunately without some danger. During the reconstruction in August, Ephraim Ghent a citizen of Cape Elizabeth and a veteran of the revolution, missed his footing while crossing in the dark and fell to his death.

By the 1830's the pigs had ceased to run at large and oxen were restricted to certain areas. The alewive fishery was still important enough to warrant the continuance of three town fish wardens but the steady enroachments of dams and other obstacles was slowly spelling its doom. The town tired to regulate the fishery but met with ever increasing opposition from those inhabitants whose land adjoined Alewive Brook. For awhile the town enforced a closed period on penalty of a ten dollar fine but that too was soon dispensed with.

Previous to 1831 the town cared for its poor by farming them out to the lowest bidder with the provision that if they were mistreated the Overseers of the Poor would remove them at the expense of the bidder. The town of Cape Elizabeth received in 1831 the Thomas Jordan farm and proceeded immediately to remodel it as a Poor Farm. Two years later an addition was built to serve as a House of Correction. Fortunately its need was never greatly felt. The Poor Farm, however, was soon a going concern and proved to be an excellent investment for the town. Despite these accomodations the town continued to entrust some of their wards to private individuals. A rather poignant indication of this was a notice that appeared in the *Eastern Argus*, Friday, 18 January 1839. One John Babb of Westbrook informed the public that ". . . a lad about 16 years of age, named Francis Battersbee, bound to the subscriber by the town of Cape Elizabeth . . .", was a runaway.

One function that was always the occasion for a general holiday was the annual militia muster. The town supplied the militiamen with provisions, cartridges, and a cash payment of twenty-five cents for the day they spent on active duty. Any man who failed to appear for muster was subject to fine. Prior to 1832 the two companies maintained in Cape Elizabeth were drawn indiscriminately from the town in general. In 1821 Captains Simon W. Gregg and Woodbury Jordan commanded two militia companies. At that time they were part of the 1st Regiment, 2nd Brigade, 5th Division of the Maine State Militia. Upon occasion the town played host to other militia units. Such an instance occured on October 2nd 1827, when the Portland militia regiment, with a company of artillery, was reviewed and inspected on the common in front of the meeting house.

By 1832 the town was maintaining and drilling three infantry companies. Cape Elizabeth was divided into three geographical areas with a company raised in each. The South Company was commanded by Captain Benjamin Waterhouse, the Middle Company by Captain John Kilbourn, and the North Company by a Captain Pratt. These companies remained in force until the Civil War. However, after 1843 participation became purely voluntary, for that year the state abolished compulsory attendance.

There was one business venture organized at Cape Elizabeth in this early period that occasions a great deal of wonderment. On the 11th of February, 1834, the State Legislature incorporated the Portland and Cape Elizabeth Coal and Railroad Company, with Abner Bagley, Edward Howe, Woodbury Storer, Jonathan Dow, Rufus Emerson, Christopher Wright, Eliphalet Greely, John S. Bagley, John Pennel, Moses Hall, Michael H. Bagley and Nathan Howe, as corporate members. It was their purpose to mine coal on Abner Bagley's Cape Elizabeth farm. They also received permission to build a railroad from the diggings to Fore River and there to construct wharves, building, etc. This act was preceeded by an enthusiastic article in the *Daily Advertiser* of Portland. It designated the company's founders as William Coolidge and Seth Mason of Portland and revealed further that stock had been sold, with the value immediately climbing to one hundred per cent above par. A few days after this account another appeared and announced that during the mining operations a fine marble quarry had been discovered. The last mention so far discovered of this remarkable mineralogical "flyer" is an act of the State Legislature reducing the number of directors from nine to five.

The astonishing part of these particular mining operations is that later geological surveys have revealed no coal deposits nor large veins of marble. In addition to this the geological formation of Cape Elizabeth is of an earlier period than that in which coal deposits were formed. Therefore it creates some wonderment as to what could have been mistaken for coal in sufficient quantity to warrant the establishment of a mining corporation. The inclination would be to call it a phony stock deal were it not for an earlier venture with similar aims.

Between 1748 and 1756 strenuous efforts were made to establish a coal mine in the vicinty of Spring Point. A company was organized with Ebenezer Roberts, Jr., Joseph Weston, Elisha Parker, and Archelaus Stone, as the principal share holders. An outcropping of ledge was the basis for their enthusiasm but other than that nothing more is known. Apparently, like the later attempt, this too was unsccessful. With reference to both operations it remains a mystery as to what they considered as coal in deposits large enough for commercial exploitation.

At the town meeting of April 17th, 1837, the first faint traces of pending urbanization is discernible when it was voted to build a town house. Previous to this time the town had gathered in the combination meeting house and church on Meeting House Hill that had been built in 1733. When torn down it was approximately sixty feet by fifty feet, with a front entrance including a porch, and two side entrances. This early building was unpainted, did not have a steeple, and gave the impression that it was two stories high by displaying two rows of small windows. Inside there was an old-fashioned high pulpit and big square family pews in which half of the occupants had to sit with their backs to the speaker. In 1835 this venerable building was torn down to make way for a new church more suitable to the times. Under the building were found stumps of a few of the oak trees that furnished the original timbers.

The town meetings for 1835, 1836 and April of 1837 were held in the Friends Meeting House that stood in the old Quaker burying ground, now Bay View Cemetery. At the 17th of April, 1837 meeting Sylvanus Higgins, William Cummings, and Lemuel Cobb were constituted a committee to select a suitable and central location for the structure, and to superintend the actual construction. They chose a lot at the corner of the Hannaford and Village Roads, for which they paid twenty five dollars. The town contracted with Sylvanus Higgins to build the new meeting house for $675. He cut the timbers for the frame on his farm and proceeded to erect a one story, barnlike structure, thirty feet by forty feet. The first meeting held in the new house was on the 11th of September, 1837 for the purpose of electing a governor and other officers.

At the same 17th of April meeting the town voted to receive its share of the surplus revenue. Congress had passed the Surplus Revenue Act in 1836 dividing a national treasury surplus among the various states. The citizens of Cape Elizabeth appointed James Dyer as their agent, authorizing him to retain enough to cancel out the town's debt and to finance construction of the new meeting house. After these deductions had been made the remaining surplus was to be distributed among the inhabitants with one person receiving less than fifty dollars nor more than two hundred dollars.

The procedure to be followed was laid out at the 2nd of April meeting in 1838. The census of 1830 was to be the basis of those eligible; however, those persons who had not paid their taxes were to have the amount owed deducted from their share of the surplus. At the next meeting on the 24th of April it was decided that beginning on Thursday the 26th actual distribution would begin in the presence of the agent, selectmen, and tax collector. As cash was limited, the needy would be paid first, and those not in distressed circumstances were to receive a town order payable in four months. Agreeable to this procedure the town was sectioned off and a certain day designated for each section. The eastern part received their share on Thursday, the 26th, the southern part on Friday, and the northern part on Saturday. Therefore, by Saturday the 28th the surplus revenue had been apportioned out and, as no grievances are recorded, was satisfactory to the citizens.

The new meeting house was not overlooked in the excitement created by the surplus revenue. At the 24th of April meeting it was stipulated that the building could not be used as a schoolhouse, but that it could be occasionally utilized for religious services and by persons who wished to learn to sing. The key to the meeting house was entrusted to William Tobey subject to regulation by the selectmen.

Cape Elizabeth soon experienced a closer connection with Portland. In February of 1842 the Portland, Saco and Portsmouth Railroad began running regular trains between these points and passed over a tressel to Turner's Island, Cape Elizabeth, thus passing through the northwestern corner of the town. At the junction of Evans Street and the railway tracks the Cape Elizabeth Depot was soon erected with a smaller way-station at the Elm Street intersection. Shortly afterwards an enginehouse was established at Turner's Island and several engines were later constructed there. The fare from the Cape Elizabeth Depot to the State Street Depot in Portland was ten cents each way.

In 1845 Cape Elizabeth as usual elected its own town officers at the regular spring meeting. This particular meeting was the first Monday in April instead of the first Monday in March. The officers elected differed very slightly from those elected in the early years. The selectmen were still three in number with a town clerk and treasurer. There were also a superintending school committee of three, nine pound keepers, three tythingmen; three surveyors of wood and bark, six surveyors of lumber, three fishwardens and three constables. The offices of surveyors of highways, fence viewers, hogreeve, and field driver were combined and fourteen men appointed to carry out the collective duties required. The selectman had by this time absorbed the offices of tax assessors and overseers of the poor. The offices filled, however, varied somewhat from year to year but remained basicly the same.

The usual appropriations were made for the poor, schools, town charges, etc. Hogs were no longer permitted to go at large, neat cattle or oxen were closely regulated, and the pound keepers' yards or barns continued to be substitutes for a regular pound. As in several years previous the town declined to grant any liquor licenses for the retailing of alcholic beverages thereby displaying a spirit of abstinence quite different from that of earlier years.

Once again it was necessary to rebuild Long Creek Bridge and late in 1845 five hundred dollars was appropriated for the project. The new bridge was constructed by William Low to the town's specifications. It was supported by eight-foot thick stone abutments and towered twenty feet above the creek. When it was completed the bridge was quite an imposing structure as compared with the previous accommodations. Two covered sluice-ways were incorporated into the bridge. One was used by Skillin's saw mill but the other's use is unknown. Apparently a substantial dam had been constructed by this time just above the bridge. The builder, William Low, later obligated himself to keep the bridge and its approaches in good repair throughout his lifetime with suitable appropriations from the town.

One very interesting company that was organized in this period was the Great Pond Mining and Agricultural Company. It was incorporated by the state legislature on the 25th of June

1849 for the purpose of cutting and processing peat-moss, mining iron and other minerals, and cultivating cranberries and similar agricultural products. It was also granted permission to dam the outlet of Great Pond to create extensive bogs for the raising of cranberries, etc. The town had by this time apparently given up the alewive fishery as not profitable enough to regulate. The last reference made to it in the town records is in 1842 when the fish wardens were cautioned against the expenditure of money.

This new venture was soon doing business under the active leadership of John D. Buzzell and George W. Smith. Almost immediately they erected buildings on the height of land at the pond's northeastern end. Their chief product was charcoal made from burnt peat moss and a fertilizer concocted from decomposed peat moss. The following year the company published an interesting brochure stressing the medicinal value of the charcoal as a deodorant and disinfectant. Included also were testimonials from several promient Portland physicians and businessmen. An interesting newspaper account also appeared in Portland about the same time and elaborated upon the aims of the firm. This article also called the public's attention to similar enterprises in England that were carrying on identical operations.

The charcoal was marketed in barrels containing one hundred and fifty pounds apiece. The finished product sold at two cents a pound with a reduction of ten per cent on orders of five or more barrels. Apparently the volume of business was more than satisfactory for in the spring of 1851 the works at Cape Elizabeth were enlarged and ads appeared regularly in the *Portland Evening Advertiser*. These ads stressed for the first time the value of the company's fertilizer especially when mixed with guano. The Portland outlet was William O. H. Gwynneth's "Agricultural Warehouse and Seed Store" at 27 Market Square.

One very fascinating gentleman who was associated with the Company was Francis O. J. Smith of Portland, often referred to as "Maine's greatest failure." He invested heavily in this firm, in the Cumberland and Oxford Canal, and in other business ventures but somehow was never able to achieve a sustained financial success. Smith published in Boston in 1852 a laudatory pamphlet on the company in an attempt to obtain new investors and more orders. It was, however, a futile move for the company was evidently beginning to feel a severe recession despite the fact that the State of Maine had endowed it with a five year tax exemption.

The last official record that is available of this company's endeavors is a financial return made to the state in 1852. In this report the amount of capital was fixed at $100,000 with $82,185 paid in. A list of stockholders was included giving John D. Buzzell and George W. Smith, both of Cape Elizabeth, and John G. Myers of Boston as the controlling shareholders. The Hon. F.O.J. Smith owned ninety shares with Benjamin C. Cummings, George F. Shepley, Sylvester B. Becket, George W. Nichols, and L.D.M. Sweet, all promient Portland businessmen, also listed as stockholders. After this return was made the company apparently ceased operation and nothing more is heard of its products. Just exactly what occurred has unfortunately been obliterated by the passage of time, but the fact that it failed within a decade is quite well established.

It is evident however, that the cultivation of cranberries was a flourishing business for some years. In J. A. Carnes' delightful little book, *A Trip to Portland,* he describes these operations at Great Pond in some detail. "October 8, (1857). Took a ride in Mr. Chamberlin's carriage . . . to visit the extensive and beautiful cranberry meadow, of which we had heard so much; and a beautiful place it is, indeed; being perfectly circular, and surrounded with trees. It was once the bottom of a large pond from which the water was drained, leaving a field beautifully adapted to the purpose for which it is used. It covers a larger surface than Boston Common, and has banks of about six feet in height . . . men, women, and children of all ages and sizes, numbering some fifty or sixty, were stooping down in the swampy meadow gathering the delicious and ripened fruit; for here I observed the cranberries were perfectly red, and larger than those generally brought to Boston Market; While the produce of the labor lay along the meadow, enclosed in bags tied at one end, and holding about two bushels each. The persons engaged in this work receive two cents per quart forgathering, and I am informed a smart picker will gather a bushel and a half in a day. There were two overseers present; one a very large man, with bushy whiskers and moustache, but very pleasant and polite. He requested us to gather some as samples, and some of them I found to be almost as large as seedling strawberries. He said he expected to obtain in this meadow from four to five hundred bushels which would amount to a very pretty sum, at four or five dollars per bushel. They all seemed contented with the price paid for picking the berries."

Unlike some of these early business ventures Cape Elizabeth

was expanding and prospering especially in its northern section. The town had been, up to this time, fairly stationary as far as any indications of business vitality is concerned. Just prior to 1850, however, two extremely enterprising and energetic gentlemen appeared on the scene bringing with them a welcome stimulation of business. They were George W. Turner and James B. Cahoon, both well-established merchants and residents of Portland. These gentlemen had sufficient foresight to see that the growth of Portland in business and population would eventually have repercusions in Cape Elizabeth. As co-partners they purchased extensive tracts of land in the vicinity of what is now Knightville and Ferry Village in South Portland. By 1850 they had erected over twenty buildings, established a steam saw-mill; a chain-cable factory that also made iron ship fittings and tools; an extensive shipyard; and a steam ferry, the *Elizabeth,* that ran regularly between Cape Elizabeth and Portland. Unfortunately Turner died before the venture was really started but the co-partnership lasted out the five-year limitation. Their holdings were soon enhanced by the establishment of another shipyard by Thomas E. Knight close by Portland Bridge.

This new firm of Turner and Cahoon quickly divided much of the land up into house lots and advertised them for sale during March, April and May of 1850. Every consideration was given to mechanics, craftsmen, etc, as an inducement to settle in the "New City" by way of long term payments in the purchase of land. Without a doubt these two men did more toward developing Cape Elizabeth in these years prior to the Civil War than any other man or group of men. It can truthfully be said that they precipitated the inevitable movement toward urbanization that was to grow with such rapidity in the years to come.

Travel had so increased over Portland Bridge by this time that the frequent toll payments were an abominable nuisance. Therefore, agitation was begun to make the bridge a public thoroughfare with no toll charges. This thorny question made its first appearance at the town meeting held the 21st of December, 1850. At this meeting the citizens cast 177 yeas to 44 nays in favor of appropriating $5000 to purchase stock in the bridge. Shortly before the meeting $5000 had been raised by private subscription for the same purpose. Despite the lethargic attitude of the inhabitants of Scarborough and Portland, also heavy users of the Portland Bridge, the citizens of Cape Elizabeth set to work in earnest to make it a free bridge. As the possibility existed that their attempts would be unsuccessful they were prepared, if necessary, to build another bridge.

Success was not forthcoming as in May of 1851 the town petitioned the legislature for permission to raise more money and to purchase Portland Bridge. As this too achieved no immediate results the inhabitants drew up a plan to constuct a bridge from Turner's Island to some point on the Portland side just above the existing bridge. This structure was to be of the solid type with outer walls of stone and a filled center of rubble.

Fortunately the State Legislature acted in time to forestall the necessity of building this solid bridge. On the 30th of March, 1853, the town of Cape Elizabeth was granted the enabling power they so much desired and they immediately purchased Portland Bridge, conveying it almost instantly to the Commissioners of Cumberland County as a free bridge.

In the period that saw the citizens almost despairing of purchasing Portland Bridge a movement was started to purchase Vaughan's Bridge. Subsequently, at a meeting held the 13th of September, 1851, $1500 was appropriated to purchase the stock of this bridge. This however was not sufficient and it was raised to $2500 with the idea of also conveying this bridge to the county commissioners. The project was vigorously pursued but as usual it was time consuming despite the fact that it received a great deal of support in Portland.

In the interim the town had other pressing matters to attend to. The annual meeting of 1852 held on the 22nd of March transacted the usual business but also included an interesting list of fines on impounded "beasts." The owner of an animal thus confined was required to pay the selectmen for keeping it at the following rates: for a horse, twenty-five cents per day; a cow, a cent and a half per day; a hog, six cents per day; an ox twelve and a half cents per day; and a sheep, four cents per day. These routine matters were overshadowed by events of graver proportions. By an act of the State Legislature the farm of Thomas Broad with parcels of land belonging to Joseph and Silas Broad lying in Cape Elizabeth, was set off to the town of Westbrook. The inhabitants of this section must have been nursing their disaffection for sometime as two previous attempts had been made much earlier to accomplish this end. In 1775 they sought annexation to Falmouth but the move was vetoed by the other citizens of Cape Elizabeth. The next venture in this direction was at the 28th of January meeting in 1825. It was put to a vote and promptly defeated eighty-eight to seven. After the "fait accompli" of 1852 the town acknowledged the fact in a petition to the Legislature asking for an abatement of its state and county taxes. The success of these inhabitants was to pale into insignificance however when a greater and more flagrant disaffection occurred in the years to come.

The proprietors of Vaughan's Bridge expediated matters somewhat, late in 1853, by offering to surrender the bridge to the county commissioners. The State Legislature acted quite promptly and on the 17th of April, 1854 authorized the county commissioners to accept the structure. Immediate repairs were necessary before the bridge was a satisfactory thoroughfare. The town of Cape Elizabeth received 1,156 feet to maintain and Portland received 1,408 feet. About one thousand feet of new surface was put on the bridge and a forty-two foot draw was located over the deeper western channel. Much of the old cobbwork was removed and replaced by piling. The construction work was done by the contracting firm of John Brackett and William Low of Portland. After Vaughan's Bridge had been renovated they started long needed repairs on Portland Bridge.

The ramp leading from the bridge to York Street was discontinued by the county commissioners despite the heated protests of the Cape Elizabeth citizenry. The Portland end of the bridge was thus lowered to Canal Street and necessitated a hazardous crossing of the railroad tracks. This intersection became at once the scene of frequent accidents and soon received the grisly title "Gridiron of Death." As the number of railroad tracks increased the situation was to grow worse proportionately before this dangerous crossing was remedied in 1874.

There occurred in Cape Elizabeth early in 1855 an incident that produced a great excitement both in this town and in Portland. As usual the farmers were doing their spring plowing and at Richmond's Island Solomon Hanscomb was no exception. On the 11th of May, 1855, accompanied by his two young sons, he was plowing on the island's northwesterly slope. The area had not been touched by the plow for many years and consequently Mr. Hanscomb was cutting some rather deep furrows. He was holding the plow as his twelve year old son drove the team when the boy noticed an old broken jug lying bottom up in the freshly turned earth. With the cry "I've found it" he picked up the earth filled jug and carried it to his father. The boy was alluding to the old traditional stories of the islands hidden wealth. With a cursory glance Mr. Hanscomb declared it to be an old rum jug, placed it upon a nearby rock pile, and proceeded with the plowing. His other son, too young to assist him in his labors, climbed up on the pile of rocks and began to playfully pick the packed earth from the jug's interior. The boy had not progressed more than half way to the jug's bottom when he came upon a quantity of coins and a ring. One can easily imagine the excitement this caused when the boy conveyed the discovery to his father.

Assisted by two other men Mr. Hanscomb immediately spaded up the area where the jug was found but no further coins were unearthed. They did turn up some broken pottery, clay pipe fragments, part of a large green bottle, an iron spoon, nails, spikes, charcoal and a quantity of beach stone. This was evidently the site of an early cellarless building. Upon closer examination it was discovered that the jug had apparently been shaped like a globe lantern, was of common manufacture and originally held about a quart. Some of the jug's broken pieces were found nearby and from the appearance of its fractures this had not been the first year that a plow had disturbed it. One crack was new as though caused by its recent encounter with Mr. Hanscomb's plow.

The coins numbered fifty-two in all; consisting of twenty-one gold pieces in good condition and thirty-one silver coins greatly discolored. At that time their total monetary value was approximately one hundred dollars. The silver consisted of four one-shilling pieces, seventeen sixpences, one groat or four-penny piece, and two half groats of the reign of Elizabeth; four one-shilling pieces, and one sixpence of the reign of James I; with one-shilling and one sixpence from the reign of Charles I. The earliest silver coin is dated 1564 and the latest 1625.

The collection of gold pieces is made up of ten sovereigns and three half sovereigns of the reign of James I; seven are sovereigns of the reign of Charles I; and one is a Scottish sovereign. The earliest of these is the Scottish coin dated 1602, and as the others are undated they can only be placed in the reigns of the rulers pictured thereon. The gold pieces exhibit less wear than the silver ones and were not as badly tarnished.

In the pot the coins were so arranged that the gold lay on one side and the silver on the other with the ring in the middle. This ring is a combination wedding-signet ring of fine gold weighing eight penny-weight, four grains. The signet is oval in shape and measures six-eights of an inch by five-eights. On its outer surface edge is an ornamental border and in the center are the initials G. V. with a cord passing between them containing a tie at the top and a love knot at the bottom. Engraved inside the ring is the word "United," followed by the figure of two entwined hearts and the message "Death only Parts." The workmanship is remarkably good with the letters well-formed and sharply cut. The initials undoubtably represent the persons whose hearts are "United," but as to who they were it has to date been impossible to determine.

The theory generally accepted in reference to this collection of valuables is that it probably was part of Walter Bagnall's assets. This was first expressed by Portland's eminent historian William Willis. His solution as to the origin of this cache is that it was most likely concealed by the Indians that slew Bagnall and his servant. The fact remains, however, that the treasure, in all probability, belonged to "Great Walt" and was either lost or hidden at the time of his demise. It is safe to say that the chances of tracing its early history are practically nonexistant. The ring and some of the coins now repose in the vaults of the Maine Historical Society.

One interesting sidelight in reference to the finding of this jug and its valuable contents appeared late in 1868. One of Portland's most prolific nineteenth century writers, Charles Parker Illsley, used it as the basis for a fascinating novel entitled "Treasure Trove or the Signet Ring." Unfortunately its only appearance in print was in the *Lewiston Weekly Journal* that presented it in serial form from Thursday, November 26, 1868 to and including Thursday, April 22, 1869. Each installment was of considerable length and it most certainly would have made quite a book as the novel was divided into fifty substantial chapters.

As the town attained the mid-century mark its expansion was gathering speed whereby Cape Elizabeth was literally increasing by leap and bounds. With the coming of the railroad, the opening of two free bridges, and the establishing of a new steam ferry, it became increasingly easier· to develop the commercial potentialities of the town. The Portland, Saco and Portsmouth Railroad was leased jointly to the Boston and Maine and the Eastern Railroad. In 1853 they facilitated the establishment at the Cape Elizabeth Depot of the first post office within the limits of the town. Prior to this time one had to travel to Portland for the mail, but with the opening of this post office the mail coming by train from Boston or Portland was deposited at Cape Elizabeth Depot for distribution.

Another sign of rapid expansion was the almost unbroken

line of shipyards from Ferry Village to Turners Island. During these years this section of the coast resounded to the caulkers' hammer and the shipwrights' adz from early in the morning to late at night. Many were the fine ships built in these extensive yards. Close by the ferrylanding was the new marine railway capable of handling a vessel up to one thousand tons. These and many other operations employing large numbers of men made this northern section the busiest part of the town. By 1860 the rapid growth was more than evident. That year Cape Elizabeth was designated by the state as a "Banner Town" when it was ascertained that in the ten year period from 1850 to 1860 the town's valuation had experienced an increase of three hundred per cent.

Upon this note of impending expansion the town greeted the memorable year of 1861. Before these normal proceedings could be pursued further the grim spectre of Civil War raised its ugly head. At 4:30 a.m. on the 12th of April the rebels commenced their bombardment of Fort Sumter and with it the war of the rebellion. Three days later President Lincoln issued a call for seventy-five thousand volunteers and almost immediately enlistment activities were begun in Cape Elizabeth. At the 7th of May meeting the town voted to provide assistance for the families of those men who entered the Union forces.

Once again Fort Preble became the scene of intensive martial activities. The state of its defenses was not as dilapidated as might have been expected. In 1816 the works had been extensively repaired. The soldiers of the garrison attended to much of the renovation themselves by building a small hospital, a mess-hall, storehouse, blacksmith's shop, carpenter's shop, guard houses, and sentry boxes. Additional to this they constructed a sea-wall, parade ground, and carried out some extensive landscaping. What had been left of old Fort Sumner on Munjoy Hill in Portland was salvaged and incorporated into this reconstruction of Fort Preble. At that time the fort was garrisoned by a company of the 1st Regiment U. S. Artillery. Thirteen years later, in 1829, the fort had received twelve 24-pounders as an addition to its armament. Ten were placed in the main work and two in the southeast battery. This same year a company of the 3rd Regiment, United States Artillery replaced the company from the 1st Regiment. These troops remained six years, departing in 1836 for Florida and the Seminole War.

The Fort was not remanned until 1839 when once again it became necessary to repair and remodel it. The old ramparts were razed to the ground and built anew with an added thickness of earthwork. Also remodeled were the powder magazines and barracks. During the Mexican War two new batteries were added mounting twelve and ten guns respectively. It was not long, however, before the fort fell into disrepair and dilapidation. When the 17th Regiment U.S. Infantry took over the fort in July, 1861, its armament consisted of but twelve 24-pounders, plus one 8-inch Columbiad and one 8-inch Seacoast Howitzer both dismounted. The magazines were empty of powder, with the shot supply much depleted, consisting only of a small quantity of 24-pounder balls and a few 8-inch shells. As this was to be the headquarters of the 17th Infantry the repairs and reconstruction were pursued with feverish intensity. The post was soon restored to first class order and once again became a formidable military establishment.

Almost at once a system of night signals was arranged with the mail steamers and other vessels to prevent the possibility of enemy ships slipping by in the dark. The incoming vessel was to give five whistle blasts of one second duration each when abreast of Cushings Island. The guards at the fort would then examine the oncoming vessel and if satisfied would show a blue light. The vessel in question would acknowledge with one whistle blast before proceeding into the inner harbor. If suspicions were aroused at Fort Preble the vessel would be stopped and its commanding officers ordered ashore to the fort's wharf. These signals were often changed to prevent the Confederates from learning and using them.

Despite these martial activties there were moments of relaxation at the fort. Especially delightful were the polished concerts given by Poppenberg's Band that was stationed at the post. People came from Portland, Cape Elizabeth, and the outlying towns to hear these Sunday concerts. On one occasion a program was given devoted to the favorites of George Washington as set down in manuscript form by Drum Major Elijah Kellogg of Washington's Headquarters Guard. Drum Major Kellogg was the father of the famous Harpswell author Reverend Elijah Kellogg. Another long remembered Poppenberg concert was one consisting entirely of hymns sung frequently during the Revolutionary War and the War of 1812.

Late in 1861 the State established a training camp at Cape Elizabeth in the locality now known as Ligonia, or Kerosene Corner, South Portland. About seventy-two acres of level land, extending from a small creek that flows in the rear of Calvary

Cemetery to a branch of Fore River, and bordering on the State School for Boys property, had been enclosed and was known as Baldwin's racing track or the Cape Trotting Park. This area was leased by the state and called Camp Abraham Lincoln. The name was soon changed, however, to Camp Berry in honor of General Hiram G. Berry of the 4th Regiment Maine Infantry, and a native of Rockland, who was killed early in the war. The Camp's first Commandant was Colonel John Lynch who took active command early in 1862. Ten large wooden barracks were built running east and west, accommodating about one hundred men each. They were one story buildings, sheathed with unplaned boards, and inside double deck bunks lined all four walls. In the winter these barracks were heated by large stoves placed in the center of the building. In addition to this there were eleven two-family dwellings forming "Officers' Row". They were cottage-like structures but substantially built. Between the groups of buildings was a large parade ground upon which a full regiment could perform its military evolutions.

Regiments destined for service in the South were mobilized at Bangor, Augusta, and Cape Elizabeth. Eastern regiments camped near Bangor, those recruited in central Maine were quartered at Augusta, and the men enlisted in western and southwestern Maine gathered at Camp Berry, while the regiments were formed and trained. When a regiment was ready to depart for the front it marched over Vaughan's Bridge to Commercial Street and boarded the trains at the old Transfer Station.

During the summer months the capacity of the camp was increased by the addition of an extensive tent colony. With this method it was not uncommon to have two regiments encamped and training at the same time. As a consequence the parade ground was the scene of constant activity from dawn to dusk. Here the daily grind of drill by squad, by company, and by battalion was pursued. Officers as well as enlisted men had to learn these details so necessary to military discipline. Early in the war drillmasters put them through their paces, but as the war wore on experienced officers, who had seen service and had become seasoned veterans, took over this work.

The first regiment to rendezvous at Camp Berry was the 10th Maine Regiment of Infantry. Although this regiment and many succeeding ones bivouaced at Camp Berry in Cape Elizabeth, it was always designated as Portland in official documents. Closely following the 10th was the 12th Maine Infantry and the 1st Maine Battery of Mounted Artillery. At about this same time

Fort Preble was also pressed into service as a training center only on a far smaller scale. The 2nd, 5th and 6th Maine Batteries of Mounted Artillery were encamped there for short periods of time early in 1862. As the war progressed the regiments came and went with regularity at Camp Berry. Other well known Maine detachments that trained there were the 17th, 23rd, 25th, and 27th Maine Regiments of Infantry. The 4th Maine Battery of Mounted Artillery also experienced the rigors of camp life at this military site.

As 1861 drew to a close approximately ninety-three Cape Elizabeth men had entered their country's service. They were distributed fairly well among the various regiments with the largest number serving in the 5th Maine Regiment of Infantry. This regiment participated in three years of war and distinguished itself at such battles as Bull Run, West Point, Gaines' Mill, Charles City Cross Roads, Crampton Gap, Antietam, Fredericksburg, Salem Heights, Gettysburg, Rappahannock Station, Wilderness, Spottsylvania Court House, and Cold Harbor. This same year also found Cape Elizabeth men serving in Company B of the Home Guard on duty at the harbor defenses of Portland.

The following year witnessed an increase in its contributions to the Union armies. One reigment in particular that was raised late in 1862 contained thirty-three Cape Elizabeth men. This was the famous 17th Maine Regiment of Infantry. Company E was made up almost entirely of Cape men and was commanded by two fellow townsmen Captain Ellis M. Sawyer and 1st Lieutenant George W. Ficket. It was mustered into the service of the United States on the 18th of August after a brief period of training. On the 21st they left the state for Washington, D. C. and the South. In the three years that followed the 17th quickly took its place as a veteran regiment sustaining heavy losses in the process. It fought in some extremely bloody engagements such as Fredericksburg, Chancellorville, Gettysburg, Wapping Heights, Auburn Mills, Locust Grove, Mine Run, Wilderness, Coal Harbor, Peterburg, and Hatcher's Run. The Cape Elizabeth men in Company E received their share of casualties. Captain Ellis E. Sawyer was instantly killed by a musket ball while leading a charge at Locust Grove, Virginia, and Sergeant Charles H. Waterhouse was mortally wounded. Privates Edwin E. Anthoine, George W. Doughty, Andrew W. Jordan, and John T. Lombard were also wounded. At Gettysburg the company lost Private Arthur A. Harmon, killed, with Corporal

George F. Small and Sergeant Oliver E. Jordan among the wounded. These are only a few of the many Cape men who were wounded during the war. Of the thirty-three men from the town of Cape Elizabeth in this company only five emerged unscathed. Three other Cape men escaped by the ignominious act of desertion. The regiment was mustered out of the United States service on the 4th of June, 1865, and arrived in Portland the 8th. They were welcomed as conquering heroes and marched down Congress Street with the citizens wildly cheering them. Probably never had a returning regiment been so enthusiastically received in Portland.

At the three town meetings held in 1862 the war, with its inherent difficulties, was much in evidence. The annual March meeting held on the 27th provided five hundred dollars for the families of men who volunteered for the Federal service. However, the number of enlistees had so increased during the year that at the 9th of December meeting it was voted to raise $2000 for the support of the soldiers' families. This rapid increase in the number of men serving in the Union ranks was due partly to the town's granting of a bounty of one hunderd dollars to each volunteer payable when mustered into United States service.

Without a doubt the town bounty was instrumental in the formation of a new regiment at Camp Berry. This was the 25th Maine Regiment of Infantry, the second of the eight nine months' regiments mustered into United States service and the first to leave the State. It is safe to say that there were more Cape Elizabeth men in the 25th than in any other Maine regiment. They numbered fifty-six in all and were largely concentrated in Companies H and I. The 25th was mustered in on the 29th of September, 1862 and left for Washington the 16th of October, where they remained until March 24th, 1862 engaged in guarding vital Long Bridge across the Potomac. On the 24th they joined the Army of the Potomac and marched to Fairfax Court House in Virginia. Before they could proceed further south their term of service expired and they returned to Arlington Heights, at Washington, before being seen home by railroad. The regiment arrived in Portland July 3rd and after marching to City Hall, escorted by the Portland Band, the city authorities held a collation in their honor. Although the 25th participated in no engagement it faithfully performed the various duties assigned to it.

The harsh realities of war were brought home to the people

of Cape Elizabeth and vicinity early in the summer of 1863. The Confederate privateer *Tacony* under Lieutenant Charles E. Reed, C. S. N., was at that time operating with impunity off the coast of Maine. It was not long before she was heavily laden with the spoils of many captures. Due to the fear of detection by Federal cruisers Lieutenant Reed captured the schooner *Archer* of Southport on the 24th of June, transferred all their equipage to her and burned the *Tacony*. The *Archer* was then headed for Portland, for the express purpose of cutting out the United States revenue cutter *Caleb Cushing* and destroying the uncompleted gunboats *Pontoosic* and *Agawam*, moored at Franklin Wharf, along with any other available vessels.

On the night of the 26th they sailed boldly into Portland Harbor, under the very guns of Fort Preble, disguised as a fishing schooner. About two o'clock in the morning a detachment of the rebels boarded the *Caleb Cushing* and noiselessly overpowered the crew. As the wind was practically non-existent boats were lowered and, assisted by the *Archer*, the cutter was warped out of the harbor via Hussey's Sound. By dawn they had attained the open sea just beyond Outer Green Island. She was soon sighted by the lookout at the Portland Observatory who immediately sounded the alarm. The Customs Collector Jedediah Jewett rose to the occasion and at once organized a suitable force for pursuit. A messenger was dispatchd to ready men and guns of the 17th Regulars at Fort Preble to board a steamer at the fort dock. Another messenger hastened to Camp Berry to obtain a detachment of men from the 7th Regiment Maine Infantry bivouaced there in the process of reorganization. The 700-ton side wheel steamer *Forest City* of the Boston Line was commandeered along with the steamer *Casco* and sent to Fort Preble to load the waiting soldiers. At the fort the *Forest City* took on two 12-pounder field guns, thirty-five soldiers, and forty muskets via the *Casco*. The men of the 17th Volunteers were placed aboard the screw steamer *Chesapeake* of the New York Line and soon followed the *Forest City* out of the harbor. Accompanying the *Chesapeake* were the two tugs *Uncle Sam* and *Tiger*. The *Forest City* reached the *Caleb Cushing* first but were driven off by balls from the cutter's 32-pounder. As the rebels could not find the shot locker, and as the rest of the "task force" was bearing down on them, they freed their prisoners, set the cutter afire and abandoned ship. The *Cheasapeake* picked up the rebels while the *Forest City* rescued the released prisoners. At 1:48 p.m. the cutter was blasted to atoms when the fire burned through to the powder magazine, and at 2:00 p.m. the *Archer* was captured without a fight by the *Forest City*. With this the fleet returned to Porland and the rebel prisoners were transferred for confinement at Fort Preble. They consisted of Lieutenant C.W. Reed, Second Officer E. H. Brown, Master's Mate J.W. Billups, Master's Mate N.B. Pryde, Master's Mate J.W. Matherson, and twenty seamen.

These developments produced a great excitement among the inhabitants especially when augmented by wild rumors relative to the thwarted intentions of the Confederate raiders. The temper of the citizens of Cape Elizabeth and vicinity reached such a degree of intense hatred that Major George L. Andrews, Commandant of Fort Preble, found it necessary to keep half the garrison on guard not only to insure the confinement of the rebels but for their own protection. The mutterings of the citizens had become so ominous that on the 29th of June he deemed it expedient to communicate with Major C. T. Christensen, Assistant Adjutant General, Department of the East, in New York City, suggesting that the rebels be removed as quickly and quietly as possible to safer quarters. The confederates greatly aggravated the situation by plotting an escape. They succeeded in bribing a civilian employee at the fort to assist them and attempted to interest a guard with similar inducements. However, the soldier proved to be of truer metal than they anticipated. This unnamed patroit feigned acceptance of their overtures, learned their plans, and promptly reported the developments to Major Andrews. The prisoners were immediately mustered and searched for weapons. Such a move was quickly justified as two pistols were discovered among the rebels' effects. Despite these disturbing developments the government was agonizingly slow in removing the Confederates and it was not until late in July that they were transferred to Fort Warren in Boston Harbor.

Fort Preble was also the scene of a stark military necessity in this eventful summer of 1863. It graphically displayed to the rebel prisoners and Union soldiers alike that the Federal Army was waging total war. This was the execution of Private William H. Laird of Berwick, Maine, for desertion. Previously the government had been very lenient with deserters, but the time had arrived when it was absolutely necessary to impress upon the troops the magnitude of this military crime.

Private Laird enlisted in Company G, 17th Maine Regiment, at the age of 27, and was mustered in on the 18th of August, 1862. He volunteered as an infantryman but for some forgotten reason was tranferred to the artillery. This was distasteful to him and he protested, maintaining that the govenment could not transfer him without his consent. The man was not overburdened with common intelligence and could neither read nor write. Unfortunately the men of his company ridiculed him unmercifully which added greatly to his discomfort and discontent. When this treatment became more than he could bear he simply packed up and went home.

It was not long before the military authorities sought him out and arrested him. Although the arresting officer maintained that Laird resisted him, the unfortunate man always claimed this false and was substantiated by others. However, he did acknowledge his desertion and deeply regretted it. A court martial which convened at Augusta adjudged him guilty, and sentenced him to be executed at Fort Preble.

The Reverend Edwin C. Bolles, pastor of Portland's Congress Square Universalist Church, was selected as his spiritual advisor and became greatly interested in his case. As Laird appeared to be without friends, and since the clergyman believed that the sentence was too severe, the Reverend Bolles obtained the signatures of many influential citizens on a reprieve petition. Despite these attempts the day of execution arrived with no word of commutation. On the afternoon of July 15th he was led into the outside court of the brick fort and placed in a kneeling position beside his coffin. Not over fifteen people were present as the date of execution had not been disclosed. Dr. Samuel Tewksbury of Portland was the attending physician. Private Laird was a man of good physique and countenance in these his last hours and bore himself with courage and resignation. His only request was that the firing squad, consisting of twelve soldiers from the 17th Regulars under a Lieutenant Henry Inman, should do its duty effectively. They fired, killing him instantly, and he was pronounced dead at 3:00 p.m.

Previous to his death Laird had dictated two letters to the Reverend Bolles to be forwarded to his mother and sister after the execution. Before the letters were mailed the Reverend Bolles added a letter giving an account of the Private's manful end. By some mistake these missives were delayed, and the first knowledge that Laird's family had of his execution was the arrival of the casket at the Berwick Depot. Tragic though it is, the fact remains, that a reprieve did arrive shortly after the sentence had been carried out. The reprieve had been dispatched from New York

Breakwater Light, also known as "Bug Light." Circa 1890.

Original crew of the Cape Elizabeth Lifeboat Station, From the left: Maurice Jordan, Joseph Staples, Sumner Dyer, Samuel Angell, Jesse Barker, Woodbury Pillsbury, Capt. Horace Trundy. Foreground: Trundy's dog Rover. Photo taken in October 1892 by Everett Smith of Portland.

Dyer's Cove showing Cape Elizabeth Lifesaving Station and fog signal building with steam whistle. Circa 1893.

The Cape Cottage as it appeared in 1852 after its reconstruction by John Neal.

in sufficient time but the telegraph lines were down, cut by the rabble participating in that city's notorious draft riots. The maniacal mobs had in reality destroyed another life. This made the matter a great deal more distressing and deep sympathy was expressed for Laird's family. Without a doubt the man should never have been shot, but unfortunately war is just what General Sherman termed it.

As the war progressed Cape Elizabeth continued to do its part. There was hardly a public or private meeting held that did not involve some direct reference to the rebellion. At the March meeting in 1864 five hundred dollars was appropriated to aid the volunteers and at a meeting held the 11th of June the Selectmen were instructed to enlist the town's quota of troops in anticipation of a call from the President. The sum of $1800 was set aside for recuiting purposes, especially in the filling of this new quota. The town clerk was also instructed to procure a book in which to record the names of, and all information about, those men who were serving or who enlisted in the future in the Union Army. This was soon done and the book is still preserved.

In August of this same year the town sent Captain Ezekiel Wescott and Dr. E. Hutchinson into the South as its official representatives to recruit troops in sufficient numbers to fill the town's quota. This was done pursuant to the War Department's General Order No. 227. Both Dr. Hutchinson and Captain Wescott were supplied with ample funds to pay the enlistees the Maine state bounty. The pressing need for troops continued throughout the remainder of the year. At the November meeting it was decided to pay recruits $100 for each year of their enlistment up to and including the third year. One interesting item to come out of this particular meeting was the fact that the citizens of Cape Elizabeth voluntarily contributed money to ease the town's financial burdens brought about by the large enlistment bounties.

That magnificent organization, the United States Sanitary Commission that did so much to ease the life of the Union soldier in the field, was not forgotten by the townspeople. The women picked lint, rolled bandages, knitted socks, and generally assisted wherever possible. The men give what they could in the way of food stuffs from their rock-ribed farms. Many were the barrels of potatoes, apples, and mixed vegetables, to say nothing of the kegs and boxes of dried produce, that they turned over to the commission. Truly it is a record of which to be proud.

The year 1865 opened with a fresh call for troops and once again the town set about the arduous task of recruitment. Before the quota could be filled it was found necessary to raise the bounty five dollars per month. Even then the men did not exactly flock to the colors. At this time, as was the case throughout the entire war, some of the more "indispensable" men hired substitutes rather than submit to a draft call. Just exactly how many men were drafted and how many enlisted it is practically impossible to determine.

However, before further martial activities became necessary the rebel army under General Robert E. Lee capitulated at Appomattox Court House on the 9th of April, 1865. With the ending of this fratricidal conflict the town of Cape Elizabeth returned immediately to prosaic municipal matters such as the appointment of two constables to keep Ferry Village affairs on a peaceful basis; and the support of schools, roads, bridges, and the poor.

Despite the cessation of hostilities the recent war was all too vivid to many Cape citizens. Of the approximately two hundred and thirty-nine Cape Elizabeth men who saw active duty in the Union armies, five were killed in action, five were mortally wounded, twenty-one were wounded and lived, thirteen died of disease, and nine were listed as deserters. Quite naturally there is no way to positively verify these figures but they are a fairly accurate representation. Soon after the war the veterans began to organize under the banner of the G.A.R. thus perpetuating the cause for which they fought.

The closing years of this decade witnessed the emergence of a movement that launched within the limits of this town a storm of controversy far surpassing anything previously experienced. Under the impact of the various and sundry issues incident to this movement neighbor fought neighbor and many families were split into vociferous factions. This was of course the urbanization of one section, at the expense of another with the ultimate result being the secession of the urbanized group. This then was the subject that overshadowed every other, both national and local in Cape Elizabeth during the remaining years of the nineteenth century.

Chapter IV

PAINS OF URBANIZATION

With the termination of the Civil War era, the town of Cape Elizabeth contained several areas which were urban in character. They were in reality clearly defined villages, the most active of which was Ferry Village, located in the area previously designated as Purpooduck, not far from Spring Point. It had the added advantage of being in close communication with the city of Portland by way of the ferry. Here could be found inexpensive rents with pleasant surroundings and convenient retail shops. There were also two constables on active duty who constituted the first fulltime police force in Cape Elizabeth. As a consequence, people began to settle here who were employed in Portland and commuted via the ferry, thus creating the first truly suburban area in Cape Elizabeth. An extensive sewerage system was laid out in the village and $800 was appropriated in 1870 to begin construction, making it the first section of the town to be so provided. That same year its population was extensive enough to warrant the establishment of two post offices, one bearing the official name Ferry Village, located in the village proper, and another at the ferry landing officially called the Cape Elizabeth Ferry Post Office.

At the Cape end of the Portland Bridge another settlement, Knightville, was more than evident. This village, named for the prominent local master shipwright Thomas E. Knight, was so far advanced that A, B, C, D, and E Streets were accepted by the town in 1866. It, too, had its retail shops and sported the busiest pair of hay scales in the entire town. By 1874 it had reached such a stage in its urbanized growth that a village reservoir became necessary for fire protection. As the population grew and the constabulary increased throughout the town, a base of operations became necessary. Therefore, in 1878, Knightville played host to the town's first building erected solely for purposes of incarceration. The new police station was a single story office located on Church Street, measuring 18 by 26 feet. It contained four cells, each 4 by 7 feet, equipped with iron-grated doors. The cell block was connected by a passageway five feet wide with the court room located in the front of the building. This front room measured 13 by 17 feet. From contemporary reports it is evident that the structure presented a neat and trim appearance. This flourishing little village also had its own post office, opened in 1875, and officially designated as Knightville.

Further along the shore line in a westward direction was another village, somewhat smaller than those previously mentioned, located at Turner's Island. This little village was named in honor of George W. Turner who in partnership with James B. Cahoon, helped to bring about the early urbanization of northern Cape Elizabeth. It was at this point that the Portland, Saco, and Portsmouth Railway trestle entered the Cape from Portland. Turner's Island, rather thinly populated, merged about this period with the settlement at the Cape Elizabeth Depot to form Pleasantdale. Improvements became necessary here, and in 1872 the town appropriated $200 for a sewer to serve Turner's Island.

Following the tracks of the Portland, Saco and Portsmouth Railway inland to where they intersect the junction of Summer and Brown Streets locates the Cape Elizabeth Depot. When the railroad was built in 1845 it so facilitated travel to and from this section of the Cape that a Depot was shortly constructed. However, as the number of dwellings increased the need for an all inclusive name was felt and consequently the name of the Depot post office, that had been established in 1853, was changed to Pleasantdale in the summer of 1869.

Still another settlement was located at the Cape Elizabeth end of Vaughan's Bridge. This was the industrial community of Ligonia. In 1866 the newly created Portland Rolling Mill Corporation purchased Camp Berry of Civil War fame and turned its approximately eighty-five acres into a "Company town." They divided it up into avenues, streets, and lots, refurnished some of the houses that previously made up Officers Row, and turned the abandoned barracks into serviceable dwellings. Added to the original buildings were nine single houses, twelve double houses, and three six-family houses.

Most of the houses were built on one long main street called Center Avenue, which ran east and west with a few shorter streets branching off at right angles. The houses were all painted a warm, dark barn-red producing a slightly monotonous effect, but as time passed, here and there certain families continued to live in the same dwelling for a generation or longer and quite naturally these homes became individualized to some extent with gardens, lawns, and trees.

A schoolhouse was also erected and served as the local primary school with children from the entire region attending. Many of the pupils lived on the "Old Camp Ground" and some of them used their fifteen minute recess period to hurry home so that they could carry hot dinners down to the mill for their fathers and perhaps a boarder as well.

Another addition the company made was a large two-story hall. In the auditorium, on the second floor, church services were often held as well as recreational activities. A general store occupied the ground floor and functioned as "company stores" usually do.

Across from the row of houses was an extensive baseball park. Large crowds often attended the Saturday afternoon games producing a rather animated assemblage. A great number of the better players were "mill hands". The team, known as the "Irons," had its own uniforms and soon outgrew the amateur class.

To this settlement the mill owners applied the name "Ligonia," possibly in commemoration of an earlier community. However, as the number of families increased in the immediate vicinity of this "company town," the name Ligonia became a geographical generalization loosely applied to that entire area.

One factor that accelerated the growth of these early suburban beginnings was the introduction of new industries into the nothern perimeter of the town. There were already established a few small industries that employed a limited number of people. One of these was a brewery located at the junction of the Brewery Road, now Highland Avenue, and the Ocean House Road. It was built in 1857 by Gibbs and Robinson of Portland for the manufacture of ale. After a short period of time the brewery was purchased by James McGlinchy of Portland; and under his management, approximately 180 barrels of excellent ale were turned out each week. It received a fairly wide spread distribution throughout the states of Maine and New Hampshire. The mash, after the extraction of the ale, was sold locally as cattle feed and was considered by many to greatly enhance the flavor of the milk.

Sometime during the seventies, the manufacturing of malt beverages was prohibited by amendments to the prohibition law and as a consequence, McGlinchy's Brewery was forced to suspend operations. The plant remained closed until 1881 when it was leased by Perry and Flint of Portland to be used as a canning factory. They apparently prospered on a minor scale until 1883, when on September 1st of that year the structure was destroyed by fire. The canning concern lost 187,000 cans, a large number of boxes, some produce, and all their machinery. They had about $10,000 worth of insurance that partially compensated them for their loss, but the heavy losers were the McGlinchy heirs who lost over $50,000 worth of brewery equipment that had very little insurance protecting it.

Another local industry that was somewhat active during this period was the small brickyard that had been started in the late fifties, by Christopher Dyer. It was situated between the Portland, Saco, and Portsmouth Railway right of way and Barberry Creek, in Pleasantdale. Although its production was at times quite large, most of the products were sold locally.

The first large industrial plant to be established in Cape Elizabeth was the Portland Kerosene Works. They erected their buildings on the south bank of Fore River, occupying about two acres of land just east of the Cape end of Vaughan's Bridge, in 1859. At first they manufactured their oil from Albert coal and provided the first dependable supply available for local use. Early in the sixties they shifted over to the refining of crude oil brought in over the railroad from the Pennsylvania fields. It was not long however before they began to employ ships in this carrying trade. The firm was prosperous enough to contribute appreciably to the income of Cape Elizabeth and also furnish their investors with an excellent return. Needless to say, with an ever expanding local market, the Kerosene Works continued to be an active concern well into the ninties, producing a constant supply of kerosene, naptha, and parafine.

The Portland Kerosene Works had been in operation only a few years when another large industry was located at the Cape. The Portland Rolling Mill was incorporated in March of 1864 to manufacture railroad, bar, hoop, and other iron products. However, after construction was begun in 1865 at a point just west of the Cape Elizabeth end of Vaughan's Bridge, on the south bank of Fore River, it was found necessary to increase the firm's capital from $200,000 to $300,000. This was achieved in February of 1866 by an act of the state legislature, that also authorized the company to construct a railroad trestle, for the convenience of the mill, not less than three hundred feet west of Vaughan's Bridge. It was also stipulated that the bridge be constructed on spiles and be provided with a suitable draw. By thus locating the plant an opportunity was thereby afforded to supply it with coal or iron by water as well as by rail, and to ship products out of the state in the same manner.

The works, erected under the direction of John Bundy Brown of Portland, were completed early in 1866. Originally the main building, measuring 200 by 90 feet, was of wooden construction, with a slanting roof, and with a wing 75 feet square. It housed the furnaces, rolling machines, and a stationary steam engine of 400 horsepower. Production began in June and within a few years the company was using approximately 5,000 tons of pig iron, 12,000 tons of old rails, and 12,000 tons of bituminous coal per annum. By 1875, production amounted to about 14,000 tons of rail each year having a total value of over a million dollars. The plant by that time employed nearly two hundred men with an annual payroll of $160,000. Most of the workmen first employed were of Irish, Welsh, Polish, or German extraction and experienced iron workers. Although the company's products were widely distributed, their greatest market was in Maine, Massachusetts, and Canada.

The early processes of unloading, by hand, the iron bars that had been imported from New Jersey, the manfacture of the pig iron into wrought iron, and the rolling and shaping of the iron into a finished product, forms a very interesting part of the plant's history.

Despite the fact that smelting the ore removed a large part of the impurities, the pig iron retained so much sulphur, phosphorus, carbon, and silicon, that it was unfit for most purposes unless purified. The iron, after purification, was known as wrought, or malleable iron, and was placed on the market in the form of iron rails, plates, bars, and rods.

The wrought iron was made by breaking the pig iron into chunks and placing them in a furnace, the length of which was somewhat greater than its height, and equipped with a sand or iron floor and vaulted roof. The fire was located at one end and the flue at the other; and as the fire passed under the roof, it heated the iron placed in the center of the furance. A quantity of iron rich in oxygen or magnetic ore was always included and as the chunks of pig iron became soft, the oxygen from this united with the impurities and formed cinder.

The puddling process was quite difficult and required a great amount of skill on the part of the workmen. As the pieces began to soften, the puddler stirred them vigorously with a large iron rod inserted through a hole in the furance door. The pieces were formed into balls of sixty to eighty pounds preparatory to being seized by large tongs and rushed to the "squeezer."

As the iron still contained impurities in the form of cinder that had to be expelled before it cooled, the "squeezer" played an important part. By means of this machine the heated iron was rolled into a cylinder and at the same time continually reduced in size. When the cinder had been removed, the iron was placed between rolls and worked into bars. These bars were cut up, reheated, and rolled again, the final rolling leaving the iron in the form desired for market. The rolls were so constructed as to shape the bar into various shapes. Throughout the entire process the men wore large leather aprons to protect them from the multitude of flying cinders.

The individual on which the success of the entire puddling process hinged was the puddler. It was his duty to determine the exact time when to remove the soft iron ball from the furance. He did this by closely watching the color of the melting iron as he worked it. A moment too soon or too late would spoil the entire lot. It is rather unnecessary to say that these early iron workers had a knowledge of their trade that was extensive in the least.

From its inception to 1878, the mill was managed by John B. Brown, the Portland financier. At that date the name of the firm was changed to the Ligonia Iron Company with George E. B. Jackson, president of the Maine Central Railroad, named as president of the works. Somewhat later, in 1880, it again assumed the name of the Portland Rolling Mills under the ownership of Seth and C. R. Milliken. They expanded production to include the manufacture of bar and angle iron of the type used in the construction of bridges, buildings, etc., along with fish plates and railroad spikes.

On a somewhat smaller scale, industrially speaking, was the old tide water mill at Knightville. The dam on which the mill rested had been considerably remodeled and repaired, holding back quite a body of water. The flowage of Mill Creek, also known as Lawrence Creek, Meadow Brook, Sawyer Brook, and Trout Brook, increased somewhat the length of time which the mill could be worked on at each tide.

Shortly after the Civil War, machinery was installed in the old mill to manufacture wooden spools. This venture was, however, of short duration for in 1868, Edward Oxnard of Portland reconverted it to its former status as a grist mill. In 1875 the establishment became the property of the John J. Lappin Company, but its days as a paying grist mill had passed. Larger mills, selling bulk flour through retail stores brought about its eventual failure.

In later years the source of power for the mill was changed over to steam and probably accounted for its destruction in 1892. On Wednesday, December 21st the old mill caught fire and was totally destroyed before fire-fighting equipment could be dispatched from Portland. When the steam pumper finally arrived, all that remained to be done was to water the ashes. This it did, making it the first time that water from Sebago Lake was used to extinguish a fire in Cape Elizabeth. Despite the disastrous fire, there is evidence that the mill was rebuilt.

There was one other interesting business venture that made itself felt in the early days of this period. This was a revival of interest in converting the Spurwink salt marshes into meadow land. In February of 1876, the state legislature incorporated the Cape Elizabeth Dyking Corporation. The express purpose of the firm was to erect and maintain a dyke and water sluices in the Spurwink River to shut out the salt water. The cost of maintenance was to be obtained by taxing those individuals who owned the fresh water marshes and meadow lands created by dyking the river. Like its predecessor of 1821, this attempt also ran its course in the space of a few years.

All things suffer from the ravages of time and the Portland Bridge was no exception. Consequently in May of 1866 extensive repairs were begun on this important thoroughfare much to the gratification of the Cape Elizabeth citizenry. About two hundred feet of the bridge was torn up and a program of complete rebuilding commenced. Repairs progressed at the proverbial snail's pace and after the bridge had been closed to traffic the greater part of a year, the number of irate citizens grew appreciably as the summer of 1867 approached. Feeling ran especially high when it became evident that the independent ferry operators that ran between the Cape and Portland were charging fares greatly in excess of the rates set by the county commissioners. Fortunately repairs were completed and the bridge reopened by mid-summer, thereby precluding action by the inhabitants.

Within the space of a few years, Portland Bridge was once again in the news, this time involving its Portland terminus. In 1855 that end of the bridge was lowered for the convenience of the public. This necessitated a crossing of the railroad tracks on Canal Street, now Commercial. As time went on, a perfect network of rails cut across the grade crossing over which the people were obliged to travel in entering and leaving the city. Accidents of increasing frequency and of a wide variety soon won for that intersection the ominous title, the "Gridiron of Death."

Agitation for the correction of this dangerous situation erupted in September of 1871. The conditions became critical in 1872 and public indignation had attained such a magnitude that action was finally obtained. The city of Portland, under considerable pressure, contracted with the Eastern Railroad Company to secure and maintain safety of travel over the gridiron. It was at this point that the railroad company agreed to build an overpass from Clark Street to a point near the draw of the Portland Bridge and also to establish a detour around to the east into State Street, so that the heavy traffic could be routed over but one track. The overpass was finally constructed in 1874.

To make a way of easy access to the Clark Street overpass, Beach Street was discontinued and York Street laid out much as it is at the present time. Wooden steps were built from the foot of Brackett Street over the railroad tracks for pedestrian traffic to the bridge and Canal Street; and in 1876, a footway was extended across the bridge proper. This stop-gap aid served as a matter of safety for a few short years. As an added safety factor, gas lamps were installed on the bridge and lighted for the first time Thursday, February 17th, 1876.

The last major improvement to the bridge prior to separation occured in 1893 and 1894. In February of 1893, the United States government ordered the County Commissioners to construct a new draw in the bridge with two openings of not less than seventy feet in the clear, and make such other general improvements as was necessary to put it in first class condition. The government also stipulated that the work had to be completed within one year of the construction order.

The top priority rating given this project by the county commissioners must have been somewhat gratifying to the citizens of Cape Elizabeth when a comparison is made with the time consumed by previous improvement activities. Despite the time limit imposed, the last granite block in the stone supporting pier was was not cemented into place until Saturday, March 31st, 1894. The finished pier measured 22 feet at the base, 21 feet at the top and 45 feet in height. It was not until Sunday, May 6th, that the new iron turntable type draw was swung into place atop the granite pier. The draw had two clear spans of 70 feet, with a combined length of 192.5 feet. With the draw in place the work was rushed to completion, and by late summer the bridge was open once again to vehicular traffic. The new iron draw was installed by the Boston Bridge Company. By this time the bridge had been reduced to a quarter mile in length as a large part of its original span had been filled in.

Cape Elizabeth's other main artery of transportation, Vaughan's Bridge, also required extensive repairs in this same period. In 1855, the old cobb work had been renewed and strengthened with piling. Further alterations were carried out in 1861 when it was widened to four rods. The span was shortened to 1,400 feet by dumping large quantities of gravel on each side of the cobb-work portion at each end. The spaces under the arches connecting the cobbs were also filled in and the water diverted through the spiling further out. These repairs were not too satisfactory as the fill had a tendency to settle each spring, creating serious obstacles to travel.

The overall instability of the bridge was amply demonstrated on November 12th, 1861, when a violent storm, accompanied by an unusually high tide, swept away a large portion of the structure. The town officers took prompt action and the bridge was soon reopened to traffic. The repairs made necessary by the storm cost the town about $900. A large amount of gravel was hauled for fill, the work of widening was completed, and the bridge was in somewhat better condition at that time than it had been for years. At this point the structure consisted of two rods of cobb-work and two rods of gravel, extending outward to the spiling at the center, with Cape Elizabeth responsible for 615 feet of the total span beginning at the southern end.

The last appreciable addition that Cape Eilzabeth made to Vaughan's Bridge took place in 1874. In the fall of that year, the town erected street lamps on this portion of the span. They were furnished by the New England Gas Light Company of Boston and had the improved "Solar Burner" that gave a bright steady flame, free of smoke. The lamps were first lighted in November, 1874. Previous to that time, the traveler literally placed his life in jeopardy if he attempted to cross on a particularly dark night.

This same year, 1874, also had its melancholy aspects, for on Friday, January 23rd, the venerable Town House at Town House Corner, was reduced to ashes in the course of an outstanding conflagration. This was the barn-like structure that had been erected in 1837 by Sylvanus Higgins.

The fire broke out about nine o'clock in a large grocery store owned by John L. Parrott, located just below the Town House on the Ocean House Road. A neighbor, Frank W. Dyer, discovered the fire and succeeded in turning out the neighborhood. He also furnished his team, and word was sent to Portland for assistance. A large crowd gathered and attempted to save the building, but as the wind was blowing fresh, the flames spread so rapidly that it was useless to attempt to save the store. Therefore, all hands turned to and successfully saved the vauable stock of goods the store contained.

The store was a two and half story building, with a dance hall on the second floor. The nature of the building's construction probably accounts for the rapid spreading of the fire. From the store, the flames jumped to an older store immediately adjoining it. In a very short space of time, both buildings were all ablaze. It was at this point that the Town House caught, despite the efforts of the citizenry. As these structures were beyond saving the fire-fighters turned their attention to James W. Harmon's carriage and blacksmith shop, situated close by. Blankets were placed on the roof and by keeping them constantly wet the flames were kept from the building. If this structure had ignited it would have been impossible to save several houses in the immediate vicinity. The steam pumper Casco 5 was dispatched from Portland but before it could get beyond the Portland Bridge it was turned back with the news that the buildings involved had been reduced to embers for want of water.

To many Cape Elizabeth citizens the Town House fire was not as calamitous as one might expect. There had been some agitation as early as 1871 for the construction of a new Town House. It had for many years been altogether too small and inconvenient to accomodate the increasing business and population of the town. At some meetings it was very difficult for the moderator to decide a yea or nay vote in the packed building. Occasionally there was so much confusion that the voters were ordered outside to form lines on opposite sides of the road before an accurate vote could be taken.

The town therefore was not completely unprepared for the sudden loss of the Town House. At the March meeting in 1871 a committee of three had been appointed to investigate the propriety of building a new Town House. They were also instructed to have plans drawn up and ascertain the expense. However, with a new Town House now a necessity, it was voted on the 26th of March, 1874 to build a new one and to borrow $12,000 to cover construction costs. Part of the sum thus appropriated was used to purchase additional land to accomodate the contemplated structure. Accordingly one acre was obtained at Town House Corner from Henry Nutter.

Plans were submitted by Francis H. Fassett, a Portland architect, and were accepted by the building committee. Contracts were subsequently let to S. C. Chase of Portland for the masonry work and to William Rand of Cape Elizabeth for the carpentry. Owing to the sudden death of Chase, his contract was assumed by Knight, Redlon & Company of Portland.

When the building was completed late in 1874 it certainly presented an impressive appearance. It stood facing the Hannaford Road, now Sawyer Street, about 200 feet north of the Ocean House Road and close by Bay View Cemetery. The new brick Town House was 49 feet in width on the street side and extended back 84 feet. The entrance also faced Sawyer Street, and was equipped with a double door totaling eight feet in width, a commodious entry way to say the least. This door led directly into an auditorium on the first floor that measured 46 by 60 feet and was 13 feet in height. It was here that the meetings were held. The town offices were located on each side of the entrance, and apparently were 13 by 18 feet. The selectmen's room, had a large vault and provided for the first time a safe repository for the town records. On the second floor was another hall, 47 by 52 feet and with a height of 14 feet. It was designed as a high school, with a recitation and a clothes room adjoining. All in all it made a convenient and attractive Town House. Not the least of its assests was its commanding location. From the second floor an extensive view of the harbor, ocean, and surrounding countryside could be had. That this new building became a center of activity is attested by the town records. In March of 1875 it was voted that the Town House could be used for meetings, schools, etc. at the discretion of the selectmen and at a price fixed by them to cover lighting, heating, janitor service, and up-keep. However, dancing assemblies, dancing schools, balls, "Negro concerts," and the like were prohibited. At the same meeting it was also voted to establish a free high school to be located on the second floor of the Town House.

The same year that the citizens voted to rebuild a new Town House, they also appropriated funds to construct a new almshouse. The old Thomas Jordan farm had been used since 1832, but its condition no longer warranted its use. Consequently in the spring of 1874, the old Jordan place was torn down and a new building 36 by 46 feet, two stories in height was erected about thirty rods to the west. The new almshouse was built under the supervision of the selectmen, by William D. Murray of Cape Elizabeth, from plans drawn up by Francis H. Fassett of Portland, and cost approximately $4,000.

This new poor farm proved to be a fairly profitable and self-sustaining undertaking. Using the year 1882 as an illustration, the farm produced that season about 45 tons of hay, 300 bushels of potatoes, 20 tons of cabbages, plus a large crop of squash, and other assorted vegetables. That year the farm and buildings were valued in the assets of the town at $7,000.

To conclude the commentary on the industrial growth of this era, it is of interest to note a few industries that proved to be all too ephemeral in nature. Probably the most outstanding example was the erection of a plush mill, on the Hovey Farm late in 1892. It was designed to manufacture plush, an item used extensively in the period as a covering for upholstered furniture. However, it was not until early in 1893 that the plant was ready to function; and in March of that year, its owner, Isaac C. Atkinson of Portland, invited a select group of local businessman to a collation in honor of the event.

Despite this auspicious beginning the factory, extensively equipped as it was with the latest in looms, dye vats, packing room, and a huge stationary steam engine, to say nothing of a large generator that made the plant electrically self sufficient, did not prove to be successful industrially. By April, operations were suspended entirely and in October the corporation was declared insolvent. The reason behind the failure of this industry, that certainly should have proven successful in the age of plush furniture, was attributed to a lack of operating capital.

The plush mill remained empty and idle until early in 1895 when it was sold to the John P. Lovell Arms Company of Massachusetts. They were able to begin production by the fall of the same year.

Another concern, somewhat more successful, carried on an unusual and novel business in this same period. This was the Portland Extracting Company whose continued prosperity depended largely on the labors of the individuals incarcerated in the Cumberland County jail at Portland and the Androscoggin County jail at Auburn.

The prisoners were employed in cutting heel taps from scrap leather, a waste product of the shoe factories. As the high grease content of the leather interfered with the manufacture of the finished heel it was imperative that this substance be removed. Therefore, approximately two tons of taps from Portland and three tons of taps from Auburn were shipped each week to this Cape Elizabeth concern for that express purpose.

At the Portland Extracting Company the bagged taps were allowed to soak over night in large tanks of naptha. When the soaking process was completed the naptha was drained away and the heel taps were dried in the vat by steam heat. The processed taps were then shipped back to their respective points of origin to be made into finished shoe heels.

From the still into which the used naptha was pumped about 600 pounds of grease per ton of heel taps was extracted. This waste product was then sold to various tanning concerns, soap manufacturers, and furriers, as a lucrative side line. Another feature of this company's operations was the cleansing of clothing, carpets, and furniture in naptha baths, thereby anticipating the modern dry-cleaning establishment.

The closing years of the nineteenth century found the town of Cape Elizabeth exhibiting examples of an increased social awareness on the part of its inhabitants. The temperance cause received considerable support in this period, especially in the Ferry Village section.

The first group organized in Cape Elizabeth with total abstinence as its basic tenet was the Temperance Watchmen Club No. 49 formed at Bowery Beach on the 7th of March, 1850. With reference to the records of the club, regular meetings were held up to and including Saturday, June 3rd, 1854. The meetings were apparently quite lively with temperance and prohibition the main topics of discussion. It is evident that the efforts of the organization were not always successful as the recorded minutes contain frequent references to back-sliding members and intemperate citizens. Subjects other than "demon rum" were often debated by the members at the weekly meetings. The Fugitive Slave Law was unanimously condemned at the meeting of February 21st, 1852. On the 6th day of March, 1852, the members by a vote of 23 to 9, declared the removal by force of the American Indian from his natural place of abode to be a crime against humanity on the part of the United States. The question of capital punishment was briskly debated on the 13th of March, 1853, and by a majority vote of 24 to 17, it was decided that life imprisonment was more desirable. For a club with such an active membership it seems strange that the meetings were terminated so abruptly.

The Independent Order of Good Templars was the next organized attempt to curb alcholic intemperance in Cape

Elizabeth. Lodge No. 25 was organized on the 9th of October, 1864 in Thompson Hall, over Charles A. Tilton's store at Ferry Village. Within a year, the membership had so increased that it outgrew these quarters and agitation was begun to raise funds for the construction of a new hall. By 1866, enough money was available to cover the basic expenses, and as a consequence Seaside Hall was erected at a cost of $5,364.50 by the members themselves.

The organization continued to grow, and in a little less than two decades the original Lodge No. 25 numbered 205 members. The same period also witnessed the formation of two more lodges, one at the Town House and one at Pond Cove.

In January of 1872, the Ferry Village Temperance Reform Club was organized by Captain W. Dyer with total abstinence as its guiding principle. It proved to be the first club of this particular type formed in the state of Maine. By March of 1873, the membership of this organization contained 170 Ferry Village citizens. On Saturday the 26th of April in this same year, a Washingtonian meeting was held in the village and proved to be a great success. The temperance sentiment continued for at least a decade or two before any decline in enthusiasm was readily apparent. Another reform club was organized in Ferry Village on the 25th of September, 1876, and 728 individuals signed its cold water pledge. Hardly a meeting went by without new names being added to the list or new members enrolled to the accompaniment of "Yes, We'll Sing Forever, No Brown Jug for Me." There were also, quite naturally, a few individuals who consistently refused to participate in these expressions of total abstinence and who proved to be a thorn in the flesh. When the temperance element, with due reference to the saloons, made known its motto "we bend the knee, but not the elbow," one wit among the tipplers remarked that it apparently referred to a habit of drinking from the bung of the barrel.

Temperance sentiment was probably at its height when, on Wednesday, April 30th, 1884, the twenty-fifth quarterly convention of the temperance reform clubs of Cumberland County met at the Methodist Church on High Street in Ferry Village for a three day conference. Following closely on the heels of this gathering was the formation, in this same village, of a club for the express purpose of furthering the cause of prohibition. Calling themselves the St. John and Daniel Club this group sought the complete removal of the alcoholic menace from the community. On the whole the temperance movement continued with enthusiasm to the close of the century, but its place in the minds of the people was gradually eclipsed by the separation agitation.

Various fraternal orders also made their appearance in this same period. The Freemasons resident in Cape Elizabeth felt the need of a local lodge and as a consequence, nine Master Masons met at the selectmen's office on September 25th, 1875, to decide on a course of action. Before they could organize it was necessary to secure a suitable hall, therefore they petitioned the selectmen to call a town meeting for the purpose of considering the propriety of the Freemasons engaging the attic rooms of the Town House as a Masonic Lodge. A meeting was held on Thursday the 5th of October and it was voted to allow the Freemasons the use of the rooms in question.

After some debate, the Cape Elizabeth Freemasons afixed the name Hiram to their Lodge and then proceeded to petition the Grand Lodge of Maine for recognition. The dispensation was granted the petitioners under the date of November 1st, 1875, thereby officially creating Hiram Lodge No. 180. The first regular meeting was held on November 4th 1876, with Gordon R. Garden, Worshipful Master, presiding. This Lodge immediately became very active and by 1890 its membership had increased to one hundred and fifty-three.

The Knights of Pythias were also active and Bayard Lodge No. 44 was established at Ferry Village on January 25th, 1884. By 1887 they were prosperous enough to erect a hall for meeting purposes at the corner of High and Preble Streets.

Two other fraternal groups, the Patriotic Order of the Sons of America and the United Order of the Golden Cross, were also active. The former organized about 1877, met regularly in Tilton's Hall. The later instituted somewhat later, approximately 1880, also met fairly regularly. Both orders were represented by a sizable membership. It should be pointed out however, that both of these groups had their base in a bigoted dedication to white, Anglo-Saxon, Protestant, anti-foreign principles.

One source of pride and enjoyment afforded the citizens of Cape Elizabeth in the closing decades of the century were the brass bands organized in the various sections of the town. The first to be formed was the Union Brass Band of Ferry Village. It owed its inception to the efforts of John Emery, a cornet player of considerable talent. Recruiting several of his fellow townsmen, they became quite a polished group as the result of instruction provided by Charles Grimmer, a former member of Poppenberg's Band that had been stationed at Fort Preble during the Civil War. They held their rehearsals in Union Hall adopting its name for their band. Like so many other brass bands of this era they were called upon very frequently for social functions, parades, and political rallies. In the summer months they gave periodic concerts on the lawn of the Peoples Methodist Church in Knightville. After eight years they dissolved with many of the members joining bands in other sections of the town and in Portland.

Two years later, in 1882, another band was organized in Ferry Village by Clarence Merriman and John F. Merriman. Known as Merriman's Band they practiced in Union Hall under the guidance of John Cole and Frank Collins, two promient Portland bandsmen. In due course they became quite proficient and were soon giving concerts from a bandstand built by appreciative Ferry Village citizens. As their fame grew Edward Hays built them a second bandstand at Dog Corner, now known as Willard Square.

This band also had the distinction of being one of the best dressed musical organizations in the town. They purchased the uniforms discarded by the old Portland Light Infantry. The uniforms consisted of light blue trousers with a wide red stripe down each leg, dark blue coat with gold braid down the front and large gold epaulets, and a wide white leather belt. For head gear they wore tall fur shakoes with a white plume for the men and a red plume for the band leader.

Much in demand for political gatherings and parades, Merriman's Band was undoubtedly the most popular within the town. They participated in many a social function not only in Portland but in other sections of the state. When they disbanded about 1892 they were sorely missed.

A third band flourished for a similar period of time at Town House Corner. Known as the Town House Band they took their inspiration from Merriman's Band and were also instructed by Frank Collins. Under the leadership of Philip Robinson they practiced constantly in a room at the Town House and in due course were giving spirited concerts throughout the town. During the summer they gave weekly concerts at a bandstand built for their specific use at Bowery Beach. However, like the others they flourished but briefly dissolving about 1890.

In 1884 yet another band was born. Organized at Ligonia by the men of the Rolling Mill it was named the Ligonia

Cornet Band. Its leading figure was William J. Lewis, known to the bandsmen as "Bill John" Lewis. Despite the fact that he was only fourteen years old and the members of the band were at least twice his age, his was the guiding hand. In addition Lewis organized a male chorus of fifty voices from among the Welch iron workers, and, with the band, they gave many polished and delightful concerts.

Unfortnately Lewis moved to Virginia in 1889 and shortly thereafter the band ceased to exist. In later years "Bill John" Lewis was the leader of the Richmond Light Infantry Band that achieved nation wide fame. Although he returned to Ligonia late in life he did not revive the band of his youth.

The last band to be organized in this era came to life in Knightville in 1885. Instruction was provided by Charles Howe of Portland and their early practice sessions were held in a room over a harness shop at Knightville Square. Shortly after the band was formed they erected a small building with a large piazza close by the Knightville end of the old Portland Bridge. Here they practiced and on frequent occasions gave concerts using the piazza as a band stand. Like the other bands they traveled far and wide. participating in a large variety of public, as well as private functions. Again like its local counterparts its life was brief and they disbanded about 1894. Their little band building was later moved to Knightville Square and converted into a hardware store.

The laboring man too, was very active for a brief period, and was represented in the town by the Knights of Labor, Assembly No. 5230. It was, however, not long in evidence as the group gave up its charter and disbanded in February of 1887. At that point the treasury contained approximately thirty dollars which was donated by the members to the town for the purchase of a set of encyclopedias to be used in the public schools.

The tillers of the soil were a little more successful in banding together. In 1882 the Patrons of Husbandry made its appearance in Cape Elizabeth and a local Grange was instituted at the Town House the same year. The organization did not at first attract very many members. After drifting along a few years the Cape Elizabeth Grange was reorganized at the Spurwink District School in 1889. That same year a Grange Hall was erected and dedicated at the junction of the Spurwink and Fowler Roads. Once again enthusiasm apparently lagged and it was necessary to reorganize a second time in 1915. Shortly after this date the Grange Hall was sold to Phineas Sprague of Boston and meetings were subsequently held at the Town Hall. In later years a financial arrangement was worked out with Sprague and meetings were resumed at what is now Sprague Hall.

A high degree of sophistication had certainly been attained, when on Saturday, the 22nd of October, 1881, the *Cape Elizabeth Sentinel*, a weekly newspaper of four pages, hit the street. Published by Frederick H. and James H. Harford at Ferry Village, it represented the ultimate in the poignant journalistic wit and humor typical of the late nineteenth century. This delightful little paper sold at four cents per copy, thirty-two cents for three months or $1.25 per year and was considered by the citizenry as well worth the price.

The *Cape Elizabeth Sentinel*, was not however, the first newspaper to be published in Cape Elizabeth. On the 1st of July, 1868, there had appeared an eight page, thirty-two column sheet, dated in Cape Eilzabeth and called *The Casket*. It was published by G.M.D. Libby, and was printed at the office of B. Thurston and Company of Portland. It did not survive long enough for a second issue to appear. Judging from the tone of the editorial that appeared in *The Casket* the publisher realized that it was the first and last edition. One article was devoted to the old Town House with its inadequate facilities, and recommended dividing the town up into wards to better accomodate the voters. Another article entitled "Portland and Its Suburbs," written by George W. Libby, called attention to the desirability of constructing a municipal park in Cape Elizabeth. There was also an enlightning article on "Profane Swearing" by Henry H. Osgood. Local advertising occupied one column with advertisements by Portland merchants filling the remaining space. One copy of this interesting journalistic experiment is known to exist at the present time.

Another short lived predecessor of the *Cape Elizabeth Sentinel* was the *Suburban Times*. The pre-publication prospectus described it as a four page weekly paper, representing Ferry Village, Knightville, and Ligonia, to be published at Ferry Village every Friday, The first issue was scheduled to appear on Friday, March 14th, 1879. However, as no copy or recollection of this paper survives, it is extremely doubtful if it ever appeared.

The *Sentinel* was soon expanded in format, larger offices obtained, and a press, used briefly by the *Portland Sunday Union*, was purchased so that the actual printing could be done at Ferry Village. Within a comparatively short period of time, the paper reached a circulation of 1,500. It is safe to say that there were few pubic questions on which the *Sentinel* did not take a definite stand by presenting an impassioned commentary. During its lifespan the paper backed many groups and projects, not the least of which was its own baseball team.

Modern columnists would certainly be risking prompt legal action if they tried to match the candid remarks of some contributors to the *Sentinel*. One column in particular, entitled "Wheat and Tares," written by Harcus A. Hanna, had at times a vitriolic quality which made it not only substantial reading but pungently challengeable as well.

The paper was published regularly until the first decade of the twentieth century when it changed hands and suspended publication for a time. However, the old appeal and spirit was gone and by 1912 the *Sentinel* ceased publishing for good. No complete file of this paper could be located at this writing. As far as can be ascertained no more than thirty-five issues of this worthy journalistic achievement are preserved.

There was one other newspaper that devoted its columns to the news of Cape Elizabeth and vicinty. This was the *Coast Watch*, fifth and last in a series of weeklies, published by Libby and Smith of Portland. The first issue appeared on Friday, September 27th, 1895, and the paper ran until 1916. When this paper began publication it so incensed the owners of the *Sentinel* that they started the *Deering Enterprise* to compete with the Libby and Smith paper that served the Deering section. Despite a good start the *Coast Watch* was never able to equal the vivacity and flavor of the *Sentinel*.

Of all the local problems that attracted the attention of the *Sentinel* and its editors none elicited more purple-prose than the matter of ferry service to Portland. Throughout the eighties and nineties column after column was devoted to the need for improving this vital form of transportation. No occasion was ever overlooked, nor any opportunity allowed to pass, in keeping their public well informed on this issue.

Actually the ferry was almost as old the community itself. In the colonial era irregular ferry service existed at Purpooduck as early as 1678. The unsettled nature of the times brought frequent interruptions and as a result nothing permanent was effected until the incorporation of Falmouth in 1718. In May 1719, John Pritchard, residing on the Neck, became the first officially appointed ferryman. This policy of regulating and supervising the ferry service by municipal fiat had been sanctioned by the Massachusetts General Court in 1639. When Cape Elizabeth was set off as a district in 1765 the maintainance of the ferry became a matter of constant concern to the selectman, subject to regulations voted at the town meeting. Until it came within realm of state control the ferryman was granted his franchise by the town and a bond taken to ensure proper service as sell as a safe, convenient landing place.

In 1719 John Sawyer had built a large crib-work wharf close by the foot of what is now Sawyer Street. It was here that the ferry landings were made until late in the century. Across the harbor a public landing was maintained at Ferry Point on the east side of Clay Cove. After the Revolutionary War the ferry was operated for many years by Capt. Cary McLellan, a prominent citizen of the town. He made regular crossings to Ingraham's Wharf using an open boat propelled by sail or oar. In 1787 a new landing place was constructed near Sawyer's Wharf, on flats purchased from the estate of Christopher Strout. Also, that same year Capt. McLellan was awarded the ferry franchise for a period of twenty-five years and greatly expanded at his own expense, the facilities of the ferry landing. Eight years later he surrended his franchise and the town awarded him fifty pounds as compensation for the improvements he had made. He was succeeded by Jonathan Sawyer who held the post until 1800.

In the early decades of the nineteenth century it was customary to grant the ferry franchise each year to the person who offered the highest sum for the privilege. Although the town continued to keep the ferry landing in some semblence of repair very little attention was apparently paid to the service provided by the ferryman. Contemporary comments are extremely critical of the irregular schedules, exorbitant rates, and and indifferent comforts provided by those who exploited the ferry franchise. One extremely vocal patron penned a letter to the editor of the *Eastern Argus* in February 1820 in which he noted that "the negligent, irregular, and shameful manner in which the Cape Elizabeth Ferry has been attended for several years past, is a subject of just complaint . . . and a notorious disgrace to the town." He then discoursed at length and in detail on the situation explaining why sweeping reforms were badly needed. Apparently his appeal fell on deaf ears for no change is discernable in the annual recommendations of the selectman, accepted at the town meetings.

When Portland Bridge was opened in 1823 the ferry declined

still further as a convenient mode of transportation. In 1827 James Mariner received the franchise with a bid of eleven dollars. Three years later however, the possibilities of change are discernable when with a bid of $274 Col. Solomon Cutter obtained the franchise. As was usually the case he hired a ferryman, in this case Alfred Stanford, supplied him with a boat, paid him a salary, and collected the revenue. In this case however, the colonel must have been a far sighted man anticipating the spread of commercial activity to Ferry Village. Just three years before a bid of only $11.00 had won the ferry franchise. The town also realized the potentialities of urban growth and mercantile expansion for in 1843 a new granite faced retaining wall was constructed at the ferryways by the local masons Jonathan Nichols and Ebenezer Smith.

In conjunction with their plans for developing the commercial enterprises they envisioned at Ferry Village the two Portland merchants George W. Turner and James B. Cahoon also initiated a drastic change in the ferry situation. The town had previously returned its responsibility for the ferry to the state. In February of 1847 the state legislature granted a charter to the Portland and Cape Elizabeth Ferry Company whereby they were empowered to operate a ferry for the transportation of passengers, animals, freight, carriages, carts, wagons, etc. The rates were also fixed, hopefully covering all combinations and contingencies. In addition, the hours of service were specifically established, subject to periodic review by the legislature. If the company was derelict in its duty it was liable to a fine of ten dollars for each offense.

The new firm immediately began construction of a new ferryboat close by the ferry landing. On Saturday, 17 June 1848, the 147 ton side-wheel, double-ended steam ferry *Elizabeth* was launched. She was the first such vessel to be employed on the waters of Portland Harbor. Under the command of Captain Noah B. Knight she was immediately put into service running regularly every fifteen minutes, 6:15 a.m. to 8:00 p.m., between the ferry ways and Maine Wharf.

Apparently, the ferry was not as financially successful as had been anticipated. When the partnership of Turner and Cahoon was dissolved, due to the death of Turner, the ferry company was declared bankrupt. In 1852 the town of Cape Elizabeth appropriated $1500 as a grant, payable in three annual installments, to assist Joseph W. Dyer, Henry Goddard, and Benjamin W. Pickett, in their efforts to keep the *Elizabeth* in service. Two years later the town was authorized by the state legislature to continue this financial aid. Unfortunately the *Elizabeth* was destroyed by fire while tied up at the ferry ways late in 1856.

The following year a new firm was chartered by the state, the Cape Elizabeth Steam Ferry Company, on terms identical to its predeccessor. A new ferry, the *Little Eastern*, 32 tons, was built at the Dyer Yard and launched in June of 1857. Somewhat smaller than the *Elizabeth*, she was named *Little Eastern* as a humorous comment on the failure of a Portland business combine to have the city utilized as a Canadian winter port by the gigantic English steamer *Great Eastern*. The new ferry went into service 2 July, 1857 following a schedule similar to that previously used. No major change was effected until 1864 when the side-wheeler *H. H. Day*, 49 tons, also built at the Dyer Yard, replaced her. Financial problems once again became acute and in 1866 the town pledged an annual subsidy of $200 for the next five years. The following year the state authorized an increase in the rates to further lighten the financial burden. Despite this assistance the company did not prosper and the service deteriorated rapidly. By the spring of 1870 public indignation in the vicinity of Ferry Village was sufficiently inflamed to warrant protest meetings. As the ferry company was now completely unable to continue operations the town was forced to take action. The following year the town borrowed $4100 to repair the ferry landing to accommodate a new boat operated by Randall, McAllister, and Company of Portland. This new boat was a small fifty-four foot passenger screw steamer, *Josephine Hoey*, that formerly ran between New York City and Governors Island in New York Harbor. She now made regular trips between Custom House Wharf and the ferry landing.

The same year, 1871, John B. Curtis and Capt. Benjamin J. Willard purchased the charter of the now defunct ferry company, changed its name to the Portland and Cape Elizabeth Ferry Company, purchased the *Josephine Hoey* and went into business. Four years later they added the *Mary W. Libby* another small passenger steamer. During the summer months in subsequent years this second steamer was used on a variety of routes in Casco Bay and along the coast.

In 1879 dissatisfaction with the ferry once again became a heated issue in the northeastern villages of the town. Not only did the service leave much to be desired but the rates were now considered to be unnecessarily high. The citizens demanded that the rate be reduced to three cents. At first the company argeed to accept this rate but only during off-hours. This did not prove acceptable to the citizens and a protest meeting attended by over two hundred was held 2 October at Ferry Village. Such a vigorous display of united sentiment had its affect and the company agreed to the three cent unlimited fare. The service however continued to be rather poor and despite repeated demands no boat was added to accommodate vehicles, teams, etc.

Thus it was that when the *Cape Elizabeth Sentinel* was born in October 1881 an impassioned issue was already before the people. As the editors were local citizens not connected with the ferry interests they instantly joined the cause for an improvement in this vital form of public transportation. After a great deal of agitation, aided and abetted by the *Sentinel,* a large protest meeting was held at Union Hall in Ferry Village, Saturday evening 31 January, 1885. With Dr. J. W. Lowell as chairman a series of resolutions were adopted after several very partisan speeches. Outstanding among the resolutions were the heartily endorsed sentiments that the "citizens of Ferry Village . . .in public meeting assembled, hereby enter our protest against the present conveyance across Fore River as provided by the Portland and Cape Elizabeth Ferry Company." This was followed by the declaration that "patience has ceased to be a virtue" and that "improved accomodations must be provided . . .earlier in the morning and later in the day." The resolutions were than embodied in a petition to be forwarded to the state legislature. In conjunction with the protests the charter of a new company, to be known as the People's Ferry Company, was read and unanimously endorsed. It is interesting to note that one of the most vocal participants at this meeting was the editor of the *Sentinel* Frederick H. Harford, who in addition was one of the prospective incorporators of the new ferry company.

The People's Ferry Company was duly incorporated by the legislature in March, 1885. At a town meeting held that same month it was voted to lease exclusive rights to the use of the ferry landing for a period of ten years, at an annual rental of one dollar, to this new firm. The incorporators of the People's Ferry Company were Charles A. Tilton, Tristram G. Hutchins, Dr. David A. Kincaid, Aurelius V. Cole, Rotheus M. Cole, Caleb Dyer, Nathan R. Dyer, William Spear, Albert M. Spear, Andrew W. Smart, M. Sanders Small and Frederick H. Harford. On Friday evening 6 March, 1885, a gala celebration was held at

Ferry Village with bonfires, artillery salutes, and a torch light parade in honor of the company. Later in the month work was commenced at Bath on a double-ended, side-wheel, steam ferry boat for the line.

This new vessel, the *Cornelia H.*, named for a member of the Spear family, was launched late in May. On her maiden voyage to Portland she proved to be rather hard to manage due to the absence of a keel and her shallow draft. In entering Portland Harbor the ferry collided with two island steamers, the *Express* and the *Gordon*, before reaching her berth at Custom House Wharf. The *Cornelia H.* went into service on Friday 12 June but continued to be somewhat cranky, repeatedly abusing Custom House Wharf and colliding with other steamers. Also, she had a tendency to yaw quite badly under way. One local wit recommended that the company adopt the words "none can tell where fate will bear me" as its motto. However, a heavy keel was shortly added to the vessel eliminating these navigational problems. By this time the Portland and Cape Elizabeth Ferry Company had been absorbed by the Forest City Steamboat Company which continued to operate the *Mary W. Libby*.

One problem that still faced the People's Ferry Company in its desire to provide the best in accommodations and service was the establishment of an adequate landing on the Portland side. With this in mind the firm petitioned the County Commissioners to lay out into the tide waters of Portland Harbor a ferry landing suitable for teams and foot passengers, near the site of the early municipal landing at Ferry Point. This landing had been abandoned in 1847 when the first steam ferry went into service.

The heavy traffic at Custom House Wharf prompted a change in the projected ferry landing and Portland Pier was selected by the petitioners. However, the County Commissioners ruled against the construction of such a landing as an unwarranted expense. Needless to say the battle was again joined and the people of Ferry Village decided to appeal the decision to the Supreme Court of Maine. The hearing opened 30 March, 1886 before three commissioners appointed by the court. After lengthy deliberation a report was submitted by the commissioners urging the court to rule in favor of the People's Ferry Company. The Supreme Court accepted the recommendations of the comittee and ordered that a suitable landing be constructed by the city of Portland, at Portland Pier. The following March, 1889, the town of Cape Elizabeth appropriated $2000 to be used for the building of a suitable ferry way at the old landing.

In April construction began at Portland Pier of a satisfactory ferry ship. Before the work had progressed very far a group of dissatisfied Portland taxpayers headed by Neal Dow filed a bill in equity with the Supreme Court seeking an injunction to halt construction. He set forth as his primary objection, that he as a "citizen of said Portland, and an owner of property liable to taxation on account of said highway and ferry landing, is in danger of suffering great wrong and irrepairable injury." This request was met with outraged opposition from a wide variety of sources. The city was petitioned to continue with the construction of the ferry landing regardless of Dow's remonstrances. After a lengthy hearing the court ruled against Dow and his supporters thereby clearing the way for completion of the alterations to Portland Pier. Once again the *Sentinel* and its Ferry Village supporters were jubilant hailing if for the final victory it truly represented.

The ferry landing and waiting rooms were completed in October 1889. When completed the ways were 100 feet in length, built of southern pine and supported by trusses, with a maximum rise at low tide of one foot in ten. The owners of Portland Pier were also compensated by the city with a payment of $15,586 for the damages they sustained. The formal opening of the new ways occurred Monday, 5 November, just in time to replace Portland Bridge, temporarily closed to traffic due to damages to the draw inflicted by a passing schooner. The first team to cross on the ferry was driven by Ira Clay hauling a hogshead of molasses to Ferry Village for Aurelius V. Cole.

Three years later in April of 1892 the *Sentinel* reported with obvious satisfaction that the *Cornelia H.* was carrying an average of sixty teams a day, half of which were double teams in addition to approximately 1,400 passengers. Disaster struck unexpectedly early in the morning Saturday 3 September. Moored at her dock near the landing at Ferry Village the *Cornelia H.* took fire and before help could arrive was a mass of flames. She burned to the water line taking with her much of the ferry landing, waiting room, and part of an adjoining fish market. It was only through the heroic efforts of Portland firemen that the wharf and a nearby schooner were saved. As a temporary measure the steamers *Isis* and *Chebeague* were pressed into service as ferries.

Two months after the fire the People's Ferry Company sold its charter to Charles M. Jones, treasurer of the Brooks Arms and Tool Company. He in turn immediately sold it to George S. Hunt and James P. Baxter of Portland. The new owners began at once to negotiate for the construction of a larger double-ended ferry to replace the late and now lamented *Cornelia H*. Also, the town of Cape Elizabeth at a special meeting held 3 December, 1892, voted to borrow the funds necessary to repair the ferry landing. Shortly thereafter the work thereon was initiated by Nathan Dyer, low bidder on the contract. In March of the following year the New England Shipbuilding Company of Bath completed and on the 23rd launched the new ferry, to be known as the *Elizabeth City*. She was immediately towed to Portland to have her engines, built by the Portland Company, installed. Throughout this period the steamers *Alice* and *Winter Harbor* had served as ferries, with the opposition boats *Josephine Hoey* and *Mary W. Libby* enjoying an improved patronage.

The *Elizabeth City* was completed late in May and on 2 June made a shake-down cruise up the harbor and down among the islands of Casco Bay. She went into regular service Saturday 24 June with loud hosannas from the *Sentinel* and its partisans. This new vessel proved to be such a faithful and dependable public carrier that it easily gathered most of the business. This, in conjunction with a decline in the population of Ferry Village, coupled with advent of the trolley line, ultimately drove the opposition boats off the run. The new owners of the Portland and Cape Elizabeth Ferry Company charter, the Casco Bay Lines, ended their service to Cape Elizabeth on Sunday 7 April, 1895. In return the People's Ferry Company agreed to refrain from any participation in the Casco Bay business. Unfortunately troubled years lay ahead for the *Elizabeth City*, with declining revenue an ever present problem. She was finally withdrawn from service in January 1912 and was sold to a New York firm in June of the following year by her owner James P. Baxter.

The civic awareness of the Cape Elizabeth citizens was embodied in two associations that were very active in this era. At a large and enthusiastic meeting held at Union Hall, Ferry Village, on Saturday the 25th of January, 1890, it was unanimously voted to form a Board of Trade. A total of thirty-five citizens were immediately enrolled as members and they promptly elected Charles A. Tilton, President; Marcus A. Hanna, Edward C. Reynolds, and Andrew J. Cash, Vice Presidents; plus sixteen Directors. The subject of introducing Sebago Lake water into Cape Elizabeth was brought up but bound over for later consideration. This particular question, despite its innocent connotations, was to be the basis for impassioned debate in the months to come.

Of equal importance was the Cape Elizabeth Village Improvement Association that was formed early in 1892. They initiated an efficient system of municipal rubbish removal at Ferry Village and began an earnest effort at public beautification of this urban area. At the instigation of this group attractive flower beds and shade trees were added to the grounds adjoining the various schoolhouses.

As has already been pointed out, the citizens did not neglect the social aspects of community life. There were of course various groups, other than the fraternal and church organizations, that catered to special interests. The Ladies Aid Society met regularly at Ferry Village, with two other groups of women, the Samaritans and the Evergreens, meeting at Ferry Village and Point Village respectively. The two latter societies were instrumental in rescuing Mount Pleasant Cemetery from a condition equally as deplorable as that which now exists in the Eastern and Western Cemeteries of Portland. It was through their efforts that the Mount Pleasant Cemetery Association was incorporated as a legal entity in 1874.

Prominent among the social groups with a specialized appeal, were the Cape Elizabeth Gun Club and the Cape Elizabeth Wheelmen. The members of the first named organization were known among the "gunnin" enthusiasts for their markmanship. The latter club, pursuing a non-violent kind of recreation, certainly must have been made up of individuals gifted with uncommon stamina. A fairly rugged constitiution was a prerequisite when one ventured forth on the unpaved highways, in the bone-shattering velocipedes of that era.

It is estimated that in a two year period 1885 to 1887, the Ferry Village area experienced more general expansion and real estate development than in the previous fifteen years. This sudden growth was the result of a gradual increase in population throughout the whole town. Consonant with this growth was a change in the postal system. The first move in this direction was the establishment of a post office at Bowery Beach in 1876. The settlement at Point Village was also warranted as large enough to need postal facilities. As a consequence, a post office was opened Monday, 26 May, 1884, coinciding with a change in the name of the village, and officially designated as Willard. The two post offices at Ferry Village and the Cape Elizabeth Ferry were amalgamated into one office in 1887 to be known as South Portland. This was the first offical appearance of the name, as suggested for the area by the *Cape Elizabeth Sentinel,* that was to receive wider acclaim in the months to come. Still another alteration was the opening of a new post office in 1889 at Town House Corner, bearing the generalized name of Cape Elizabeth. Needless to say, this abudance of postal facilities frequently caused considerable confusion, delay, and no end of profanity, when some individuals, for example, persisted in addressing a letter to Willard, Cape Elizabeth, or to Bowery Beach, Cape Elizabeth. Despite the appearance of these new geographical expressions, many of the older Cape citizens continued to gave their place of origin either Spurwick or "Pooduc."

In this period of urbanized growth, agitation was initiated for the erection of a monument honoring the soldiers and sailors from Cape Elizabeth who participated in the Civil War. The suggestion as first made by Albert D. Boyd, soon evolved into a public project. Subsequently, a meeting was held at the Town House on August 8th, 1891, to consider the matter and plan a fund-raising campaign. Another meeting was held on the 17th of August at the Town House whereby further plans were made pursuant to the projected monument. A mass meeting was finally achieved, and on August 22nd the general public turned out in large numbers to be addressed by General Charles P. Mattocks, Augustus F. Moulton, William B. Clifford, and Colonel Jared A. Smith, on the desirability of erecting such a memorial. Incidental to the meeting, the Cape Elizabeth Soldiers and Sailors Monument Association was organized on September 30th, 1891, with Edward C. Reynolds, President; Noah B. Knight, Secretary; and William B. Jordan, Treasurer. The by-laws and constitution of the Portland Soldiers and Sailors Monument Association were adopted and with this the organization was duly incorporated.

Most of the necessary funds to cover construction costs were obtained by solicitation. However, the town of Cape Elizabeth donated $800, William Widgery Thomas of Portland gave $200, and the various social organizations in the town subscribed substantial sums, with certificates for membership in the association issued for all amounts received.

On March 5th, 1895, the North Congregational Church donated a lot of land on which to erect the projected monument. This piece of land, on which the memorial was eventually placed, was designated as being a triangular plot directly in front of the church, bordered on one side by the Mitchell Road and on the other by the Shore Road. As later events demonstrated, this location proved to be the most desirable.

The monument was completed and erected late in the summer of 1896. Like so many others to be seen throughout the state of Maine the memorial consists of a substantial granite base topped by the life size figure of a Union soldier standing with his rifle at ease. The Cape Elizabeth statue stands six feet two inches in height and is cast in white bronze. The pedestal on which it rests measures approximately thirteen feet six inches from the base to the cap-stone, with an earthwork foundation that rises four feet above the ground level, and is encompassed by granite curbing. The material used in the construction of the pedestal is highly polished Hallowell and Quincy granite.

Dedication services were carried out Saturday afternoon the 29th of May, 1897. The occasion proved to be a memorable one with over two hundred Grand Army men from Portland, South Portland, and Cape Elizabeth participating. They assembled at the junction of Cottage Road and Broadway, and then, accompanied by Merriman's Band, marched up Meeting House Hill to the exercises. The citizenry also turned out in large numbers with the day proving to be an enjoyable one for all concerned.

The matter of fire protection had been one subject that disturbed the people of Cape Elizabeth for many years. With the overall expansion that was going on in the northern reaches of the town, the inhabitants of this area finally took matters into their own hands and formed fire companies for their mutual protection.

In the summer of 1892 there was considerable talk in Ferry Village of the urgent need for organizing some sort of a fire company. Consequently a call was issued requesting the citizens to meet in Union Hall on the evening of September 21st to discuss ways and means.

The meeting was well attended and so enthusiastic were the participants that an organization was immediately effected under the name of the Volunteer Hose Company No. 1. The first Foreman was F. L. Paige, with D. V. Willard, First Assistant; A. A. Cole, Second Assistant; W. E. Nason, Clerk; and J. H. Harford, Treasurer. The membership of the company was limited to forty. At a meeting held on the 15th of February, 1893, a constitution and a set of by-laws were adopted. Work was then begun to put the company on its feet, financially speaking. The sum of $529.73 was realized through a benefit fair, and, coupled with the money raised by popular subscription, the organization was provided with sufficient funds to establish itself.

The first purchase of apparatus was made on October 15th, 1892, when $150 was invested in five hundred feet of hose. It was not a very imposing beginning, but with a little ingenuity the members were able to construct a hose cart. Further equipment was purchased in March of 1893 in the form of several single ladders plus a forty-six foot extension ladder. This did away with the disadvantage of borrowing ladders, only to replace them, when they gave way through their over zealous use by the fire-fighters.

Another fire company was organized at Willard simultaneously with the one at Ferry Village. Despite the fact that its preliminary meeting antedated that of the Vounteer Hose Company, it was officially designated as Willard Hose Company No. 2. It was tentatively formed on the 28th of September, 1892, when nine inhabitants of Willard met at the home of Willis F. Strout to discuss the organization of a hose company. However, due to limited attendance the meeting was adjourned until Saturday, October 1st. At this meeting the offical formation took place, but in the interim a company had been organized at Ferry Village. In honor of his untiring efforts, Willis F. Strout was elected as the Willard Company's first Captain.

A hose cart and five hundred feet of hose was soon purchased to properly equip the company. On the 29th of October, land on which to erect a hose-house was donated by E. L. Pilsbury and by election day the building had been constructed. The original structure measured approximately thirty feet long and twenty feet wide, with a substantial expansion taking place within the next few years.

Before concluding this section on the original fire companies, mention should be made of the one organized at Knightville. This company, while in no way a political organization, owed its inception to politics. In the spring election of 1894 the Republicans upset the usual Democratic majority and carried the town of Cape Elizabeth. They expressed their jubilation by kindling several immense bonfires. which in the course of the celebration, got beyond control. As a consequence, Matthew's Grain Store went up in flames incurring a loss of several thouand dollars. All attempts to extinguish the blaze were futile and the building burned to its foundation.

This disaster demonstrated to the citizens of Knightville

View of the Cape Cottage after the addition of a mansard roof. Circa 1885.

Wood-cut of the Ocean House at Bowery Beach. Circa 1855.

Summer view of the Ocean House. Circa 1880.

Gathering of the Venerable Cunner Association and Propeller Club at Hannaford Cove. August 1889.

the need of establishing a volunteer company. The matter was informally discussed and late in the spring of 1894 the Knightville Hose Company was organized. Subscription papers were circulated and enough funds were secured to cover the purchase of a hose reel and a few hundred feet of hose. By fairs and entertainments, the total amount for the purchasing of apparatus, was increased to $600.

In June of 1894, the company decided that a hose-house was essential for storing the equipment. Within a short time the members erected an adequate building with the cost of materials the only expense incurred. By way of conclusion, a reference should be made to the Knightville Hose Company's original officers, they were: James L. Turner, Captain; S. W. Place, First Assistant; W. P. Brown, Second Assistant; John E. Moulton, Treasurer; and E. J. Farrell, Clerk.

Before taking up the division of the town, it is proper to discuss the one incident that proved to be more of a deciding factor than any other in bringing about the actual separation. This was the vehement controversy raised over the introduction of Sebago water. In reality, the basis of the trouble was not the water itself but the outlay of money necessary to make it available to a limited portion of the population.

As the process of urbanization transformed the villages in the northern reaches of Cape Elizabeth, various civic embellishments became necessary. Over the years certain items appeared in the town warrant that, while they brought improved living conditions to the villagers, only added to the tax burden of the rural citizens. In other words, while everyone was forced to pay the tax as assessed, only a limited number of the inhabitants benefited from the improvements.

The citizens of the outer Cape had, down through the years, patiently borne the expense incurred by laying out new streets, building sidewalks, maintaining a police force, constructing an extensive sewerage system, erecting street lights, and various other improvements to the urban community, without directly benefiting therefrom.

Their balking at what augered to be a new and larger expenditure is not to be wondered at. As the citizens warmed to the question, old grievances reappeared, tempers flared, and partisan feelings increased in intensity. The *Cape Elizabeth Sentinel*, pursuing its well established policy of never occupying neutral ground, joined the villagers in their agitation for Sebago water. Their colorful editorials and the various "Letters to the Editor" that they published further incensed the already impassioned citizenry. Quite naturally the villagers had some arguments definitely in their favor. Some parts of Ligonia, Cash's Corner, Pleasantdale, Turner's Island, Knightville, South Portland, and Willard were closely settled with the houses very near together. Their use of wells as a water supply left much to be desired. It was also impossible to overlook the advantages to be gained through the introduction of hydrants, not only in fire protection but subsequently in the reduction of fire insurance rates. Lastly, with reference to the matter of taxation, the villagers certainly had a telling argument when they made the point that the farmers, through the nature of their employment, had the benefit of the then current custom of working on the roads to alleviate their tax burden. It was an advantage that those employed in urban pursuits certainly did not have.

The matter of introducing Sebago water into the town of Cape Elizabeth was not a new one as it been considered and acted upon in previous years. At the annual meeting held on Monday the 6th of March, 1882, the town voted to . . . "allow the Portland Water Company to lay down, in and through the streets and highways of the town, pipes, aqueducts, and fixtures for the purpose of conveying a supply of pure water to the town . . ." As the cost of installation was to be borne by the Portland Water Company and not by the citizens, no opposition was heard. Contract and rate disputes prevented the project from suceeding at this time.

The water company tried again in 1887. Early in that year the Company circulated a petition through Knightville and Ferry Village to determine the number of people willing to pay for Sebago water. If the demand proved great enough the company would install the water mains at their own expense. The rate to individual consumers would be an annual levy of ten to twelve dollars per faucet. Apparently the response was not satisfactory as the firm again failed to carry its plans to fruition.

These attempts proved quite conclusively that private subscriptions alone were not sufficient to bring Sebago water to the villages of Cape Elizabeth. Therefore, to achieve this objective the town must lend its support and with this in mind a town meeting was called for Friday, the 15th of April, 1892, to decide this vital question. It was quite apparent to everyone that whatever the result of the contest, it would present a genuine hardship to the defeated faction. It would be a burden to the farmers if they were required to pay for an improvement in which they could not share and it would be detrimental to the villagers to force them to continue with their inadequate water supply. The town of Cape Elizabeth was a house divided as the date approached for deciding this momentous question.

Probably no other meeting in the history of the town ever attracted a larger crowd of opinionated people than the one that assembled at the Town House early in the afternoon of Friday the 15th of April, 1892. At precisely two o'clock, Noah Knight, the town clerk, with some difficulty called the meeting to order and read the warrant. He was immediately interrupted by Albert D. Boyd, one of the more vehement anti-water men, who arose and read, despite frequent interjections and asides from the opposition, a protest against the legality of the meeting. Apparently the town officials were unimpressed as they immediately proceeded with the business at hand.

Next in order was the election of that vital official, the moderator. The people of the outer Cape put forward Charles E. Jordan as their candidate and the villagers nominated Thomas B. Haskell. The secret ballot was employed and the voting immediately became a rapid fire operation with no check list employed. The final count read 430 votes for Haskell and 172 for Jordan. Thus the pro-water faction won the first contest.

With the election of the moderator the next point of business was the reading of the projected contract between the Standish Water and Construction Company and the town of Cape Elizabeth, which, among other things, obligated the town to pay an annual hydrant rental of $1,500 for twenty years. At the conclusion of the reading Albert D. Boyd again arose and launched into a bitter denuciation of the project, its backers, and the water company despite the cautioning of the moderator not to indulge in personalities. Although he was interrupted several times by "valuable advice" and "timely suggestions" from his opponents, Mr. Boyd succeeded in delivering a very colorful oration. Various men replied to this speech in kind with the ultimate result of intensifying the degree of feeling on both sides.

When at last the check list appeared and preparations were made for the crucial vote, the excitement had reached a fever pitch. For this historic vote George C. Mountfort and Eliphlet C. Robinson were chosen as checkers and counters. During the process of voting several voters were challenged, with pandemonium barely averted on each occasion. One man actually fainted in the crush of humanity at the ballot box. It required the combined services of the moderator, plus several constables, to maintain some semblence of order. After the polls closed late in the afternoon the citizenry partially regained their composure as they anxiously awaited the tabulation. The final vote was annonced in due time and proved to be a substantial victory for the pro-water men. Of a total vote of 742 there were 547 yeas and 195 nays. Complete confusion followed the announcement of the results with the victors cheering lustily. An impromptu celebration was immediately organized by the pro-water group. This was followed in the evening by a colorful display of fireworks set off by the joyful villagers to commemorate the event.

Pursuant to the contract, the Standish Water and Construction Company proceeded to construct a system of water mains to supply South Portland, Willard, Town House Corner, Turner's Island, Pleasantdale, Ligonia, and Cash's Corner, with Sebago Lake water for domestic purposes, the extinguishment of fires, and the supply of shipping. The company also installed fifty 3-nozzle hydrants, four public drinking fountains for either man or beast, and three public fountains for the exclusive use of humans. A stand pipe with a capacity of 600,000 gallons was erected on Meeting House Hill just a short distance, ironically, from the residence of Albert D. Boyd.

The water was finally turned on, with a pressure of sixty pounds, Saturday the 27th of August, 1892. A sum of eight dollars per annum was established as the rate for one family using one faucet. In closing it is interesting to note that in compliance with the contract only laborers from the town of Cape Elizabeth were employed in the actual construction and due to local prejudice no Italian workers were hired.

With the termination of the water dispute it became increasingly apparent to many citizens that the time had arrived to alter the political structure of the town of Cape Elizabeth. Various ideas had been broached on this particular subject in the years immediately following the Civil War. The first definite move toward separation, however, occured in 1854, when a group of Ferry Village citizens, headed by Nathan Dyer, petitioned the state legislature to divide the town or at least allow them to secede. This attempt proved to be abortive.

It was not until October of 1873 that another plan was formulated to divide the town. This time, however, the disaffected section sought annexation to Portland. In that month a meeting was held in the Council Chamber of Portland City Hall. A Committee consisting of Colonel R. S. Smart, B. W. Frickett, A. V.

Cole, John Brewer, W. B. Thompson, D. W. Kincaid, and Dr. J. W. Lowell of Ferry Village; Nathaniel Shannon, and B. F. Pritchard of Knightville; Cyrus Cole, E. H. Watson, Charles L. Litchfield, and W. W. Fickett of Turner's Island; William Atwood, G. R. Gardiner, and John Thomas of Ligonia, met with the Mayor and a special committe appointed by the City Council. After considerable discussion pro and con the meeting was adjourned.

Later in the month an evening meeting was held at Portland City Hall. At eight o'clock an hour after the meeting began, a torchlight procession from the Cape, headed by Chandler's Band of Portland, appeared on the scene. Making up the parade were 100 men, with torches, from Ligonia, under the leadership of John W. Thomas; plus 200 men, with torches, from Ferry Village, Knightville, and Turner's Island. The company from Ligonia carried a large transparency, bearing on one side the legend "Annexation means Prosperity." When the meeting was finally called to order the Council Chamber was rather solidly packed. Mayor Wescott introduced the various speakers all of whom favored the projected plan of annexion. Among the speakers were such influential Portland citizens as Benjamin Kingsbury, Charles P. Kimball, Israel Washburn, Jr., George W. Woodman, Francis O. J. Smith, and Nathan Webb. The meeting adjourned, however, without formulating any definite plan of action.

The citizens of Cape Elizabeth who opposed annextion of any portion of the town to Portland were sufficent in number to take counteractive measures. At a town meeting held on Tuesday the 23rd of December, 1873, it was voted that:

> ... The municipal officers and representative elect of the town of Cape Elizabeth, be and are hereby instructed by the inhabitants of said town, in a public meeting duly warned and assembled for that purpose, to employ their best means and influence at every time and place to discurage and prevent the whole and every movement tending to awaken or develope disaffection, sectional strife, and antagonism among the people, or to affect the division and partition of the territory of Cape Elizabeth.

With this declaration in mind the pro-annexationists were apparently discreet enough to await further developments.

There was still another school of thought that attracted many Cape residents by proposing an alternative to annexation. This group recommended that the town change its form of government to that of a city. From their point of view, Cape Elizabeth had outgrown the system of town administration. According to this quite vocal faction civil affairs would run more smoothly if guided by a mayor with approximately seven aldermen and twenty-one councilmen. By dividing the area up into wards and precincts a more efficient manner of voting would be inaugurated, thus giving larger voice in the government to those individuals unable to attend the periodic town meetings. The name of Elizabeth City was given considerable thought as a fitting appellation. Even the *Cape Elizabeth Sentinel* devoted considerable column space to the encouragement of this plan, prophesying in January of 1889 that, should this change occur, people would regard the Cape as the "Brooklyn of New England."

It has already been noted that the settlement of the Sebago water dispute made it more than evident to many citizens that some readjustment was necessary especially with reference to the tax situation. Consequently, early in 1893 South Portland again took the initiative and this time sought to secede from the rest of the town. There was very little opposition voiced in the other villages. Thus began the final move that resulted in the division of the old and honorable town of Cape Elizabeth. Despite an apathetic attitude exhibited by many citizens, a few staunch defenders still continued to resist all attempts at altering the structure of the town. When the hearing relative to a city charter came before the state committee on legal affairs, A. F. Hannaford, Clement E. Staples, and W. H. Clifford appeared on behalf of those who had faith in the old town and succeeded in having the charter petition bound over to a later committee. From these indications it is evident that the separatists, annexationists, and city charter men certainly had to overcome some stubborn resistance before they could hope to accomplish their aims.

The efforts of the separatists were finally successful in inveigling a majority of the citizens to sign petitions urging a division of the town. There was still some hesitancy on the part of a few people but the majority seemed willing to acquiesce. One citizen of the outer Cape, a little more articulate than his fellow townsmen, composed an appropriate bit of doggerel that expressed an opinion held by many:

> O fractious village on the flats,
> Forever wanting something new,
> We are tired of your endless spats,
> And wish to be well rid of you.

The reference was made of course to South Portland. The last important public discussion of the question was a meeting held at Union Hall in South Portland on Wednesday the 22nd of January, 1895, to consider the "Charter for Division." Various remarks were made; but the general consenus of those present, surprisingly enough, was in opposition to a division of the town and in favor of a city charter. However, despite the conflicting view points, the legislature of the state of Maine, acting on petitions requesting separation legally divided the town of Cape Elizabeth as of the 15th of March, 1895. The northern part, which at that time consisted of approximately 8,000 acres became the town of South Portland, and the southern portion containing approximately 7,000 acres retained the old name of Cape Elizabeth.

With the passage of this act, the barrage of printed and verbal invectives gradually subsided as the various factions ruminated on the degree of success or failure that they had achieved. The utterances of the *Cape Elizabeth Sentinel* became almost prosaic in nature and generally speaking most of the citizens were willing to let bygones be bygones. Practically everyone, especially in Cape Elizabeth, now turned to the various problems resulting from separation.

One interesting sidelight of the division of the town involved a cultural loss of immeasurable value to the citizens of both Cape Elizabeth and South Portland. Early in 1895 Tristram Frost Jordan of Metuchen, New Jersey, author of the *Jordan Memorial*, a genealogy of the Jordan family of Cape Elizabeth, made arrangements to purchase land at Town House Corner for the erection of a library. This edifice, to be called the Jordan Library, was to be the repository of this gentleman's extensive library and large collection of genealogical material. As a final gesture he was prepared to bestow a liberal endowment fund upon the library for the yearly purchase of new books. The partitioning of the town so disgusted Mr. Jordan that he withdrew his generous offer and ended all negotiations forthwith.

With the separation of the town agriculture once again became the predominent industry of the Cape. From the very earliest period subsistance farming had sustained and nurtured the citizens of Cape Elizabeth. As the nineteenth century advanced a more diversified form of agriculture became apparent with market gardening quickly assuming a position of importance.

In 1857, J. A. Carnes had described in his book, *A Trip to Portland*, some of the more prominent agricultural features that impressed him. He noted that in his travels about the Cape ". . . several patches or fields of pumpkins and cabbages met my view as I passed along . . . There were of the former at least ten cartloads, and of the latter more than one thousand in number, varying in size from six inches to a foot and a half in diameter, each weighting from two to twenty-five or thirty pounds." On another occasion he wrote that ". . . vegetables are raised in abundance and the most luxuriant crops of grass I ever beheld, two crops already having been mowed, and there was then a growth of velvety thickness, so that it was with difficulty we could wade through, it set so closely together. Here were pumpkins of the richest golden hues, squashes of every kind and color, weighing from ten to fifty or sixty pounds, cabbages of various descriptions, some of them weighing from fifteen to twenty-five or thirty pounds, and rutabagas, turnips, onions, potatoes, tomatoes, etc., in abundance." During one of his frequent walks Carnes relates that ". . . in a valley sheltered by a hill inclining to the west was a rich patch of golden pumpkins and squashes (for which Cape Elizabeth is so famous) fully ripe and ready to be gathered and harvested for fall and winter use."

In a letter to the *Daily Eastern Argus* of Portland, dated 18 August, 1875 yet another observer commented at some length upon the agricultural scene.

> Cape Elizabeth contains about 13,000 acres, and a large portion of them are well cultivated. The soil is a red, brown and black loam . . . every time we look over the farms and gardens in this town the conclusion is forced upon us that Cape Elizabeth is one of the best, if not the very best, farming towns in our country. A very abundant crop of hay has been secured, and other crops are growing vigorously. But we are sorry to notice that rust has fallen upon the potato vines and the late planted will be of little value. . . and the farmers must rely on their early planted potatoes. Barley and oats are looking finely, and those who had the courage to sow wheat will be generously rewarded according to the present prospects. But alas, we believe there are only two in town who ventured to sow wheat, and our friend Chamberlain of the Ocean House, is one of them, and his wheat looks finely. It is seldom that better fields of wheat are seen in the West. There are larger ones of course, but very few fields will yield so much to the acre as Chamberlains, as the prospect now is.

This diversified combination of market gardening and subsistance farming characterized the agricultural activities of Cape Elizabeth throughout most of the century. Very little change was evident until early in the present century. Evidence of this is found in the occasional comments that appeared in the local newspaper such as the following that was printed in the *Daily Eastern Argus* on Tuesday 13 August, 1895. "One of the recent exports to the West Indies were nearly thirty-five hundred heads of cabbage that were carried by the bark *Ethel Boynton.* They were raised mostly at Cape Elizabeth." Again in 1912 we find the weekly newspaper *Coast Watch* noting that ". . . in spite of the drought the Cape crops are in a good condition. The well cultivated acres of potatoes, squash, and cabbage look as if this part of the state would be in no danger of a famine, if all outside supplies should be cut off." To even the most casual observer of today it is more than evident that no major changes have been made as to the crops under cultivation in Cape Elizabeth."

One fascinating side-light pertaining to the raising of such bountiful quantities of cabbages in the later years of the nineteenth century was the part played by a humble citizen named Sam Taylor. For many years he traveled throughout the city of Portland making nocturnal visits to a large proportion of its dwellings. With great celerity he removed the night soil carrying it away in a large dumpcart. When he had completed his alloted rounds Taylor would take his redolent cargo to the cabbage fields of the Cape. Contemporary reports wax eloquent as to the magnificent cabbages this fertilizer produced.

The most successful farm organization to function for any extended period of time in Cape Elizabeth was created in conjunction with the town of Scarborough. In 1875 a group of far sighted men organized the Scarborough and Cape Elizabeth Farmers Association. For the next thirty years the group held a two or three day fair late in September or early in October. On land leased from Walter B. Nutter at Pleasant Hill, Scarborough, the Scarborough and Cape Elizabeth Fair became an enthusiastically anticipated annual event. Premiums were offered on a great variety of exhibits varying from fifty cents to ten dollars. Among the more prominent exhibits featured were the following: best team of working oxen and working horses; draft, fat, and matched oxen. Also included were cows, heifers, bulls, sheep, swine, family horses, colts, stallions, mares, and domestic fowl. In addition there were premiums for the best in fruit, butter, cheese, grain, vegetables, carriages, harnesses, plus household and fancy articles.

One very popular feature of the fair was the horse racing program. Purses of twelve dollars for first place, five dollars for second place, and three dollars for third place, were available in the trotting horse event open only to four year old colts owned and kept within the limits of the two towns at least sixty days prior to the race. Purses were also available in the "Grand Sweepstake" ranging from twelve dollars for first place, to eight dollars for second place and three dollars for third place. This was followed by the "free for all' with purses of twenty five dollars for first place, twenty dollars for second place and fifteen dollars for third place. Interspaced between the heats were "scrub races" that invariably offered much amusement. As one observer put it they were races "between plugs that had seen twenty summers and had never been known to have trotted inside of eight minutes." Another wag refered to the program as the "agricultural horse trot." The track was half a mile in length, somewhat heavy of grade and sandy at some points. However there was plenty of room for two horses all the way and a third had frequent opportunity to pass if the nag possessed the necessary speed.

The exhibition of manufactured articles, fancy work, produce, etc. was held in the society's hall close by the fair grounds at Pleasant Hill. The premiums were limited to one per item with the prize forfeited if it was not collected within sixty days. Also, exhibits were limited to the citizens of the two towns, with members of the society admitted free of charge. On most occasions it was necessary to erect a tent immediately adjacent to the hall to handle the immense quantity of agricultural produce entered in competition.

Special forms of entertainment were occasionally supplied. The Scarborough Brass Band was always a popular embellishment adding immensely to the festive atmosphere of the fair. Another successful and warmly appreciated feature were the culinary triumphs that were offered for sale. No great stretch of the imagination is required to visualize the enthusiasm that must have been engendered. It was truly the high point of the fall season, and perhaps of the entire year, for many of the citizens in these two neighborly towns. Regrettably the twentieth century brought a decline in the fortunes of the society and it suspended operations forever shortly after World War I.

In that equine age it was only natural that a great many people were deeply interested in the different varieties of horseflesh and their relative capabilities for speed. It has already been noted that the track at Pleasant Hill was heavily patronized. Attendance frequently exceeded 4,000 when competition was particularly keen. There were other manifestations of this interest as well. As early as 1857 the Island Mile Track in Ligonia, located where the Bancroft Martin Mill now stands, was very popular. Other less sophisticated sites, such as the frozen surface of Great Pond, occasionally witnessed some very spirited trotting races.

Under these circumstances a considerable degree of interest was aroused in 1891 when it was revealed that a professional track was to be built in Cape Elizabeth. Under the auspices of the Maine Mile Track Association the construction of a mile track on the site of what is now the Rigby Rail Yard was contemplated. Among the early supporters of the track were the racing enthusiasts Gen. Charles P. Mattocks and John F. Haines. The association was duly incorporated, with capital stock of $25,000 to sell at ten dollars per square. Approximately 85 acres of land was purchased with shares of stock from H. N. Jose south-east of Skunk Hill, now Thornton Heights.

Actual construction of the track was entrusted to Seth Griffin of Joliet, Illinois. His experience in the building of race tracks was very extensive, having constructed the mile track at Nashville, Tennessee, the Ha-Ha Track at Minneapolis, a half-mile track for William Rockefeller at Greenwich, Connecticut, and the track at Narragansett Park, Providence, Rhode Island.

In constructing the track at Rigby Park, as it was to be called, Griffin utilized a system that was peculiarly his own. After excavating the bed of the track, he took tough fibrous turf, cut in pieces about a foot square and laid them edgewise, closely packed, throughout its entire length and breadth. On top of the turf foundation Griffin spread a four inch surface of loam that would pack down, producing ultimately a tenacious spongy mat so essential to the faster tracks of that era. A high water table was necessary to retain the springy quality of the track and was easily achieved at the Rigby site. When finished it was oval in shape with curved ends of seventy rods each in length, the straight sides being ninety rods each in length. This track was considered by Griffin to be his masterpiece, the "acme of tracks," as he expressed it.

The stables were constructed early in 1893 by Henry Soule of Portland. The first to be built was 240 feet in length and 40 feet in width, with the side facing the track two stories in height to accommodate offices and waiting rooms. Three more stables were soon added raising the total number of stalls to one hundred. Approximately 125,000 board feet of lumber were consumed in the construction of these buildings.

The official opening of Rigby Park occurred on Saturday 12 August 1893 with some three thousand spectators on hand to watch the great Maine stallion Nelson attempt to break his Grand Rapids record of 2:10. The fame of Rigby Park spread quickly throughout the nation and it was soon considered by many to be the fastest track east of the Mississippi. In the few short years of its life it proved to be immensely popular if not a financial success. One highlight of its history was the world record time of 2:05 set by the champion pacer John R. Gentry on the 23rd of September in 1896.

Overwhelming financial troubles soon proved to be insurmountable. After five colorful and spectacular years Rigby Park closed in 1898. For the next twenty five years the area was deserted and neglected. In 1923 the present Rigby Railway Yard was constructed by the Maine Central Railroad on the site.

Having sustained no serious ill effects Cape Elizabeth emerged from this painful period of urbanization, internal strife, and separation, into a new and prosperous era, unhampered by inner conflicts. As the post-separation years grew in number it became increasingly apparent to the stalwart citizens of Cape Elizabeth that the partitioning of the old town had its advantageous aspects and that the benefits accruing thereby were well worth the struggle. The future certainly augured well for the town as the last years of the nineteenth century ran their alloted course.

Before proceeding further with the modern era it is necessary to pause and examine some of the more specialized areas of historic importance. In the chapters that follow we will explore the rise and decline of summer tourism, the maritime heritage, as well as religious and educational endeavors. The concluding chapter will of necessity deal with the growth and development of suburbia, a trend that is destined to obliterate completely the Cape Elizabeth of the past. It is hoped that the verbal vignettes to follow will, to some small degree continue to awaken a spark of historical awareness in the minds of those unfamiliar with the life that has vanished in this venerable town.

Chapter V

WATERING PLACES

I

As the nineteenth century entered its third decade a new era emerged that found Americans enjoying a high standard of living and more leisure time. This trend soon manifested itself in an extraordinary enthusiasm for travel and recreation. Added incentive was provided by revolutionary improvements in transportation. New turnpikes and canals, the steamboat and the railroad were working wonderous changes in American life which affected business and industry as well as recreation.

In 1825 the appearance of a little booklet called *The Fashionable Tour* had revealed the new trend and one observer declared that the American people were carrying their desire for travel "to a passion and a fever." It was now possible for almost every one to undertake trips of which an earlier generation would hardly have dreamed. "There is scarcely an individual in so reduced circumstances," marveled one visitor from abroad, "as to be unable to afford his dollar or so, to travel a couple of hundred miles from home, in order to see the country and the improvements which are going on."

When longer jaunts were not possible a days outing in the country was not only fashionable but the epitome of enjoyment. The picnic excursion throughout the summer months was immensely popular in the eastern states and was one recreation enthusiastically enjoyed by the citizenry of Portland. No area was quite as delightful, nor as inviting, as Cape Elizabeth with its natural charms. The quiet rural scene, the beauties of its seashore, and the hospitality of its people, to say nothing of its close proximity, proved irresistable for many. The prospects of a bountiful picnic lunch, fishing for cunners, gambolling in the frigid ocean, or picking wild fruits and berries, were looked forward to from week to week as the memorable highlights of the summer season.

One delighted excursionist, signing himself "Julip," wrote to the editors of the *Eastern Argus* extolling the pleasures of an outing at the Cape. His letter, printed by the editors 14 July 1825, describes a visit with Joshua Freeman, keeper of Portland Head Light:

> In these sissling-hot days, I know of no excursion so pleasant as a jaunt to the Light House. There our friend Freeman is always at home, and ready to serve you,
> 'With bak'd and broil'd and
> Stew'd and toasted,
> And fried and boil'd, and
> Smoked and roasted.'

There you can angle in safety and comfort for the cunning cunner, while old ocean is rolling majestically at your feet, and when wearied and fatigued with this amusement, you will find a pleasant relaxation in tumbling the huge rocks from the brinks of the steep and rocky precipices which dame nature has kindly placed there for your accommodation. Are you fond of sea-bathing? No place better than Ship Cove, near the Light House. Are you fond of cool punch, London particular, old cognac, and a hundred of etceteras, no man is better provided with these articles, than Captain Freeman. . . In short, Messrs. Editors, of all the retreats from the heat, dust and confusion of this dull town, I know of no equal to a ride or sail to the Light House and earnestly recommend it to all poor devils who, like myself, are afflicted with the dyspepsia, gout, or any of the diseases to which human flesh is heir.

Sentiments such as this were echoed far and wide. One other visitor who frequently enjoyed Capt. Freeman's open-handed hospitality in this same period was a very young and very serious Bowdoin College student. In the years to come the world would know him as one of America's best loved poets, Henry Wadsworth Longfellow.

As the Cape's salubrious summer climate became more widely known and appreciated, visitors from greater distances began to seek out lodgings for a more extended stay. Many of these early tourists found comfortable and most enjoyable quarters in the humble farm houses of the area. It was only a matter of time, however, before some enterprising citizen recognized the monetary gains to be derived from an attractive hostelry.

In June of 1825, the first such commercial venture was inaugurated. Close by the head of the Bowery Beach Road, Ebenezer Dyer, Jr., opened a modest boardinghouse which he called The Bower. He described it as "having the beautiful beach of Cape Cove on the one side and the Great Pond on the other." It met with instant success for in August of this same year a letter appeared in the *Daily Eastern Argus* entitled "Will You Come to The Bower?" The letter depicts in glowing terms the joys to be derived from such an outing. The author, "Auscanius," begins by saying:

> The great subject of conversation, at present, in almost every circle, is the pleasantness of a ride to The Bower. In order to satisfy myself of the truth and propriety of the high-wrought description of this romantic place I lately took a horse and chaise and bent my course towards the Nahant of Maine. I can now with truth say that the one half was not told me.

This introduction is followed by a fascinating vignette of his trip across the Cape and the hospitality of Mr. Dyer.

Such laudatory comments were apparently not without effect for in June of 1829 The Bower is described by its new manager, Alexander H. Piper, as having been expanded and improved. The cuisine must have been impressive for so modest an establishment for the advertisement further states: "The larder will be furnished with the best the market affords, and with every variety of the season, and the bar with the best wines, etc., in the country." From contemporary descriptions, this hostelry was apparently a rather small two story residence facing the road, with attached outbuildings and a barn at the back.

Although The Bower may have prospered in a very quiet way it never attained the status or stature of some of the later summer hotels. During the years from 1835 to 1838 it was used as a private school for boys. It wasn't until 1847, however, that advertisements again appeared offering summer accommodations. By this time the name had been changed to the Bowery House and it was described as having been "fitted up in good style" under the management of Henry Bodge. It must have gradually declined in popularity for no further notices appear until 1900 when its sale by Alfred E. Haskell to A. Scott Jordan was reported in the *Eastern Argus*. Like most of the summer hotels that flourished in Cape Elizabeth the Bowery House vanished in a blaze of glory. On the 8th of July 1909 a defective chimney set the house afire and the entire structure was quickly burned to the ground. Nothing now remains of this early hostelry except the name Bowery Beach and an overgrown cellar hole.

By 1835 Cape Elizabeth was well established as an excellent location for outings and protracted summer visits. The summer of 1836 must have witnessed quite a significant increase in the number of summer visitors for the citizenry felt sufficiently imposed upon to convene a special town meeting. The meeting was held on the 12th of September and resolutions were drafted attacking the rather raucous antics of Sunday revelers. Specifically, the citizens deplored the disruption of Sunday church services by noisy groups traveling through the countryside. This lack of consideration on the part of the pleasure seeking public produced a stinging editorial condemnation in one of Portland's religious newspapers, the *Christian Mirror,* when the resolutions were duly published.

It was at this time that the first true summer hotel in Cape Elizabeth was nearing completion. This was the soon to be famous Cape Cottage known in later years throughout the United States and Canada for its informal but comfortable accommodations.

In 1833 the Cape Cottage Company had been formed by John Purington, Benjamin Knight, and Anthony Strout with capital of $6,000 raised by selling shares of stock at $50.00 each. The site selected for the hotel was immediately adjacent to Maiden Cove, approximately where the Lloyd Knight residence now stands. In earlier years members of the Strout family lived in a farm house that stood on the same spot.

Actual construction was begun in the summer of 1835, however, it wasn't until the following summer that guests were actually received. This first building was a three story wooden structure, painted white with green shutters, and faced the open sea. A wide veranda extended across the front; its roof supported by columns made from young trees with the bark removed and the limbs partially chopped off. The roof of the building was surmounted by a large cupola that offered a marvelous view of the harbor, islands and the sea. At first the name Acadian Grove was used but the simpler Cape Cottage replaced it for the opening of the 1836 season. From the beginning it was very popular with the people of the Portland area. Comments in the Portland papers praised its accomodations and spoke in glowing terms of the natural beauty to be found surrounding the Cape Cottage.

The following year, 1837, Anthony Strout took a large mortgage on the property in lieu of payment for the land he had conveyed to the Cape Cottage Company. Later the same year he sold the mortgage to one of Portland's most fascinating literary figures, John Neal. Within a relatively short period of time, Neal acquired a controlling interest in the company and quickly emerged as its most energetic champion. In this same year Edward Bracket of Portland established a regular shuttle service between the city and the Cape Cottage. His conveyance was a beautifully decorated barge, drawn by four horses, that left the city at 9:30 a.m. and 2:00 p.m., with return trips at 11:30 a.m. and 5:00 p.m. every day. His fare was twenty-five cents per person each way. This was, incidentally, the first of many barges that served the Cape's summer tourist trade for years to come, surviving until the advent of the electric trolley and the automobile.

Within a remarkably short period of time the Cape Cottage was the busiest summer resort on the Cape. Improvements were instituted in 1838 to further enhance the comfort of the visiting public. A wharf and bath-houses were built at Maiden Cove, and an access road was opened to the main thoroughfare. The common pleasures of eating, sleeping, and conversation were featured, infrequently interrupted by walking, riding, fishing, playing games, or sea bathing.

In 1839 John Neal leased the Cape Cottage to William Stephenson of Portland, a man of great experience in catering to the needs of the tourist. His notices in the Portland papers emphasized the special consideration he gave to sea food dinners and private parties or banquets. Also stressed were the wines and spirits available for the connoisseur.

This was also the year that a very distinguished couple spent eight rather fascinating weeks as guests at the Cape Cottage. On the 17th of July the English phrenologist George Combe and his wife arrived from Conway, New Hampshire. His impressions and experiences are memorably preserved in his fascinating three volume study, *Notes on the United States of North America, during a Phrenological Visit in 1838-39-40*, which he published in 1841.

His descriptions of his visit are in definite contrast to the glowing testimonials written for local consumption. On the 28th of July he noted:

> I am now blind in one eye, and lame in both feet, from mosquito bites. We rise at five o'clock in the morning, and see the sun ascend in beautiful majesty from the Atlantic Ocean, which is spread beneath our windows. We breakfast at seven, dine at one, drink tea at six, and go to bed at nine o'clock. My time is spent preparing the manuscript of my lectures on moral philosophy for the press, in reading, and in maintaining correspondence with my friends in Europe and the United States. But for the mosquitoes, this place would be a paradise of beauty and delight.

Anoher interesting experience that enlivened his stay was a seasonal north-east "line storm" that occured on the 1st of September. Although it may not have been any more violent than the usual, to Combe it was memorable incident.

> Last night the wind increased to a heavy gale from the north and and north-east, accompanied by a tremendous rain. Cape Cottage, a frame-house of three stories, clap-boarded, vibrated to its foundations, and our bed shook beneath us. The rain streamed through the roof, penetrated the room above ours, and fell in large drops on our floor. The windows leaked, and the wind roared through our apartments, as if they had been Eolus's cave. The storm continues this day, and the sea comes rolling in from the Atlantic in stupendous waves, and breaks with terrific grandeur against the rugged cliffs that skirt the shore.

During his period of residence Combe was visited by various admirers with whom he had corresponded. One frequent visitor was John Neal of Portland the owner of the Cape Cottage. Neal was intensely interested in phrenology and had on one occasion tried to use phrenological evidence as the defense attorney in an assault case. Also, assisted by two Portland physicians, Dr. Albus Rea and Dr. Jesse W. Mighels, and Neal, Combe instructed a group of interested local gentlemen in the science of phrenology by dissecting a human brain.

One other fascinated visitor to seek out Combe at this rustic retreat was the great nineteenth century American educator Horace Mann. They had met during Combe's tour of the United States and a warm friendship quickly developed. Even though they never met again after Combe returned to England, Mann was sufficiently impressed to name his first born son, George Combe Mann.

Of all the descriptions of his visit that appear in Combe's journal none is more charming or revealing than that extracted from a letter written by his wife. The lady in question was the former Cecilia Siddons, a daughter of the famous English actress Sarah Siddons. In a letter dated 12 September she expansively relates:

> Here you may picture us quietly seated in our summer retreat, a handsome, rather large cottage built of wood, clap-boarded, and painted white, with those green outside window-shutters which give such an air of coolness and neatness to New England cottages in general. Cape Cottage stands upon Cape Elizabeth, a projecting point, jutting out into Casco Bay.... The Americans have improved the name of the cape by changing the Indian 'Pooduc' into 'Cape

Elizabeth'; but they have been less successful with the islands to three of which they have given the unpoetical, appellations of 'Hog,' 'House,' and 'Bang' . . . .

The land that skirts the coast is like our English downs, grassy and gently undulating, with here a projecting rock and there a little pool. If affords pasture to cattle, sheep and horses, and is all open to the footsteps of the wanderer. Beyond this, the country is divided into small farms, the possessors of which are also many of them fishermen, whose neat white cottages gleam forth from amidst brushwood, tall Indian corn, and rather stunted trees. As we range along the shore, one ear drinks in the murmur of the waves and the splashing of oars, whilst the other feeds on the notes of American robins, the sharpening of scythes and the lowing of herds. . . .

A profusion of wild flowers, some of which are cultivated in gardens at home, may be gathered on the downs and in the fields, Our parlor is generally adorned with bouquets of them including fragrant dog-roses that grow even in the clefts of the rocks quite down to the margin of the tide. Wild raspberries, of excellent quality, wild strawberries, and the whortleberry, or Scotch blaeberry, abound everywhere. They and excellent sea-fishing, attract numerous parties of pleasure from Portland, who arrive, some in handsome barges by the bay, others in equipages of all varities of form by the road; they spend a few hours rambling singly or in groups, give liveliness to the scene, and return home in the evening. The fields also are alive with grasshoppers. . . . As you walk along, you encounter also whole clouds of primrose-coloured butterflies, and pale blue dragonflies. These are harmless. I wish we could say as much of those bloodthirsty mosquitoes, which infest us everywhere, and seem as if sent to remind us, amidst all these sweets, that we are still in a world of mingled good and evil. My poor husband has lain on the sofa for three weeks, lame with their bites on his ankles and is only now again able to walk. My own eyes have often been closed up for days by the mountainous swellings with which they have been encircled, but thanks to Providence, the mosquitoes have generally taken them in turn, and left me one at a time fit for use. We have learned, however, to exclude them from our rooms. We have nailed catgut muslin over every window through which they find it difficult to squeeze even their slender bodies and this, with ablutious of camphorated spirits, nearly frees us from their in-door intrusion. . .

But it is time that I should introduce you to the interior of our cottage. It would never do for an American rural retreat; for although a 'public house', as they name a hotel, it is of such moderate dimensions, that the family of one of the ministers of Portland, that of a Senator from Maine to Congress, and ourselves, with the landlord and his family, fill it. . .

We boast of no finery in our cottage, but it will vie with a palace for order and cleanliness; our fare is not such as would suit a London alderman, but it is abundant, savoury, and well-cooked. Air, exercise, and minds agreeably occupied, yet void of care, give an exquisite relish to our dinners of fresh fish, (cunners and pollocks caught by the rod on the rocks, by the master of the inn, his son, or their boys), our 'chower;' or fish-soup, our young Indian corn, and our squash, the last a very delicate vegetable, I assure you, notwithstanding its frightfully vulgar name. Fowls, turkeys, beef, veal, and mutton, make up our fare, and we are in no danger of suffering want either of substance or variety in our meals. . . .The only drawback, besides the mosquitoes, to our enjoyment, is periodical visitations of dense fogs. They come so regularly every Monday, that we at last reckon them as due on that day. . .

After an eventful sojurn of eight weeks the Combes left on the 12th of September, returning to Portland by boat. They spent six days there before taking the steamboat for Boston. As they departed Combe noted in his journal that they ". . . sailed past Cape Cottage and the scenes which we had so abundantly enjoyed. We took our last look at them with regret, and breathed forth our best wishes for the success and happiness of our late excellent host and his amiable family." Thus ended what is in all probability the most detailed early account that exists of a visit to the Cape Cottage. Truly, it must have been a remarkable adventure for this English gentleman and his wife accustomed as they were to the refinements of London society.

That the Cape Cottage continued to enhance its superior reputation is more than verified by the letters that continuously appeared in the newspapers waxing eloquent as to the advantages to be found there. In July of 1840 a communication appeared in the *Bangor Whig* and once again William Stephenson was flatteringly endorsed: "He understands how to cater to the wants of all, his charges are light, and the temptations he offers irresistable."

One highlight of the 1840 season was the appearance of a fairly large number of whales cavorting in the waters immediately in front of the Cape Cottage. According to the newspaper coverage they were a source of amazement and some entertainment for a considerable portion of the month of July. One of the whales, measuring fifty-seven feet, was harpooned and towed away to Wood Island. Although acclaimed as "sea-monsters" their true identity soon produced a decline in the excitement that had initially gripped the local citizenry.

About 1843 operation of the Cape Cottage was taken over by Frederick D. Byrnes of Portland who also operated an oyster bar on the corner of Federal and Temple Streets. During his period of management, which lasted until 1848, many changes were instituted to increase the volume of patronage. His advertisements stressed such advantages as expanded accommodations, bowling alleys, quoit games, a good stable of horses, and a fine wharf at Maiden Cove. It is also apparent that his kitchen and bar were outstanding features of the establishment. With reference to the latter it must have functioned a little too successfully as the selectmen at a town meeting held 11 September 1843 were instructed "to acquaint the manager of the Cape Cottage with the local liquor laws." Regardless of such details letters from appreciative patrons continued to appear in the local newspapers. One unusual visitor in this era was the chief of the Cherokee Nation, John Ross. Although his sojourn was limited to a few days in August of 1844, he was momentarily the object of considerable interest to the many who flocked to the Cape Cottage to meet him.

Unfortunately for the continued success of Byrnes, disaster struck in the spring of 1847. On the 10th of March at about 3:00 a.m., a fire of undetermined origin broke out and before any aid arrived the main building burned to its foundation. The stable, bowling alley, sheds and barns were saved. As the house was fairly well insured rebuilding began at once and a smaller but adequate Cape Cottage opened late in the summer of the same year.

For the next two seasons the tourist trade was unusually light despite the addition of regular steamer service to Portland. As the roads, to use the words of an observer, were "frozen ruts in the winter, oceans of mud in the spring and fall, and seas of dust in the summer," this was indeed a blessing. The vessel was the little paddlewheel steamer *Experiment* of 63 tons built at Pittston, Maine in 1844. She was advertised in the summer of 1849 as running regularly between Portland, and the Cape Cottage wharf, twice a day on Monday, Wednesday, and Friday. The fare was $.12½ each way, with special rates for parties and excursions. On Sunday she made the run every fifteen minutes.

Despite such an attraction, the loss of revenue was sufficient for the owner John Neal to offer the property for sale in August of 1849. However, disaster struck again before any transfer of the property could be accomplished. On September 18th fire broke out in either the kitchen or bar room and spread rapidly throughout the house. The entire set of buildings were a total loss and very little furniture was saved.

Undaunted by this second catastrophic fire in a little over two years Neal quickly set about the task of rebuilding. The new Cape Cottage that arose on the site of its predecessors was a grander structure in every way. The main building, completed in the fall of 1850, faced the sea as did earlier ones. It was a three story structure constructed of field stone and was gothic revival in style. The third story was quite unusual in that it had twin gables, facing the front and back and at right angles to the axis of the building. The following year a large wooden, unattached, three story cell was added at the back crowned with an observation platform, surmounting the ridge pole. Verandahs were also constructed running across the front of the main house and along the north side of the ell. In addition, commodius sheds and stables were added along with a bowling alley, and a new bath house at Maiden Cove. Truly, these new accomodations eclipsed those of former years.

In 1851 Alexander Foss was engaged as a year-round resident manager. He continued in this position until his death in August of 1864, with very few interruptions.

When the Cape Cottage reopened in 1851 an omnibus was placed in service operating to and from Portland with three round trips each day, except Sundays and holidays when more frequent trips were made. The fare was $.25 each way.

Once again a spate of letters and editorials appeared in the local newspapers describing in great detail the open-handed hospitality, thirst quenching refreshments and cold collations, and bountiful menus. People from distant points in the United States from Canada and Europe, as well as the local citizenry, descended upon the Cape Cottage in unprecedented numbers. It was the beginning of its most prosperous era. Apropos of this was the spectacular celebration staged on Bunker Hill Day in 1852. The festive occasion was high-lighted with a concert by the Portland Brass Band and a "grand display" of fireworks in the evening.

However, the large number of summer tourists sorely tried the patience of many Cape residents. At a town meeting held the 7th of May 1853 the following was adopted by popular vote and printed in the *Eastern Argus*:

> Whereas it has become the constant and increasing practice of persons to stroll from the City of Portland especially on the Sabbath, crossing fields, taking down bars and fences, fishing, setting fires, playing ball and sometimes insulting persons passing to or from meeting, to the great annoyance of the citizens of Cape Elizabeth and injuring of farmers living in the vicinity of the Rail Road and Portland Bridge; therefore: Resolved that as citizens of Cape Elizabeth living near the city or otherwise, we will not only use all milder means, but in our individual capacity will countenance and

sustain those who shall be obliged (as we certainly will) to resort to legal measures to rid themselves of such trespassers.

Unfortunately the situation was not in any way profoundly altered. The friction and altercations between citizens and tourists would continue to disturb the town well into the twentieth century. Only with the coming of suburbia would it gradually subside.

In August of this same year the Cape Cottage was sold by its owner John Neal, for $12,000, to a successful young business man of Bangor, John Goddard, who had established a reputation in the thriving timber trade of northern Maine. Further expansion of the facilities and other improvements were forthcoming. Also, for greater convenience, the wooden ell was permanently attached to the main building. As in the past the house opened in May and closed in October, but received special groups or parties during the rest of the year.

Throughout the decade of the fifties a succession of managers were in brief attendance. One of the more dedicated was Charles H. Adams the proprietor of the Elm House in Portland. In this same period omnibus, coach and steamer service were maintained to Portland during the summer months. The steamer in question was the little 87 ton sidewheeler, *Teazer,* built in Farmingdale, Maine, in 1852.

In 1857 the Cape Cottage was visited briefly by the traveler J. A. Carnes of Boston. In his entertaining little book, *A Trip to Portland,* he discusses in great detail his five day visit to Cape Elizabeth. On Sunday the 4th of October he drove out to the Cape Cottage where he explored the beaches and surrounding area, commenting on the fauna and geology of the region. Of the house itself he noted that ". . . not a boarder or living thing now dwelt within its deserted rooms."

In the spring of this same year John Goddard, the owner of the Cape Cottage, began the construction of a large and roomy residence close by the northern edge of Ship Cove. The house was built in the grand manner of the era, and was designed by Charles A. Alexander of New York. This gentleman was the architect who designed such Portland landmarks as St. Stephens Episcopal Church, the Libby mansion, John B. Brown's "Bramhall", and the Falmouth Hotel. Unfortunately only the Goddard mansion and St. Stephans have survived cultural indifference and the wrecker's hammer.

When the Goddard mansion was finished in the spring of

1858 it immediately became an object of considerable architectural interest. The main house, its three story tower, plus the ell and stables, were all constructed of native stone. Here John Goddard and his family resided for many years. Ultimately the federal government purchased the property for Fort Williams. During the Civil War Goddard was appointed Colonel of the First Maine Regiment of Cavalry. However, he never saw any action, soon returning to his now extensive local business interests. He died of a heart attack on the 27th of March 1870 after attending the funeral of a daughter who had succumbed to scarlet fever while a student at Westbrook Seminary.

The Goddard mansion was the first such residence to be built within the town. In the years to come similar homes would be constructed by other affluent families, but none ever matched the proportions of this magnificent residence. After years of use and abuse by the federal government it has recently become the property of the town. Perhaps now its future will be brighter. The mansion was also, incidentally, the locale of a mystery novel, *Midnight at Mears House*, written by Harrison Holt of Portland and published in 1912.

From the sixties through the eighties, the Cape Cottage continued the success it had achieved earlier. Under the management of Alexander Foss service and cuisine achieved a degree of excellence that prompted patrons to return summer after summer.

In 1870 the property was taken over by Van Valkinburg and Co. and continued to serve the public under various managers. However, in 1874 the Cape Cottage experienced financial difficulties that kept it closed until the summer of 1879 when it reopened after undergoing extensive renovation. This included the removal of the severe, double gable roof, and its replacement by a mansard roof that provided much needed additional space. Also installed for the first time was a central heating system.

With Frank L. Foss as manager prosperity returned and for the first time in some years accommodations were available both summer and winter. A telephone was installed in 1881 to further expand its accessability to the public. Four years later it was sold by the Colonel's widow, Mrs. Lydia L. Goddard to Charles W. Goddard and others for $25,000. In 1885 Benjamin C. Gibson became manager and enjoyed a minimum of success for a short period of time.

As the decade of the eighties drew to a close the Cape Cottage reverted to its earlier status of a summer hotel. Under various managers a degree of financial success was maintained. This continued to be the situation into the early nineties.

The final demise of the venerable Cape Cottage occured in the fall of 1894. Like so many other similar hostels its existence was terminated by a spectacular fire. About 11:30 p. m. on Sunday the 21st of October the flames were discovered by people living nearby but the fire was too far advanced to combat with any chance of success. The fire raged most of the night and by dawn nothing but ashes and ruins remained. Thus it was that after a career of sixty years the Cape Cottage with all its fond recollections passed into history. The name, however, survived and its locality is now known simply as "Cape Cottage."

II

In the early years of tourism the unique charms of the "Outer Cape" were not long in being discovered. It was only natural that a competitor to the Cape Cottage should evolve in this area of scenic beauty. Late in 1848 Abia Chamberlain began the construction of a hotel on a spot close by the eastern end of that beautiful beach known as Cape Sands, Cape Cove, Seal Cove, Bowery Beach, and more recently as Crescent Beach. It wasn't until early in June of 1849 that the Ocean House, as it was named, announced in the local newspapers that it was ready to receive its first patrons.

From the very beginning the Ocean House catered to a clientele more interested in a family style vacation. The transient visitors who frequented the Cape Cottage were somewhat less inclined to seek the quiet solitude and peaceful relaxation for which this house soon became famous. The gentle ocean air and the rural environment readily lent itself to a satisfyingly indolent sojurn.

During the winter and spring of 1851 Abia Chamberlain greatly improved and expanded the accommodations. In a detailed advertisement he describes the Ocean House as being three stories in height with a cupola on the roof, and measuring 62' x 32'. Attached to this main house was a three story ell that measured 46' x 25'. The entire structure containing sixteen rooms for guests, two ladies parlors, a large parlor for gentlemen, and a very large dining room, ran parallel to the road that skirted the edge of the beach. Separating the road from the beach was a granite retaining wall parts of which can still be seen. A verandah extended along the beach side and the front that faced toward the sea.

In addition to the main house there was large barn and stable, a four lane bowling alley, together with a fish house, ice house, and a bath-house. For recreation various carriages and boats were always available.

The buildings occupied only a small part of the 115 acres owned by Chamberlain. Much of the land was under cultivation and supplied the kitchen of the Ocean House with a large variety of fruits and vegetables in season. The proprietor also maintained a stable of horses and a sizeable herd of cattle.

The cuisine was apparently on the hearty side, probably prompted by the invigorating sea air. The proprietor featured beef in various forms, fowl both domestic and wild, as well as a wide variety of sea food, all served without wines or any type of liquor. Not unmindful of public relations, Chamberlain invited the editors of the various Portland newspapers to sample his culinary achievements on Thursday the 5th of June in 1851. It must have been a tremendous success judging from the fulsome editorial description published shortly thereafter. The editors good-naturedly chafed one another with comments on the prodigious appetites they had displayed.

Management of the Ocean House was assumed by Abia's son Joseph P. Chamberlain late in 1851. He ably directed the affairs of the house for the next twenty-five years, ever mindful of the excellent reputation well fixed in the public mind. Visitors from many distant points, especially Canada, returned year after year. However, unlike the Cape Cottage the season never began much earlier than May or extended much beyond the middle of October. In 1852 Manager Chamberlain arranged regular omnibus service to and from Portland. This was replaced in 1856 by a Concord coach that made one round trip a day. The fare was $.75 one way or $1.00 for the round trip. The coach was continued in service every year that the house was in operation.

One rather observant visitor who spent five days at the Ocean House in 1857 was the traveler noted earlier, J. A. Carnes of Boston. He arrived at the house on Sunday the 4th of October, and, as he was the only guest, he was, to use his own words, " . . . domiciliated as one of the family, and therefore felt perfectly at home". On the subject of food, Carnes enthusiastically states "I sat down to as fine a dinner as the most fastidious epicure might desire. It consisted of black ducks, sand birds, or peeps, pumpkin and mince pies, a good cup of coffee, etc., and I assure the reader, if he had followed me through my desultory rambles over Cape Elizabeth, that I did ample justice to the choice and delicate viands placed before me by the lady-like proprietress of the House."

While residing at the Ocean House Carnes spent his time wandering far and wide through the fields and along the shore of the "Outer Cape." He commented at some length upon the scenic beauty he encountered, the prosperous farms, and the industrious fishemen. Of the citizenry he says:

> A happier race of people I think I never saw than those I found while rambling over the shores of Cape Elizabeth, either among the peasants, or the fishermen who draw their sustenance from the surrounding waters of the bay and ocean. As regards general intelligence, there cannot be found, as far as my observation extended, a more exalted race of people on the face of the globe, in their situation in life. . . Here the peasant and fisherman feels contented and happy with his lot, for he sees an equality around him which makes him satisfied with his position among his fellowmen.

On one of his jaunts, Carnes visited Richmond's Island, spending most of one day with the owner and occupant of the island Dr. John M. Cummings. The doctor had purchased the island in 1843 for $3500., and in 1856 had built a house, with barns and out buildings, as a permanent residence. A graduate of Bowdoin College in 1833, Dr. Cummings practiced medicine and surgery in Portland for twenty years before retiring to Richmond's Island. Visitors to the island, such as Carnes, invariably received an open-handed welcome from this solitary resident. Seldom leaving the island for any length of time, Dr. Cummings lived out the rest of his life there, dying at his residence on the 30th of March in 1878, at the age of 66. His home, much abused, neglected, and weather beaten was torn down in recent years. The only inhabitants in recent years being two brothers by the name of Jordan who used the island as a base for fishing activities, during the summer months.

It was with great reluctance that Carnes made his departure on Friday, 9 October 1857. Laden with about twenty pounds of butter, besides his luggage, he returned to Portland and from there took the steamer *Lewiston* back to Boston.

With the Ocean House a well established institution very little change in the annual routine occurred throughout the next two decades. Although Proprietor Chamberlain acquired two partners, his was always the guiding hand. In August of 1875 one visitor contributed a few remarks to the *Eastern Argus* that reveal the general tenor of life at the house in this period. Speaking of the guests he noted that ". . . they are about equally divided between Americans and Englishmen from Canada, and a jolly company they are. The Ocean House has always been a favorite resort of the English gentleman who generally knows what good cooking is and here they get it. This house is admirably located for all the purposes of a life by the seaside, and the Canadians found it out years ago."

Late in the following year Chamberlain retired and sold the business to his son-in-law Col. Andrew J. Nichols of Natick, Massachusetts. This gentleman had pursued an extraordinary career before becoming proprietor of the Ocean House. In 1853 at the age of seventeen he went to California, remaining there almost a decade. He was employed aboard the steamer *Golden Gate* and nearly lost his life when it burned at sea. After that he served as purser on the steamer *Constitution* that ran between San Francisco and Panama. Experiencing strong Union sympathies Nichols returned to Maine in 1863 and was commissioned a 1st Lieutenant in Company B of the Second Regiment Maine Cavalry. After service in Florida and Louisiana he was discharged in 1864. He returned to the South after the war and opened a business in Savannah, Georgia. Within a year he traveled to the continent and England almost dying of cholera in Liverpool. After his marriage in 1867 Nichols and his bride moved to California where he became assistant Secretary of State. However, in 1870 he was back in Natick, Massachusetts as an active member of the Union Lumber Co. Before becoming proprietor of the Ocean House in the spring of 1877 he made still another visit to California. During the winter of 1876-77 Col. Nichols erected a comfortable home just north of the Ocean House on the corner of what is now Fessenden Road and Ocean House Road. Here he resided most of the time until his death 30 November 1880, at the age of forty four.

Under the guidance of Proprietor Nichols the Ocean House quickly took on a more cosmopolitan and sophisticated air. In February of 1877 he lavishly entertained a group of leading businessmen and newspapermen of Portland. Their description of the festivities certainly bespoke a new era of entertainment in the history of this quiet hotel. Within a comparatively short period of time Col. Nichols was well known among his neighbors as "quite a sport."

The new proprietor also renovated and modernized the Ocean House with the intention of expanding the facilities for transient clientele. Greater emphasis was placed upon coach service to and from Portland with a marked increase in the number of round trips each day. Also more attention was given to sea food on the menu, with clambakes and shore dinners a featured attraction. That these alterations enhanced the already excellent reputation of the house is borne out by a note in the *Eastern Argus* Thursday 13 June 1878. On that date it was reported that approximately 2,000 people had taken dinner or supper at the house so far that season.

After the death of Col. Nichols in 1880 operation of the Ocean House was taken over by three experienced hotel men, Freeman Mason and John McMillan of North Conway, New Hampshire, and C. H. Osgood of Portland. With Osgood as resident proprietor the house continued to be immensely popular especially with the Cape Cottage experiencing minor operational problems. In 1885 C. D. Dresser of Portland replaced Osgood, leasing the property until 1892.

On the 16th of December that same year the Ocean House experienced the fate of so many summer hotels. About 5:30 a.m. a fire was discovered in the building but by that time it was so far advanced as to render all efforts to quell it hopeless. The entire structure was completely destroyed with very little of the contents saved. No attempt was ever made to rebuild and the last of the surviving outbuildings were removed about 1901. Nothing now survives to indicate that the Ocean House was ever there, nothing that is, except the stone retaining wall that was built between the road and the beach.

III

From the early days of the Cape Cottage to the present time social, fraternal, professional, and cultural groups have frequented Cape Elizabeth as the ideal setting for their occasional outings. With the passing of years it became in many cases an annual institution, a tradition to be cherished and perpetuated as long as members survived. For the most part these groups sought out such hospitable resorts as the Cape Cottage or the Ocean House. In a few instances the social organizations erected their own places of refuge where the cares of the world were momentarily excluded.

Of the various social groups that frequented the inviting shores of the Cape none have ever matched the permanence or conviviality of the Venerable Cunner Association and Propeller

Club. The first meeting of which there is any record occurred at Portland Head Light on the 7th of August 1845. On that date Lewis B. Smith, Samuel Thurston, Francis E. Pray, George B. Eaton, Francis Pennell, and John Miller, all of Portland, to quote the record, ". . .to escape from the heat of the city . . . sought this retreat, and did fish, smoke, cook, eat, and drink and nothing worse, all for twenty-five cents each." This first meeting also produced the first of many song fests, with "Brother Eaton" serenading his fellow revellers with the first song, "We'll chase the Buf-fa-lo." The name of the club, incidentally, was derived from their fishing activities and the joyous salutes they rendered to the steam "propellers" of the Boston line as they sailed past Portland Head.

The first elected officers were Commissary, Treasurer, and Secretary, with Fireman and Waterman added in 1847, Steward in 1850, and the exalted office of Potato-Peeler in 1851.

In the early days of the Cunner Club, as it was soon called, the outing began in the early dawn at Monument Square. There they boarded a hay-rack or barge and rode to Portland Head. If an overnight visit was planned they either pitched a tent or sought lodging with the keeper of the light. The days were spent in various forms of "recreation and relaxation." During the fifties the annual outings were held for a few years at Diamond Island. This proved to be unsatisfactory however and the outings were resumed at Portland Head. By this time the first Tuesday in August had been established as the annual "anniversary outing", with most of the members assembling the night before. During the years of their residence at Portland Head the "Cunners," gradually, constructed a rather sizeable cairn as a permanent memorial. The corner stone was laid the 2nd of August 1859, with appropriate ceremonies, and a tin box of "valuables" placed beneath it. Over the years the members continued to add to the memorial until it ultimately reached a height of several feet. Late in the nineties, after the federal government purchased the area, the remnants of the tin box was retrieved from beneath the corner stone. Although the papers contained therein had long since disappeared the following valuable relics were recovered: three periwinkle shells, two peach stones, one ox shoe, and eighteen coins of little intrinsic value.

As the membership and activities expanded a foreign correspondent was appointed in 1879 and a few years later it was decided to move permanently to Long Point near Trundy's Reef. Here in 1888 a cottage was constructed to serve the needs of the club more completely. While the cottage was being constructed the *Eastern Argus* commented that "the Venerable Cunner Association and Propeller Club are building at Long Point, Cape Elizabeth, a cottage to be ready for occupancy on Fast Day. Mr. John L. Shaw, chairman of the building committee, is overseeing the work from the Observatory." Prior to the move the outings were held at various suitable sites such as Bluff Cottage near Peabbles Cove. In the future, when the "anniversary outing" was held at the new cottage, it was named, for the occasion, in honor of some departed or honored member. By this time the membership had increased to twenty-five and henceforth this was constituted as the maximum number.

With the coming of the twentieth century the list of "original Cunners" dwindled very rapidly. By 1904 Samuel Thurston was the only survivor of the six charter members. The rapid flight of time had produced a new generation of members equally as eager to carry on the now time-honored traditions of the Cunner Club. About 1916 seven acres of land were purchased at Long Point and a new cottage constructed thereon. It is here that the "Cunners" meet to this day.

In the later years of the nineteenth century other social groups established "cottages" for the summer comfort and relaxation of their members. Early in the seventies a group of ten Portland men formed the Bluff Cottage Club. Not as exclusively inclined as the "Cunners" they entertained with an unrestrained hospitality. At their cottage, located near the famous "Cunner Rock" clam-bakes and shore dinners were lavishly produced by the club's culinary expert George D. Robinson.

Throughout the summer months the members gathered once each week to partake of a dinner, with cunners invariably the "piece de resistance", followed by spirited games of whist. One articulate member, the amateur poet and musician John Shaw, composed a poem of several verses entitled "A Song to the Members of Bluff Cottage," in which he wove the name and occupation of every member. The first verse will serve to give the general tone:

> In good Bluff Cottage on the Cape
> image us to be,
> The jolly ten convivial souls all
> gathered by the sea,
> To rest awhile from city life, from
> care and dust and heat,
> And pass the pleasant hours
> away in this our cool retreat.

Unlike the "Cunners" the Bluff Cottage Club faded into history as the twentieth century progressed.

A third club to seek the salubrious climate of the "Cape Shore" was once again, a group of young men bent upon a spree of fishing, gormandizing, and camaraderie. This was the Ironclad Club, organized early in the seventies. Within a year or so of their inception they constructed a comfortable stone cottage on the shore close by the southern edge of what is now Delano Park. They named their retreat Ledge House and took great pains to preserve the rusticity that surrounded them. The interior was dominated by a large fireplace that served not only as a center of warmth and comfort on grey days, but as a kitchen as well. The name, Ironclad Club, was derived from the ironbound door and shutters that protected the cottage from the weather and uninvited guess. An early member and benefactor was Henry Goddard who made the land available as a site for the cottage. Other charter members were Eli Webb, Augustus P. Fuller, James R. Hawkes, Andrew A. Sawyer, Alexander Huston, George Goodrich, Andrew P. Morgan, Thomas A. Roberts, Charles B. Pettengill, William Senter, James A. Jack, and J. R. Corey, all of Portland.

About 1908 the land and cottage became the property of William Chenery. During the years of his "stewardship" the spot was much frequented by a jolly group of naturalists such as Perley Cummings, Thomas K. Jones, and Arthur Norton. However, the inexorable march of time so reduced the membership that in 1921 the property was sold to Lyman B. Chipman who remodeled and enlarged the cottage into a comfortable summer residence.

While the era of the summer outing club was getting underway, various individuals were, in a very quiet way, establishing summer residences along the inner "Cape Shore". In the early fifties William H. Stephenson of Portland purchased a tract of shore property slightly south of the juncture of the present Cottage Road and Preble Street. He occupied what was known as the "Widder Webb" house as a summer residence until 1869 when he constructed a cottage more suited to his needs. Unfortunately the cottage burned during the first season of its use and in disgust Stephenson sold the property to his brother Albert who also experienced the same misfortune, but had the temerity to rebuild.

In 1881 Albert Stephenson sold his adjacent pasture to Prentiss Loring and three years later sold an additional tract to Mrs. Mehitabel Baxter.

Members of the Ironclad Club in residence at their stone cottage. Photographed in July 1877 by Charles B. Conant of Portland.

Summer residence of Sylvester B. Beckett built 1871-74 and known as "Beckett's Castle". Circa 1876.

Residence of Colonel John Goddard built 1857-58. Circa 1868.

View of Cape Cottage Casino, showing facade added in 1899, and trolley park, from the roof of the theatre. Circa 1900.

Within a short period of time Prentiss Loring and his brother Charles had constructed summer homes adjacent to the Stephensons. The Charles Loring residence was partially built of material from an old manse in Yarmouth that he had recently torn down. The cottages were supplied with water from a marvelous spring, the source of Stony Brook. Close by the mouth of the brook Albert Stephenson built a pond which he stocked with ducks. The constant clamor of the birds aroused his ire however and with a shotgun he transfered their habitat to the kitchen.

The Loring property was sold in 1899 to George H. Archibald of Manchester, England, who soon tranformed it into a palatial summer home which he named Cragmoor. The former Charles Loring cottage he relocated and named Yellow-Head Cottage. This in later years was the Sylvester Judd Beach residence.

Another area of summer cottage activity was located in the vicinity of Glen Cove, just north of Maiden Cove. Here Capt. Green Walden built a rustic retreat in 1853. This gentleman spent most of his adult life in the U. S. Revenue Service, many years of which he served as Captain of the Revenue Cutter *Morris,* based at Portland. He placed an iron naval cannon in front of his cottage, facing the sea, and added many nautical embellishments over the years. Unfortunately, the place was totally destroyed by fire in the summer of 1888 some years after the death of Captain Green.

Immediately adjacent to the Captain, Caleb Carter and Edwin Churchill built a lovely cottage, designed by the architect Charles A. Alexander, also in 1853. This cottage was known as Glen Cove, hence the name, and is currently the Maj. Gen. John W. Gulick residence. Also nearby was the cottage of George Owen.

As the century progressed cottages sprang up between Glen Cove and the Stephensons. In the next few decades such names as Ledgelawn, Huntcliffe, and Graesmere, were recognized as the epitome of gracious summer living. With the coming of the twentieth century many of these "summer places", as well as those in other areas, were renovated and converted as year round homes.

One of the most unusual, and certainly one of the most picturesque, summer residences to be constructed on the Cape Shore was that built by Sylvester B. Beckett a few yards south of the Ironclad Club. A man of many talents, Beckett was for many years a prominent local journalist as well as an artist, litterateur, and amateur ornithologist of some distinction. The cottage, a story and a half building, constructed of field stone, was commenced in 1871 and finished in the summer of 1874. An outstanding feature of the cottage was a square three story tower. From the very beginning the cottage was known as "Beckett's Castle," and quickly became a favorite resort of the literati of Portland. On the day of its formal dedication late in the summer of 1874, Beckett's close friend, the editor of the *Portland Transcript*, Edward H. Elwell, composed and delivered a lengthy poem entitled "The Tower by the Sea."

During Beckett's lifetime the occasions for social gatherings were frequent and highly prized. The assemblages were those of kindred spirits with congenial tastes. Among those often in attendance were the artists John B. Hudson, Harrison Bird Brown, Charles Frederick Kimball, and Franklin Stanwood, as well as the journalists Charles Parker Ilsley, Hobart W. Richardson, and of course Edward H. Elwell.

Beckett's Castle was famous for its expansive dinners cooked in primitive fashion in a large fireplace. Many a savory chowder and stew was brought to life on his hearth. A Dutch oven had its place before the coals for baking and roasting, with a portly coffee-pot perched upon the "hob" to absorb the heat of the blaze. Around the table gathered many a trencherman, while the host carved the turkey which had been roasted a deep brown on a spit. Good food and drink, bright talk and good stories, interesting personal experiences, recollections of travel and adventure, made every such gathering a memorable experience. When Beckett died on December 2, 1882, the Castle passed to his daughter, Mrs. George W. Verrill. Her son, George B. Verrill, who inherited it in turn, ultimately sold the property to Col. Walter Singles, in whose family it now remains as a summer residence.

As would be expected, some of the summer cottage colonies forming along the Cape Shore sought to preserve the exclusiveness and sylvan beauty of their surroundings. Such was the case in 1885 when the Delano Park Association came into being. The area involved had been part of the homestead farm of James Delano and was conveyed by his heirs to Charles Payson and others. Actually, the region soon extended from the vicinity of the Ironclad Club north along the shore to the boundary of Fort Williams.

Residents of the Park would be responsible, in common, for the care and upkeep of all roads while at the same time sharing in common the rock-bound shore. Also each member was required to keep his property in good repair and to construct no additional buildings unless approved by the Association. In addition no transfer of property could be carried out without the consent of the trustees.

The first cottages to be built in Delano Park were: the George F. Morse residence erected in 1886, John Calvin Stevens architect, now the home of Mrs. John C. A. Brady; the Rev. Frederick M. Houghton residence constructed in 1886, John Calvin Stevens architect, which stood just east of the present Donahue cottage; the Elias B. Dennison house built in 1886, now demolished, but which stood a few hundred feet northwest of the Morse residence; and the lovely Charles A. Brown cottage, designed in the Queen Anne shingle style by John Calvin Stevens, erected in 1886, and now the summer home of Mrs. Charles L. Donahue.

A short distance beyond Delano Park at Pond Cove in this same era, the Portland financier Henry St. John Smith constructed his beautiful and palatial residence, "Belfield." Built in 1886, Smith occupied it until his early death in 1896. In later years members of his family continued to reside there, but unfortunately in 1937 it was demolished. This lovely home was also designed by John Calvin Stevens in the Queen Anne Revival shingle style.

IV

The middle years of the nineteenth century brought a great proliferation of summer hotels as well as cottage colonies. About 1860 close by the south side of what is now Montgomery Terrace there was built the rambling Cliff Cottage. Overlooking the harbor it commanded a fine view of the islands and the open sea. Catering largely to transient guests it is quite apparent that this hotel did not receive the patronage accorded the Cape Cottage and the Ocean House. With George H. Bailey as resident proprietor it did attain a moderate degree of prosperity. Unfortunately, the Cliff Cottage was totally destroyed by fire on Saturday 15 March 1873.

Despite this disaster the Cliff Cottage was rebuilt and limited success was achieved from the late seventies through nineties. During the spring of 1900 Glen Cottage and Sunnybank Cottage were constructed as annexes, each containing ten rooms. At the same time the main house was completely remodeled and all the buildings were electrified. The accommodations would now handle a maximum of seventy-five people.

The following year, Charles B. Dalton the owner and proprietor, in seeking a more extensive patronage, changed the name of the hotel to the Cliff House. In his rather lavish newspaper notices Dalton emphasized as advantages of the house ". . . one hundred rooms, electric lights, an orchestra, unsurpassed cuisine, perfect sanitary arrangements, salt and fresh water baths, large ocean frontage, fine beach, ... with low rates for June and September." In addition a steam heating system was installed to extend the season and to make limited use of the house during the winter months possible. So many of the guests were Canadian citizens that Dominion Day now became a featured celebration of the house. Truly, the first decade of the twentieth century was the most properous era for the Cliff House. The only misfortune of this period was the destruction by fire of the building that housed the bowling alleys, billard rooms, and kitchen, on Thursday 7 June 1906. Although fire companies from South Portland eventually reached the scene the building was a total loss.

By 1911 the locale around the Cliff House was so extensively built up with cottages that it was named Ottawa Park. Unfortunately, the house itself had fallen on rather poor times and had closed its doors in 1910. Three years later the property was purchased by Jabez True of Portland. The summer of 1913 the Cliff House was managed by the Peaks Island Hotel Company which also operated as summer hotels the Peaks Island, the Coronado, and the Union House. This resurgence of activity was abruptly halted the following spring. On Saturday the 13th of June 1914, fire broke out in the Glen Cottage about 2:00 a.m. and quickly spread to the Cliff House and Sunnybank Cottage. Despite the fact that fire companies were rushed to the scene from Fort Williams and South Portland all three buildings were reduced to ashes. No effort to rebuild was forthcoming and in later years the area became the site of several suburban residences.

Generally speaking, the decades after the Civil War were years of success for those who catered to the summer trade. In August of 1866 the *Eastern Argus* made some interesting observations pertaining to the clientele then frequenting the Cape.

> Our Canadian friends, who had been so cousinly during the past few years, have decidedly given the cold shoulder this season. . . . . Their absence is generally attributed to those terrible fellows, the

Fenians. We are sorry to lose them, for though their clothes did not fit them and some little snobbishness would crop out, they were good fellows in the main. They were sharp at a bargain, however, and generally speaking the host's charges for 'lunch', 'wine', etc., were few and far between. Their places. . . have more than been filled by southern people, who far from not being sufficiently reconstructed financially to afford the fashion and foolery of Saratoga, are finding out what real comfort and enjoyment is . . where fashion is dethroned and common sense reigns supreme.

A popular bit of doggerel that was often quoted through the years expresses quite well the feelings of the family man who sought the cooler climes of the Cape shore. With due apology to Alfred Lord Tennyson it is as follows:

>Break, break, break
>On thy cold, gray sands, O sea!
>And a trunk of shells for Molly,
>And a board bill long for me!
>
>O well for the fisherman's boy,
>Singing with heart elate!
>But I'm off the toiling city,
>Send the board bill on by freight!

Among the less pretenious summer colonies was the quiet little settlement at Pond Cove located a mile beyond the Cape Cottage. Early in the seventies James and Samuel Safford of Portland built the Picnic House about where the George S. Drake residence is now located. In 1878 the house was leased by Capt. Billy Broughton who specialized in Cunner fries and fried clams. During his period of tenure it was known as the Cove House. However, the following year it was once again managed by the owners, the Safford Brothers. One speciality of the house was a delicious clam chowder made from the famous Spurwink or Scarboro Clam. So celebrated was this delicacy that some local bard penned the following verses, entitled simply *The Scarboro Clam*:

>You may sing of your "Providence oysters,"
> Or boast of your roasted "spring lamb,"
>There's no dish or compound that ever was cooked
> Comes up to the "Scarboro Clam."
>
>When deliciously made in a chowder,
> Or boiled, and picked out of the shell,
>Or when taken and fried brown in batter,
> There's no dish that tastes half so well.

> Then too, there is something peculiar,
>   Of them you don't sicken or cloy;
> You may eat them for weeks in succession,
>   And the more their taste you'll enjoy.
>
> So brag of your Thanksgiving turkey,
>   Served up with its cranberry jam,
> There's nothing will equal, in my estimation,
>   The honest old "Scarboro Clam."
>
> You may scoff at my song and my rhyming,
>   And brace your shocked nerves with a dram,
> But yourself and your pocket would be better off,
>   If you took to the "Scarboro Clam."

Although the Pond Cove House was not equiped for anything more expansive than day outings, picnics, clam bakes, etc, it did enjoy a brisk business. This was especially true during the period when Mel Blanchard served as manager and host.

In 1883 the Safford Brothers sold all of their shore frontage, some sixteen acres, to various Portland residents for the construction of summer cottages. Within a relatively short period of time Pond Cove became a thriving community of comfortable summer residences.

Early in the nineties the Pond Cove House was considerably rebuilt and expanded, after a fire that did extensive damage, to accomodate over-night guests. Under new management it opened in the spring of 1895 as the Sea View House. It was a two and a half story building with a mansard roof, and a two story porch overlooking the Cove. Various Portland groups used the Sea View House as their summer outing headquarters. Among those in frequent attendance were the members of the Portland Wheel Club. In their *Road Book for Cycling . . .*, published in 1895, they noted that special rates were available to the members of the cycling fraternity. Unfortunately, the Sea View House was not as successful as expected and it was sold at auction 17 June 1897.

A few years later the house was opened again, this time as the Belmont House. In 1902 it was operated as a year-round hotel by John W. Swett of Portland and received a large amount of patronage from the various road companies that played at the Cape Theater. Its success was very short lived however, for a fire broke out early in the morning on 20 July 1903 that burned the building completely to the ground. As was the case in so many other instances it was never rebuilt.

One group that continued to enjoy Pond Cove was the

Argonaut Association of Portland. Organized in 1883 to further a common interest in aquatic sports they maintained a suit of rooms on Union Street as their headquarters. From early spring to late fall, the Argonauts occupied their cottage at Pond Cove seldom leaving it idle for any length of time. They continued summer visits for some years not terminating them until their cottage burned 26 April 1918.

Of the many social organizations that thronged to the Cape in this era probably none had a more hilarious time than the Richmond's Island Associates. At first composed entirely of young Boston men, when organized in 1891, it quickly attracted a fairly sizeable number in Portland. Limited to one hundred male members the association erected a cottage on Richmond's Island in 1899. Every third weekend of the summer months the men would gather at the island with their guests. Usually the Boston contingent would come to Portland on the steamer or sail their yachts directly to the island. High on the list of entertainment was a huge clam bake, with an inexhaustable supply of refreshments. From the reports that appeared occasionally in the Portland newspapers conviviality reigned supreme.

V.

Toward the close of the nineteenth century the electric trolley began to appear as a rapid means of public transportation, and with it a new recreational facility known as the trolley-park. This new conveyance revolutionized the tourist industry by providing a vast new medium of Sunday and holiday entertainment. Steam boat and even railroad excursions had long been possible but here was a far easier and cheaper means of getting away from the city. The trolley ride was an outstanding feature of week-end merriment, and the trolley parks to which the leisure seekers were carried, became the holiday mecca of the multitude. A writer in *Harper's Weekly*, impressed by the immense crowds that throughout the summer took advantage of these facilities, described the trolley-parks as "the great breathing places for the millions of people in the city who get little fresh air at home." Yet another observer declared that such recreation yielded more enjoyment "than all the courtly balls and fashionable dissipation indulged by fortune's favorites."

Not slow to grasp the potentialities to be developed in Cape Elizabeth a group of Portland men and others in 1881 formed and incorporated the Cape Elizabeth Railroad Company. Although surveys and other preparations were forthcoming no actual construction was initiated, despite the fact that the state legislature granted the company an extension of time to 1887. Two years later, the Cape Elizabeth Shore Railroad Company was incorporated to accomplish the same objectives. However, it wasn't until the spring of 1895 that tangible signs of activity was discernable. A building was constructed in Knightville to house the generators and by the end of October the tracks ran from Willard in South Portland to Monument Square.

When completed early in 1896 the line began in Portland at the foot of Preble Street, ran up Preble to Oxford Street, along Oxford and up Elm Street to Monument Square where waiting rooms and offices were soon established. From Monument Square the tracks ran down Federal Street to Market Street, down Market to Fore Street, along Fore to Cross Street and then down Cross to Commercial Street. After crossing the old Portland Bridge the line ran through Knightville to Broadway, thence to Willard Square via Sawyer, Pickett, and Fort Streets. Somewhat later in 1898 the route was extended to Willard Beach (Simonton's Cove) and up Angell Avenue to Cottage Road. Tracks then were laid from the corner of Cottage Road and Broadway to the corner of Angell Avenue and Cottage Road, thence on to Cape Cottage. The following year the Portland Railroad Company assumed control of the line and by the summer of 1909 track was laid to the Cape Elizabeth town hall. In the first decade of this century there was a great deal of agitation and sympathy for an extension of the line beyond Cape Cottage and from the town hall to Bowery Beach. However, despite a spirited effort the tracks never passed beyond Fort Williams or the town hall.

The coming of the electric trolley soon awakened a new interest in the Cape Cottage area. After the destructive fire of 1894 that swept away the famous hostelry, people continued to frequent the region on picnics and other outings. The year after the fire Charles Hannaford continued to operate a regular barge service from Portland and various groups held annual field-days there as usual. In 1897 George D. Robinson of Portland purchased the property from James P. Baxter in conjunction with the Cape Elizabeth Railroad Company. The previous year the trolley company had built a lavish $30,000 Casino at Willard Beach, South Portland, to stimulate summer business. As a result fares increased from 191,714 in 1896 to 503,900 in 1897. Needless to say these figures accelerated construction at Cape Cottage. Early in 1898 work progressed very rapidly and by May the Cape Cottage Casino was ready for occupancy. Designed by John Calvin Stevens, the Casino was an imposing wooden structure of two full stories, plus a ground level, with wide verandahs surrounding it on all sides. In conjunction with the Casino a summer theater designed by a Colonel Wood was also erected early in 1898 at the south-west corner of what was now Cape Cottage Park.

The season of 1898 was a very busy one at the Park partially as a result of the burning of the Willard Casino in January. Despite a major rearrangement of financial affairs and ownership, improvements advanced very rapidly. The Portland Railroad Company began construction of a loop that would deposit passengers at the entrances of the Theater and the Casino, and an aviary of exotic tropical birds was installed. Landscaping, the planting of flower beds, trees, and scrubs, the erection of auxiliary buildings, and the laying out of walks, proceeded with great speed. The formal opening of the Casino occurred on Tuesday the 21st of June 1898 with a huge clambake for two hundred and fifty people. Five special cars were required to bring all the guests from Portland.

The opening of the theater was also an affair of considerable excitement. When completed late in May 1898 it was a large wooden box-like structure. On the front of the building was a broad portico that led directly into the foyer of the theatre. From the foyer two flights of stairs led up a large balcony. The main floor plan was similar to that of the Jefferson Theatre in Portland. There were also three boxes on either side of the main floor. The total seating capacity was 1024, with standing room for quite a few more. The stage was somewhat smaller than that of the Jefferson but ample enough for the summer stock companies destined to play there. The drop curtain was a magnificent affair, painted by a New York artist H. Logan Reid, portraying Sappho the ancient Greek lyric poet. On either side of the stage were located five dressing rooms, and in front was a large orchestra pit. Officially the theatre was known at this time as McCullum's Theatre, named for the nationally known Portland actor associated for so many years with the Jefferson Theatre, Bartley McCullum.

The first stock company arrived on Wednesday June 1st, and with McCullum as manager, opened Saturday the 11th with Myron Leffingwell's *The Dawn of Freedom,* a Cuban drama of contemporary interest. Unfortunately, opening night did not go off without a hitch. The hand operated drawbridge on Portland

Bridge opened for a ship and could not be closed again for three hours, forcing the theatre goers to use the ferry. Overloaded cars at the ferry wharf caused a spreading of the rails and more delay. The first act, forty minutes late, was interrupted by a blown fuse and trolley lamps were pressed into service to illuminate the stage. However, due to the delay the theatre issued, upon demand, tickets good for another performance. On this memorable occasion fare to the theatre, including admission and return trip, was twenty cents.

It is an understatement to say that the theatre was well patronized from the very beginning. The week ending Saturday 2 July, 1898 produced 6741 paid admissions. Throughout the rest of the summer the trolleys were hard pressed to accommodate the crowds which attended the matinee and evening performances.

This first season featured as stars William A. Pascoe, Lisle Leigh, Mabel Taliaferro, and Bartley McCullum. Among the popular attractions were such great favorites as David Belasco's *May Blossom,* the younger Alexandre Dumas' *Camille,* Harry and Edward Paulton's *Niobe,* William Howarth's *The Ensign,* and Dion Boucicault's *The Shaughraun.* This tremendously successful season ended on Saturday the 10th of September with standing room only every night of the final week.

One highlight of the season began in a spectacular way and almost ended on a note of tragedy. A Private Nute of Battery E, 2nd U. S. Artillery, stationed at Portland Head, planned a balloon ascension with a parachute descent for the afternoon of Wednesday 17 August. Unfortunately someone partially severed his supporting rope with the result that it parted when Private Nute was only a few yards off the ground. The intrepid aeronaut landed in a heap entangled in the parachute, but fortunately escaped with bruises and minor lacerations.

The second year was much like the first with plays by David Belasco, Augustus Thomas, Dion Boucicault, Bronson Howard, James Sheridan Knowles, and others. This was the first season that the trolleys ran straight through to the theatre without a long detour through South Porland. It was now possible to leave Monment Square and be at the theatre twenty minutes later. Among the featured stars were such names as Bart and Tommy Reynolds, James Horne, Jimmy Bankson, Beatrice Ingram, Robert Wayne, Lisle Leigh, and of course Bartley McCullum.

The theatre continued to prosper and soon became an

established summer institution. In 1901 the Portland Railroad Company assumed full ownership and it was henceforth known simply as the Cape Theatre. Through the years that followed it was operated jointly by the manager and the trolley company. The financial arrangement was usually based on receipts, with the manager receiving the income from the reserved seat tickets and company making its profit on the combined admission-round fare tickets. It should be noted that the only unreserved seats were in the rear of the balcony.

Despite its initial success the Cape Theatre was never a great money maker. The biggest week in its history began Monday 27 July and ended Saturday, 1 August 1908. A total of 9400 people attended the theatre that week with 1350 on Saturday evening alone. A total of twenty seven trolleys were necessary to remove the crowd on that memorable night. Unfortunately this was never repeated and the average day always produced a much smaller number. The weather was always a decisive factor from the standpoint of attendance. During the runs of some of the most lavish and expensive productions the weather would be wet, and foggy, and as a result the audiences would be disastrously small. On the other hand in periods of bright and balmy weather the theatre would be thronged. Such fluctuations did not seriously worry either the company or the managers in the earlier years. Many of the managers were delighted to be spending the summer with their families at the seashore and were content to make a comfortable living out of the theatre.

Although Bartley McCullum came and went as resident manager, there were others who successfully directed the affairs of the Cape Theatre. Among them were such capable men as E. V. Phelan, Bide Dudley, and W. Natt Royster. Under their careful guidance the works of William Gillette, Dion Boucicault, George B. McCutcheon, David Belasco, Gilbert and Sullivan, William H. Crane, Richard Mansfield, Victor Herbert, Augustus Thomas, William C. Fitch, and George M. Cohan, were given repeated productions. Among the more popular troupers, in addition to those already noted, were Helen Marr Wilcox, Sidney Toler, Henrietta Brown, Gertrude Bondhill, Harriett Worthington, Willard Blackmoor, John Meehan, Bert Lytell, Tom Reynolds, Emma Salvatore, Genevieve Reynolds, Lester Lonergan, George Murray, Robert Baillard, Mae Hosmer, and Maude Edna Hall.

The era of World War I and the advent of the automobile

saw a decline from which the Cape Theatre never recovered. In 1913 vaudeville acts and movies replaced summer stock with very little success. The years of 1914 and 1915 were a small gain through the medium of musical comedy. The following year was poor due partially to a lengthy strike that tied up the trolleys. In 1917, the theatre was not visited by professional summer stock, but was used occasionally by various amateur groups such as the Maine Masque of the University of Maine. Interspersed between groups were movies, jazz band concerts, and porch dancing. During the war year of 1918 the theatre was pressed into service to entertain the troops stationed at Fort Williams. Concerts and other cultural events were staged at various times by the War Camp Community Service. After the war the theatre closed its doors for good ending a great and sparkling era in public entertainment. Early in the summer of 1921 the end came and before the month of June was over the Cape Theatre disappeared forever under the wreckers' hammer.

The other great tourist attraction of Cape Cottage Park, the Casino, experienced its greatest popularity while the Cape Theatre was at its height. The restaurant became widely known for the superior quality and variety of its cuisine. The great speciality of the house was a heroic shore dinner, a gastronomic delight. From the very beginning the business, professional, civic, fraternal, and social organizations fully utilized the facilities for their summer outings. Under the management of Charles Richenberg the first full season, 1899, was a spectacular success.

In addition to the Casino and the Cape Theatre there were bathhouses, gazeboes, and refreshment stands to further enhance the enjoyment of the visiting public. Across Shore Road from the theatre was a two story structure recently erected by Joseph W. Armstrong who maintained a restaurant on the first floor and a dance hall on the floor above. Immediately adjacent was a small, attached, single story building in which, on 14 July, 1899, Armstrong opened the Cape Cottage Post Office. Lastly, a large circular gazebo-like popcorn stand was functioning just east of the theatre under the management of Charles Chase. Thus it was that by the season of 1900 Cape Cottage was well established as a large and active trolley park with entertainment ample enough for the most demanding tourist.

During the summer months people from near and far considered a day or an evening at Cape Cottage the absolutely perfect form of relaxation. Beginning with an exhilarating ride out on the open trolley, followed by an ample dinner at the

Casino, with a concert by Callahan's orchestra, or the Worcester Empire Trio, than the theater, perhaps an additional refreshment, and a leisurely ride back to the city on the trolley. This was life at its best, sophisticated living in an unhurried age that vanished with the Great War.

Under the management of experienced restaurateurs such as Alfred H. Hatch who established and nurtured its fine reputation for over a decade, and Gen. R. E. Graves of Graves and Ramsdell, the Casino generally experienced one excellent season after another. The season usually began early in June and ended shortly after Labor Day.

The managment never rested on their laurels but were ever active, expanding and improving the facilities. In 1912 a wharf and float were constructed at Maiden Cove to accommodate the steamers *Madeline, Cliff House,* and in later years the *Admiral.* Taking the steamer to Cape Cottage Park, via Peaks and Cushings Island, and then returning on the trolley after dinner and the theater, was a very popular pastime. Other popular attractions were private dinner and dancing parties, evening concerts by Chandler's Band, and visits to the second floor art gallery of the nationally known photographer Fred Thompson.

During the war year of 1918 the Casino was temporarily converted into a Hostess House by the Women's War Council, largely through the efforts of Mrs. John F. Thompson and Mrs. Herbert J. Brown. A canteen, hostesses, and an atmosphere of relaxation contributed to the well-being of the various service men stationed in the Portland area.

The following year, 1919, the Casino was back in business under the management of Edwin L. Field. However, the automobile enabled the traveling public to go further afield and as a result business persistently declined. In 1922 Harry E. Baker, formerly of the National Cash Register Co., purchased the property but after two rather poor seasons he closed the doors of the Casino for good. Now that the property was no longer in the hands of Cumberland County Power and Light, successor to the Portland Railroad Company, the tracks were taken up and the era of the trolley park at Cape Cottage faded into history.

VI

With the coming of the twentieth century tourism at the Cape began to change. Despite the gradual disappearance of the more imposing summer resorts the general public continued to frequent the usual haunts of earlier days. Cottage colonies were still increasing. Early in the first decade the Cunner Cottage near Peabbles Cove began to acquire neighbors. Within ten years the area was rather heavily populated with summer residences of various types. One of the more prominent was Wildwood Cottage built in 1910, by a group of South Portland people. Consisting of eleven members the Wildwood Club leased the land from George Peabbles and constructed a roomy cottage, 18' x 28', with a large living room and separate rooms for each member. They also purchased a fifteen foot launch which they kept at the cove.

Smaller summer hotels were also becoming more noticable. Near Cape Cottage Park the Owl's Nest was opened about 1899 and was a popular spot for "young sports" from Portland. In 1924 it was purchased by Edwin L. Field who expanded it considerably and renamed it the Cape Cottage Hotel. He also constructed a store on the corner of what is now Surf Road and Shore Road which, in 1916, served for a time as the Cape Cottage Post Office.

Further out on the Cape, just beyond the Town Hall and on the opposite side of the road another small hotel came into being. The old home of Edward Hill, converted and altered, was opened as the Central House early in 1905. Although its location was auspicious its active life as a hotel was very brief.

In this same period a center of purely local social activity was Seaside Hall, near Bowery Beach. A large two story building built in 1912 by Otis M. Wheeler, played host to many a jovial gathering. The first floor was used for business purposes with the floor above used for social events. One group that used the hall very frequently was the fraternal order, the Knights of the Maccabees. It was totally destroyed by fire on Friday the 24th of October, 1913.

The natural beauty of the "Outer Cape" attracted not only those inclined to recreation but neophyte movie companies as well. As early as 1910 scenic shots were made and two years later the Lublin Manufacturing Company of Philadelphia used Maiden Cove as a locale for the production of a melodrama entitled *The Doctor's Debt*. The scenes shot at the cove portrayed ". . . a bold, bad villain stealing the battery box from a motor boat; a beautiful fisher girl, a veritable water-nymph, frantic because she had no means of power to drive the boat; an old fashioned Maine doctor sorely vexed and much perplexed because he could not get to a patient dying from dyptheria across the harbor."

Again in the spring of 1914 James A. Herne's marine drama *Hearts of Oak* was partially filmed at Richmond's Island and Watt's Ledge. The scenario was that of a ship wreck, with Watts Ledge utilized in this capacity. The sixty-five foot sloop *Excelsior* was totally wrecked and sank in the process of filming the scene. This was followed five years later by yet another sea drama, this time it was Jack London's *The Star Rover*. The film was produced by the Shurtleff Company with several Cape locations being pressed into service.

As the twentieth century advanced the area available to the public was rapidly reduced. The construction of substantial suburban residences, with extensive peripheral acreage, and rather palatial summer homes closed vast regions previously available to the casual visitor. By the late forties the general public was hard pressed to find ocean frontage open to them. Late in 1955 the State Park Commission opened negotiations with the federal government for the purchase of approximately forty acres at High Head. The site had no bathing area but it did have about 2,150 feet of magnificent ocean frontage. Actual work was started in the fall of 1957 and by the spring of 1961 the park was ready to receive the general public. Since its dedication in June of 1961 Two Lights State Park has been extraordinarily popular with approximately 70,000 visitors during the 1963 season. Such figures certainly testify to the wisdom of the State Park Commission in acquiring this spendid site for the enjoyment and recreation of the avearge citizen.

Another area currently under development by the State Park Commission is Crescent Beach State Park. Originally, in 1956, the town was given the opportunity by the state to develop the area as a municipal park, however, the town refused to act. The state was forced to take appropirate action to perserve the area for the enjoyment of future generations. The beach had been cited earlier by the National Park Service in its report *Our Vanishing Shoreline* as one of the sixteen Atlantic and Gulf Coast areas given top priority in its drive to acquire sites suitable for public recreation. In 1959 the town voted 176 to 74 in favor of Crescent Beach State Park but unfortunately the state legislature neglected to appropirate any funds for its creation. Finally in November of the same year Gov. Clinton Clauson, a Democrat, authorized the initial purchase of the property to make the park a reality at last. The area involved represents approximately 3,800 feet of usable beach plus space for fireplaces, tables, bath houses, and a section for parking. Work has progressed slowly and it is now anticipated that a formal opening dedication will occur in the summer of 1966.

Thus it is that the scenic beauty and noble vistas of Cape Elizabeth will be preserved from the inexorable march of suburbia. The mushroom like proliferation of housing developments, with delightfully euphonius names, have turned the once predominently rural "Outer Cape" into a "sleeper-community." Were it not for the foresight of a few dedicated individuals the shores of Cape Elizabeth would soon have been beyond the reach of all but a few members of our affluent society. Now the joys of days gone by will have some meaning for the generations yet to come.

Chapter VI

SHIPS AND THE SEA

The maritime history of Cape Elizabeth is almost as old as the first permanent settlements on the Maine coast. As previously noted visitations to this section of the coast were especially frequent at the dawn of the seventeenth century. It was only natural that the first adventurous souls would be fishermen seeking more fruitful rewards for their arduous labors.

As the sixteenth century drew to a close some unknown mariner discovered that cod frequented the coastal waters of Maine in great numbers during the winter months. With the gradual expansion of the fisheries in the following century came voyages of exploration, one of the most memorable being that of Captain John Smith. His expansive and enthusiastic descriptions of the coast and his frequent comments upon the rich harvests of fish stimulated the interest of many an English merchant. Among them was Sir Ferdinando Gorges who soon invested in a ship and sent her on a fishing voyage to the coast of Maine.

In 1620 James I conferred upon Gorges, and his associates in the Plymouth Company a monopoly of fishing rights in seas that bordered their grant. This monopoly was rather brief, however, for in 1624 the English Parliament rescinded it thus opening the coast to any fisherman with the courage to venture forth.

A new era dawned in the next decade that greatly altered the fisheries of the Maine coast. Previously, fishermen from the ports of western England had visited the coast only long enough to catch and cure their fish, returning to England as soon as their holds were filled with no definate plans to return. It was only natural that various English merchants should seek a more systematic approach to the taking of fish from these teeming waters. Within a short time semi-permanent stations, or factories, began to appear at several points along the coast of Maine.

Thus it was that Robert Trelawney and Moses Goodyear established a station in 1632 on the hospitable shores of Richmond's Island. Under the direction of their resident factor, John Winter, the station soon became the largest and most flourishing on the coast. Much of the correspondence that passed between Winter and Trelawney has been preserved, as noted in an earlier chapter. Thus it is that we are able to reconstruct the myriad activities that constituted the life of such an active fishing station.

In this era more fish could be taken within a few leagues of Richmond's Island than at any spot along the coast. Winter soon found that it was very profitable indeed to keep boats constantly at sea on the fishing grounds. Almost at once great quantities of dried fish were being shipped to southern Europe. Among the reports that Winter submitted to Trelawney we find the names of many vessels such as the *Angel Gabriel, James, Fellowship, Hercules, Hunter, Lion,* and *Margery,* which were actively engaged in this trade. There was, in addition, a very busy coasting trade carrying fish as well as other products to the Kennebec, to the Bay Colony, to Virginia, and occasionally as far south as the West Indian Islands.

The average fishing boat of this period was a vessel of approximately 200 tons burden, carrying a crew of about fifty men. Each crewman contributed toward the coast of provisions and received, as his wages, a share of the profits derived from the voyage. Toward the end of the seventeenth century, the ships used in the coastal fisheries were somewhat smaller and were often described as shallops. Such vessels usually carried a crew of four.

As a general rule, three fishing voyages were made each year. Most of the fish were taken with hand lines and then carried ashore to be washed, salted, dried on flakes, and sorted. Of primary value were the full grown solid fleshed fish that were easily saleable especially in the Catholic nations of southern Europe. Next in importance were the so called "refuse fish", perfectly edible but not so solid and full fleshed. Also in this category were those that were slightly discolored or salt-burned. Such fish soon found a ready market in the West Indies as food for Negro slaves. Last were the "dun" or dark fish, generally pollock, caught in the summer months and sun cured for sale in southern Europe.

Most of the fish were heavily salted or dried before being shipped to distant markets, but some, known as "cor-fish" or corned fish, were packed whole in brine. Other types, unfit for food, were tried out for the oil they contained which was sold as "traine" and made a rather valuable export.

The station at Richmond's Island was not destined to be a permanent settlement. The death of Robert Trelawney, and financial problems, brought a decline in activity; and when Winter died in 1645, the area was soon abandoned. The buildings that survived despite the neglect were burned during the Indian War of 1690.

It was not until 1718 that living conditions returned to anything that resembled a normal state. As settlers returned, it was only natural that they should attempt to resume activities forcibly abandoned in years past. With regard to the sea John Josselyn in 1638 speaks of many men as being both farmer and fisherman, a description that was equally applicable in the early years of the eighteenth century.

Early in the eighteenth century many men turned to the sea as a primary source of livelihood. How many shipped out of the port of Falmouth is, of course, unknown. However, it is safe to assume, from the meager records that have survived, that fishing and foreign voyages were not an uncommon way of life. Prior to the Revolution, Cape Elizabeth, interestingly enough, was the scene of an extensive commerce with the West Indies. As noted in an earlier chapter, the center of this activity was Simonton's Cove. While the people on Falmouth Neck were busily expanding the masting trade, Ezekiel Cushing and William Simonton were rapidly transforming this placid cove into the most thriving maritime center of that era in the region of Casco Bay.

The vessels that these gentlemen employed in the West Indian trade were by later standards surprisingly small. For the most part they were large sloops, or two-masted schooners and brigs. The average burden of these vessels never exceeded 200 tons. They were also, to a large extent, constructed locally, although the details of this activity are very sketchy. However, according to local recollections, a Capt. John Robinson constructed some rather small vessels at Ship Cove near Portland Head. In later years, bits and pieces of marine hardware were turned up by the plow, along with rusted tools, in the level meadow that previously existed at the head of the cove.

The cargoes exported by Cushing and Simonton were rather varied. Judging from the manifests of this era, sawed lumber, and shingles were much in evidence. Also common were hogshead, tierce, cask, and barrel shooks with the staves jointed and crozed, hoops shaved, and the heading fitted, all ready to be assembled. Another common cargo was salt or dried codfish often shipped in "drums" of from five to eight hundred pounds each. On the return voyage these vessels brought cargoes of molasses, sugar, treacle, and other West Indian products. Many of these return cargoes were undoubtedly disposed of in the more populous ports of southern New England, or in New York. This flourishing trade could not, and did not survive the Revolutionary War. When peace returned in 1783, the center of trade and commerce was soon re-established across the harbor, with Simonton's Cove surviving merely as a resort for fishing vessels.

Before proceeding further, it would be of interest to examine a little more fully these two rather remarkable merchants of the early eighteenth century, Ezekeil Cushing and William Simonton. Of the two, Cushing was by far the more influential and affluent. He was the youngest son of the Rev. Jeremiah Cushing of Scituate, Massachusetts, and was born 28 April 1698. On 1 April 1720 he married Hannah Doane of Plymouth who bore him eight children. After residing at Provincetown, Massachusetts for several years, Cushing moved to Cape Elizabeth about 1740. He built a very comfortable home on a point of land between Stanford's Ledge and Spring Point. The house faced the south and apparently was the first two-story house in that section of the Cape. In later years the roof was lowered giving it the appearance of a story-and-a-half house. The building was still standing in the early years of the nineteenth century. However, by 1870, nothing but the cellar hole remained.

Within a short period of time, Cushing was flourishing as one of the most prominent, if not the leading, merchant of Cape Elizabeth. In 1754, when Gov. William Shirley visited Falmouth to negotiate with the Indians, he dined with Cushing on the 23rd of July. Two years later, when the French and Indian War was renewed, he was commissioned a colonel of militia by the Commonwealth of Massachusetts. His service was of brief duration, but, like many a colonial officer, he was forced to pay off his men at his own expense, and then wait some years before being reimbursed.

The West Indian trade was not without its losses. According to Parson Thomas Smith, Col. Cushing lost a sloop and a Negro slave in the 1760's to a French man-of-war. His commercial activities, however, were varied enough to cover such occasional losses. One interesting maritime business venture that he was involved in was coastal whaling. Unfortunately, it, too, brought its moments of grief to Cushing for in 1769 his son Nathaniel was killed while harpooning a whale near Portland Head.

Real estate was another source of interest to Colonel

Cushing. At one time he owned, in addition to his holdings in Cape Elizabeth, Bang's (Cushing's), Long, Marsh, and Overset Islands in Casco Bay. When he purchased Long Island, the tradition is that he contemplated buying land on the Neck but considered the Island a better maritime investment. In 1760 he sold Cushing's Island to Joshua Bangs. Incidentially, it should be noted that this Island was not subsequently named for him but for a member of a distant branch of the same family. Cushing's older brother, Ignatius, was, for many years, an inhabitant of Long Island.

In the area of public service, Col. Cushing was also a prominent figure. He served for nine years as a selectman and two years as treasurer of Falmouth. In addition, he served as the judge of the Court of Common Pleas for five years.

As was the case with many colonial men of means Cushing was an owner of Negro slaves. On one grim occasion, 15 September 1745, his five-year-old son Nicholas was accidentally killed with a pistol by one of his slaves. When Cushing died in 1765, he left two slaves, Cato and Philis, to his son Thomas, and a four year old Negro girl, Dinah, to his wife Mary.

The family of Col. Cushing was both extensive and interesting. Of his eight children by his first wife, Hannah, the most prominent was his eldest son, Loring, who graduated from Harvard College in 1741, but died of wounds after the Battle of Saratoga on the 9th of October, 1777, at the age of fifty-six. His wife died 7 June 1742 at the age of thirty-nine. Her grave is the oldest known burial in Mount Pleasant Cemetery at Meeting House Hill in South Portland.

The Colonel's second wife was the former Mary Parker, a widow, of Boston and a daughter of Dominicus Jordan. They were married 1 April 1746 and were blessed with three sons. Their eldest son, John, saw arduous service in the Revolutionary War, and their second son Thomas was lost with the privateer, *Cumberland,* in 1778. It was their youngest son, Nathaniel, who was killed while harpooning a whale.

When Ezekiel Cushing died on the 7th of May 1765 at the age of 67, the town of Cape Eilzabeth lost one of its most extraordinary colonial citizens. Certainly, he was one of the most distinguished men in the Falmouth Neck region, a leading figure in the pre-revolution society of Falmouth, as well as an official of the crown. In addition, his style of living was according to contemporary accounts, both gracious and expansive, never oblivious to amenities expected of his station. Even his passing was in the proper style. An appropriate coffin was constructed by Enoch Moody of Falmouth for Cushing at an expense of eight pounds, an indication of the Colonel's standing in the community as the average coffin never exceeded nine shillings in cost. His final resting place is now unknown as is that of his second wife.

Somewhat eclipsed by his affluent competitor, William Simonton was, nevertheless, successful in an ephemeral way, never achieving the stature that was Cushing's. He arrived at Cape Elizabeth in 1718, with his brother Andrew, as part of a group of twenty-one families of Scotch-Irish Presbyterian's from northern Ireland. His way of life and his demeanor were modest indeed, but he prospered in both the West Indian and fishing trades. When Simonton died in 1784, at the age of one hundred years, he left behind a large and active family with many descendants.

On a more modest scale were the maritime activities of John Mariner and his son, Joseph. The first of the name to settle in Cape Elizabeth, John was born in France and emigrated to the American Colonies with his father the Rev. John Mariner, a Huguenot minister, after the revocation of the Edict of Nantes. The family settled in Gloucester, Massachusetts about 1685 with young John taking to the sea at an early age.

As master of a coaster, John made enough voyages to Falmouth to become convinced that his future might be brighter in that area. He received grants of land at what is now Ferry Village about 1720, and ten years later moved his family to these holdings. Mariner constructed a substantial home and garrison house or "watch-box." He flourished in the coasting trade and was sufficently prosperous to be considered one of the town's wealthier citizens. While on a voyage to the West Indies in 1748, John Mariner and his vessel vanished without a trace.

Mariner's son, Joseph, inherited his father's house, holdings, and fleet of coasters. He soon became one of Cape Elizabeth's most energetic and enterprising citizens. Besides operating a tavern in his home he kept his coasters continuously employed, making personal voyages in the schooners *Neptune* and *Molly*. During the Revolutionary War he was an ardent patriot despite the fact that he lost most of maritime property. In the years that followed the war, he took an active part in the fisheries with the aid and assistance of his son, Silas. Throughout the rest of his life Joseph continued as an influential citizen, dying in 1811 at the advanced age of ninety-three.

Although not as prominent as his father, Silas prospered as

an "amphibious farmer". During the War of 1812 he was taken prisoner in the privateer *Teazer* along with Isaiah Jordan and James Loon, also of Cape Elizabeth. After several months of imprisonment at Halifax, they were exchanged. He died in 1873 in his eighty-second year.

The Revolutionary War ended a prosperous era of maritime activity. Beginning with Capt. Mowatt's destructive assault upon Falmouth, shipping gradually vanished from the waters of Casco Bay. The coast of Maine was disasterously close to the course usually taken by British naval vessels and privateers sailing between Halifax and their southern stations or cruising grounds. In addition, privateers loitered, sometimes for days on end, around the outer limits of Casco Bay, gobbling up coasters and fishing vessels that had the temerity to venture forth.

During the war, many Cape Elizabeth men shipped in the various privateers that hailed from Casco Bay, often with tragic results. In 1776 alone, approximately forty-two men were killed or captured while serving in this capacity. The heavy loss in shipping soon made it almost impossible to put to sea and survive. By 1781 there were but twenty-four tons of shipping still extant at Cape Elizabeth. Even this was lost before the war ended with the Treaty of Paris in 1783.

It was late in the decade of the eighties before any signficant maritime activity was revived in the vicinity of Falmouth. The depression and hard times that followed the war gravely altered prospects of rapid recovery. In addition, it was extraordinarily difficult for the fishermen to fit out suitable boats with the necessary gear for a resumption of their badly needed harvests of the sea.

In these dark days, the only gleam of hope to be found was in the rumors of impending war between England and France. The possibility of supplying the belligerents in neutral bottoms made many a merchant pause for thought. It wasn't until the spring of 1793 that the long anticipated hostilities broke out, destined to continue almost without interruption for the next twenty-two years. Thus was inaugurated a "heroic age" of soaring profits and high adventure that was to last until 1807 when Thomas Jefferson, attempting to preserve "freedom of the seas" for the United States, withdrew American vessels from foreign trade. These were the marvelous years of neutral profits when, despite the frequent seizure of ships and cargoes by one or the other of the belligerents, many a fortune was made trafficking in the necessities of life. So eager were the citizens of

Cape Elizabeth to participate in this maritime resurgence that they, at a special town meeting held the 17th of September 1793, drew up the following declaration:

> In consequence of a Letter Circular from the Hon. Thomas Russell Esq. Chairman of the committee for the commerical interest in the town of Boston, a number of the inhabitants of this town met and being impressed with a sense of many advantages that will arise in the United States in observing a strict neutrality towards all the belligerent powers, unanimously voted the following resolves:
> Resolved: 1. .That we will to the utmost of our power, strictly attend to the pacific system injoined by the President in his late Proclamation.
> Resolved: 2. That we heartily concur with our fellow citizens of the town of Boston, in their late doing relative thereto; and that we will endeavour to detect all such as may in the smallest degree violate that neutrality we so highly approve.
> Voted unanimously, that the above resolutions be printed in the *Eastern Herald.*
> A true copy from the records.
> Ebenezer Sawyer, Town Clerk.

As was to be expected, shipping and its attendant industries were soon flourishing in the area of Falmouth Neck, providing many opportunities for employment to the men of Cape Elizabeth. This maritime activity was frought with many dangers. Both England and France soon began to issue a multiplicity of regulations designed to harass the enemy. Primarily concerned with the war effort, they gave very little thought to the injuries visited upon the merchant fleet of the United States. They were slightly deterred from absolute indifference by various economic considerations. The United States was one of the largest purchasers of England's industrial products and, with many markets now closed by war, the nation was to a degree a valuable customer. In addition, American neutral bottoms were of great assistance to the French in transporting precious cargoes of sugar and coffee from their Caribbean possessions, and to a lesser degree in their coasting trade when the might of the British Navy made the tricolor a risky ensign to flaunt anywhere at sea. The United States was, therefore, very useful but, as it sorrowfully discovered, not indispensable.

Gradually, the transgressions of the belligerents forced Jefferson and Madison to attempt commercial coercion. The embargo, Non-intercourse, and Macon Acts were a disaster in reverse. Instead of working any miracles abroad it brought maritime ruin and stagnation to the United States.

With foreign trade thus drastically reduced, "coasting voyages" were the only answer. In clearing for Maine ports to the eastward, many local skippers developed "errors" in navigation that took them to Passamaquoddy Bay and its adjacent waters. A clandestine trade was soon flourishing as Yankee products were exchanged for the wares of England and its West Indian islands. Within a short time, Halifax became a teeming entrepot, well supplied by the "coastal trade."

As restrictions on foreign trade were reduced with each passing year, American foreign trade tried to adjust and respond to a rapidly changing international situation. Now that England was the almost uncontested "mistress of the seas," her efforts to maintain an adequate naval force at sea were difficult indeed. One ever-present problem was the constant need to obtain trained seamen to man the warships of England's far flung fleets. A partial answer was the heavy impressment of sailors from the merchant vessels of the United States. Many English seamen were deserting the "bloody floating barns" of the British Navy, seeking a freer life aboard American merchantmen. This manpower loss was incentive enough and the practice of examining American merchant crews for the detection of "deserters" became routine for many short-handed captains of the Royal Navy. It mattered not if the individual in question was native-born or naturalized as long as he was an experienced seaman. The apprehension of genuine deserters was exceedingly difficult, with the result that in any case where nativity was at all in doubt, the individual was automatically impressed into His Majesty's service.

It is impossible to determine exactly how many Cape Elizabeth men were forced to accept involuntary servitude aboard British warships. However, the experiences of one such individual survives, and although his service was mercifully brief, the incident was not uncommon.

Early in 1806 Mark Dyer, Jr., at the age of twenty-five, shipped aboard the Portland schooner *Sea Gull* as a seaman. With a cargo of barrel shooks the vessel made a rapid and uneventful passage to Havana, Cuba. Here, the shooks were landed and a cargo of molasses taken aboard for the voyage home. As the schooner cleared the harbor, it was hailed by the frigate *H. M. S. Shamrock,* and a boarding party was sent to check the meager crew of the *Sea Gull.* The only hand to be impressed was Dyer, and he soon found himself an unenthusiastic member of the frigate's crew. The *Shamrock* then entered Havana harbor to continue her "recruiting" activities. That night Dyer was confined below decks, under guard, with other impressed men to forestall any chance of escape. However, while ashore at Havana, Dyer had acquired a small amount of cash from the sale of some goods he had carried with him aboard the *Sea Gull*. With this he convinced the sentry to look the other way while he slipped over the side. Despite the fact that the sentry almost immediately sounded the alarm, and that a boat was lowered to look for Dyer, he managed to swim to the ship *Quaker Lady,* of Philadelphia. He was quickly concealed aboard the ship, and, although it was boarded by a party from the *Shamrock,* he eluded detection. In due course, the *Quaker Lady* sailed and Dyer ultimately returned to his home none the worse for his harrowing adventure.

This long era of neutral profits and maritime complications finally produced the War of 1812. It was not an inevitable conflict despite the impassioned response awakened by the slogan "Free Trade and Sailors' Rights." The truth of the matter was that our problems on the high seas involving Great Britain were at a very low ebb. Actually, this totally unnecessary declaration of war was largely the work of truculent elements on the western frontier who were casting covetous eyes on Canada. The shipping interests of New England were antagonized to an unbearable degree and were frequently more hostile to "Mr. Madison's War" than to England. Until 1814, no serious effort was made to blockade the New England coast and the "Quoddy" trade flourished as before. Despite this lukewarm enthusiasm for the war, privateering became, for a few short years, a flourishing enterprise. The contribution of the Casco Bay area to this "war effort" consisted of forty-five vessels ranging in size from the *Hyder Ally* of 367 tons to the tiny *Lark* of only four tons. With speed the most desirable attribute, ships were rapidly constructed, often of green, unseasoned wood. Crews were easily signed on from the vast number of unemployed seasmen and cruises hastily inaugurated.

Among the first of the privateers to be constructed was the schooner *Dart* of forty tons built in Cape Elizabeth, near the blacksmith shop of Joseph Dyer at Ferry Village, by Ezekiel Dyer, early in 1812. Within five weeks of the day her keel was laid, the *Dart* was ready for sea. She was long and low with a pinky stern but carried two naval guns and a sizeable crew of approximately forty-six men. Her masts were hinged just above the deck to facilitate concealment should it be necessary to hide from some resolute pursuer in a secluded cove or inlet. The

Dart also carried long sweeps to furnish a "white ash breeze" should the vessel find itself becalmed at an inopportune moment. Her owners were Joseph Cross, and others, of Portland, and her first shipper was Capt. John Curtis, also of Portland.

The first cruise of the *Dart* began on the 27th of July 1812 with the Canadian West Indian trade as her primary objective. Her first prize was the brig *Howe,* captured off the coast of Newfoundland on August 22nd and sent to Portland with Eben Sweat in command. The following day, the *Dart* sighted the brig *Hector* and after a long pull with the sweeps and a brief but spirited engagement she too became a prize. On the 25th a small shallop was seized and then released with the crews from the first two prizes. Two days later, the brig *Eliza* was taken and forwarded to Portland under the command of Stephen Veazie.

On the last day of August, the *Dart* made what was to prove to be her most memorable capture. She sighted, off Cape Ray, the brig *Dianne,* from London to Quebec, and, after a chase of five hours succeeded in making her a prize. The brig's cargo turned out to be two hundred and twelve puncheons of rum. She was soon underway again, bound for Portland with William Thomas at the helm. After marooning the crew of the *Dianne,* the *Dart* headed back to Portland arriving on the 11th of September, thus completing what was to be the most successful cruise of her career.

The *Dianne's* cargo of approximately 17,800 gallons of rum produced something of a sensation in Portland. It was soon discovered to be of superior quality, probably due to a long period of aging in some London warehouse. From the very first, "Old Dart Rum" was a spectacular success, and its ambrosial qualities were long remembered by local connoisseurs. It was retailed from the "original casks" for many years. These casks, incidentally, are suspected of having been as prolific in the production of rum as the hold of the *Mayflower* was in producing heirloom furniture.

The subsequent career of the *Dart* is unknown. She sailed from Portland late in 1812 and vanished at sea without a trace. As no record of her capture or fate is known, it is assumed that she foundered in a North Atlantic gale and sank with all hands.

One of the most daring captures of the war was carried out by Cape Elizabeth men in these opening months. Somewhere to the south the British ship *Rollo* had captured a Philadelphia vessel, put a prize crew aboard, and ordered her to Halifax. Off the Cape shore, she hove to and sent her prisoners in, but the wind died before she could get underway again. Sometime during the day, as she lay becalmed, Captain John Chitty, with eight other men, rowed out near her in a whaleboat and spent the remainder of the day pretending to fish. Under cover of darkness they rowed stealthily up to the prize-ship and boarded her in a rush demanding immediate surrender in the name of a "well-known privateer." The astonished prize master relinquished the ship at once under the impression that a formidable privateer was lying alongside. After seizing the arms of the ship, the captors dropped their disquise and ordered the prisoners to hoist the whaleboat aboard. The evening breeze had meanwhile sprung up enabling Captain Chitty and his men to work the ship into Portland Harbor. Of the members of this adventurous Cape Elizabeth crew, Captain Chitty was afterward commander of the privateer sloop *Lilly* of Portland, while Jot Sawyer was boatswain in the New York privateer *Teazer;* a Mr. Wormal and Ezekiel Jordan were also members of the whaleboat crew.

The spring of 1814 brought maritime stagnation to the port of Portland. The British blockade was extended north to Passamaquoddy Bay in April, and in September the seventy-four gun ship of the line *H.M.S. Bulwark* hovered just beyond the entrance to Portland Harbor, making periodic forays along the coast. All of the Maine coast east of the Penobscot River was British territory. The coasting trade, that had been active with the tacit approval of English officialdom, now ceased altogether. A British landing in the Portland area was expected daily throughout most of September.

As the invasion scares and alarms began to subside, some movement of trade was resumed, not by way of the sea but by land. The blockade was still very much a reality, and voracious Canadian privateers thronged the coastal sea lanes. Under these conditions, merchants were forced to resort to the slow and arduous movement of goods in a variety of carts and wagons, drays and pungs, drawn by oxen or horses. To the stranded seamen, these vehicles offered some employment and were soon dubbed "mud clippers." Known more formally as the "Horse Marine" these conveyances now crowded the roads of Maine from the Penobscot south to Portland, Boston, New York, and beyond. Some of the local newspapers printed regular reports of this commerce under the heading "Horse Marine List." A typical report was that of 6 November 1814 in the *Portland Gazette*.

Arrived Kennebunk at noon, two horse cutter "Timothy Pickering" and "Quincy Cannon Ball", Commodore Delande from Portland to Boston. Spoke on her passage sixteen ox schooners from Bath, cargo, tin plate, all well. Also saw on the Scarboro turnpike a suspicious looking cutter which was escaped by superior sailing.

Both the United States and Great Britain were, by now, heartily sick of this unnecessary war, and when the deliberations at Ghent produced a cessation of hostilities, very few dissenting voices were heard on either side of the Atlantic. When the news reached the District of Maine, a universal feeling of relief and delight pervaded the coastal communities. With great enthusiasm, idled thousands now returned to the ways of the sea. In a remarkably short time, the fisheries, coastal trade and packets, deep sea voyages and West Indian cruises, were revived. Once again, "nautica mystica" became an overpowering incentive which many a seafaring citizen of Cape Elizabeth could neither resist nor deny. The villages along the Cape Elizabeth shore of Fore River and Portland Harbor were the "homeport" of many a seafarer throughout the remaining years of the nineteenth century.

For the next fifty years the great bulk of maritime activity in the Portland area was centered upon the West India trade. This was a great age of individual initiative, responsibility, and proficiency on the high seas. Without such qualities, success was elusive indeed. Under ordinary circumstances, two voyages a year was the general average. A vessel would clear the port of Portland the latter part of December and arrive at the islands early in January. She would land her cargo and load again fast enough to complete the voyage late in February. A second trip would be immediately undertaken, with the vessel returning the latter part of April. During the summer months there would be no voyage until the yellow fever and hurricane season ran its course, thus giving many a mariner the opportunity to plant and harvest a crop at home.

Most of the West India cruises were undertaken with no particular port in mind, forcing the ship master to rely upon his experience and training in seeking a market that offered the greatest opportunities. These voyages were frequently anything but a pleasure trip. On many occasions dull and depressed markets gravely affected financial success. In addition, navigational hazards in the form of reefs and shoals were an ever-present menace to the unwary. Lastly, piracy in the early years of this era, was a factor that could not be ignored with a ghastly fate awaiting the ill prepared or unsuspecting mariner.

The ships and rigs common to the West India trade are now but a matter of history. Generally speaking, they were small vessels, averaging between 200 and 400 tons in size. Being very full bodied and drawing very little water, they could receive or discharge sizeable cargoes in fairly shallow water.

The most common type of vessel was the brig, more of these being constructed in Maine than anywhere else. A full-rigged brig carried fore and main masts, with three spars each and was entirely square-rigged except that the mainmast carried a standing gaff to which was bent a fore-and-aft sail called a spanker.

Next to appear was the hermaphrodite brig. Actually, this was a cross between a brig and a schooner. Its distinctive feature was that it was square-rigged on the foremast and fore-and-aft rigged on the mainmast. Her economical operation made her a very popular type, as few men were needed to operate her. A varition of this rig was the "jackass brig." She carried one or more square sails on the mainmast.

Yet another popular type was the Maine brigantine. She carried the sails of a brig on her foremast, but her mainmast consisted of two spars having the rig of a topsail schooner with at least one square main topsail and sometimes a main-topgallant sail. This vessel was considered to be somewhat more weatherly than the others as the large fore-and-aft sail was a powerful pusher when close-hauled to the wind.

The eighteen thirties, forties, and fifties were years of extraordinary maritime activity in Cape Elizabeth. The port of Portland served as an entrepot for a vast northern area. The White Mountain Road was the main artery of commerce for northern New Hampshire and Vermont during the winter months. The "up-country" men brought their product to the Portland market where it was exchanged for flour, salt, fish, and such West India goods as coffee, rum, molasses, and sugar. Completed in 1830, the Cumberland and Oxford Canal also contributed its share of cargo for the holds of the West India brigs. Still later, the coming of the railroad opened yet larger areas to the port of Portland.

Of all the West India products, coffee, molasses, and rum led the field. As the years passed, coffee and rum declined in popularity, with molasses assuming a pre-eminent position in the manifests of the West India brigs. In this respect, the port of Havana had long been a favorite with the shipmasters of Maine. As early as 1826, over one-tenth of the total shipping tonnage to enter this harbor hailed from Maine. With the rapid increase in the sugar and molasses trade that occurred in the forties and fifties, Cuba turned more and more to Maine for her sugar boxes, molasses hogsheads, and tierces. The port of Portland quickly monopolized the shook trade and became a collecting center for transhipment. The shook was a package of red-oak staves and headings, numbered and ready to be assembled as a hogshead, cask, barrell, etc., when needed. They ranged in price from 50 cents to $1.50. Since the going rate was approximately 30 to 35 cents for the rough stock, shook makers such as James McKensey of Knightville and William D. Strout of Ferry Village, who could complete four or five sets a day, made a good day's wage.

Throughout this era, molasses was very cheap, bringing about fifty cents a gallon retail, and was therefore consumed in enormous quantities. A valuable derivative of molasses was raw brown sugar. This was known in the West India trade as "muscovado" and was produced by draining the molasses through holes in the bottom of the hogshead after crystallization had begun. Most of the muscovado came from Matanzas in hogsheads weighing about half a ton. Refinement of the raw brown sugar produced the luxury product, white sugar. It was usually marketed in a cone or loaf at a much higher price.

The process of refining sugar offered relatively high profits, and the Portland merchant, John Bundy Brown, with this in mind, constructed in 1845 what was probably the third sugar house to be built in the United States. Over a period of time he developed an efficient process that produced a high quality granulated sugar. His famous Portland Sugar House was eight stories high and consumed 30,000 hogsheads of molasses a year, with a daily output of 250 barrels of sugar.

The demands of Brown's Sugar House, coupled with the needs of the back country and other sugar refineries, soon made Portland a molasses port that was a close rival of New York. The national total in 1860 was 31,000,000 gallons, with New York in first place with 8,500,000. In second place was Portland with a total of 5,700,000 gallons. Unfortunately these prosperous times were not destined to survive the Civil War.

As early as 1853 there were signs of commercial disaster. In 1857, a financial panic struck the United States that was followed by several years of calamitous depression. The economic dislocation was partly American and partly European in origin. During the fifties, the United States experienced a period of tremendous economic expansion. The productive capabilities of the nation's economy had been greatly expanded in all fields; in industry, in transportation, in agriculture and in shipping. To a large degree, these capabilities had been very much overexpanded; that is, the economy now produced far more of everything than the country could use. The business, or the demand, to sustain the enlarged facilities simply did not exist.

Never, since the days of the embargo, had the port of Portland presented so depressing a picture. Many ships literally rotted at the dock. These were the vessels that had, such a short time before, been busily loading and unloading cargo for the West Indies and other distant ports. Freight, which had been scorned at sixty dollars a ton, was now almost impossible to obtain at ten. In various foreign ports local ships lay idle at anchor, hoping for cargoes that would at least pay their expenses home.

These difficult days were soon followed by another disaster, the Civil War. The heavy toll of shipping, even though greatly overrated, exacted by such Confederate commerce raiders as the *Florida, Alabama, Tallahassee,* and *Shenandoah,* produced futher suffering and distress. These losses precipitated a "flight from the flag" of extraordinary proportions. For every vessel of the United States destroyed by the rebels, eight others were lost through transfer to foreign registry. All told, approximately 1,613 vessels or 774,000 tons of shipping were "sold foreign."

Those great and beautiful sailing vessels, the full-rigged ships and barks which had been the pride of the old merchant marine and the backbone of foreign trade, were the hardest hit. After the rebellion had been crushed and the seas were free of Confederate raiders, Congress acted in behalf of the shipbuilders and forbade the return of these now foreign vessels to American registry.

In addition to these disasters, there was the phenomenal growth of steam navigation. The age of steam had arrived and with it the eclipse of the great age of sail. As the nineteenth century drew to a close, the activities of the port of Porland were so altered in character as to abruptly terminate the maritime significance of Cape Elizabeth's northern villages. Even through the coasting trade and foreign voyages were to some extent revived, the great seafaring generation was past. The days when over thirty shipmasters called Ferry Village their "home port" was now a matter of history. This village, and the others like it, became, instead, quiet suburban communities with the call of

Seaward side of Cape Cottage Casino showing piazzas added in 1899. Circa 1900.

View of the Cape Theatre, photographed by H. A. Roberts of Portland, 24 June 1899.

Fort Preble, showing Rodman-gun emplacements facing Simonton's Cove. Circa 1865.

Ten-inch disappearing gun in process of being reloaded, Battery DeHart, Fort Williams. Circa 1912.

the sea being answered primarily by humble fisher-folk and coasting skippers. Truly, the great age of sail had given way to a much less colorful and more prosaic way of life.

II

Far less spectacular but just as vital in its own way to the maritime economy of Cape Elizabeth and the port of Portland were the fisheries. After the decade of the Revolution many returned to the old way of life of farming and fishing by turn to sustain them. The observations of J. A. Carnes in 1857 reveal a situation that had existed for more than a hundred years and would continue throughout the nineteenth century. He accurately noted that:

> . . . the fisherman here at Cape Elizabeth is not only a fisherman, but at the same time a farmer, for he cultivates his patch of ground, he drives his "team a-field," at the proper season, plants his seed for vegetables, etc.; and when the time arrives for fishing, he either takes his rod and line, and from the rocks that bound his shores, angles for "cunners," (as they call them at the Cape, or in our cities better known as perch,) which frequent all the little basins or inlets, or, if the weather be favorable, he launches his wherry, or flat-bottomed boat, and, going a mile or so from the land, throws his heavy lead into the deep, and afterwards, with his tiny boat almost filled to the thwarts with cod, haddock, hake, &c., pulls to shore with his treasure from the sea, and often realizes from the sale of his fish, caught in a very few hours, sufficient for the support of himself and family perhaps for a month or more. Thus among these industrious and contented people there is no such thing as abject proverty, so often found in our great cities. . .

In addition to such part-time activities the commercial fishery attracted many of the hardier seafarers of the Cape. The Treaty of Paris that ended the American Revolution secured to the fishermen, largely through the efforts of John Adams, their immemorial right to take fish anywhere in the sea where they "used any time heretofore to fish." Encouraged by this, fishermen once again began to frequent the Grand Banks, and, by 1790, despite their lack of money and equipment, re-established a large proportion of their former prosperity.

The loss of the British West Indies was partially compensated for by Federal assistance. In 1789 Congress passed an act that provided a bounty of five cents per quintal on dried or salted fish exported from the United States. At the same time a duty of fifty cents per quintal was levied on imported fish. Three years later the law was altered, granting a bounty to vessels employed in the cod fishery. The annual rates were: one dollar per ton for vessels between five and twenty tons, one dollar and fifty cents for those between twenty and thirty, two dollars and fifty cents for vessels in excess of thirty tons. The maximum grant for any calendar year was fixed at one hundred and seventy dollars.

The bounty was applicable only through the four months when the cod fishery was at its most active stage. The vessels were required to be actually engaged in fishing, within a certain distance of the land, for a total of one hundred and twenty days, and to be adequately equipped. The shoresman was also required to make an oath as to the amount of fish each vessel landed for curing.

The primary reason for confining the bounty to the cod fishery was quite simply that this was the most valuable fish, not only for domestic markets but export as well, and could be obtained in large quantities only at a great distance, thus necessitating larger vessels with rather elaborate outfits. The heavier species of cod, averaging two and a half or three feet in length, and weighing from thirty to fifty pounds were generally taken by "going over the bay", i. e. from the Bay of Fundy, Bay of Chaleur, Seal Island, Grounds off Cape Sable, Straits of Belle Isle, Grand Banks of Newfoundland, George's Banks, Straits of Labrador, LeHarve Banks, Bar Quereau, and the coast of Labrador. These banks or grounds were shoal places, rising gradually from the ocean depth, many far beyond the sight of land, with a great fluctuation in depth from one to fifty-six fathoms. The largest fish were taken on the Grand Bank. The Labrador fish were smaller, not much larger than a haddock. Generally, the deeper the water the larger the fish.

Early in the nineteenth century, to outfit a vessel for a "vyge" to these distant ground, required an expenditure of from eight hundred to fifteen hundred dollars in proportion to the size of the vessel, the number of crewmen, and the distance to be traveled. Fishing the grounds closer "in-shore," such as Matinicus, Sou' Sou' West, Spot of Rocks, Saturday Night Ledge, Kettle Bottom, Cashe's Ledge, Sagadahoc, Mistaken Ground, and New Ledge, was less expensive.

Most of the fishermen existed in very modest circumstances "poor, yet making many rich," as one author described it. The initial expenses of a voyage were met in a variety of ways. Often, some affluent local merchant would either furnish the necessary gear or would extend credit based upon the anticipated profits of the voyage. One common method was to outfit "at the fifths." The owner or owners would supply one-fifth of the salt, provisions, lines, nets, bait, etc. and receive in return one-fifth of the total catch. The crew furnished the other four-fifths of the outfit and received that proportion of the proceeds. Each man's share was based upon the number of fish he caught. Not only was it profitable to be "handy with a line," but to be known as the "high-liner" (i.e. catch the largest number of fish) was a great honor indeed. Each man was also responsible for his personal "kit", which usually included warm clothing, "monkey-jacket" (pilot-cloth peacoat), thigh-length boots, a barvel (leather apron), lines and knives. The skipper, who provided his own charts, log book, quills and ink, and was responsible for navigation, received as extra compensation every sixty-fourth quintal. Also, the "salter," whose status was roughly that of first-mate, was given a barvel and a pair of boots as an indication of his special value. Another valuable member of the crew was the cook who had the distinction of being the only one to receive monthly wages. Occasionally, if his duties permitted, he also fished, and his wages were less. If he was a good cook, no deduction was made, and he could indulge his fishing talents to the fullest.

Between 1797 and 1807, the tonnage of fishing vessels hailing from the port of Portland reached a maximum of about 2,927 tons. This growth was terminated by the embargo era and "Mr. Madison's War." After the war, recovery was agonizingly slow. Under the terms of the Anglo-American Convention of 1818, fishing in Canadian waters by American fishermen was sharply restricted. To partially mitigate these curtailments, Congress increased the bounty rates, continuing them for a considerable portion of the nineteenth century.

In this era Simonton's Cove and Seal Cove had the most active fishing fleets at the Cape. Some of the vessels were owned in Portland, but many were the property of several individuals who fished on shares. One of the most fruitful, and largely unsuspected, primary sources that provide a wealth of detail as to the lives of these fishermen, and the vessels they sailed, are the books of the Rev. Elijah Kellogg, Jr. His series on Casco Bay, altough written for a juvenile audience, are filled with data and descriptions based on his own recollections and observations, as well as those of his father. Coming to Portland in 1787 as pastor of the Second Parish Church, the Rev. Elijah Kellogg, Sr., occupied a prominent position in the community until his death in 1842 at the age of eighty-one. The author, having been born in 1813 and spending much of his adult life in the Harpswell area, had a close personal contact with the way of life he so clearly portrays. Using Kellogg's books as source material it is relatively easy to piece together and reconstruct a picture of the men, vessels, and activities, indigenous to the fisheries.

Between the Revolution and the War of 1812, little if any change was evident in the various types of fishing vessels. The ships that frequented Canadian waters and the Banks were barrel-bottomed schooners, a far cry from the sleek Gloucester boats of a later day. Two early types were the Chebacco boat and the Dogbody.

The Chebacco derived its name, Indian in origin, from a parish in the present town of Essex, Massachusetts. They were seldom over forty feet in length but were considered excellent sea boats. Generally, they were buff in the bow, with neither bowsprit nor jib, carried two stout masts stepped well forward, and had a high, sharp, pink stern. The stem came up about two feet above the deck with a mortise and truck in the top to facilitate hauling in the anchor cable. Beside the stem was a plank with a space between it and the stem to receive the cable when the boat lay at anchor.

At the stern, a small area was decked over and equipped with a hatch to serve as the salt-locker. Immediately forward was a standing-space eighteen inches wide running athwart-ship with the decking almost resting on the ballast. Next came a large kid (pen), into which the fisherman threw his catch. Forward of the kid was the hold, decked over with a hatch directly aft of the main-mast, where the fish could be sorted and salted after being headed, cleaned, and split. Just ahead of the hatch was another kid and standing space. In the bow was the cuddy, a tiny cabin, with the over-head a mere nine inches above the level of the gunnel. Here were located four narrow berths and lockers; and a fireplace with a brick or plastered-over wooden chimney.

Hatches covered the standing spaces, and kids effectively blocking access to the cuddy as well as the salt-locker. When thus battened down, in rough weather, the gaff-rigged sails closely reefed, and a good hand at the tiller, the Chebacco "would live, go safe, and beat off a lee shore."

The Dogbody was almost identical to the Chebacco except that it had a square stern rather than a pink-stern. Both were often classified, by the rig, as cat-schooners.

Among the fishermen, the Chebacco and Dogbody were

much favored until the decade of the 1820's. At that time, they were gradually replaced by the "full-rigged" jigger and that great "work-horse" of the fisheries, the famous Pinky. Until the early fifties it led the field in popularity and was built in a vast variety of sizes ranging from twenty to one hundred tons. The hull was very full in the bow, very sharp aft, deep, and of substantial beam. Thus it was, that in heavy weather they could scud handily to windward or ride easily at anchor in rough seas.

The Pinky was equipped with a simple schooner rig. The bowsprit was carried high to prevent fouling the anchor cable when riding out a heavy sea. The timbers were sharply gathered in at the stern, extending well beyond the sternpost, terminating in a high peak. This pecularity was the source of the name Pinky. The overhang at the stern served as a support for the boom when the vessel was not underway, and, being open at the bottom, functioned as a convenient, if somewhat breezy, "comfort station" for the men. When sailing deeply laden, this sharp stern slipped easily through the water and was especially safe in a following sea. As Kellogg describes it, the Pinky "steered like a pilot boat, and did not leave a wake bigger than a shad."

The interior arrangement of a Pinky was not unlike the Chebacco boat and involved an ingenious utilization of all available space. Immediately beneath the limited deck space at the stern was the salt-locker. A hatch was placed below the tiller to ship the salt, sometimes as much as sixty hogsheads, and a sliding door admitted the salt to the hold for the use of the "salter." Forward was the cuddy, comewhat more commodious than that of the Chebacco. Between the cuddy and the well-deck was a locker for the storage of fire wood, supplies, and spare gear. Within the cuddy, berths were placed along the sides two tier high, four to a side with berths across the forward end. The space beneath the lower berths served as lockers for provisions and personal effects. The foremast was in the center of the cuddy. Built around it was a small circular table that could be slid up the mast and buttoned to the overhead when not in use. Detachable legs were also used in rough weather to steady it down. Holes were occasionally cut in the table to hold dishes and bowls; otherwise every man took his food or mug in his hands, bracing himself at best he could. The space around the table was narrow enough to utilize the berths, as improvised settles, with the skipper occupying a seat of honor forward. On his right, sat the salter. Frequently, a plank was placed athwart-ship between the after berths as additional seating space. The mess-gear consisted of simple plates, mugs, pannikins, knives, forks, and spoons.

On the starboard side of the cuddy, between the berths and hatch, was a small brick firepalce. An iron bar was built into it to support a multi-purpose iron pot. A flat-bottom iron kettle with a flat cover served as a Dutch oven. Suspended over the fire with coals heaped on the cover biscuits, pies, meat, and beans could be baked in it. An iron tea pot was also standard equipment.

The basic diet consisted of fish, beans, potatoes, salt pork, salt beef, corn and barley meal, molasses, rum, and tea brewed so strongly that "it would bear a flatiron." Occasionally, luxuries such as cheese, butter, wheat flour, onions, and a bottle of pearlash for shortening, would be included in the larder. Among the dishes favored by the fishermen were the harslet of porpoise fried with onions, and Indian bannocks (small cakes of baked corn meal), cod head stew, corned halibut napes and fins, fried porpoise steaks with onions, smoked halibut, mackerel, or herring, duck or goose stew, fried cod tongues, pork steak fried with onions, stewed beef, hash, and baked or stewed beans. If they touched at any of the bird islands or the coasts of Newfoundland and Labrador, the fishermen would collect bird's eggs or barter a leg of mutton. A special treat was "scourer", made by boiling corn meal with salt pork, and eaten with molasses.

The deck plan of a Pinky was designed to facilitate, as much as possible, the task of fishing. Along both sides of the vessel were the kids with space between each one for a man to stand and fish. Cleats were fastened to the deck between the kids to provide the men with a firm footing once the fishing began. Immediately adacent to the centrally located main hatch was a large kid running athwart-ship. At the end of each day's fishing the men would transfer their catch to this kid with the number of fish caught by each man carefully recorded by the captain.

The method of fishing to be employed was quite different on each bank or ground. On the coast of Labrador a vessel could anchor in the easy waters of a bay or inlet. The vessels could be anchored on the Grand Bank of Newfoundland and in the Bay of Chaleur but the seas were considerably rougher. On the Seal Island Ground and in the Bay of Fundy, they were forced to drift. In such circumstances the fore sheet was eased off, the mainsail guyed out, and the helm put down, thus enabling the vessel to draft lee bow to the tide. The men could only fish from the weather side with half the usual crew unemployed as their lines would be carried beneath the vessel. Needless to say a far larger catch could be obtained at anchor.

The hazards encountered in fishing were many and varied. Tides that ran with the force of a great river, violent gales or storms, heavy breaking seas in shoal waters, icebergs, and collisions in the shipping lanes, were common dangers. To succeed under such adverse conditions the captain of a fishing vessel had to have prudence, resolution, good judgement, and a thorough knowledge of the tides, currents, shoals, rocks, habits and feeding-grounds of the fish, and the bait most attractive to them, if he was going to obtain a full fare of fish.

Once the desired grounds had been reached and the "killick" let go with plenty of cable, preparations were made for fishing. The main boom was placed on the top of the "pink", where a groove had been made to receive and hold it, the sheet hauled down, with the balance of the sail reefed as taut as possible. With the helm lashed amidships, the vessel would lie easy in the water. The foresail was completely furled, the gaff lashed to the boom, and the boom tightly lashed to a large pair of wooden tongs fastened to the cleats on the deck, to prevent its slatting and to keep the sail clean. Next, a barrel of salted clams was opened, lines and gaffs broken out, and "killers" or short clubs distributed so that the men could quickly dispatch the thrashing fish as they came aboard. This was followed by "chalking for berths," i.e., drawing lots for the best fishing stations between the kids. The captain had first choice and usually selected a place midship as this was considered the best spot for fishing. After that, the men took their places according to lot, the least desirable being the two forward berths.

At the end of the day, with the catch concentrated in the large kid amidship, the task of dressing and salting got under way. Still wearing the calf-skin barvels that enveloped them from chest to knees, and thigh length boots that effectively excluded water and gurry, the men took up their new stations. At least seven men were required to make up a proper "dress gang." Boards were laid on the midship kid to form cutting tables. Generally, the "throater" began the process by opening up the fish, making a deep cut at the neck, and removing the tongue if the fish was a cod. Next the "header" broke off the head, removing the entrails but saving cod livers for oil, and passing the fish on to the "splitter," usually the captain, who cut away the backbone and than tossed the now completely dressed fish into the hold. Assisting in the process was the "idler" who kept the "throater" supplied, removing the debris, and packing the livers and tongues. Once the operation began a steady stream of fish poured down the hatchway to the "Salter" who, assisted by the cook, carefully piled them, skin down, alternating napes and tails, and constantly sprinkling the proper amount of salt over them.

In addition to cod, halibut were occasionally caught, weighing upwards of two hundred pounds. They were cleaned, dressed, cut into strips, and salted with the rest. The strips were later dried or smoked and then divided among the crew. Also, when hake were caught, the livers were saved and lamp oil rendered from them. Herring, when encountered, were taken in nets from the stern of the vessel and cut up for bait. When the men were fishing, mackerel were often attracted by the bait that washed from the hooks. They were easily caught in large numbers to be eaten by the crew, cut up for bait, or salted down with the rest of the catch.

Once loaded, the vessel returned to port and landed the cargo at a flake-yard for proper curing. Shortly thereafter, the profits of the voyage were distributed. After reducing the catch to dollars and cents, the captain's share was deducted, plus the cost of salt, provisions, gear, etc., and the wages of the cook. The remainder was then divided among the crewmen with each man's share based on the total number of fish he caught. The government bounty due each crew was paid out at the Portland Custom House each year usually in January.

It was not uncommon for the fishermen to bring home small cargoes of fish for their own consumption. The cod tongues, halibut strips, hake livers, mackerel, and haddock were not the only items brought home from the banks. Also in great favor were the backbone of sharks for the making of canes, Gut-of-Canso whetstones from the Bay of Chaleur, bird's eggs, the nose of a sturgeon for the center of a ball to give it bounce, and sea duck feathers.

Another enlightening source of information of the fisheries is an entertaining little book written by Captain Benjamin J. Willard, a life time resident of the Simonton's Cove area. Born in 1828, he went to sea at the age of eight. In the spring of 1838, he shipped out in his father's Pinky, the *Lively*, fishing the in-shore grounds. Three years later, he was again at sea, this time in another Pinky owned by his father, the *Martha Washington*. On this voyage he caught what must have been a record cod on the Mistaken Ground. With the assistance of other crewmen, the fish was landed and was estimated to weigh 130 pounds. When cleaned and dried, its weight was a remarkable seventy-five pounds.

In addition to voyages to the banks, Willard also fished for cod throughout the Casco Bay region. One of his favorite spots was Trundy's Reef where cod could be found in great quantity when the Alewives were running up the brook to Great Pond. In addition, he fished for lobsters along the Cape shore, selling his catch to a smack that made regular trips from Boston to Portland during the summer.

The summer of 1844 found Willard fishing for himself in a large Hampton boat, a gift from his father. In this very able boat, he fished the White Head Ground and Drunken Ledge for cod. With James Cobb as a partner, Willard landed large quantities of mackerel during the months of August and September. Using a mackerel jig, i.e. a small hook with its shank enclosed in a sinker of lead, they occasionally made an unusual catch; for example, they once took aboard about 1,400 pounds of mackerel between daylight and noon off Hue and Cry Shoal.

The mackerel fishery was uncertain indeed with years of plenty alternating with years of famine. Appearing from some unknown source early in April just south of Cape Hatteras and moving leisurely northward along the coast in May and June mackerel could usually be found off the Delaware Capes and in the area off Cape Ann. Through July and August, they congregated along the coast of Maine and in the Bay of Fundy. During September and October, the schools frequented the Bay of Chaleur. Late in the fall, they returned southward with the fishermen pursuing them as far as Cape Ann or the Nantucket Shoals.

Not only were the mackerel taken with the jig, but the older method of "chumming" was commonly used. Placing fish scraps, menhaden, porgies, clams, or gurry in a "bait-mill", i.e. a box with a revolving shaft, to which short knife blades were attached, running through it and working between other knives fastened to the bottom, a hash like mixture called "chum" was produced. Casting it over the surface of the water they would, if fortunate, "raise a school." When this occurred the water would literally boil with mackerel, and, by flinging their lines, with more chum, into the mass, they would catch the mackerel in great quantities until the school moved away.

Yet another method was known as "drailing." Lashing short

"drail-poles," with lines attached about a foot apart, at right angles to the side of the boat the fishermen, under close reefed sails, would move slowly along trolling for mackerel. The lines fastened to the "drailpole" had another tied to them running to the side of the boat so that they might be hauled inboard to remove the fish without unshipping the "drail-pole." Baited hooks, jigs, and chum were all utilized when fishing by this effective but rather slow method.

Once the fish had been taken aboard they were dressed, salted, and barreled, with each man marking the barrels that contained his catch. The year 1831 was probably the banner year for the old-time mackerel fishery. In that year alone, approximately 186,548 barrels were landed by the fishermen of Maine. This record was not exceeded until late in the century when the purse seine had replaced the old hand-line methods. In these early years, the best fishing grounds were the waters around Cape Elizabeth, Casco Bay, Seguin, Matinicus Rock, Monhegan Island, and Mount Desert Rock. An indication of the activity that prevaded this branch of the fisheries is revealed in Sylvester B. Beckett's *Portland Book for 1850-51*. Under the heading 21 October, 1849 he notes that "a fleet of three hundred vessels was seen off our harbor from the Observatory today, catching mackerel. To the naked eye, they presented the appearance of an immense city."

About 1865, the purse seine made its appearance on the coast of Maine and quickly revolutionized the mackerel fishery. By the eighties the purse seines commonly used were upwards to 1,300 or 1,400 feet in length and about thirty feet deep. They had cork floats attached along the top to keep the edge on the surface with lead weights along the bottom, thus producing a wall net. Around the bottom edge, rings were fastened with a purse line running through them. When a school was encircled with a net, the purse line was hauled up tight like a pucker-string, shutting the bottom of the net and effectively trapping the fish. Under ideal conditions as many as seven hundred barrels of mackerel might be taken in this manner. With such large quantities, it was usually necessary to transfer the fish to a "bag net," lashed alongside the boat until they could be dressed and salted.

A variation of the purse seine, the gill-net, made its appearance in this same era. As the name implies, the small mesh of the net ensnared the fish at the gills. These walls of net were set when the schools were present and hauled once a day often with spectacular results.

It should also be noted that the purse seine greatly expanded the herring industry. As the nineteenth century advanced, the sardine-packing business launched in the eastern part of the state spread to the port of Portland and proved to be remarkably profitable.

Late in the fifties, the cod fishery also experienced extensive changes. The Pinky, although it remained much in favor with the local fishermen until late in the century, was slowly replaced by larger fishing schooners. The early square-sterned models with short, high quarterdecks and known as "hell-tappers" gradually evolved into a type referred to as the "sharpshooter." The name was derived from their characteristic sharpness in deadrise and waterline.

This was the era when the banks became the haunt of the dory-fishermen. Each vessel carried up to fifteen dories nested in stacks on deck. When the grounds were reached, the vessel anchored and the dories were launched. The fishermen quickly dispersed over the sea to commence operations. Generally, the men handled two lines apiece, each equipped with multiple hooks and a 3½ pound lead. With a line in each hand, they moved them slowly up and down within a few feet of the bottom. When a fish took the hook, he would quickly cleat the other line and haul in one or more codfish. After returning the rebaited hooks to the depths, cod would often be waiting on the other line. Thus it would go until the dory was full to capacity with upwards of 1,800 pounds of cod. At the end of the day, the schooner would run down the line of dories, picking them up with their day's catch. In fog, or when suddenly engulfed by storm, fishing could be a very difficult task. Under such conditions, the solitary fishermen had to rely on the skill and experience of their skipper, helping to guide him in with stentorian blasts from a conch shell.

An average trip to the banks lasted approximately ten weeks. Some of the more skillful skippers would "wet their salt", i.e. ship a cargo, in as little time as seven weeks. Many of the local skippers were referred to as "Sunday Keepers," that is they fished only Monday through Saturday. It should be noted that each working day was usually filled with as many as eighteen hours of dangerous, back-breaking toil. In the winter months, the extra hazard of darkness and cold added immeasurably to the routine perils of the deep.

Early in the sixties, hand-lines slowly gave way to tub-trawls on the banks and the in-shore grounds. Such trawls were heavy lines laid along the bottom with three foot ganglings bent on every six feet, a hook attached to the end of each one. An anchor and a buoy was fastened to both ends of the trawl. Usually, a dory carried two men and four to six tubs. Each tub carried a baited and carefully coiled trawl. When laying out the trawl the fisherman would work the dory slowly to leeward to keep the line straight and taut. After about an hour the trawl would be either under-run, i.e. pulled across the dory, the fish removed, and paid-out again, or taken in and re-coiled in the tubs after removing the fish. These methods, although well adapted to the offshore banks, were utilized by local fishermen on the inshore grounds. As the nineteenth century began to wane, most of the men continued to fish the inner banks in the old manner frequently shipping out in Pinkys or small schooners and using the hand-line.

One product of the inner banks that sustained many a fisherman in this period was the haddock. In earlier days this fish had been considered something of a nuisance and either thrown back or set aside for the use of the crewmen and their families. However, in the seventies, "finnan haddie" became very popular, thereby providing a market for freshly caught haddock. The tub-trawl proved to be well suited for the taking of large quantities on the inner grounds. Such fish, known as "shore haddock" were considered a superior variety. Much of the fishing was carried on during the winter months with the "haddockers" making short runs of approximately twenty-four hours. As haddock was now more popular and brought a higher price than cod, these cruises were endured for many years.

In the eighties, the firm of Lewis, Chase, and Whitten maintained a flourishing trade in fish on the southern edge of Simonton's Cove. They had erected extensive fish houses and flakes in 1884, closely supervised by the selectmen who by tradition regulated the use of such tidal frontage. According to the *Portland Board of Trade Journal*, this firm was very active keeping a fleet of seven vessels constantly engaged in the cod fishery. In 1888 their flake-yard covered three acres, and that year they cured 15,000 quintals of cod. During the height of the season, they employed as many as twenty men in curing and packing fish for market. The name Gurry Cove, so frequently used in the nineteenth century to denote what is now Willard Beach, and was earlier Simonton's Cove, is an indication of its extensive envolvement in the fisheries. The word "gurry" is an old term meaning fish offal or refuse. It must have existed in great quantities to warrant its use as a name for so large a cove.

An interesting footnote relative to the fisheries at Cape Elizabeth involves historic Richmond's Island. For many years in the first half of the twentieth century, two brothers, George W. Jordan and Walter R. Jordan Jr., spent their summers fishing the adjacent waters. They lived in the ell of the old Cummings house and spent their days either lobstering or tending the pound they maintained on the southwest shore of the island. The pound angled out from the shore in a semi-circle a short distance south of the breakwater. Actually it was a wall of net supported on the surface by kegs and weighted on the bottom. It was situated in an ideal spot, effectively blocking a natural course fish followed in entering Richmond's Island Roads. Periodically the circle was closed, the nets hauled in and the catch loaded into dories. The fish were many and varied with mackerel, cod, and pollack predominating, although an occasional Atlantic salmon or horse-mackerel was taken. The Jordan brothers were forced to abandon their activities late in the forties due to the infirmities of old age.

The lobster fishery, for some reason, has never received the fulsome attention devoted to other branches. Ever since the early explorers and settlers learned from the Indians that the lobster was an extremely edible form of sea food, it has been a highly prized addition to the diet of many New Englanders. The first reference available relative to the lobster is to be found in Rosier's narrative of Weymouth's voyage to the coast of Maine in 1605. In this account he notes that "...towards night we drew with a small net of twenty fathoms very nigh the shore; we got about thirty very good and great lobsters...which I omit not to report, because it sheweth how great a profit the fishing would be..."

Although no lobster industry was forthcoming lobsters were, nevertheless, greatly enjoyed by the early coastal colonists as a delightful source of food. In 1638, John Josselyn, in his account of a voyage to New England, comments at some length on the plentiful supply of lobsters to be found in waters adjoining Cape Elizabeth. This continued to be the case for at least the first century of the colonial era. It was extremely easy to gather lobsters from tidal pools or spear and gaff them in shallow water. After many violent storms, great quantities of lobsters were thrown upon the beaches and gathered up by the colonists as fertilizer for their crops. From the scraps of evidence available the situation was not significantly altered until late in the eighteenth century.

In the years that followed the Revolutionary War, the shores of Cape Elizabeth and the shoal waters of Casco Bay were described as superior areas for the taking of lobsters. A limited market was available for the meat and for live lobsters, but problems of transportation precluded any possibility of expansion. The methods used in catching them in this early period reflected the great quantity available and the ease with which they could be taken. Until the second decade of the nineteenth century a hoop net was the most common device. Using an iron ring, or the wooden hoop from a hogshead, a hoop net approximately three feet in diameter would be fashioned. To this hoop was attached a net bag with an average depth of about two feet, with two wooden hoops or lines crossing at right angles twelve to fifteen inches above the center of the net or suspended from the point where the hoops crossed above. As there was no way of closing the mouth of the net, it had to be constantly watched. In this era, the average lobster weighed from five to fifteen pounds, with those of two pounds or less being thrown back as too small to be worth keeping.

About 1830, a lobster trap or "pot" made its appearance in the Casco Bay area and was quickly adopted as a valuable addition to the fishery. For the next fifty years, very few changes were made in the shape or form, of the trap. In this period lobster traps were usually four feet in length, two feet wide, and eighteen inches in height, with a semicylindrical shape. The framework of the bottom consisted of three strips of wood, often oak or hemlock, with a hole bored through each end to receive the hoop. The hoops were oak, ash, birch or hemlock branches bent to the required shape while green, with the bark left on. Three such hoops constituted the frame of the trap. To this frame were nailed ordinary house laths of spruce or pine, or hardwood withe-rods, with oak laths gradually introduced as the industry developed, about two inches apart. On the bottom were nailed heavy strips of oak or ash to serve as runners to protect the trap while resting on the ocean bottom. In each end of the trap a net funnel or "head" was placed as entry ways. These were knitted of two-strand manila twine and when finished were about a foot long tapering to a diameter of six inches. The mesh was approximately an inch square with an iron or wooden hoop inserted in the small inner end to keep it open. The heads were kept taut within the trap to provide an easy crawl-way for the lobster. At the top of the trap a door, three or four laths wide, running the full length, was built in with leather hinges and a cleat or button to keep it closed. In the center of the trap was a wooden or iron rod eight to twelve inches long extending upwards, with a large barb in the end, on which the bait was impaled. Several flat stones or bricks were fastened or built into the bottom as ballast to keep the trap from drifting.

From the very beginning, variations in the form of the trap were evident as the fishermen experimented or indulged their personal preferences. In some early types, the trap was upwards of seven and half feet in length with five frames set at equal distances apart. There were four heads, one attached to each frame except the center one and pointing inboard. As the lobster had to pass through two heads to reach the bait it was thought his chances of escape were much less. Also, a few traps were constructed from time to time with wooden heads carefully constructed of narrow laths. In addition, some square traps were built with an opening in the top but were generally found to be less successful than the standard type.

Various kinds of bait were used from the earliest days of the fishery. Most common were cod, hake, and halibut heads, along with sculpins, flounders and cunners. As time went on halibut heads led the list. Also, small mackerel and herring were used after being allowed to stand in brine for a few days. When "ripe" enough they were packed in small-mesh bait bags or slatted wooden bait boxes and secured in the trap.

Down to about 1860 it was customary to fish the traps individually. To each was fastened five to fifty fathoms of six thread "pot warp". This buoy line was usually attached with a clove-hitch to an end bow where it entered the bottom cross member. The buoy was often a testimonial to the individuality of the lobstermen. Fashioned in a variety of spindle shapes and painted with distinctive, contrasting colors, each man's buoy was clearly distinguishable from that of his competitor. About a third of the distance between the buoy and the trap a cork or bottle "floater" was bent on to keep the line from fouling on the bottom when the tide dropped.

Early in the decade of the sixties many fishermen began to fish their traps in large groups called a trawl or "ground line." As the lobsters gradually declined in number the trawls increased in size until in some instances as many as fifty traps would be involved. The traps were attached to one another with thirty feet or more of line, with a buoy at each end of the trawl. Under ideal circumstances a man could work along emptying and baiting one trap at a time without removing the entire string.

In the more popular fishing areas the trawl became something of a problem, with one lobsterman unknowingly laying his trawl across that of his neighbor. The results were frequently a spectacular snarl involving cut lines, heated altercations, and generous quantities of invective. When such circumstances developed, single traps or bull-trawls, i.e. two traps with one buoy, were the only alternative. Generally, the ledges, kelp beds, and shoal waters of Cape Elizabeth were not conducive to the use of large trawls.

Most of the lobster fishing was carried on from early spring to late fall. In this period the lobsters frequented the shallow inshore waters and with the pleasant weather of these months, fishing was rather easily pursued. During the winter months the lobsters had a tendency to move into the deeper water of the off-shore grounds or ledges. The winter fishery always attracted relatively few men except during the era of the great lobster canneries. The combination of bad weather and light catches prompted many lobstermen to haul up their gear or at least visit their traps two or three times a week rather than every day as was customary during the regular season.

In the area of Cape Elizabeth and adjoining waters a variety of sailing vessels were used, prior to the coming of the gasoline engine, in the lobster fishery. Small square-sterned sloops of from five to seven tons were often used, with the famous Friendship sloop predominating late in the century. Some of the smallest were little lapstreak, center board boats, sixteen to twenty-five feet long, with a gaff-rigged sail. The able Hampton boat proved to be immensely popular. Also found in great numbers were lapstreak dories and little double-ended rowboats. The former came in many sizes but the latter averaged fifteen to sixteen feet in length. The double-enders or "peapods" were frequently described as having a "rocker bottom" due to its well rounded sides, flat bottom, and slightly elevated ends. Although rowing was its common motive power a small sprit sail and center-board were standard equipment.

As early as 1830 well-smacks from Boston visited Cape Elizabeth to purchase the accumulated catch of the lobstermen. From spring until fall the smacks came with regularity increasing in number with each passing year. Between sales the local lobstermen kept their daily catches alive by storing them in large specially constructed, partially submerged crates called lobster-cars. The claws were carefully plugged to keep mayhem at a minimum. By 1846 the smackmen were paying the fishermen $4.00 per hundred lobsters. This was not altogether satisfactory and after prolonged negotiation the price became $1.12 per hundred pounds. In this period a lobsterman fishing approximately fifty traps could catch from 1,200 to 1,500 lobsters in about ten days.

Early in the decade of the forties the lobster canning process was introduced in Maine from Scotland, first at Eastport in 1843 and then at Harpswell six years later. A third cannery opened at Carver Harbor in 1851 and a fourth at Southwest Harbor in 1853. At most of the canneries lobsters were only part of the total pack, with sardines, clams, fish, vegetables, and fruits packed in season. Most of the canneries were built and operated by firms in Portland or Boston. At first the lobsters used for canning averaged in weight from three to ten pounds apiece. However, as transportation improved and demand for live lobsters grew the canneries took smaller and smaller ones until finally they were processing lobsters of a pound or less. Beginning in 1883 laws were passed establishing minimum sizes to preserve the fishery from extinction. Such laws were progressively strengthened and thereby greatly reduced canning activities. The decline was so rapid that the last lobster cannery closed its doors in 1895.

In the years that followed the Civil War the port of Portland quickly developed as an entrepot for the lobster fishery. Individual lobstermen from the Cape could now sell their catches directly to the fish merchants. By 1880 the total annual weight of lobsters landed at Portland reached 1,900,000 pounds and eighteen years later had increased to 6,145,821 pounds. Needless to say the lobster fishery had come of age.

As is often the case with natural resources the average citizen is apt to be a bit callous unless restrained by law. This proved to be the case with the lobster industry of Maine. In 1823 the first conservation law was passed by the state legislature prohibiting non-residents from fishing in Maine waters unless authorized by local town officials. This was in reality a re-application of a similar Massachusetts statute passed in 1812. Between 1823 and 1872 no attempt was made to limit the size or type of lobster taken or the method of catching them. The first real conservation effort was embodied in the law of 1872 that prohibited the keeping of "seed" or female lobsters. This law was replaced in 1874 by a new statute that established a closed season each year from 1 August to 15 October. In addition, it now became illegal to keep any lobster less than ten and a half inches in total length between 15 October and 1 April. The canning industry was then prohibited in 1883 from processing any lobster with an overall length of less than nine inches.

During the seventies and eighties minor alterations were made to existing statutes, but it was not until 1889 that seed lobsters were again protected. In 1895 a permanent year-round size limit of ten and a half inches overall was established by law. That same year a Maine coastal warden service was created to enforce the various regulatory laws.

The method of measuring lobsters remained unaltered until 1907 when a carapace measurement of four and three-quarters inches, from the end of the nose to the center rear of the body shell, was established as the minimum legal size. Eight years later the first licensing laws were passed and in the years that followed became increasingly exclusive.

In 1919 the current method of measuring a legal lobster was fixed by law. The minimum was three and a half inches from the eye socket straight along the center line to the rear of the body shell. A double-gauge lobster measure was instituted in 1933 on the assumption that large lobsters were desirable breeding stock and must therefore be preserved. The maximum measure was four and three-quarter inches. Between that date and the present time other adjustments have been made until now the double-gauge is a minimum of three and three-sixteenth inches and a maximum of five and three-sixteenth inches.

The twentieth century also saw some major changes in the methods employed within the lobster fishery. Generally speaking the techniques were unaltered but the equipment was somewhat improved. The introduction of the gasoline engine added mobility and efficiency. The lobsterpot, although basically the same, did undergo some refinements. Shortly after World War I the "parlor" or three head trap became common. Instead of an opening at either end, both ends were slatted across, and two openings made in the sides with the heads opposite one another. The third head was attached to the center frame and extended back into the trap. The number of "escapes" from this trap was much less than that of the two header and had the additional advantage of retaining the catch if the lobsterman was forced to miss a day in hauling his pots. A variation of the parlor trap that soon appeared was the flat or trapezoidal shape. They proved to be very popular in shoal water and had the desirable feature of being easily stacked or stored.

Although the Maine lobster, Homarus Americanus, may not be as plentiful as in earlier times, its popularity has not diminished. Today as in years gone by the lobstermen of Cape Elizabeth set their traps in the coastal waters. Essentially they are hardy and persevering fishermen utilizing techniques perfected or discovered by past generations. Aided by modern equipment they have expanded the industry far beyond the modest beginnings of a century ago. Most of the professional lobstermen are now located at Seal Cove. During the summer months they must compete with the suburban diletante whose nuisance value is exceeded only by his brashness. Fortunately, with stricter conservation and licensing statutes, the future belongs to the professional.

Somewhat less colorful than the lobster fishery but just as vital to the economy of the town for many years was the clamming industry. From the earliest of times many of Cape Elizabeth's sandy coves produced a rich and succulent harvest. Local market's consumed most of the annual take. The cod fishery alone absorbed hundreds of barrels of salted clams for bait each year. As an item in the diet of the local populance it was devoured in quantities equally as great. At best clam-digging was a cold, wet, back-breaking task, with its hours of employment governed by the tides. During the winter months it was comparable in discomfort to life in a dory on the banks. Many of the clam-diggers were lamed with rheumatism and arthritis by middle age, resulting from a prolonged exposure to cold and damp. The financial reward never fully compensated them for the hours of toil expended. In the fall of 1836 for example they refused to sell or dig unless an increase in prices was obtained. The *Portland Daily Press* lent its editorial support and a slight advance in earnings was granted to the chronically depressed diggers.

The coming of the summer visitor and the popularity of the shore dinner brought an increase in the consumption of clams. One very plentiful source was the Spurwink River estuary. The Scarborough clam as it was called, either shucked or in the shell, was a perennial favorite. Steamed-clams, clam-chowder, clam-fritters, and of course the expansive clam-bake, were a widely touted gourmand's delight.

One much-to-be-lamented consequence of the twentieth century surburban growth has been the exhaustion of the clam flats. In a rather belated attempt to protect this industry the town, in March 1899, voted "that people living out of this town be prohibited from digging clams during the year, and that we have a close time from the first day of September, provided that during said close time citizens of this town may dig clams for their own family use." Four years later the closed period was increased, beginning 1 April and ending 1 October. This continued in force until 1931 when it was voted to impose no closed period upon the citizens of Cape Elizabeth. The last such attempt at regulation was passed by the town in March 1936, after that date no further action was taken. Pollution and a complete lack of conservation principles have currently eliminated the local commercial clam-digger. In recent years the state has interceded in an attempt to resuscitate this valuable natural resource. Perhaps in the years to come citizens yet unborn will experience the enthusiasm of an earlier day for that delicious mollusk that could once be taken in uncounted millions from the tidal sands of Cape Elizabeth.

III.

From early colonial times, shipbuilding was an industry native to the coast of Maine. The first vessel to be built within the present limits of the United States was the thirty ton pinnace *Virginia* built by the Popham colonists near the mouth of the Kennebec River in 1607. As the settlements grew and spread along this "rocky, poverty compelling coast" it was only natural that men should turn to the sea and the building of ships.

The first ship to be built in Cape Elizabeth was apparently constructed at Richmond's Island. Although very little evidence exists to substantiate it, several competent historians are of the opinion that one George Richmond resided briefly on the island about 1620. During his short stay it is believed that he built a small vessel of some sort and then vanished from the scene. The only indication of his presence is the fact that the island now bears his name.

Later in the seventeenth century, during John Winter's tenancy at Richmond's Island, more definite shipbuilding activities were pursued. The Trelawney papers and Baxter manuscripts clearly reveal those pioneer efforts. In the spring of 1636 Winter made plans for the construction of a bark and requested that his employer, Robert Trelawny, ship out to him the necessary supplies. The timber was apparently cut locally but no work was commenced until the "chaine bolts, nails, spikes, tarr, and pitch" arrived from England. The bark, designated as the *Richmond*, was built during the winter of 1636-37 and launched fully rigged on the following tenth of June. A cargo of wine, oil, and earthenware was put aboard, and she sailed the 20th of June, under the command of Narias Hawkins, for Massachusetts Bay.

Despite the fact that this first venture was not an unqualified success, the *Richmond* continued to make frequent coasting voyages until 1639. During a cruise to Virginia in the summer of that year the stoutness of her construction was drastically tested. She was overtaken by a severe storm that heeled her over to such a degree that her ballast shifted and her main mast had to be cut away to right her. With a jury rig the *Richmond* returned successfully to the island, her cargo of Indian corn intact.

Late in 1639 the bark sailed for Plymouth, England with a cargo of pipe staves, and never returned. Her subsequent history is unrecorded, but it is known that she was confiscated by the government of Oliver Cromwell.

In 1640 preparations were advanced for the construction of a second and larger vessel at Richmond's Island. The plans were drawn by Trelawny's master builder Stephen Sargent. By July, the frame was up and partially planked. All of the timber had been cut and was stockpiled on the island. As far as can be ascertained, the ship was approximately fifty feet long at the keel and had a beam of eighteen and a half feet. She also had two decks, with four and a half feet between them, a forecastle and quarter-deck and a nine-foot depth of hold. This new vessel, referred to as a ship and also christened the *Richmond*, was launched 15 July, 1641.

A cargo of salt fish, traine, and fish peas was shipped while the carpenters were still completing their labors. She sailed later in the month for Bilbao, Spain under the command of Stephen Sargent and disappeared forever into the limbo of unrecorded history.

Very little maritime activity was discernable until the Indian Wars had passed and resettlement had been accomplished. In the second decade of the eighteenth century a re-awakening of commerce occurred and with it an increase in shipping. Practically no information survives as to the shipbuilding activities that were carried on throughout the eighteenth century. It can only be surmised that such men as Ezekiel Cushing and William Simonton constructed small vessels for their own use. Unverified local traditions identify Ship Cove, as a place where sloops, shallops, and small schooners were built prior to the Revolutionary War. In the remaining years of the century evidence seems to indicate that boats and various small vessels were constructed in the locality of what later became Ferry Village.

About 1810, Ezekiel Dyer, who resided on Thames Street in Portland with his son the master shipbuilder Lemuel Dyer, and who also operated a marine railway at Clay Cove, began in a very modest way to build ships near the ferry landing at Cape Elizabeth. Although he remained a resident of Portland it is known that he built three small vessels over a period of four years. In 1810 he launched the brig *Cordelia* of 185 tons. She must have been an able craft, for thirty-eight years later, despite two fires at sea and extensive rebuilding in 1837, she sailed on her ninetieth voyage to the West Indies. She was finally condemned in 1849 as no longer seaworthy, and broken up.

As previously noted, Dyer built and launched the famous *Dart* for Joseph Cross and others of Portland in July 1812. This vessel was followed by the schooner *Hound* of thirty-one tons which he launched late in 1813. These were apparently the extent of his shipbuilding efforts at Cape Elizabeth. Although the site was abandoned by Ezekiel Dyer, his family in later years established one of the most active shipyards to grace the port of Portland in the same section of Ferry Village.

Late in 1845 two prominent merchants of Portland, George Turner and James B. Cahoon, formed a partnership for the purpose of developing a shipbuilding center at Cape Elizabeth in the vicinity of Ferry Village. A contemporary observation that appeared in the *Eastern Argus* noted that "for twenty-six years the place has been entirely stationary, with hardly any indications of business vitality. During that whole period, we cannot ascertain that a single private residence has been erected." Within eighteen months the firm of Turner and Cahoon erected over twenty buildings. Close by the base of the Stanford Ledge Breakwater, facing the harbor, in the north-east corner of Ferry Village they established their shipyard, with George Turner and the master shipbuilder Benjamin W. Pickett, formerly of Newburyport, Massachusetts, in charge.

Pickett was thirty years old when he joined the firm, with over twenty years of shipbuilding experience behind him. He had been educated as a marine architect and draughtsman, quickly establishing a reputation as an expert in his field. While in Newburyport he had successfully operated a shipyard with his brother.

In addition to three sets of shipways and a long cobb-work dock for outfitting the completed vessels, the firm also constructed a shop and mould loft one hundred feet in length, a steam sawmill, and a machine shop equipped to produce chain-cable, hardware, and edged tools. Despite the fact that George Turner died very suddenly early in 1848, work at the yard did not falter but forged ahead under Pickett's direction.

The first vessel off the ways was the steam ferryboat *Elizabeth* of 147 tons. Launched on the 17th of June, 1848, she immediately began running between Ferry Village and Portland. Late in 1849, three vessels were launched. The first to take to the water was the ship *Caroline Dow* of 515 tons sliding down the ways on the 6th of November. She was shortly followed by the brig *Fortunio* of 202 tons, and on the 27th of December they were joined by the ship *George Turner* of 518 tons, named for the deceased partner. The *Fortunio*, incidentally, was the first vessel to sail from Portland around the Horn to California during the Gold Rush. After the completion of these three vessels, Benjamin W. Pickett purchased the yard from James B. Cahoon, then Mayor of Portland, and continued ship construction until 1868.

In 1850, Pickett constructed three more vessels that were an outstanding testimonial to his skill as a master shipbuilder. The first to be launched was the ship *Frank Johnson* of 529 tons. She entered the water at twelve noon on Saturday, the 30th of March, just seventy days after the laying of her keel, and was described as a "white oak ship." Closely following the *Frank Johnson* was the clipper bark *Jasper* of 300 tons. She was launched 5 October, 1850, fully rigged and coppered. According to the *Eastern Argus* she "slipped into the water with a curtsey that would have done credit to a French danseuse." The third ship of that year was the *Adonis* of 538 tons, also built of white oak. Her launching occurred on Saturday, 1 June, 1850.

The following year again witnessed three launchings at the Turner and Cahoon yard. The first off the ways was the copper-fastened, white oak bark *Parodi* of 528 tons on 17 March, 1851. The next launching occurred on the 18th of September and was the 160 ton schooner *Georgia*. The last vessel of the year was the largest that had been constructed in the district up to that time. This was the ship *Grecian* of 1150 tons described in contemporary newspaper accounts as a clipper and launched Saturday, 27 September, 1851. She sailed immediately for New York where she was quickly sold for $60,000. Shortly after the sale, the *Grecian* sailed for California.

Other vessels known to have been constructed by Pickett are the ship *Forest City*, 492 tons, in 1852; ship *Cumberland*, 1066 tons, in 1853; brig *Scotland*, 284 tons, in 1854; bark *Ellen Stevens*, 354 tons, in 1856; bark *Charles Edwin*, 344 tons, also in 1856; brig *Thomas Owen*, 289 tons, in 1860; bark *Hunter*, 396 tons, in 1862; brig *Mary N. Locke*, 312 tons, in 1863; bark *Arte-*

misia, 447 tons, in 1865; and the bark *Lizzie H. Jackson*, 504 tons, in 1866.

Although Pickett continued as a shipbuilder until 1868, his later efforts are obscure. In his declining years he was in the real-estate business at Ferry Village and represented Cape Elizabeth in the state legislature on various occasions. He died Monday, 28 December, 1891, at his residence on Front Street and was buried in Newburyport, Massachusetts.

It would be well before proceeding further to examine the shipbuilding scene of which Cape Elizabeth was an integral part. From the very beginning, the emphasis in the Portland area was on shipping rather than on ship construction. Despite this situation, the port of Portland made a very significant contribution to the shipbuilding supremacy of Maine. Many maritime historians believe that the state did not play a prominent role until after the clipper ships decade of the fifties. In the annual tabulalation of ships constructed, Maine took the national lead as early as 1820 when 27,705 tons of shipping, valued at slightly in excess of a million dollars, were built. From 1820 to the end of the age of merchant sail the state never abdicated its supremacy. For the next thirty-two years, the annual tonnage and total value quadrupled. Although it may have been partially true as pertaining to Cape Elizabeth, it was not the annual clipper ship boom that was responsible for Maine's lead in tonnage. This is indicated by the returns for 1849 before the boom period actually began. In that year, the state was in first place with 82,256 tons, New York was second, Pennsylvania third, and Massachusetts fourth.

The year 1854 was the height of the clipper ship era and was actually the last year that witnessed the frantic construction of such vessels primarily for speed. In that year, Maine produced 168,631 tons of new shipping or a total of 350 vessels, two-thirds of which were square-rigged. By comparison, the state built almost three times as much tonnage as New York and close to four times as much as Massachusetts. As revealed by an examination of the figures the supremacy of Maine as a shipbuilding center, in 1854, at the height of the construction boom, is indisputable. This overwhelming superiority was not an ephemeral oddity. Actually, it reflected a constant and sustained rate of growth that had been evident for decades.

After the clipper ship era and throughout the remaining years of the age of sail, shipbuilding was centered almost entirely in Maine and Massachusetts, with Maine increasing in national reputation until at the end of deep-water merchant sailing ship construction in the United States, it launched about seven-eighths of all square-riggers constructed in this country. The shipbuilders concentrated on the building of square-rigged ships designed to provide the maximum in economic operation and cargo space. The type of vessel that gradually evolved was the "Down Easter." They were fast, able, handy, three-masted, full-rigged ships, adapted to a small crew and capable of carrying large cargoes anywhere in the world. The "Down Easter" represents the disdain widely felt by Maine shipbuilders for the emotional, impractical, and unprofitable clipper ship type as well as its deep-seated trust in the practicality of sturdy, hardworking, unpretentious square-riggers. What they lacked in aesthetic qualities and "clouds of canvas" they more than compensated for in the counting house until they were displaced by the age of steam.

Generally speaking, the various shipyards at Cape Elizabeth exhibited standard ideas, methods, and materials common to Maine. This is attributable in part to their location and common source of supply. All of the yards in question were located on the southern shore of Fore River. They were protected from the sea by crib-work retaining walls pierced at intervals with openings called slips. At each slip, piling was driven to support the heavy bed timbers and the ways. In addition to the usual shops, lofts, and sheds, each yard usually had a large crib-work wharf for the fitting-out of vessels and the landing of supplies.

Most of the timber used in these yards was brought by ship or canal boat. Until early in the fifties native timber predominated with southern pine the only major exception. White ash was used for oars or sweeps, elm for keels, tamarack or juniper for knees, locust for treenails or thole pins, spruce for spars and joists, yellow pine for decking and planking, white pine for masts and large spars, and white oak for stem and stern pieces as well as frames. Most of the special hardware, sails, cordage, windlasses, anchors, capstans, oakum, billetheads, stern-pieces, and figure-heads were obtained from the shops of Portland.

The men who labored in these yards were quite generally skilled craftsmen. Much of the work was done by hand and required an expert, well experienced eye. Although they all worked together, each had his own particular job in which he was pre-eminent. An examination of the early directories reveals a great many men, residing in the northern villages of the town, engaged in various shipbuilding crafts such as shipwright, ship-carpenter, block-maker, rigger, caulker, shipsmith, sailmaker, boatbuilder, and shipjoiner. In the forties such skilled workers received a dollar a day with a gradual rise to $3.50 a day in the fifties. Apprentices, helpers, and ordinary laborers were compensated with a daily wage of seventy-five cents. The working day was usually long by modern standards, generally from dawn to dusk, well into the fifties when it was reduced to a flat ten hours. Breaks for breakfast and lunch never exceeded forty-five minutes.

The actual construction of the ship started with a half-model, lift-model, or plans, devised by the master shipbuilder. The half-model was fashioned from a solid block of wood and then sawn transversely at designated intervals to obtain the shape of the frames. The lift or water line model was cut longitudinally thereby permitting an accurate projection of the shape of the hull from the model to fullscale drawings on the mould loft floor. The technique of designing a vessel by half-models was no easier than using plans except perhaps that it required a little less experience to judge the lines when worked out in this manner. Ordinarily, a master shipbuilder, such as Benjamin Pickett, would construct the model and lay out the plans. Needless to say, as competition became more acute in the fifties the carefully executed model or plan was not widely circulated especially if the vessel was a great success.

After the half-model was completed, the next step was to "take off and lay down" the lines full size on the floor of the mould loft. As this was a difficult and very exacting undertaking, it was customarily performed personally by the master shipbuilder. With the completion of this task a complete set of plans showing the size, shape, and form of the frames, timbers, keel, stem, sternpost, and deck beams would be clearly laid out on the mould loft floor. This was followed by the construction of patterns or moulds from these lines that would be used in the actual building of the vessel. In many instances, the moulds were taken into the back country where the timber was carefully selected to fit, then cut, squared, shaped and numbered before being transported to the yard.

Once the timbers were on hand, the keel was laid upon the ways well blocked to provide space beneath for the ship carpenters to work on the hull. Generally, the keel was inclined slightly toward the water, about five-eighths of an inch to the foot, to facilitate the launching of the completed vessel. The keel was usually of well seasoned oak superimposed upon a false keel of elm. To his keel the oak sternpost and deadwood were now fastened with long iron bolts or wooden pins.

Next came the process of framing up. Fashioned in the exact shape called for by the moulds, each frame was worked into position on the keel and held by shoring timbers. This was followed by the placing of cant timbers to support the stern. Once the frames were in place and steadied by strips of temporary planking, the keelson was bolted to the keel. This was a massive timber that provided additional rigidity and longitudinal strength to the vessel. The long timbers such as side keelsons and bilge stringers were then added followed by the setting of the stern. This was actually a timber of three or more parts, built of the best white oak, held together with pins and firmly fastened to the keel so that together they formed one continuous piece. Next to be installed were the knightheads, bow cants, deck beams, figurehead or billethead, and scroll work.

Work now began on the outside of the hull. Men with adzes smoothed the timbers in preparation for planking. The plankers were specialists who through long experience could twist and bend the heavy planks to fit the curves of the vessel. It was hard, grueling work calling for men of great strength. To make the plank more workable it was frequently softened in a long steam box and then at the proper moment rushed, with the cry of "hot plank," to the hull to be forced tight against the frame by many hands. Below the water line the planks were held in place by locust treenails and above by treenails of oak. Iron or copper bolts and spikes were utilized only at the plank ends and butts. Once the planks were on, the caulkers followed along driving oakum into the seams and covering them with melted pitch or tar. Lastly, the shipjoiners smoothed the surface of the hull in preparation for painting.

While the planking was in progress, the decks were laid and caulked. Then the forecastle and cabins were built, rudder shipped, pumps, windlass, and anchors installed, and the masts frequently stepped. On many occasions, the ship was fully rigged and the sails bent on prior to launching. Also at this stage, the ship's boats were finished and shipped. The boatbuilders, such as Nathan Dyer, Thomas Simonton, Richard Lee, and George Soule, were men of rare talents. A ship's boats were often a matter of much pride and objects of widespread admiration.

With the vessel fully equipped and brightly painted, a day and hour for launching was set, usually at flood tide. Such an event was a gala occasion. The yard and the ship would be gay with bunting. People turned out in a holiday spirit. To the builder, a launching was relatively routine but requiring much forethought and careful planning. A master shipcarpenter was put in charge of the actual mechanics of the launch.

On top of long massive timbers that served as the ways were placed short timbers or slides fitted with flanges to hold them in place. The slides were built up to fit snugly against the bottom of the vessel. Beneath the top block and its lower neighbor, and between the lowest block and its upper neighbor, were inserted large wooden wedges. Purpose of the wedges was that as they were driven into each set of blocks, the ship would be lifted free of the bed timbers. The tops of the ways were heavily greased with tallow to facilitate an easy run for the slides.

Approximately half or three-quarters of an hour before high water, the master shipcarpenter and his crew would go beneath the vessel and, working forward from the stern, would split the blocks upon which the keel now lightly rested. As the men moved toward the bow, the settling of the ship completely on the slides would be accompanied by heavy creaks and rumbling groans. The gradual rending of timber and the first tremors of life along the keel would warn the men that it was time to leave. Slowly at first but with increased momentum, the vessel would start its smooth run down the ways. At the first sign of movement, the spectators would break into lusty cheers celebrating the birth of yet another "ocean queen." In the space of a moment, if all was well, the vessel would be safely afloat in her native element surrounded by floating blocks and restrained by heavy mooring lines firmly anchored to the shore, leaving only the smoking ways to mark her passage.

During the summer of 1850, another important shipyard was established on the southern shore of Fore River near Ferry Village and slightly west of the Turner and Cahoon yard.

Early in July, Joseph W. Dyer began the dismantling of his old yard at the foot of Mountfort Street in Portland. The filling in of the old waterfront and railway construction, plus the easy availability of shore-front at Ferry Village prompted the change. By September, Dyer had transferred most of his equipment and property to the Cape. The *Eastern Argus* noted on the 20th that he had recently laid the keel of a vessel of approximately 1000 tons. This was destined to be the ship *Corinthean* that Dyer would launch in August 1851.

This new Dyer yard was in reality the continuation of a family trade that had now entered its third generation. As mentioned earlier, Ezekiel Dyer, a native of Cape Elizabeth who moved to Portland in 1815, had constructed the *Dart* and other vessels early in the nineteenth century close by Ferry Village. His son, Lemuel, born at Cape Elizabeth in 1786, established with his father's aid a shipyard at what was then known as Clay Cove. Also in conjunction with his father, he built a marine railway slightly to the west of the cove, which became Ezekiel's responsibility. Between 1808 and 1824, Lemuel had six sons all of whom subsequently became involved in shipbuilding. Early in the forties, his third son, Joseph W., who had been born in 1814, established a shipyard at the foot of Mountfort Street not far from his father's home on the north-east corner of what is now Fore and India Streets. After the death of Lemuel in 1847 from the blow of an axe while cutting ship timber in Hiram, his grandfather Ezekiel having died in 1839, Joseph continued in business alone. He was undoubtedly assisted by other members of the Dyer family for in this period there were twenty men of that name resident in Portland in the immediate vicinity of his yard who were listed in the directories as shipcarpenters. In addition, the family also included six boatbuilders, plus a shipwright, a shipjoiner, and a naval architect. With such talent at his disposal, Joseph W. Dyer certainly had no difficulty in obtaining skilled practitioners in the art of shipbuilding. Although he transferred his yard to Ferry Village, Joseph continued to reside in Portland.

The first vessel to be launched from the new Dyer yard at Cape Elizabeth was the ship *Corinthean*, 1098 tons, slipping from ways, fully rigged, on Friday, 29 August, 1851. The *Eastern Argus* described the ship in glowing terms.

> ... she is constructed of the best of pasture white oak, has a frame of extraordinary strength, is square fastened and that in the heaviest and most substantial manner, and as to excellence of model is pronounced by by nautical men to be second to none built in this district.
>
> In her internal arrangement, her accomodations for her crew, her steward's department, her passenger's quarters, etc., advantage has been taken of all the acknowledged and tried improvements of the day. Her cabin is an elegant room with doors and panels of polished branch mahogany and rosewood with pilasters of the same materials, having gilded capitals, and is furnished with carpets, sofas, and other furniture in keeping; and those conversant with such matters say it would be difficult to designate a point where she could be improved.
>
> She is 172 feet 9 inches in length, 37 feet 3 inches in breadth, and 19 feet 7½ inches in depth, and of course tons, 1098 34/95ths.
>
> The doors, panels, and cabinet work in her cabins were furnished by Mr. Walter Corey of this city."

She has cleared for New Orleans with a full complement of passengers and now lies, waiting a wind, in the harbor. May she prove a source of prosperity to her enterprising builder and owners.

The maiden voyage of the *Corinthean* to New Orleans was accomplished in the rather good time of eleven days. She quickly proved, according to subsequent reports, a profitable investment for her owners, "the heirs of Lemuel Dyer."

Two years later in 1853, Joseph W. Dyer launched two sturdy barks and one of the most beautiful ships ever built in the port of Portland. On Saturday, 15 January, the bark *Faith*, 300 tons, left the ways, followed shortly by the *Macon* of 325 tons. Late in the year, on Thursday, 3 November, the ship *Portland*, 998 tons, with the lines of a clipper was launched. According to the *Eastern Argus* it was a major event:

> ...witnessed by several hundreds of our citizens who went over to Cape Elizabeth for that purpose, besides hundreds more who stood on our wharfs or occupied the roofs of the buildings. It was a beautiful and most successful launch. She slid down the ways easily, dropped her stern gracefully in to the water, and moved swiftly off eastward. She then made a curve and sailed up the harbor. The Portland is of an elegant model, and we think will prove to be one of the handsomest and staunchest ships ever build by Joseph W. Dyer. That is, we know, saying not a little, for there are no better crafts built anywhere than such as come from his yard. In that respect, he fully sustains the reputation of his venerated father....

This lovely ship was built for the Portland merchants Nathaniel F. Deering and Jacob McLellan. Unfortunately, her subsequent career and fate is now unknown.

Despite the fact that he launched but one vessel in 1854, it was in many respects a memorable incident. During the summer, the bark *White Sea*, 577 tons, entered the water of Portland Harbor with the usual crowd of spectators on hand. Among the spectators was the New York artist John W. Hill who sketched the entire scene in minute detail. The sketch was later reproduced by Charles Parson, a famous lithographer, and published by the New York firm of Smith Brothers and Company in 1855. The print is an extraordinary study of Portland Harbor. In the foreground is the bark *White Sea* resting on the ways just prior to launching. Standing just off-shore writing for the bark is the steam tug *Tiger* of 58 tons built in 1851 at Philadelphia for William Willard. She was the first propellor tug in Portland and was operated by Willard until late in the century. Further to the right is the steam ferry *Elizabeth*, built by Turner and Cahoon. Far along near shore to the right is the yard of Benjamin W. Pickett. Off to the distant left is the old Portland Bridge. Generally speaking it is one of the finest portraits of Portland Harbor ever done. The print, produced in 1855, was an instant local success and is today a highly cherished bit of Portlandiana.

Although Dyer was appointed a U.S. Inspector of Steamboat Hulls in 1852, a post he held the rest of his life, he continued to be actively engaged in shipbuilding until he died 19 November, 1883. In 1855, he built the ship *Kate Dyer*, 1278 tons, and launched her late in December. She was built by the Dyer family and sailed under the command of Joseph's younger brother, Ansel. Her life was unfortunately brief for she sank in November, 1866, as the result of a collision off Fire Island, New York. The *Eastern Argus* described the *Kate Dyer* as "massively timbered, and heavily bolted and braced . . . beautifully proportioned . . . Her finish is in accordance with her size and strength. The cabin is like the drawing room of a palace."

The following year, Dyer built the ship *Bamberg*, 1119 tons. Other vessels were constructed in this period but no record thereof now exists. However, it is known that during this period his relatives Nathan Dyer and Nathan R. Dyer, both boatbuilders, became associated with him. Together they continued to build sailing vessels and steamboats until late in the century.

During the Civil War, Joseph W. Dyer constructed one of the five "90-day" gunboats built in Maine. These vessels were almost identical with very few characteristics to set them apart. The second of this series assigned to Maine yards was Dyer's contribution, the *U.S.S. Kineo* of 507 tons. Her keel was laid 20 July 1861 and construction pursued with great haste. The *Kineo* was of briefly seasoned white oak, the frames reinforced with heavy iron braces for maximum strength. When completed, she measured 158 feet in length, with a beam of 28 feet and a 12 foot depth of hold. Her maximum draft was approximately 10 feet. She was rigged as a two-masted schooner and during her short career it was discovered that she sailed more rapidly than she steamed. The launching occurred on the 9th of October and was a subject of considerable interest to the *Eastern Argus*.

After the launching, the *Kineo* was towed across the harbor to Portland Pier where her engines were installed early in December. She was equipped with two horizontal, back-action steam engines that turned a single nine-foot propellor. The engines, built by the Morgan Works of New York, were well protected on both sides by coal-bunkers under the assumption that they would absorb any projectiles that might pierce the hull.

On the 10th of January, the *Kineo* was turned over to naval authorities at the Boston Navy Yard and became a commissioned naval vessel on the 8th of February. On the voyage from Portland to Boston, she achieved a speed of ten knots under steam. Her original armament, as of 13 February, was one IX-inch smoothbore Dahlgren, one 20-pounder Parrott rifle and two 24-pounder howitzers.

In addition to blockade duties, this sturdy little gunboat participated in Admiral David G. Farragut's famous battle at New Orleans in April 1862. In this decisive naval engagement, the *Kineo* had one killed and eight wounded but sustained no serious damages. Although her cost was approximately $100,000, she was sold by the Navy 9 October 1866, for $14,100 at Philadelphia, thus ending a naval career of exactly four years.

The Dyer yards remained active throughout the war years and into the eighties. In 1865, Joseph W. Dyer built the bark *Wallace,* 638 tons, and the following year constructed three schooner rigged canal barges for the Cumberland and Oxford Canal. They were the *Dreadnought,* 86 tons; *Lady Woodbury,* 75 tons; and the *J. G. Craig,* 77 tons. That same year, 1866, Nathan Dyer built the screw steamer *Dirigo,* 941 tons, and five years later constructed the second steamer to sail the waters of Sebago Lake, the *Sebago* of 78 tons. Unfortunately, the life of the *Sebago* was very brief for she burned at her moorings near the Bridgton Landing in 1873. Another relative, Nathan R. Dyer, also produced some very able vessels, among them the *Maggie Ellen,* a schooner of 217 tons, and the steam ferry *Mary W. Libby,* 20 tons, both built in 1874. Yet another scion of this illustrious family of shipbuilders was Joseph H. Dyer. Born in Portland in 1824, he was educated as a naval architect and although he remained a resident of that city until his death in 1920, his contribution to the activities of the Dyer yards were varied and frequent. In later years, his fame as a designer and builder of yachts was very wide spread.

Before proceeding further, notice should be taken of two yards that were established during the boom period of the clipper ship era. Actually, this spectacular period began in 1843 as the logical result of a growing demand for shorter voyages in the China trade. Under the stimulating influence of gold discoveries in California and Australia, the clamour for speed increased until the opening of the Suez Canal in 1869. These extraordinary years were one of the most important and interesting epochs in the maritime history of the United States. After years of experi-

Steam ferry *Cornelia H.* of the Peoples' Ferry Company, built in 1885 and destroyed by fire seven years later. Circa 1887.

The "Down Easter" *St. John Smith* of Portland, 2,220 tons, in the larger graving dock of the Portland Dry Dock and Warehouse Company. Circa 1875.

View of the English steamer *Bohemian*, 1,488 tons, after it sank at Broad Cove, 22 February 1864, reproduced from *Harpers Weekly*.

The bark *Annie C. Maguire*, 1,363 tons, wrecked at Portland Head 24 December 1886.

mentation, this era produced a perfection of design in wooden sailing ships that resulted in a maximum of speed and beauty. Nearly all the true clipper ships established records for fast passages which were not equalled or exceeded by contemporary steamships. Not until late in the century did steam finally conquer sail as the most rapid form of maritime transportation.

The port of Portland produced five true clippers and all of them were built in Cape Elizabeth yards. The first to be launched came from the yard of Cornelius B. Butler and Alford Butler at Turner's Island. Here were constructed three clippers in the two year period of 1850-1851. Nothing is known as to the origin or later life of the Butlers. No records exist of their having produced any other vessels in addition to the three clippers. They are truly a perplexing historical enigma. It is quite apparent that they were experienced shipbuilders, but where they obtained this experience or where they went has so far eluded detection. There is no indication that they ended their lives in this area although they disappeared from the directories in 1858. The only surviving reference is the fact that Sally, widow of Cornelius B. Butler, died at eighty-two on 5 January 1860 and was buried in Portland's Western Cemetery.

Despite the obscurity of the builders, the vessels they constructed occupy a significant place in the annals of the clipper ship era. Their first effort was the clipper bark *Black Squall* of 420 tons. She was launched early in November, 1850, fully rigged and must have been a beautiful sight with her jet black hull and a single gold arrow running the length of her gunwales. The vessel measured 427 feet in length, with a beam of 30 feet, and a 12 foot depth of hold. The *Eastern Argus* commented that "although the *Black Squall* is not so large as some of the China clippers, yet as her accommodations are all on deck, she will carry with her great breadth of beam, a good cargo; and we think she will prove that while Maine keeps up her rank as the first state in quantity of tonnage built, she can also keep up with the times in style, strength and beauty of model and finish." She sailed for New York on 12 November and, late in December, was sold to John Codman of that city for service in the California trade. Her best run apparently occurred in 1852 when she sailed from New York to San Francisco, via Valparaiso, in 156 days.

In 1851, the Butlers launched two more clippers somewhat larger than the *Black Squall*. First off the ways was the ship *Snow Squall* of 743 tons, taking to the water on 14 July. This handsome vessel was constructed of white oak, heavily timbered and "square-fastened." She measured 157 feet overall, had a beam of 32 feet, and a 16 foot depth of hold. On this occasion, the *Eastern Argus* published a long and glowing description exceeding the usual coverage. It was noted specifically that the *Snow Squall* was "well worthy the inspection of connoisseurs in navel architecture." The article then continued by noting that

> ...She is very sharp at the bows with a lean, but handsomely graduated run, but from her great breadth of beam and fullness of bulge will be enabled to carry well, while at the same time she cannot fail of being a fast sailer. Her cabin is furnished with polished mahogany, rose and satin wood, with coving and caps and bases to the pilasters of burnish gild; the floor is carpeted with rich tapestry carpeting, and the cabin furniture is to be of a style in keeping. Between decks she is finished in better style than it was formerly the practice to finish the cabins of most of our shipping.
>
> Her spars are very long, the main yard being 65 feet in length, and she is, we believe, the first vessel ever built in this district which carried standing sky-sail poles and yards. The height of her main truck from the deck is 142 feet. She is entirely painted white with the exception of a vermilion streak along her gunwales...

The *Snow Squall* sailed for New York on Thursday, 14 August and was "hull down in the course of an hour." Her owner, Alford Butler, sold the vessel for $40,000 to Charles R. Green of New York. Under the command of Capt. Isaac Bursley, the *Snow Squall* made some rather rapid voyages, first to California and then in the China trade.

One of her most memorable passages occurred in the spring of 1859. On this occasion, the *Snow Squall* was pitted against Donald McKay's large clipper, the famous *Romance of the Seas* in a run from Shanghai to New York. The McKay clipper sailed on 21 March with the Butler masterpiece departing the following day. Although the *Snow Squall* passed her off Anjier on the 9th of April, the *Romance of the Seas* soon reestablished her lead and rounded the Cape of Good Hope May 7th, two days ahead. The South Atlantic crossing proved to be most advantageous to the *Snow Squall* enabling her to cross the Line two days in the lead on the 29th. She reached Sandy Hook on 22 June with the *Romance of the Seas*, despite her thousand ton advantage, arriving the 23rd, being 92 and 94 days respectively from Shanghai. Although these were not record-breaking passages, few vessels ever made better time over that route at that time of year. No ship could have done as well as the *Snow Squall* unless she was a superb clipper sailed to the absolute limits of her capacity. An interesting sidelight to this race involves the clipper *Malay* of 868 tons. She was a fast ship, heavily sparred, with three skysail yards, and royal studding-sails on her fore and main masts. The *Malay* left Shanghai exactly two weeks before the *Snow Squall* yet they both arrived at New York on the same day.

The year 1851 also saw the last of the Butler clippers to be built at Turner's Island. This was the ship *Warner*, 500 tons, launched late in the year. Her length was 138 feet overall, beam 28 feet, and depth of hold 14 feet. As was the case with many fine clippers, this vessel has been ignored in most of the popular accounts despite the fact that she was unquestionably of clipper build and rig. The *Warner* was sold early in 1852 to William H. Merritt of New York and immediately entered the California trade. Later that year and in 1853, she made some memorable passages between New York and San Francisco under the command of Capt. Luther Ripley, Jr. Her promising career was abruptly terminated in March, 1854, when the New York papers posted her as missing and overdue. The *Warner* vanished without a trace, quite possible a victim of the craze for speed that characterized the clipper ship era.

Yet another major shipyard flourished in this period close by the southeastern end of Portland Bridge. Here, late in 1850, Nathaniel Blanchard, one of Portland's leading ship chandlers, in conjunction with Thomas E. Knight, a master shipbuilder also of Portland, established a sizeable yard. Apparently, Blanchard furnished the capital and Knight supplied the technical knowledge.

Before settling in Cape Elizabeth, Thomas E. Knight had worked for some years with his father, Robert W., who operated a shipyard at the foot of Maple Street. It was here that he gained the practical experience that enabled him to become a master shipbuilder. The elder Knight, born in Portland in 1790, began the construction of ships early in the thirties and quickly established a reputation as a skilled craftsman.

The first vessel to be built by Blanchard and Knight was the sturdy little packet schooner, *Ezra F. Lewis*, of 182 tons, for the Portland merchant John B. Brown. She was launched on Saturday, 31 May, 1851, and immediately began regular trips between Portland and New York. Other small schooners were constructed in this period but their names are now unknown. Early in 1853, the bark *Elton*, 348 tons, was launched, and work immediately commenced on a ship of approximately 1400 tons.

Disaster struck before this ship could be finished. On Thursday, 7 July, in early morning, a fire broke out in the shed used for steaming timbers and quickly spread to the partially completed ship. Engine companies were summoned from Portland. The "Deluge," from Casco Street, started a descent of Brackett Street hill to Portland Bridge at a dead run. Unfortunately, the crew lost control and the engine capsized, after slamming into the end of the bridge railing, completely blocking access to the bridge. The accident prevented the passage of other engines for some minutes thereby enabling the fire to get well beyond containment. The shipyard was extensively damaged, the ship under construction was a total loss with great quantities of timber completely destroyed. The loss to Blanchard and Knight amounted to approximately $40,000, totally uninsured, and although it represented a staggering blow, work was nevertheless continued.

Literally from the ashes arose the finest ship that Knight would ever build and destined to be the largest clipper constructed in the port of Portland. This was the magnificent ship that Blanchard aptly named the *Phoenix*. Of 1488 tons burden, she measured 205 feet overall, with a 41 foot beam and a 24 foot depth of hold. The launching occurred early in February, 1854.

The *Phoenix* was actually built as a transatlantic clipper packet and as such soon became the property of the Red Star Line of New York. She began regular runs to Liverpool early in 1856 and continued in regular service for the next two years. Carrying a moon-sail on her main mast, a rarity even in that era, the *Phoenix* made one of the best transatlantic runs ever achieved by a sailing packet. Under the able command of Capt. John Hoxie, she arrived in Cork Harbor on 24 January, 1859, fourteen days and nine hours from Savannah, Georgia. During the passage, she averaged 352 miles a day for several days in a row, with a speed of close to 15 knots. Contemporary reports indicate that this was equivalent to a thirteen day run from New York to Liverpool. Throughout her career as a packet on the North Atlantic run, her "uphill" passages against the prevailing westerlies averaged 31 days, a remarkable record in that great age of sail and certainly a testimonial to the craftsmanship of Thomas E. Knight. In addition to her transatlantic career, the *Phoenix* made some outstanding passages from New York to San Francisco. Disaster overwhelmed her early in 1860. She caught fire at Melbourne, Australia, on 28th February and was totally destroyed.

Apparently the cost of constructing the *Phoenix,* in conjunction with the fire loss, prompted Nathaniel Blanchard to suspend his shipbuilding activities at Cape Elizabeth. In 1856, Knight built the ship *Echo* of 874 tons for Blanchard but no additional construction was forthcoming. This same year witnessed a sharp decline in the demand for large ships. The next year, 1857, produced an economic collapse followed by a protracted depression. Despite hard times, evidence exists that Knight continued to build small vessels with the aid and assistance of his father who had combined talents with him in 1854.

The Knights continued their shipbuilding activities in a modest way until 1868. On 28 July of that year, Thomas died suddenly of a stroke and was buried in Portland's Western Cemetery. His father soon retired and moved back to Portland leaving the yard idle for a few years.

Early in the seventies, the shipyard was purchased by Joshua F. Randall of Portland. He in turn secured the talents of an experienced master shipbuilder from Freeport, Daniel Brewer. While a resident of Freeport, Brewer assisted in the construction of the ships *Ocean Home* and *Kentuckian*. Later, he was active at Brunswick and built two schooners there, the *David Torrey* and the *Nellie F. Sawyer*.

Activity was thus revived at the Knightville yard and in 1874, two vessels left the ways late in the year. They were the schooner *Clara Leavitt*, of 455 tons, and the barkentine *Golden Sheaf*, of 453 tons. The following year, the ship *Alice D. Cooper*, 1392 tons, was built. Her launching proved to be a great disapointment and most embarrassing. She slid gracefully off the ways and immediately came to rest in a large mud bank. It was only after much difficulty that she was extricated and warped out into the deeper waters of the harbor.

In 1876, the 823 ton bark *Edith Davis* was launched. The following year, Brewer built two more vessels, the bark *Grace Deering*, 773 tons, and the barkentine *Carrie Heckle*, of 498 tons. The latter ship experienced the same difficulties as the *Alice D. Cooper* but was floated off a little more easily.

The year 1877 saw the final closing of the old Knight yard. Nothing now remains to indicate the colorful shipbuilding days of this locale. Shortly after the launching of the *Carrie Heckle*, Brewer moved to Portland and built a few vessels in the immediate vicinity of the old Dyer yard near the foot of Mountfort Street. Here, he constructed the barkentine *Payson Tucker* of 661 tons. Shortly thereafter, he settled in Yarmouth and worked for a few years as a master shipbuilder for Giles Loring. About the turn of the century, he returned to Portland where he died

7 September, 1901, at the age of seventy-seven and was buried in Evergreen Cemetery.

In addition to the construction of ships, the repair and rebuilding of many vessels was carried on at Cape Elizabeth in the later years of the nineteenth century. Originally established in Portland, this vital industry was transferred across the harbor during the same summer that saw Joseph W. Dyer move his yard to Ferry Village. In both cases, the cause was the same, the expansion of commercial activity and the laying out of Commercial Street.

During its period of residence in Portland, this necessary adjunct to the maritime industry was known as the Portland Marine Railway. Chartered 6 February, 1826, by William Woodbury, Philip Greely, William Swan, William Wood, and James Tucker, with a capital of $30,000, the firm built a substantial plant at Clay Cove. By August of 1850, the transfer of operations had been completed and a new company, the Cape Elizabeth Wharf and Marine Railway, was organized. With Joseph Perley directing the affairs of the firm, Nathan Dyer was appointed yard superintendent, Charles T. Talbot master workman, and William Cammett, general superintendent.

After purchasing twelve acres of harbor frontage and mud flats from Nathan Dyer at Ferry Village, the railway was built at a cost of approximately fifteen thousand dollars. As the name of the firm implies, a railway was built sloping gradually across the flats somewhat beyond the low water mark. Construction activities occupied much of the period from September, 1850, to May, 1851. One of the most difficult tasks was blasting away outcroppings of ledge and building large cobb-work wharves on either side of the tracks. In addition, a covered way of 450 feet, an engine house, plus a carpenter, blacksmith, and paint shop were built.

The method of operation was relatively simple. The vessel would first be guided onto the large cradle and firmly fixed in place. Next, cradle and ship would be hauled up the inclined track by two steam engines with a combined pull of 240 horsepower. A two and a half inch chain moving through a large sprocket wheel was utilized in moving the loaded cradle to provide a steady pull with no slippage. In this fashion, ships of 1100 tons could be drawn up high and dry in the space of twenty minutes. For the next three decades, an average of 175 ships used the marine railway each year. Being located immediately east of the Dyer yard, it was most advantageously placed to serve the port of Portland.

A general reorganization and re-chartering occurred 7 February, 1883, with the name of the firm changed to the Portland Merchants Marine Railway. The incorporators were Nathan R. Dyer, William Spear, Benjamin W. Pickett, John H. Russell, and O. B. Whitten, with Capt. Charles H. Chase chosen as president and Nathan R. Dyer as superintendent. At this time, the facilities were considerably expanded to the extent that three ships could be accommodate simultaneously. A large covered way was built to accommodate construction as well as repair work.

In 1885, the railway was leased to the George E. Hagan Co., of Bath who operated it for the next two years. At that time, Nathan R. Dyer assumed the lease and continued to run the railway until 1887. On 16 February of that year, the Portland Shipbuilding Company was incorporated by Nathan R. Dyer, Albert E. Dyer, Ralph S. Norton, John H. Humphreys, and Edmund R. Norton. This firm immediately leased the railway placing Nathan R. Dyer in charge as superintendent.

This new company proceeded to build a large number of small vessels, specializing in passenger steamers and trawlers, as well as ocean going tugs. Among them were the steamers *Madeline* and *Santa Marie* for the Presumpscot River Company; the *Louise* for the Sebago Lake Company; *Sebascodegan* and *Aucocisco,* for the Harpswell Line; the *Henry F. Eaton* for the Frontier Steamship Company of Calais; as well as the trawlers *Frank S. Willard, Nina,* and *Lizzie* for the John Willard Company of Portland. The firm was especially proud of the *Electronic,* a large passenger steamer that they constructed for the Cape Breton Railroad. One interesting project completed by the Portland Shipbuilding Company was the fitting out of the steamer *Roosevelt,* destined to carry Robert E. Peary to the arctic. Originally constructed by McKay and Dix of Bucksport, the steamer was turned over to the Portland Company when bankruptcy halted its completion. The Portland Company in turn contracted with the Ferry Village firm to finish the job. In this same era, the company sent teams of shipcarpenters to Sebago Lake and Rangeley to build various small steamers. At the height of its activity, prior to the turn of the century, approximately seventy men found employment as shipcarpenters, caulkers, blacksmiths, and machinists in this yard.

A second, and far less successful, venture in the realm of ship repair was initiated some years after the establishment of the marine railway at Ferry Village. Originally organized in 1859, the Portland Dry Dock and Warehouse Company first constructed docks and a small marine railway a few hundred feet east of the Cape Elizabeth end of the old Portland Bridge. Incorporation did not occur, however, until February 1868. Under the leadership of Capt. James E. Simpson, Lorenzo D. M. Sweat, and Charles A. Lombard, approximately twenty-five acres of mud flats were acquired the following spring. Plans for two large dry docks were drawn up by Capt. Simpson and under his immediate supervision construction began at once.

Completed late in August of 1869, the dry dock was formally dedicated on Monday, the 2nd of September. The two docks were built entirely of fill with a granite retaining wall to provide protection from wave erosion. The surface of the land was only a few yards above mean high water. The larger of the two docks was 425 feet long from caisson gate to coping. Its maximum width at the top was 125 feet narrowing to 83 feet at the gate. The sides were terraced, each step constructed of wooden planks and sloped sharply to the bottom to a maximum depth of 46 feet at high tide. In building this dock, 5,450 piles were used for the foundation and sides, with 146,000 cubic feet of timber, 355,000 feet of plank, and twenty-six tons of spikes consumed in the overall construction. The smaller dock was 175 feet in length, 80 feet in width and had 12 feet of water at the sill. Immediately adjacent to the docks was a building that housed a steam engine and pumps capable of emptying the larger dock in two hours. The total cost of the installation was approximately two hundred and fifty thousand dollars. At the entrance to each dock was a gate shaped like a semi-circular wedge that fitted into carefully prepared grooves. To admit a vessel, water was admitted to the basin through openings in the gate. Although the gate contained 200 tons of ballast, built in compartments were flooded to sink it in place. In removing the gate, the compartments were pumped dry enabling it to float. Once afloat, the gate would be warped away from the entrance to admit the vessel. Once it was carefully centered in the dock the gate would be put in place and the compartments filled allowing the gate to sink into position. Lastly, the water in the basin would be pumped out, lowering the vessel onto the blocks at the bottom of the dock.

On Wednesday, 4 September, a trial run was held to acquaint the maritime community with the method of operation. At high tide, the brig *Martha A. Berry* and the steamer *Forest City* were admitted to the large dock, end to end. In due course they were returned to the harbor waters successfully completing the demonstration. It was at that time, the second largest dry dock on the Atlantic coast exceeded only in size by the Erie Basin docks in New York.

The Portland Dry Dock and Warehouse Company did not prove to be a financial success. By 1880, the firm was close to bankruptcy but was temporarily sustained by a $75,000 bond issue and a heavy mortgage. Shortly thereafter, in 1883, the large dry dock received its single most important employment. About 10:00 p.m. on Friday, the 6th of April, the Dominion Line steamer *Brooklyn*, of 3,576 tons, outward bound for Liverpool, ran onto Hog Island Ledge. A large hole was stove in her port side just about amidship and she settled heavily in shoal water. The job of unloading and refloating her was a long, difficult task. The *Brooklyn* finally lifted clear of the ledge on the 25th of June. Warping her into the dry dock was almost as difficult as the refloating job, requiring three days to accomplish it. Approximately two months later, temporary repairs were completed allowing the vessel to sail for England to affect a more permanent reconstruction. From this job, the firm realized about $6,000, the largest single fee it ever received.

Not long after the *Brooklyn* left, Capt. Charles H. Chase leased the facilities for a period of five years. After that, both drydocks fell into disuse and were allowed to deteriorate. Finally, about 1890, the company was declared bankrupt. Shortly thereafter, the property was purchased by the Portland and Cape Elizabeth Railroad Company as the site for a power plant. After years of neglect and decay, the buildings were swept away in 1921 and work was started by the Cumberland County Power and Light Company on its now obsolete Cape Steam Station. The larger dry-dock exists to this day having been used in recent years as a reservoir for cooling the turbine condensers of the power plant.

Although shipbuilding had long since ceased to be a significant industry in Cape Elizabeth by 1890, small vessels were constructed. Most of these were built by the Portland Shipbuilding Company as previously noted. However, single individuals continued to build an occasional vessel for their own use or for speculation. Such projects were not uncommon throughout most of the nineteenth century. One very interesting incident of this type was the schooner *Triumph*, 125 tons, built by Frederick Hannaford near Pond Cove Corner in 1852. When completed, she was hauled cross country by 125 yoke of oxen to Zeb's Cove where the launching occurred. Unfortunately, the

Triumph was lost in the Bay of Chaleur in 1856 after being sold to a firm in Gloucester, Massachusetts. After the division of Cape Elizabeth in 1895, shipbuilding almost totalling disappeared. It is not an exaggeration to say that after 1877 no large ships were constructed in Cape Elizabeth and since the turn of the century, nothing larger than a boat has been built. Despite the fact that the days of greatness are long past, Cape Elizabeth did make a mighty contribution to the age of sail and to the colorful maritime history of Maine.

CHAPTER VII

PERILOUS SHORES

From the earliest days, the inhospitable coast of Cape Elizabeth with its treacherous fingers of ledge, has been a sinister adversary to the mariner who frequents the waters of Portland Harbor and Casco Bay. This was especially true in the age of sail when many a vessel was forced to brave the vagaries of the wind in trying to weather the Cape. From early September to late April, violent storms and heavy seas are always imminent. During the winter months, "north-easters" sweep the coast with great ferocity invariably accompanied by a howling blizzard and mountainous swells. At such a time, the shores of Cape Elizabeth are assaulted by thunderous surf with the off-shore ledges smothered by billowing combers. A vessel, under sail, its rigging and canvas sheathed with ice, could, in trying to beat its way into the harbor, be in gravest peril. In such a situation it was not uncommon for a ship to miss-stay on a port tack, i.e. fail to come about, and be hurled upon the ledges before anything could be done.

In the period between May and August, south-east storms, although not quite so frequent, can produce a dangerous situation. Often associated with them are driving rains, high winds, and dense fogs. Under such circumstances any miscalculation in navigation or seamanship would spell instant disaster.

Even in the best of weather, a dark night or a sudden rain squall could bring with it heart-rending grief. An extra peril also awaited the hapless mariner who inadvertently found these inhospitable shores under his lee. Thus it was that the coast of Cape Elizabeth became a source of anguish and dread to the seafarer as he set his course for Portland Harbor.

As the volume of maritime traffic increased after the Revolutionary War, the need for navigational aids was more insistent with each passing year. The advantages to be derived from the erection of a beacon at Portland Head had been recognized for some years. In 1785, Joseph Noyes, representative to the Massachusetts General Court from Falmouth, was instructed to seek the erection of a lighthouse on "Portland Point." For the previous two years, vessels up to thirty tons, not engaged in the coasting trade or fishing, had been required to pay two-pence per ton "light money," and those over thirty tons four-pence per ton. Local mariners had long objected to paying a lighthouse duty when not a single light existed on the entire coast of the District of Maine. The depressed condition of the economy forced the Commonwealth to take no immediate action. Two years later, construction was started but proceeded very slowly due to a lack of funds. At the Cape Elizabeth town meeting of Monday, 16 November 1789, Barzillai Delano, Capt. Matthew Simonton, and Lieut. John Armstrong, were appointed a committee to join with other neighboring towns in drafting a petition to the General Court seeking an appropriation "to finish the Light House on Portland Head." The petition failed to elicit any additional allocation from the Commonwealth of Massachusetts.

In August 1790, the first Congress of the United States appropriated $1500 to complete the construction. Two master-masons from Portland, John Nichols and Jonathan Bryant, were soon at work on the tower and house. The building material was rubble-stone laid up in lime from the kiln operated by Bryant near the foot of India Street. The lime was made by burning limestone brought by ship to Portland from the quarries at Rockland. Before the tower was finished, Bryant resigned from the job as the result of a dispute with Gen. Benjamin Lincoln, Massachusetts Lighthouse Superintendent, who was supervising construction for the government, relative to adding fourteen feet to the originally specified height of fifty-eight feet. This left Nichols to complete the tower by himself. The seventy-two foot tower, stone keeper's house and connecting ell were completed late in 1790, with the last stone put in place 9 October. There was now the problem of placing the lantern. By adding to the height of the tower, the area at the top had been substantially reduced and was too small to accommodate the lantern-and-lens assembly previously selected. Early in January, 1791, a smaller lantern was successfully installed, making the tower's total height eighty-seven feet. The sixteen whale-oil lamps were lighted for the first time at dusk on the tenth.

Portland Head Light was the first lighthouse to be erected on the coast of Maine and the thirteenth on the Atlantic seaboard of the United States. From the very beginning, this promontory and its lighthouse attracted large numbers of people who never ceased to marvel at the rude beauty of the locale. Over the years, it came to symbolize the stern and rugged qualities of the Maine coast. One would be hard pressed to find an object more frequently painted or sketched, photographed or filmed, than this venerable beacon.

The first keeper was Capt. Joseph Greenleaf. He received his commission from President Washington, dated 7 January, 1791. Although Barzillai Delano had been considered for the post, it was granted to Greenleaf largely because of his extensive service in the Continental Army. As keeper, he received no salary but was given leave to occupy the house adjacent to the light, to carry on whatever farming activities he desired, and to fish. His term lasted just over four years. While rowing across Fore River from Portland to Ferry Village, Saturday, 3 October, 1795, he suffered a fatal stroke. The *Eastern Argus* noted that Greenleaf "faithfully discharged his duty to the satisfaction of those who occupy their business on great waters." It is of interest to note that Miss Mary Blanche Bixby of Pasadena, California offered to sell Greenleaf's original commission to the Maine Historical Society in 1903 for one hundred dollars. The negotiations were fruitless, however, and today nothing is known about the whereabouts of this historic document.

The second keeper, Dave Duncan, served until 1796, when he was succeeded by Barzillai Delano, the blacksmith who lived close by. Like his father, Thomas Delano, he operated a smithy next to his home at what is now the first entrance to Delano Park. His house survived until March, 1878, when it was torn down.

Early in Delano's term, Benjamin Lincoln returned on a tour of inspection and after investigating the dampness within the tower, recommended that the exterior be sheathed with planks overlaid with shingles. Apparently, little consideration was given to his suggestions for no such alterations were made. The dampness persisted, however, and by 1810 much of the timbering inside the tower was badly rotted. When General Henry Dearborn inspected the tower that same year, these conditions were noted and reported, with the result that repairs were soon accomplished.

Other than routine upkeep, no major changes were instituted during the rest of Delano's tenancy. He died in 1820, and was succeeded by Joshua Freeman who, during his term of twenty years, was widely renown for his hospitality. In 1840, Richard Lee became keeper and nine years later was replaced by John F. Watts.

Two years after the appointment of Watts, the light underwent a major alteration. In August of 1850, Daniel Freeman of

Portland removed the original lantern case and replaced it with one of his own manufacture. Also installed were the recently introduced plate glass Fresnal lenses from France. The new lantern was lighted for the first time on the twenty-first.

Keeper Watts was succeeded by John W. Coolidge in 1853 who remained but one year before being replaced by James S. Williams. After a stay of less than a year, he in turn gave way to Barzillai Delano's son, James, who remained until 1861.

During James Delano's tour of duty, the government hung its first fog bell, A few yards south of the keeper's dwelling, a wooden frame tower twenty-four feet in height was erected and a 1,500 pound cast iron bell installed therein, placing it about sixty feet above sea level. The bell was rung for the first time on 20 July 1855, and henceforth in foggy weather would be struck with a wooden clapper once every thirty seconds. This bell remained in place until swept away in the great September gale of 1869. A year later, a new tower, shaped like a pyramid, was built and another cast iron bell of 2,000 pounds installed with a Stevens striker. The new bell had been cast in 1867 by Vickers and Sons, Ltd. of Sheffield, England. Although this bell was carried away during the Portland gale of 1898, it was rehung, surviving until it developed a bad crack in 1931. It was replaced by one of bronze a year later, weighing 1,010 pounds. This third bell was torn from its mooring on 3 March 1947, during the storm that wrecked the collier *Oakey L. Alexander.*

In 1861, Elder M. Jordan succeeded Delano as keeper and three years later the tower underwent a major change. As funds were not available for establishing a light ship near Bulwark Shoal, it was hoped that raising the tower twenty feet and changing the Fresnel lens from a fourth order to a second order the same purpose might be served. Late in December, 1864, the alterations were completed, a new five wick lamp burning kerosene instead of the old sperm oil or lard oil was installed, and on the twentieth the new light went into service casting its welcome beam, in clear weather, seventeen miles out to sea. The lantern now towered 101 feet above sea level.

This improvement lasted only eight years. In 1871, Halfway Rock Light was built, thereby making, according to a government survey, the second class light at Portland Head unnecessary. It was also recommended that the tower be torn down and replaced by an iron one of lesser height. The matter was referred to the naval secretary of the Light House Board. This worthy suggested that the twenty foot addition be removed and a class four lamp installed. This plan was adopted in 1882 and the following year the change was made. This quickly aroused a storm of dissatisfaction from local mariners. As this was the "heroic" age of Hale, Reed, Frye, and Dingley in Washington, Maine was not without its champions. Their influence, when mobilized in behalf of restoring the light to its former height, produced results. In August 1884, the Light House Board reversed its order of 1882 and ordered the re-building of Portland Head Light to its former class-two status. The new tower had a larger platform at its top to accommodate a bigger lantern and a more powerful lens. The reconstructed light was illuminated for the first time 15 January, 1885. At this point it was an occulting white light, i.e. the light flashes, then it occults, or goes through a period of darkness before the next flash. In the case of Portland Head, the light blazed forth every two seconds.

The year 1869 brought a keeper of rare and unusual talents to this historic beacon. This was the doughty mariner, Joshua Freeman Strout. Born 13 August, 1826, he was named for the fourth keeper at Portland Head. His grandmother, Mary Dyer, had watched the building of the light and his mother, Jane Green Dyer, had worked as a housekeeper for Capt. Joshua Freeman at the rate of fifty cents a week.

When he was eleven years old, Joshua Strout took to the sea and at eighteen served as cook aboard a tugboat. In the years that followed, he rose to the rank of master mariner and in 1854 shipped out for the first time as captain on the maiden voyage of Benjamin W. Pickett's new brig *Scotland*. During the next two years, he made several voyages to Cuba and South America in this vessel. Other subsequent commands were the schooners *Starlight, Nellie Chase, L. T. Knight, Hannah, Westbrook,* and barks *B. F. Shaw, Andres,* and *Arcadia*. A severe fall aboard the *Andres* produced complications that forced him to abandon the rigors of a life at sea. Shortly thereafter, he received his commission as keeper of Portland Head Light at a salary of $620 a year. His wife, May, was appointed assistant keeper and received $480 as an annual salary.

His thirty-five year tour of duty at the light was as memorable as it was long. On many occasions, his courage and devotion to the service took precedence over his personal safety. In the September gale of 1869, he narrowly escaped death when the bell tower was swept away by a giant comber just as he was leaving it after winding the striking mechanism. Again, with the assistance of his son, Joseph W. eighteen people were rescued from the bark *Annie C. Maguire* that was wrecked on Christmas Eve 1886, a few yards from the light. Yet another rescue was affected by Joshua's sons, Joseph W. and Gilman. The small schooner *D. W. Hammond* was driven ashore a short distance north of Portland Head in a fierce north-east "line storm" 30 November 1887. With a complete disregard for their own safety, they pulled the captain and his two crewmen from the sea more dead than alive. Rushed to the keeper's house, the exhausted, partially frozen men were quickly revived through the efforts of Joshua's wife and daughter-in-law. Even his infant grandson, Charles, took a keen interest in this humanitarian effort that was so typical of the Strout family.

In addition to the tragedies he was forced to witness in the line of duty, Joshua Strout also had to endure losses of a more personal nature. During his years at Portland Head, three of his sons were lost at sea, Charles F. on the *St. John Smith,* Stephen on the *Portland Lloyds,* and John on the *Charles Haskell.*

Much to the satisfaction of all concerned, the government tore down the old stone keeper's dwelling late in 1890 and erected on the same site a far more spacious wooden house that would accommodate the families of the keeper as well as his assistant. This building survives to this day occupied by the Coast Guardsmen who now serve as keepers of the light.

Rather late in the century, Longfellow began to repeat his jaunts to Portland Head during the summer months. He could always depend upon a warm welcome from Joshua Strout and they whiled away many an hour in pleasant conversation. The Strouts cherished the memory of these visits from the poet long after they were terminated by the infirmities of old age.

Another significant incident that occurred during Joshua's colorful career, at the light was the installation of its first fog horn. In 1872, the Daboll trumpet that had been in service at Monhegan Light was moved to Portland Head and a small engine house built to accommodate it slightly seaward of the tower. Two years later, a second-class horn replaced the original trumpet and in 1877, a 24-inch caloric engine from Boston Light installed. Within a short period of time, a Hornsby Akroyd diesel engine became the source of power for the air compressors and the Daboll trumpet was returned. No further change of any magnitude was made until 1938. In that year, an air diaphragm chime horn was placed atop a small steel tower on the northeast side of the engine house. The old Daboll trumpet was relagated to a standby status. The new fog horn actually consisted of three trumpets. The large center horn was so arranged that it could be detected near Halfway Rock. One of the smaller ones was directed toward the lightship with its twin pointed toward the southern end of Cushing's Island. This triple fog horn, a Cunningham type signal manufactured in Seattle, Washington, is still in service, emitting four-second blasts every twenty seconds. Power for the compressors has been provided by electric motors since the installation of this horn.

For the first time in its history, the light was officially extinguished by Joshua Strout on 30 April 1898. This was done to forestall easy access to the harbor by enemy warships during the Spanish-American War. Even the fog horn was discontinued. Once the Spanish fleet ceased to be a menace, the light was ordered back into service. Late in July, Keeper Strout had the pleasure of illuminating the beacon symbolizing a return to more normal times.

When he retired in 1904, Joshua was succeeded by his son, Joseph Woodbury Strout, who had replaced his mother as assistant keeper in 1877. The elder Strout moved into a new home at Cape Cottage where he spent the remainder of his life, dying at the age of 81, 10 March, 1907.

The new keeper carried on in the tradition of his father. Although born at Ferry Village in 1859, he had resided at Portland Head since the age of ten and was well versed in the requirements of the service. Like his father, he dispensed hospitality with an open hand. His reputation as a crusty salt with a rich and varied vocabulary, established him as a colorful character of great popularity. Of genial disposition with an inexhaustible store of sea tales, he was deeply admired by all who met him.

One member of the Strout family who was an unfailing source of enjoyment to all who made his acquaintance was the African grey parrot known as Billy. He was in his late thirties when he joined the family circle in 1887. The ease with which he handled lengthy phrases was exceeded only by his volubility. During his long residence at the light he never grew accustomed to foul weather. When the fog began to roll in he would ruffle his neck feathers and call out repeatedly, "Joe, start the horn, it's foggy," not desisting until his order was complied with. Following Joseph into retirement, Billy spent his declining years with the keeper's son, Charles S. Strout, at Cape Cottage. In his old age he ceased to be as garrulous but became a devoted radio fan. He survived until 1942 when he died in what must have been his ninth decade.

In 1928, after fifty-nine years of service, this remarkable family left Portland Head Light. With the retirement of Joseph W. Strout one of the most unusual eras in the history of the light passed into the realm of tradition and folklore. Never again would this famous beacon offer the warm and friendly hospitality that was extended with such generosity by the Strouts. Like his father, Joseph retired to the family home at Cape Cottage where he resided until his death at seventy-two 14 December 1931.

From 1928 to 1929 the light keeper was John W. Cameron, appointed at the age of seventy. During his brief service the source of illumination was changed from kerosene to electricity thereby increasing the candlepower of the light to 32,000 enabling it to be seen thirty miles at sea on a clear night. He in turn was succeeded by Capt. Frank O. Hilt, formerly a master mariner in the coasting trade. In 1939, during his tour of duty, the old Lighthouse Service was merged with the Coast Guard after 150 years as an independent entity.

Following Hilt as keeper was his former assistant, Robert T. Sterling, who received his appointment in 1943. By this time the light, with a second order barrel-shaped lens, had been increased to 375,000 candlepower. Keeper Sterling will long be remembered for his interesting book entitled *Lighthouses of the Maine Coast and the Men who Keep Them,* a labor of love that he published in 1935. During World War II the light was again extinguished going out 5 June 1942 and not coming on again until the summer of 1945. When he retired in May 1946, after thirty-three years of dedicated service, Sterling was replaced by an appointee from the U. S. Coast Guard, ending forever the individuality that had so distinguished the Light House Service. At the present time Portland Head is rated as second class with a flashing light that is visible thirty miles at sea under the proper conditions.

Early in the nineteenth century it was deemed advisable to construct a stone column or marker as a navigational aid at the southeast extremity of the Cape. In the spring of 1811 General Henry Dearborn conducted a survey of the area under consideration and drew up plans for the erection of the column. The contract for construction of the monument was awarded to Edward Robinson and John F. Bartlett. They in turn entered into an agreement with the two men who had sold the required land to the government, Enoch and Edward Dyer, for the necessary supplies. The Dyers furnished "undressed rocks of a good quality," with all the poles for staging, plus sand and water for the lime mortar. They received a basic fee of $135 in addition to $1.75 for each boulder delivered to the building site. Work began early in August and on 30 November 1811 the capstone was hoisted into place. When finished, the column, in the shape of an octagonal pyramid, towered fifty feet above its massive foundation. Built of rubble-stone and lime mortar, a field boulder roughly octagon in shape approximately three feet in diameter, served as its capstone. The lower half of the monument was painted white and the upper half black, with a total height above sea level of 125 feet. It stood on the site currently occupied by the eastern tower of the Cape Elizabeth Light.

Throughout the second decade of the century, maritime activity increased at a rapid rate. The *Eastern Argus* on 14 July 1825 reported that it was possible to see "with the naked eye, forty two sail of vessel off our harbor, bound out." They also noted that "within view of the telescope at the observatory, upwards of one hundred sail" could be seen. Under these conditions agitation for the establishment of a lighthouse at the tip of the Cape received wide support.

In the spring of 1827 the Federal Government approved the erection of twin towers, the first double light to be located on the Maine coast. A year later twelve acres of land, on the ridge between Staples Cove and Dyer's Cove, was purchased from Charles Staples, Edward Dyer, and Enoch Dyer for fifty dollars, and transferred to the Federal Government by the state of Maine. A contract was granted to Jeremiah Berry in May of 1828 whereby he agreed to build the two rubble-stone towers for $4,250 after demolishing the stone pyramid of 1811.

It is interesting that coincidental with the awarding of this contract was the advocacy of a plan for erecting a marine observatory on the same site. The Portland editor, John Neal, writing in his periodical *The Yankee,* tried to arouse enthusiasm for building a tower patterned after the Portland Observatory. Its primary purpose would be to relay sightings and other maritime intelligence, via marine telegraph, to its Portland counterpart for dissemination by Lemuel Moody. Nothing came of this proposal, however.

When completed in October, the two stone beacons towered sixty-five feet above the ridge and 129 feet above sea level. Running roughly east and west, they were 300 yards apart. When lighted for the first time on the 28th, the outer beacon exhibited a fixed light with its inner companion showing an occulting light, i.e. a 45 second beam followed by 45 seconds of darkness. Appointed early in the month as the first keeper, Elisha Jordan was granted an annual salary of $450 with the admonition that he "reside at the station and make it a habit to be at home." He continued in this capacity until September 1834 when he was removed, an early victim of the spoils system. His successor was Charles Staples, an active Democrat, who retained the post until his death, 14 June 1835, of cancer. During his term of service the Cape Elizabeth Lights received their first fog bell. A small building was built late in May to house the striker machinery and by early June the bell was in operation.

During William Jordan's tour of duty as keeper, the inner light was substantially changed. On 20 June 1850 Daniel Freeman of Portland installed a new lantern case that he had recently constructed at his shop in Portland. It was twelve feet high and was set with quarter inch panes of French plate glass measuring 24 inches by 30 inches. This improvement paved the way for a major change at the Cape Elizabeth Lights in 1855 when Nathan Davis was keeper.

Late in 1854 Fresnel lenses were added to both lights. Then suddenly on 20 December a public notice in the newspapers announced that after June 1st 1855 the inner light would be permanently discontinued. The outer light would henceforth be an occulting light. At the last moment a delay developed in altering the outer light that postponed the extinguishing of the inner light until 1 August. On that date the change was carried out.

In answer to the storm of protest that greeted this new arrangement, the Light House Board replied that it was instituted to avoid navigational mistakes. The board pointed out that the revolving light on the Cape was always seen quite a period of time before the fixed light was sighted. From the time a vessel picked it up, till she raised the fixed light, there was nothing to distinguish the revolving light from Wood Island Light south of Old Orchard Beach. If the vessel had lost her bearings, she could easily mistake Cape Elizabeth for Wood Island. Therefore, the board had felt justified in making the change.

As the maritime interests persisted in their demands for restoring the inner light, the Light House Board instituted another change in the spring of 1856. As of April 1st both lights were returned to their former condition. Illumination for the inner occulting light now consisted of 10 lamps with 21 inch reflectors whereas the outer fixed light had 15 lamps with 21 inch reflectors. To avoid the previous confusion the Wood Island Light now became an occulting red beacon.

During the Civil War when so many men from Cape Elizabeth responded to preserve the Union, the drain on personnel at the "Two Lights" resulted in some rather unusual changes. The assistant keeper at the western light, Asbury Staples, enlisted in the 2nd Maine Battery Light Artillery on 14 December 1861. His father, Michael Staples, assistant keeper at the western light, thereupon requested that his daughter Amelia Dyer Staples and his son Charles Wesley Staples be appointed as assistant keepers. This sixteen year old girl and her younger brother were responsible for winding the machinery that occulted the light and for cleaning the Fresnel bullseye lens. On many occasions they sat by the lens at night using its light to study school lessons. They also had the melancholy duty of draping the towers with huge loops of black crepe late in April 1865 in mourning for the martyred President Lincoln. The two white towers, thus decorated, must have been a somber sight indeed.

Later in this same year these two stone towers experienced a rather striking change of color. Four wide horizontal red bands were added to the east tower and a single, very wide, vertical red stripe was applied to the west tower. Once again they must have been striking to behold.

No further alterations occurred until the year 1873. In January of that year Marcus A. Hanna was appointed keeper. A veteran of the Civil War, he had served as a sergeant in Company B, 50th Massachusetts Regiment Volunteer Infantry. At the battle of Port Hudson, Louisiana, on 4 July 1863 he voluntarily exposed himself to heavy rebel fire to get water for his men pinned down in rifle pits. For this heroic act he was awarded the Congressional Medal of Honor. In the second year of his appointment the two stone towers were torn down and replaced by two sixty-five foot cast iron ones. The cast iron sections were manufactured by the old Portland Machine Works on Commercial Street. Shortly after the completion of the new towers the old stone keeper's house was demolished and a larger wooden dwelling constructed along with various other supplementary buildings. Originally the iron towers were painted brown but difficulty in daylight recognition prompted a change to white in July 1880.

In 1882 the Light House Board, the same year it ordered a reduction in the height of Portland Head Light, again decided to eliminate the western light at Cape Elizabeth. As was to be expected a great public outcry occurred with the Portland Board of Trade vehemently demanding that the order be rescinded. Enlisting the support of U. S. Rep. Thomas B. Reed this economy move was cancelled with congress appropriating the necessary funds. Despite this victory in keeping both towers the government once again painted them brown as less expensive from the standpoint of maintenance.

One improvement that had been badly needed for many years was the establishment of an effective fog signal. In 1869 a small building was constructed south of the towers on the edge of the shore and a large steam boiler installed. On the roof of this building a twelve inch steam locomotive whistle was placed and in foggy weather emitted a shrill eight second blast every sixty seconds. However, it was found to be inadequate and in 1874 a fog siren replaced it.

In 1886 a larger brick fog signal station was built on the same site. The steam siren, however, proved to be less than satisfactory and in 1901 the locomotive whistle, held in reserve, was restored to service. Shortly thereafter the present multiple horns were installed, operated first by steam and then by compressd air. They have a maximum range of eight miles and are easily identified by their distinctive signal, three two-second blasts separated by two seconds of silence, a seqence that is repeated every fifty seconds. The horns go into service when the old Anthony light buoy, 2.2 miles off the station, is obscured by fog.

The ever present need for maximum visibility prompted the repainting of the towers white in 1902. The matter of illumination also received constant attention, and in December 1915, the old kerosene wick lamps were replaced by oil vapor lamps using a 55 millimetre mantle. The new lamps, producing a brilliant white light, boosted the candle power of the eastern tower from 9,000 to 220,000 and the western tower from 17,000 to 110,000, a vast improvement over the sperm oil and lard oil lamps of the past, and were lighted for the first time Wednesday 4 January 1916.

The last major alteration occurred in the spring of 1924. On this occasion the western light was permanently extinguished. The changeover began 14 November 1923 when both beacons became fixed white lights thereby permitting the removal of the machinery from the western tower to its eastern counterpart. Work was completed early in May 1924 and the western light went out for the last time on the 9th. On the 15th the flashing light in the eastern tower went into service with a new and distinctive pattern. It produced six half second flashes every thirty seconds, spaced by two and a half seconds of darkness. An eclipse of fifteen seconds followed each group of flashes. Despite the inevitable protests the change was final. Currently the eastern tower, known simply as the Cape Elizabeth Light, has a first-class rating, with a group flashing, four million candlepower lamp visible under proper conditions seventeen miles at sea. Regardless of such changes this light is still called "Two Lights" by the public.

The western tower was stripped of its lantern and during World War II was used by the army as an observation post. After the war it was abandoned and gradually declined to a state of extreme dilapidation. As the Coast Guard Station at Dyer's Cove now had charge of the eastern light, the government declared the western tower keepers' quarters, and other structures surplus. The entire property, i.e. the western tower, four two-story buildings, eight one-story buildings, two garages, two antenna masts, and even the flagpole, plus 10.5 acres of land, was sold, exclusive of the eastern light, to the highest bidder in 1959.

In the middle of the nineteenth century a third lighthouse was established close by the mouth of the harbor. Prior to the erection of the light the Federal government was persuaded to build a breakwater approximately a quarter of a mile in length out along Stanford's Ledge from Stanford's Point. Once completed, a lighthouse would be placed on its seaward end. Agitation for the breakwaster was initiated early in the thirties. Largely through the efforts of U. S. Rep. Francis O. J. Smith, a Jacksonian Democrat, congress appropriated $10,000 for its construction.

The job was put out to bid in March 1837 and work began early in the summer. The projected breakwater had been surveyed and laid out in six sections, extending outward from Stanford's Point, by Col. John Anderson, U. S. Engineer. The first three sections or 172 yards built of granite blocks were completed late in 1837, thereby providing a foundation. The resident engineer, Freeman Bradford, reported to the government in November that "the portion of the breakwater already constructed has been found efficacious in keeping off the heavy swell that formerly swept over the ledge at high water, and caused much damage to the shipping in the harbor."

In August 1838 a contract was granted to Levi Strout of Cape Elizabeth and Isaac Center of Brunswick for completion of the project. Utilizing the sturdy stone sloops from Chebeague 68,176 tons of granite blocks, granite ashlar, and grout were transported from New Meadows and other places along the coast. The stone sloops were broad-beamed, full-bellied vessels designed for the specific purpose of transporting huge loads of granite.

They carried an immense gaff-rigged mainsail of approximately 1,000 square yards. The single heavy mast also served to support the derrick-boom used in unloading the cumbersome cargo. A large windlass, operated with hand spikes, furnished the hoisting power. In this manner great quantities of stone could be quickly and easily handled.

When completed in 1852 the breakwater was four hundred yards in length. It measured in width ten feet at the base and nine feet four inches at the top, with a total height of four feet. In constructing it a base of granite butters or headers ten feet long and eighteen inches thick were laid across the foundation ten to fourteen feet apart. The spaces at the sides of the wall between the headers were filled with granite blocks two feet long and eighteen inches wide. The space between was filled with rubble stone, surmounted by courses of granite blocks of various lengths. The final course was similar to the base except that the spaces between the headers were leveled off with smaller blocks. The total cost of the breakwater came to approximately $110,000.

Although anticipated for some years, a lighthouse was not built at the end of the breakwater until 1855. Constructed of wood and painted white, the octagonal tower was twenty three feet above the granite surface and twenty five feet above high water. The illuminating apparatus was sixth order Fresnel lens, showing a fixed red light, for the first time 1 August 1855 by the first keeper William Lee Willard of Ferry Village. He was followed by Paul McKenney, 1866; Stephen Hubbard, 1875; Albus R. Angell, 1877; and Parker O. Haley, 1900.

The original wooden tower was removed to Little Diamond Island in June of 1875 and replaced by an iron tower slightly larger in size. A wooden dwelling for the keeper, eighteen by twenty feet, was built on the inboard side of the tower in March 1889. Overhanging the breakwater on both sides, it survived many a storm, despite its precarious position.

In addition to the Portland Breakwater there was, for some years, a considerable amount of sentiment favoring the construction of a breakwater along the sand bar that connected Richmond's Island to the mainland. Early in the nineteenth century, large trees, stumps, and branches were anchored in place on the bar to retain it as well as to encourage the further accumulation of sand and gravel. In 1845, the state of Maine granted Dr. John M. Cummings permission to build a solid causeway along the bar, but he never carried it out. Throughout this period many small vessels took refuge from north-east gales on the south side of the improvised breakwater in what was known as Richmond's Island Roads.

Despite repeated requests for aid, the Federal government did not act until October of 1855. During that month Alexander W. Longfellow of the U. S. Coast Survey carried out a hydrographic exploration of the area relative to the feasibility of constructing a breakwater, and the potentialities of Richmond's Island Roads as a major anchorage. His findings described the ocean bottom south of the bar as blue clay covered by a thin layer of sand. Ultimately, Longfellow's survey was embodied in an excellent chart of the island and surrounding waters published by the government. The reports that he submitted were very favorable as to the desirability of a permanent breakwater. With the publication of Longfellow's survey, the $10,000 appropriated by congress in 1852 for such a project now became available. However, nothing came of the project until 1873. In the summer of that year a contract was granted and work commenced. Huge granite blocks, carried to the site by Chebegue Island stone sloops, were piled on the bar in no particular pattern. Although frequently halted by a lack of funds, the job was completed in a few years. Unfortunately, the breakwater so altered the prevailing currents that sand quickly built up on the south side, turning Richmond's Island Roads into an anchorage far poorer than before. By 1903, only the smallest of vessels could take refuge there without dragging their anchors in the soft sand bottom. Instead of creating a harbor, the breakwater produced shoal water.

The nineteenth century also brought other navigational aids to the assistance of the mariner who frequented the shores of Cape Elizabeth. As early as 1811 Lemuel Moody of Portland carefully surveyed the outstanding menaces to shipping, using the stone monument at the tip of the Cape as a guide. He designated Alden's Rock as exceedingly dangerous. A pinacle of rock three and a half miles south 61° east of the monument, covered by eight feet of water at low tide, it was impossible to detect without bearings. Farther inshore was the "Norman's Woe" of Cape Elizabeth, Trundy's Reef. Extending out from the shore for half a mile, it lay two and a half miles north 20° east of the monument. At low tide the water shoaled to fifteen feet. Three other reefs were listed by Moody as deserving careful attention. New Ledge, six and three quarter miles, north 74° with water shoaling from fifteen feet to eleven feet, about a quarter mile in length; Taylor's Reef, one mile, south 24° east, also approximately a quarter mile long; and Watt's Ledge, awash at low tide, extending several hundred yards in a south-easterly direction from the shores of Richmond's Island. Lastly, Moody called attention to Broad Cove Rock, barely covered at low water, a mile and a half north 25° east from the monument. Surprisingly enough none of these dangerous rock formations were marked for many years.

The first of these hazards to be marked was Alden's Rock. In 1835, U. S. Rep. Francis O. J. Smith was instrumental in having $1500 appropriated for this purpose in conjunction with funds allocated for the fog bell at the Two Lights. Early in August, a forty-five foot cedar spar, fifteen inches in diameter, was anchored slightly northeast of the rock. Held in place by a six hundred pound grapple and a six hundred pound anchor, the spar, painted a bright red, projected above the water about twenty feet. Fastened to the top of the buoy was a twelve foot staff to which was attached a red flag. On a clear day the Alden's Rock spar buoy could be seen six or seven miles.

This buoy was not replaced until the summer of 1855. On 6 June 1855 an iron bell-boat was anchored a quarter mile south east of the rock. The boat was painted black with the words Alden's Rock inscribed in white letters on each side. A 500 pound bell was suspended in a frame twelve feet above the water and sounded by the action of the sea. Under ordinary circumstances it could be heard a mile away. Although Alden's Rock would henceforth always be clearly marked, nevertheless, in the years to come it still claimed many a vessel. Its sinister reputation was even commemorated in a poem, entitled *Alden's Rock,* composed by the Portland poet William Cutter and published in 1849 by *Godey's Ladies Book.*

The benefits derived from the Alden's Rock buoy soon resulted in the placing of others. In 1846 spar buoys were placed at the end of Trundy's Reef and at Broad Cove Rock. Nine years later, spar buoys were also established at Eastern Hue and Cry, Old Anthony Ledge, Vapour Rock, Taylor's Reef, Bell Rock, and in 1856 at the end of Spring Point Ledge.

The last navigational aid of great significance in that pre-radar era did not appear until early in the twentieth century. On 7 March 1903 the Federal government placed Cape Elizabeth Lightship No. 74 on station, five and seven-eighths miles from the eastern Cape Elizabeth Light. As was so often the case, it had taken some years of patient but persistent badgering of the government to produce results. This first vessel was moored in 150 feet of water at 43° 31' north latitude and 70° 5' west longitude, being held on station by a five thousand pound mushroom anchor with 135 fathoms of chain. For visual identification, she was painted a dark red with "Cape Elizabeth" in large white letters displayed on each side. At night two fixed white lights burned from the mast-heads and in foggy weather her steam chime horn sounded a three second blast every twenty seven seconds. The first master of the lightship was Capt. John E. Ladd who had seen previous duty as master aboard the Round Shoal and Pollock Rip Lightships. The name of the ship was changed from "Cape Elizabeth" to "Portland" in 1910.

Life aboard the lightship was filled with routine tasks, however, it could become wildly active when storms blew in from the Atlantic. The first vessel had quite a reputation as a "roller", but she held to her station very well. During exceptionally violent storms giant combers would sweep completely over the vessel and she would be kept underway to take some of the strain off the anchor chain. On rare occasions she would tear loose and be forced to seek shelter in Portland Harbor. To serve successfully aboard the Portland Lightship a steady stomach and a well trained pair of sea-legs were prerequisite.

The current vessel on this station was built by the Bath Iron Works, Bath, Maine in 1924. A sturdy ship of 797.7 tons, she measures 134 feet 10 inches in length and is equipped with 450 hp diesel engine as well as four generators. For purposes of daylight recognition the ship is painted a bright red and displays the word "Portland" in large letters on each side. In foul weather her fog horn emits a three-second blast every thirty seconds with power enough to be heard eight miles under the right conditions. According to a crewman the vibrations from the blast are sufficiently strong to "lift you out of your bunk." Should the diaphragm horn fail a bell can be immediately placed in service that would sound twice every thirty seconds. At night, her equal interval 13,000 candlepower light is visible a maximum of fourteen miles and shows a six second flash. Before being placed on the Cape Elizabeth Station in 1952, she served at the Ambrose Light Station off New York.

As warning devices and navigational markers became well established, the greatest need yet remaining was organized assistance for mariners who came to grief in the shoal waters off Cape Elizabeth. Shore-based lifesaving operations had first been initiated in the U. S. by the Massachusetts Humane Society. Founded in 1785 this private volunteer society built its first lifeboat at Cohasset in 1807. The earliest activity by the Federal government in this area dated from 1831 when the Revenue Cutter Service instituted winter cruises to assist seafarers and ships in distress. The revenue cutter *Morris*, under the command of Capt. Green Walden and based at Portland fulfilled this duty locally during this era. In 1836 the cutters were directed to "aid persons at sea, in distress, who may be taken aboard" and seven years later became responsible for the preservation of property found aboard wrecks. Finally, in 1871 the U. S. Lifesaving Service was established as a branch of the Revenue Marine Division with the Secretary of the Treasury authorized to employ surfmen to man lifeboat stations.

Popular action for the locating of a life boat station to serve the port of Portland was launched in November of 1879. A petition was circulated by Capt. Benjamin J. Willard and forwarded to the Treasury Department but elicited no immediate response. Finally, in August of 1885 Sumner S. Kimball, chief of the Lifesaving Service, was authorized to erect lifeboat stations at Cove Island and Cape Elizabeth, Maine, as well as at North Scituate, and Portsmouth, New Hampshire. The sum of $6,000 was appropriated to cover the cost of building and equiping each station.

The Cape Elizabeth Lifeboat Station was built during the winter of 1886-87 at Dyer's Cove going into active service 1 August 1887. By this time the Lifesaving Service had become a separate bureau within the Treasury Department but continued to be supervised, drilled, and frequently inspected by officers of the Revenue Cutter Service. The first crew at the Cape Elizabeth Station consisted of Capt. Horace G. Trundy, Sumner N. Dyer, Maurice Jordan, Joseph Staples, Woodbury Pillsbury, Samuel D. Angell, and Jesse Barker.

The men who were accepted as surfmen had to be expert seamen, experienced boatmen, knowledgeable in the ways of the sea, and courageous in the extreme. Also, on occasion they were forced to serve as makeshift undertakers. In addition, they had to be strong and in the best of health, for they were compelled to submit to a thorough physical exam each year at the Portland Marine Hospital. Generally, the surfmen were all local citizens who, as fishermen and farmers, resided on the "Outer Cape."

Under ordinary circumstances their active duty began each season on 1 August and ended 31 May. They lived at the station, visiting their homes occasionally during the day or in the evening. They were constantly available however, always returning to the station for their meals and to sleep. For this, the surfmen received $65.00 a month, providing their own food, clothing, and personal gear. During the off-months, June and July, they were on call, receiving three dollars a day if pressed into service. Otherwise their time was their own.

While on active duty, their days were filled with constant drill, look-out watches, and a continual refurbishing of their equipment. Every day, weather permitting, they would don foul-weather gear and life jackets, launch their surfboat, and spend a few hours of practice at the sweeps. The surfboats were 27 foot, self-bailing, double enders; virtually unsinkable and uncapsizable. In addition, frequent drills with Lyle-gun and breeches buoy were carried on. At night a coastwatch was maintained in four-hour shifts from 4:00 p.m. to 8:00 p.m. with the men being rotated from watch to watch. Two men worked each shift, one patroling the coast to Trundy's Reef and the other to High Head. Each man carried a lantern, two flares, and a brass token which he exchanged with his companion after completing each round trip. Needless to say, it took a man of unusual stamina to face the sub-zero cold and howling gails of the winter months in keeping this constant vigil.

In 1888 a relief station was built at Trundy's Reef as a base for the frequent operations that characterized that area. Also, as the tower on the station building lacked breadth of vision a new look-out tower was constructed on a heighth of land slightly to the north adjacent to the eastern tower of the Cape Elizabeth Lights. Again, in 1891, facilities were further enlarged with the building of an addition to the station to house a work shop. At this time the station not only provided quarters for the men, but was also used to store their equipment and their surfboat. Facing the edge of the cove, with a ramp running down onto the beach, the men could launch their surfboat directly from the station in a matter of minutes.

The only major break in the regular routine occurred during the Spanish-American War. The remote possibility of a naval action and the more real probability of shipwrecks due to the extinguishing of Portland Head Light, prompted the government to keep the crew on active duty throughout the summer of 1898.

The following year, Captain Horace G. Trundy, after twelve years of arduous service, resigned his command. Immediately thereafter, he formed a partnership with George Mathews and together they purchased the tug *Wawenoc*. In the years to come Capt. Trundy and the tug were an industrious addition to the port of Portland. His place as a commander of the Cape Elizabeth Lifesaving Station was taken by Captain Sumner N. Dyer, a very capable man, with years of experience at sea.

During Capt. Dyer's long tour of duty many changes took place at the station. In December 1905 a new surfboat was delivered. One of eleven built for the Lifesaving Service by F. F. Staples of Portland it was similar to the earlier model except that it was self-righting and non-sinkable. The following year improvements in communications brought a closer working relationship with the cutters of the Revenue Service. When the surfmen went to the aid of a vessel in distress the Portland based cutter *Woodbury* would be notified if the lifesaving crew required assistance and vice versa. Together they greatly expanded and improved their already invaluable rescue operations. Yet another improvement was the issuance of a launch powered by a gasoline engine to the station in November of 1907. The surfboat with its white-ash sweeps was relegated to a stand-by status.

The year 1915 marked the end of a great era. On the 28th of January, the Lifesaving Service and the Revene Cutter Service were absorbed by the Coast Guard. Henceforth, the surfmen would be functionaries of that body, their old individuality and local associations now a thing of the past.

The development of improved communications had done much to expand the operational success of the Cape Elizabeth Lifesaving Station. The first step in this direction was the installation of a telephone in February 1888. The telephone company generously agreed to run the wire if the cost was defrayed by the subscribers. As the Federal government would not appropriate the necessary funds, local citizens raised the money among themselves. For the first three years, the subscribers would pay all maintenance costs, after which the telephone company would assume ownership and responsibility. The generosity of the local citizenry in providing this vital communications link would be deeply appreciated by many a mariner in the years that followed. In 1901, the Federal government did finance the installation of a telephone line to the relief station at Trundy's Reef.

The exposed nature of Dyer's Point adjacent to the station made it a natural location for the establishment of a weather signal tower. In February 1904 a steel mast for flags and lights was erected to give visual warning both day and night of impending storms.

To expand communication facilities further a radio station was built on the ridge close by the light towers. Actually the radio station was originally placed as a temporary installation by the Navy during fleet maneuvers in the North Atlantic between 5 and 10 August 1903. Two 150 foot antenna masts, 62 feet apart, were erected, with a radio shack located in a gully about fifty feet away. After the fleet maneuvers were concluded, the Navy decided to continue the radio installation as an experimental station. As a result, the masts were moved to a more advantageous site on the ridge, and a more permanent building was constructed to house the transmitters, generators, batteries, and crew.

Constant experimentation gradually improved transmission to the point that the broadcasting of periodic weather reports was inaugurated in December of 1905. The station also served successfully as a range finding installation in conjunction with other transmitters along the coast. As more ships began to carry radio equipment, the Cape Elizabeth station became a vital communications link throughout the North Atlantic. However, with the end of World War II the station became obsolete and was discontinued.

After the Coast Guard assumed control of the Lifesaving Station, many changes were forthcoming. In November 1933 work was started on a new station to house the crew. It was built slightly north of the original station on a site occupied for years by a two-family house. This dwelling was purchased by Vernon Reynolds and moved to a new location. The new building was a two story structure measuring approximately 25'x40' and faced Dyer's Cove. When this new building was added to the station, Capt. Charles W. Berry was in command, his crew consisting of Vernon Reynolds, John Morrison, Clarence Schwartz, Roscoe Dennison, Clarence Dunn, James McCrum, Linwood Beal, Clyde Trafton, Haskell Crane, and Earl McLaughlin. The old building continued to be used but only for storage purposes.

The end of lifesaving activities came rather quietly in 1964. The old station had been declared surplus in 1952, subsequently sold, and moved away. As of 0800 Saturday 8 February, 1964 the Cape Elizabeth Lifesaving Station ceased to exist. The base maintained by the Coast Guard at South Portland now assumed the duties and responsibilities so nobly borne in the past by Capt. Trundy, Capt. Dyer, and their interpid crews.

In the seventy-seven years of its existence the lifesaving crew carried out innumerable acts of assistance and rescue in adjoining waters. On various occasions they traveled long distances to aid those who had come to grief. One rather spectacular example was the wreck of the recently launched, Bath built, five-masted schooner *Washington B. Thomas* 12 June 1903. Laden with 4,000 tons of coal the schooner ran into heavy weather off Saco Bay and anchored to wait out the gale. Unfortunately, the anchor began to drag and in a comparatively short period of time she piled up on a reef off Stratton Island. The Cape Elizabeth crew was immediately notified and shortly thereafter Capt. Dyer with his crew departed for the scene. To reach the wreck, four horses were used to haul the surfboat overland from the station to Prout's Neck. They succeeded in saving the ship's master, Capt. William J. Lermond, and his crew. Despite their heroic efforts, the surfmen were too late to save Capt. Lermond's young wife who was torn from his grasp and drowned by the pounding surf. In this instance Capt. Dyer and his crew were on the scene three days before their mission was completed.

II

In the maritime history of Cape Elizabeth nothing is more tragic than a chronicling of the shipwrecks that occurred there. As of 1964 eighty-one known vessels, totaling approximately 23,000 tons of shipping, have been destroyed on this inhospitable coast. These marine disasters also carried seventy-nine people to a watery death.

Over the years the people of the Cape rendered whatever assistance they could to the suffering mariner. Whenever possible they saved as much as they could for the hapless seafarer, salvaging the wreckage and debris for themselves. On one occasion when the bark *Isidore* broke up on Trundy's Reef in May 1847, a large deck house washed ashore intact. It was salvaged by Freeman McKenney and converted by him into a comfortable dwelling at Broad Cove where he resided for many years.

Although there must have been wrecks in the colonial era, the earliest of which there is any record occurred 12 February 1780 at Broad Cove. This was the schooner *Nancy*, a British vessel serving as a cartel enroute from Halifax to Boston. Although the Commonwealth of Massachusetts felt honor bound to secure whatever salvage existed for the British government, the vessel was stripped bare and the hull burned for the metal it contained. Despite official displeasure, little or nothing was recovered.

Perhaps the most extraordinary of all the early shipwrecks was that of the East Indiaman, *Grand Turk*. She was built at Salem, Massachusetts by Enos Briggs for the prosperous merchant, Elias Hasket Derby. Launched 18 May 1791 she was described as a large ship, being 564 tons, too large in fact for the waters of Salem Harbor. Besides the inconvenience of her deep draft, the vessel proved to be a slow sailer. Derby sold her for $22,000 in 1795 to John Earl of New York. The new owner employed the *Grand Turk* in the China trade.

Wooden steamer *Bay State*, 1,555 tons, wrecked at McKenney's Point 23 September 1916.

Collier *Oakey L. Alexander*, 5,284 tons, beached at High Head, 3 March 1947, after her bow was carried away by heavy seas.

Painting of the clipper ship *Portland,* 998 tons, built by Joseph W. Dyer at Cape Elizabeth in 1853.

Painting of the brig *Scotland,* 284 tons, built by Benjamin W. Pickett at Cape Elizabeth in 1854.

On the voyage that brought her to Portland, the *Grand Turk*, with Capt. Barnard Magee in command, left Canton, China, 26 March 1797 and cleared Java Head 21 June. Her passage across the Indian Ocean and the Atlantic was slow and arduous. When she arrived off Portland Harbor, the local pilot, Capt. John Thurlo, brought her in and anchored her off Fish Point. The 259 day passage had worked great hardship on both vessel and crew, with three men dying of disease. Thus it was that the *Grand Turk*, flying a distress signal, put into the port of Portland for much-needed repairs and provisions 28 December 1797.

To celebrate their safe arrival, the ship's officers were the guests of honor at a dance held in the old Assembly Hall on India Street the evening of Thursday 4 January 1798. During the dance, a severe northeast gale struck the harbor. The high winds dislodged the ice at the mouth of the Presumpscot River and drove it around Fish Point hard against the *Grand Turk*. The drifting ice floes soon cut away her anchor cables and carried her across the harbor to Stanford's Ledge where she ran aground. Her guns and other heavy gear were cast overboard to float her off, but the gale drove the vessel instead over the reef inflicting grievous damage to the hull. The *Grand Turk* came to rest on Cushing's Point bilged beyond repair.

Most of her valuable cargo was saved except that which was stowed in her lower hold. Here the large hole in her bottom allowed the water to wash away chests of tea, crates of fine Chinese porcelain, and bolts of silk. Although some of this flotsam was salvaged much of it found its way into the hands of local citizens. Finery from the *Grand Turk* added a note of unaccustomed luxury to many a humble home at the Cape for years to come. Although the wreck soon disappeared, bits and pieces of porcelain could still be found on neighboring beaches until late in the nineteenth century after a violent storm.

The same year that the *Grand Turk* was lost, a small schooner came to grief at Portland Head. Wrecked on 26 November it was the first of fifty-nine schooners to leave their bones on the shores of Cape Elizabeth. Shortly after this wreck another schooner was lost at the same spot 17 December 1798. In this instance the captain's son swam through the icy waters to the shore with a line thereby enabling the others still aboard to safely reach the land.

On the 7th of April 1804 the brig *Apollo*, inward bound from Surinam with a cargo of molasses, sugar, and coffee, struck Trundy's Reef and quickly pounded to pieces. In this instance, as was frequently the case, inhabitants of the "Outer Cape" enjoyed an unexpected bounty from the sea.

The first vessel to be wrecked with a great loss of life was the Portland-Boston packet schooner *Charles*. On the night of Sunday, 12 July 1807, while seeking to gain Portland Harbor in a dense fog, she ran onto Watt's Ledge. A heavy sea was running, and she immediately began to break up. Of the twenty-two people aboard only six were able to gain the shore alive. The ship's master Capt. Jacob Adams, although he swam to safety, returned to the wreck in an attempt to save his wife and perished. Seven of the bodies were quickly recovered and conveyed to Portland where a funeral was held in the old Second Parish Church by the Rev. Elijah Kellogg on 14 July. Of the bodies recovered, Capt. Adams and his wife, Mrs. Eliza S. Hayden and her infant son Robert, were buried in Portland's Eastern Cemetery. Another victim, Miss Lydia Carver of Freeport, was buried in the little cemetery at Bowery Beach. A large slate headstone erected in her memory exists to this day. The last survivor of the wreck, Capt. Joseph Williams, died at Portland 23 March 1835 at the age of eighty-four.

In commemoration of the wreck, Thomas Shaw of Standish composed and published a twenty-nine verse epic poem as a broadside shortly after the disaster. A rather macabre and melancholy bit of ephemera, it was decorated with sixteen coffins and edged in funeral black. Another memorial broadside was a doleful elegy composed and published by Ebenezer Robbins of Portland, also in July 1807.

By far the worst of all the shipwrecks to occur at Cape Elizabeth took place the evening of Monday 22 February 1864. The screw steamer *Bohemian*, 1,488 tons, of the Montreal Ocean Steamship Company, eighteen days out of Liverpool, in entering Portland Harbor in a fog mistook the Alden's Rock buoy for the pilot boat and as a result struck the rock a glancing blow at 8:05 p.m. that opened a large hole in her engine room. The rush of water prompted the ship's master, Capt. Richard Borland, to try to beach her as quickly as possible before the boiler fires were extinguished. The vessel struck the shore at Broad Cove Rock and ran hard aground. As the *Bohemian* began to settle rapidly, the lifeboats were launched to disembark the 218 passengers and 99 crewmen. Fortunately, the sea was relatively calm and four of the five lifeboats were successfully lowered. As the boats were being loaded, panic broke out and spread quickly through the throng of 200 terror stricken Irish steerage passengers. Almost immediately boat No. 2 swamped, dumping its occupants, largely women and children, into the frigid water. In addition some began to leap into the sea with the hope of being picked up by the boats then pulling away from the ship.

Although a gun was fired, flares burned, and rockets sent aloft, no assistance was immediately forthcoming. However, as the survivors started to land, nearby residents began to gather on the shore. Large bonfires were built and as many of the sufferers as possible hustled off to shelter in local residences. Typical among the experiences of the rescuers was that of Michael Staples, keeper of the lights. He and his young son, Charles, worked most of the night helping the bewildered and frightened passengers. His daughter, Amelia, long remembered the eight begrimed stokers who slept exhausted on their kitchen floor until morning.

With the coming of the dawn help began to arrive from Portland and the task of transporting the survivors to the city was started. Agents for the Montreal Ocean Steamship Company provided shelter while local groups gathered clothing and food for the many destitute steerage passengers. The British vice-consul, Henry J. Murray, began at once to ascertain the living and the dead, as well as gather evidence, for a board of inquiry.

At the wreck bodies were being hauled ashore and carried to an emergency morgue, set up in the blacksmith shop of the Ocean House, as fast as possible. The vessel had by this time been swung around by the surf so that her bow was now pointing seaward. She rested lightly on a ledge amidship with her bow and stern about five feet off the bottom. At high tide the deck was just awash and it was thought that she could be floated off. The cargo was still aboard; only the mailbags that had been on deck had so far been removed. The Coast Wrecking Company of New York was contacted and a vessel dispatched on 25 February with equipment to raise her.

Before any effort to save the *Bohemian* could be carried out, a northeast storm swept down upon the helpless ship. The gales began Sunday March 6th. By daylight Monday the heavy seas had carried away her mizzenmast and funnel. As the day wore on, the fore and mainmasts went by the board. By late afternoon seething billows were making a clean sweep of her decks. Some time during the night, on Monday, the vessel parted midships and then split asunder lengthwise, literally breaking her into quarters. When dawn broke Tuesday morning, the sea was filled with cargo and debris from the disintegrating ship. The shore was strewn with a great variety of items from the *Bohemian's* vast quantity of dry goods that had been destined for Canadian merchants and their spring trade.

Men from the Revenue Service and soldiers from Camp Berry were dispatched to the scene to guard the growing piles of salvaged merchandise. As quickly as possible, the rescued cargo was hauled to Portland and deposited in the freight sheds of the Grand Trunk Railroad. The variety was astonishing; bolts of silks, brocades, satins, ginghams, and woolen cloth; crates of table linens and fine lace; cases filled with spools of thread, silk ribbon and celluloid combs; casks of tamarinds; boxes of dried fruit; casks of wine; to say nothing of boxed sundries. For those honest enough to turn over to the authorities the goods they salvaged, they received half of its declared value.

Swarms of small boats hovered around the wreck area, gathering in merchandise and other floatsam. Despite the efforts of U. S. Marshals and the Revenue Service the plunderers made off with substantial amounts of loot. The Revenue Cutter *Dobbin* patrolled the coast seeking caches of stolen cargo. On Wednesday 30 March they carried out a raid at Monhegan Island and seized $6,000 worth of looted merchandise. In addition, large quantities of the ship's furnishings were salvaged from the sea and carried away.

As the *Bohemian* continued to break up, more bodies came ashore and were cared for by the local undertaker, James Jordan. Many people continued to comb the nearby beaches gathering up crockery, silverware, furniture, carpets, linens, and other items with which the ship had been furnished. Souvenir hunters took away cabin doors, hardware, and all forms of wreckage as mementoes of the disaster. Some looters managed to elude the law officers and soldiers successfully making off with many valuable items. One man was apprehended on Fore Street in Portland with a wagon load of plunder. His wagon became mired, in the mud, and being forced to unload part of his ill-gotten gains in order to extricate it, was detected and quickly arrested.

The salvaged merchandise, stored in the Grand Trunk Railway sheds, was sold at public auction Thursday 31 March for the benefit of the original consignees. Although the vessel and its cargo were insured for $1,250,000 the ship owners and merchants were forced to accept staggering losses.

By this time, the destitute Irish steerage passengers who had survived, were beginning to recover from the tragedy. Local organizations such as the Irish American Relief Association, and the Ancient Order of Hibernians, provided some assistance. A few of the sufferers found shelter with acquaintances and relatives living in the Portland area. The total loss of life stood at forty passengers and two crew members. It is interesting to note that not one of the cabin class passengers was lost. Most of the victims were women and children who had drowned when lifeboat No. 2 founded.

Thirty of the deceased were claimed and interred by their families or friends. The remaining twelve were Irish passengers apparently without friends or relatives who would accept the financial responsibility of a proper burial. As a result they were interred at public expense in a mass grave at the recently established Calvary Cemetery near Ligonia. These destitute victims were Mary McDonough, age 34; Patrick McDonough, age 12; Thomas McDonough, age 6; Mary McDonough, age 7 months; Ellen Flaherty, age 18; Barbara Canavan, age 6; James Cassidy, age unknown; Thomas Kilivin, age unknown; Kebin, adult male, age unknown; and female child age unknown. It has been surmised that these victims were natives of county Galway. Tragic it was that they, forced to flee the misery and oppression of English misrule in their native land, should meet such a cruel fate literally at the threshold of a freer, more promising life. No monument has ever been erected to honor their final resting place. These "huddled masses yearning to breathe free the wretched refuse" of their native shore found nothing but an unmarked grave "beside the golden door."

Throughout the summer months, divers broke up the hull with blasting powder. In this manner, most of the ship was removed as scrap iron. Much of the metal was purchased by the Portland Company. By the fall of 1865 very little trace of the *Bohemian* remained. The figurehead, of heroic size, was obtained by Capt. Green Walden of the Revenue Service and stood for some years near his cottage at Glen Cove until destroyed by fire. A section of one of the masts was hollowed out and used as a horse trough at Pond Cove Corner late in the century. Also, a section of the vessel's propeller shaft was erected as a navigational marker at the mouth of the Saco River. Very few relics now survive, although for many years evidence of salvage was to be seen on the person and in the homes of many a Cape citizen. At the present time, the Maine Historical Society has in its collection a clock from the engine room of the *Bohemian*.

Twenty one years after the loss of the *Bohemian*, another vessel came to a tragic end under circumstances that were all too familiar. In most respects the wreck was in no way unique, for it does represent a typical marine disaster that was repeated much too often at Cape Elizabeth.

The schooner *Australia*, of 62 tons, manned by a crew of three, sailed from Boothbay Harbor 27 January 1885, bound for Boston with a load of ice in her hold and a deck cargo of 150 barrels of mackerel. Late in the evening, they raised Half-Way Rock in the midst of a north-east "line-storm." Visibility was practically nil because of a raging blizzard. The temperature hovered around zero and the sea was violently rough. Soon after leaving Half-Way Rock, the crewmen heard a steam whistle which they believed to be the fog signal at Two Lights but was in reality the Boston boat making for Portland Harbor. At this point, they tried to tack but miss-stayed. Realizing their danger, the crew began to jettison the deck cargo, hoping to make the schooner more manageable. Despite their efforts, the vessel ran upon the rocks at Dyer's Point some two hundred yards southwest of the fog station and about one hundred feet from shore. As the bilged ship began to settle, the crew took refuge in the rigging to await the coming of daylight and assistance.

At the fog-station, keeper Marcus Hanna was as yet unaware of the nearby mariners in distress. Having been on duty since midnight, he was relieved by assistant keeper Hiram Staples at 6:00 a.m. and climbed the hill to his residence. Shortly thereafter, Staples discovered the wreck and hastened to recall Hanna to aid in the rescue. As the tide receded, the two men waded through the deep snow and with great difficulty passed a line to the marooned men. By this time, the schooner's master, Capt John W. Lewis, had succumbed to exhaustion and had been swept away to his death. The two survivors, Irving Pierce and Austin Keller, were soon hauled to safety by the heroic efforts of Staples and Hanna, frostbitten and exhausted. They were immediately bedded down at Hanna's residence and in a few days were sufficiently recovered to leave for home. The schooner quickly pounded to pieces, the wreckage pilling upon the shore to be hauled away as firewood by local inhabitants.

One interesting sidelight of this disaster is the coverage that it received at the hands of an imaginative reporter for the *Eastern Argus*. Utilizing the literary talents of keeper Hanna, a rather remarkable tale of personal heroism was produced with the redoubtable keeper as the central figure. In later years additional embellishments were added and it appeared in a popular book in a much more fanciful form. Local citizens conversant with the actual facts were rather amused, if not somewhat annoyed, by both versions.

In the year that followed the tragic wreck of the schooner *Australia,* yet another disaster occurred, remarkably free of any loss of life. On Christmas eve 1886 the bark *Annie C. Maguire,* 1363 tons, ran aground and bilged at Portland Head, the ship's master, Capt. Thomas O'Neal having lost his bearings in a snowstorm. With the vessel less than a hundred yards from the lighthouse, assistance was immediately rendered by the keeper, Joshua F. Strout, and his son, Joseph. The Captain, his wife, and the entire crew were brought ashore without incident.

This vessel was the former *Golden State,* an extreme clipper built in 1853 at New York. In the great days of the California and China trade, she made some rather remarkable runs between New York and San Francisco, Shanghai and New York, London and Shanghai. During the Civil War she joined the "flight from the flag" and was sold to a Canadian firm. In later years, as the *Annie C. Maguire,* she was employed in the South American trade making frequent passages between Portland and Buenos Aires.

Although the ship was sold at auction and much of her rigging removed, very little was actually salvaged. A violent northeaster struck on Friday 31 December and within twenty-four hours she was gone. Wreckage was scattered along the coast for miles. Her mainmast came ashore at Simonton's Cove and was quickly converted into two cords of stove wood.

Another maritime disaster that was singularly free of any loss of life was the wreck of the stately steamer *Bay State* on Holycomb Reef at McKenney's Point. With Capt. Levi Forhan in command, the ship was making a routine run from Boston to Portland. An error in navigation and a mistake in identifying the Old Anthony bell buoy for the fog bell of the lightship, which had been temporarily withdrawn, brought a change of course that ended in disaster. At 3:30 a.m. on Saturday 23 September 1916 in the midst of a dense fog she struck head on, moving very slowly.

The *Bay State,* a sister ship of the ill-fated steamer *Portland* lost off Cape Cod 28 November 1898, was a wooden sidewheel steamer built at Bath, Maine, in 1895, for the Portland Steam Packet Company, the predecessor of the Eastern Steamship Company. She was registered as 1,555 tons, and measured 281 feet in length, 42 feet in width, with a 15 foot depth of hold.

At the time of her loss, she was the oldest passenger ship of the former Portland Steam Packet Company fleet. With the exception of a short period when she served as substitute on the

Bangor, Rockland, Boston route the *Bay State* piled almost continually between Boston and Portland for a period of twenty-one years. It has been estimated that she made approximately 2,400 round trips and carried a total of well over a million passengers during her career on this run.

When the *Bay State* struck Holycomb Reef, Surfman Louis Briggs of the Cape Elizabeth Lifesaving Station was on the scene. He had just punched his watchman's clock as part of his patrol when he sighted the ship steaming directly toward him. Although he immediately ignited a Corson torch, it was too late. At that very instant, Capt. Forhan had discovered his perilous situation and had rung for full astern, but this too was of no avail.

As the vessel ground to a stop on the ledge, Briggs contacted the station to the accompaniment of staccato blasts from the ship's whistle. In a matter of minutes, Capt. Sumner Dyer, with Alonzo Parker, Daniel Foss, and Fred Jordan, was underway for the scene in the surfboat. At the same time, George Staples and Willis Latham were on their way overland with the equipment necessary to rig a breeches buoy.

Simultaneously, the naval wireless station contacted the Coast Guard cutter *Ossippee* and the Eastern Steamship Company agent Herbert A. Clay. The cutter departed immediately for the wreck, followed shortly by the tugs *Cumberland* and *Portland*.

By the time Capt. Dyer was able to board the stricken vessel at 5:00 a.m. the incoming tide and heavy swells had driven her further up on the ledge despite the fact that the paddle wheels were making a maximum effort full astern. With the dawn came an increase in the wind from the eastward and heavier seas. The *Bay State* began to pound and roll quite badly under the impact of the waves. It was soon apparent that she could not be hauled off until weather conditions improved. At the same time rising water in the engine room made it imperative that the fires be drawn and the boilers blown to prevent an explosion.

It was at this point, that Capt. Forhan decided to disembark the 250 apprehensive passengers and 70 members of the crew. Shortly after 6:00 a.m. the lifeboats were lowered and the task of transferring the passengers to the tugs or nearby beaches began. However, as the seas continue to increase, it became necessary to remove the people more rapidly. On the shore, Surfmen Staples and Latham were ready and at a signal from Capt. Dyer, Staples fired the Lyle Gun, sending the first line accurately aboard. By 7:20 a.m. the breeches buoy was rigged and ready for use if it became necessary. Assisting the lifeboat and lifesaving crews were eight dories manned by Lawren Olsen, David Olsen, Charles E. Olsen, Norman Olsen, W. L. Loveitt, Arthur Bolton, Thomas Martin, and Sherman White, as well as Jack Olsen and W. S. Jones in a motorized fishing boat. Despite the dangers of the situation, these heroic men were instrumental in saving a large number of the passengers and crewmen. Although most of the people were placed aboard the tugs, some were landed at Bowery Beach, finding an hospitable welcome at the summer home of Dr. Thomas J. Burrage. The only narrow escape of the entire operation involved the lifesaving crew. When they were returning from a trip to one of the tugs a large swell carried the surfboat beneath the sponson on the port side of the steamer as the vessel rose on the crest with the result that, as the *Bay State* settled into the trough, it pushed the stern of the surfboat under water. Quick work on the part of the surfmen averted what could have been a tragedy. Once the passengers and crew had been taken off, the removal of hand luggage was started and soon accomplished.

The prevailing easterly wind gradually worked the *Bay State* around so that within twenty-four hours she lay parallel to the ledge with her port side hard aground. The absence of any immediate storm was the only thing that saved her from breaking up. However, the constant battering of the starboard side by the breakers placed her so firmly upon the ledge that any hope of refloating the vessel was reluctantly abandoned. Later in the month she was sold to the Thomas Butler Company of Boston and the job of dismantling her was commenced.

Although the ship held together, quite a bit of debris and cargo washed out of the hull. Much of this material was salvaged by people living in the immediate vicinity of the wreck. Large quantities of clothing, cases of food and liquor, as well as furnishings from the ship's interior, were rescued. Most of the flotsam was retained locally. In one instance a resident living close by the wreck realized a tidy little profit by selling several bales of underwear to Jewish merchants from Portland.

The constant pounding of the surf ultimately exacted its toll. By the last of October, most of the starboard side had been staved in with the tide ebbing and flowing through the hull. Finally on 23 November a strong southeast gale struck that carried away much of the wreck. By the time the storm had passed, half of the vessel, from just aft of the paddlewheels forward, had broken up, littering nearby shores with masses of wreckage. The weight of the engine and boilers held the stern section in place on the ledge.

During the following summer the remains of the hull was

stripped of any salvageable material and on 15 August 1917 it was set afire. The surviving fragments of the hull and the engine were blown apart with dynamite early in September. By the end of September almost nothing remained to mark the final resting place of this once proud steamer. Undoubtedly odd pieces of crockery, rugs and other relics of the *Bay State,* still exist as treasured family possessions in the homes of the "Outer Cape."

The most recent marine disaster of any significance occurred in the early morning hours of Monday 3 March 1947. In the midst of a "northeaster," the 5,284 ton collier *Oakey L. Alexander* suffered mortal damage about a mile southeast of Dyer's Point. At 4:46 a.m., as the vessel slowly breasted the heavy seas and eighty-mile-an-hour gales, approximately 130 feet of her bow suddenly broke away without warning. The bow section, loaded with 5,000 tons of coal, sank instantly.

The ship's master, Capt. Raymond W. Lewis, after ascertaining that the vessel was not sinking decided to beach her as quickly as possible. He set a direct course for the ledges at High Head but proceeded very slowly to prevent the buckling of bulkhead plates that would instantly have sunk the ship. As all the crew were aft at the time the bow section broke away there were as yet no casualties. The real heroes of the run to the ledges were Chief Engineer Winfield S. Brower, First Assistant Engineer Arthur Bradley, and Second Assistant Engineer William P. Simpson, who remained at their posts in the engine room despite the fact that the vessel could founder at any moment. Not until she reached the breakers did these men leave their posts, after first pulling the fires and setting the throttle at slow ahead.

While the *Oakey L. Alexander* was underway for the beach, the radio operator, Lorenz Connelly, began sending an SOS signal that was instantly picked up by the Coast Guard. Responding with their customary speed, men from the Cape Elizabeth Coast Guard Station were on the scene when the vessel struck. Moments later, Warrant Officer Earle Drinkwater fired a line aboard close by the stack with a Lyle gun and a breeches buoy was quickly rigged, the first man coming ashore at 8:07 a.m. the ship's master, Capt. Lewis, landed at 10:00 a.m. the last man to leave the wreck. Although their situation was extremely dangerous the officers and crew escaped without injury, the only ones requiring medical attention were two who suffered from exposure.

The ship itself was a total loss and was soon sold to a local marine salvage firm. A venerable veteran of many voyages, the *Oakey L. Alexander* had been built in 1915 for the Coastwise

Transportation Company at Camden, New Jersey, and was originally christened the *Franklin*. Subsequently, she was purchased by the American Hawaiian Line, renamed the *Nevadan*, and altered to carry general cargo to the west coast. This venture proved a failure and it was then that she was sold to the Pocahontas Steamship Company and renamed the *Oakey L. Alexander* in honor of the firm's president. Over the next twenty years she carried 400,-000 tons of coal annually to the port of Portland for the Pocahontas Fuel Company from Norfolk, Virginia. Among her many skippers was Capt. Joseph H. York of South Portland, well remembered by local maritime men, who commanded her throughout World War I.

Within a few months, the vessel's cargo of coal was unloaded by the salvage firm of Bernstein and Jacobson. After stripping her, they cut the wreck to pieces for scrap metal. Today practically nothing remains of the *Oakey L. Alexander* except a few remnants of her hull, visible only at extreme low tide.

The discoveries of the modern age have done much to mitigate the perils of the ocean, and the coast of Cape Elizabeth is now seldom the scene of maritime disaster. Although swept by the same fearsome storms and assaulted by tumultuous seas the seasons succeed one another devoid of tragedy. Its fame as a place of scenic beauty has done much to soften the memories of heartache and grief that were born among the rocks and shoals of this forbidding shore.

CHAPTER VIII

MIND AND SOUL

In the early history of education in Cape Elizabeth two prominent features are immediately discernible: first, the total absence of any organized educational effort and second, the extraordinary high rate of illiteracy. Before Massachusetts annexed the Province of Maine in 1652, no record exists of any school within the Falmouth area. Despite the fact that many clergymen carried on some attempt at education, it is doubtful if the Rev. Robert Jordan or any other minister ever did any teaching beyond his own family circle. Schools, as such, simply did not exist and anyone who acquired the rudiments of an education, was indeed fortunate.

However, when Massachusetts extended its jurisdiction to Maine, education could no longer be neglected despite the sparseness of the population. In 1642, the Massachusetts General Court had passed a law requiring parents, guardians, and masters to teach their children to read and write. Five years later, the General Court enacted a statute that became a landmark in the history of popular education. It stipulated that every township of fifty householders or more must provide free elementary education and that a town of one hundred families or over must offer a grammar school education as well. As far as the Falmouth area is concerned, these laws were an aspiration rather than a reality.

It was not until 15 September, 1729, that the town of Falmouth took any official action relative to education. In this instance, the possibility of a fine, rather than the need for a school, motivated its activity. On that date the "selectmen were requested to look out for a schoolmaster to prevent the town's being presented." There is no evidence, however, that any individual was procured on that occasion.

The first mention of a schoolmaster in the town records of Falmouth occurs in 1731. In that year, the "former schoolmaster" Cornelius Bennett brought suit against the town to obtain his lawful wages. It is apparent that he actually had to take his case to court before the town would part with the money that was due him for keeping "scool," as it was noted in the records.

In this period, the town of Falmouth instituted an educational program common in this era. This was the moving-school, a method whereby the law was complied with and each child received a few weeks of schooling during the year. The people in outlying parts of the town, such as Purpooduck and Spurwink, found the distance to the Neck much too great for the purposes of a regular school. Therefore, to serve more isolated families the teacher would move from place to place within the town, lingering irregularly for a few weeks in the various sections. Needless to say, this educational method left much to be desired. Although its disadvantages are obvious, the moving-school was not completely replaced by the district school in Cape Elizabeth until late in the century.

The town of Falmouth, in 1732, apparently engaged a teacher to pursue this particular method. In the town records for that year, a single reference reads "to see where the school shall be opened and kept and to agree upon some method to pay the schoolmaster; to see if the town will agree with the schoolmaster to preach the winter season to the people on the Purpooduck side of the river." It would appear that the town was disposed to make the schoolmaster useful in more ways than one.

The first specific mention of hiring a resident schoolmaster occurs the following year, namely, Robert Bayley, employed at an annual salary of seventy pounds. The first year he was required to teach six months in Falmouth proper, three months at Purpooduck, and three on the north side of Back Cove. In 1734, his salary was increased by five pounds and he divided his time equally between the Neck, Purpooduck, Spurwink, Stroudwater, Presumpscot, and New Casco. The next year, Cape Elizabeth having been set off as the Second Parish, he was directed to spend seven months in the First Parish and five in the Second. In 1736, he received an additional six pounds, and the keeping of a grammar school was added to his duties.

The following year, Bayley was replaced by a Mr. Sewall who, in turn, was succeeded immediately by Nicholas Hodge, a Harvard student. From this period on, the Second Parish received very little in the way of educational services from the town of Falmouth. However, as no protest or changes are evident, the citizens must have been satisfied with the meager benefits of the moving-school. At this time, and for some years to come, if an inhabitant of Cape Elizabeth wanted to provide a better education for his children, he would inevitably send them into the town of Falmouth and later to Portland. There, boarding with friends or relatives, they could attend either the public grammar school, Portland Academy, (which was incorporated in 1794), or the numerous private schools.

The moving-school was superseded by the district school system within the First Parish only, in 1762. From this date on, the Second Parish was apparently responsible for its own educational program. As no records of consequence exist, the fragmentary allusions seem to indicate that the Second Parish did nothing, utilizing the district schools of Falmouth whenever or wherever possible. The closest were on the Neck or at Long Creek.

In 1742, the inhabitants of the Second Parish had petitioned the General Court to be set off as a separate town. Although their request was denied, the reasons they gave nevertheless reflect the school problem. They were dissatisfied with, among other things, the requirement that they contribute to the support of schools that were too inaccessable and too distant to be of service. This was still a problem in 1749 when their petition for separation was again denied.

When the District of Cape Elizabeth was finally incorporated in 1765, the district school system was gradually instituted. For the next 145 years, this was to be the basic source of education for the children of Cape Elizabeth. Nothing was done, however, to divide the town into districts until 1771 when four were created, i.e. Purpooduck, Long Creek, Spurwink, and Barren Hill. In addition, a moving grammar school was created.

The first schoolmaster designated by name in the Cape Elizabeth town records was Loring Cushing. At the meeting of 23 June, 1766, it was voted that he keep a moving-school. He was not mentioned again until 6 June, 1771 when it was voted that the "District make a Present of twenty pounds Lawful money to Capt. Loring Cushing Provided he give a Receipt to this District in full for his keeping school in Said District to this day." This was the first instance wherein Cape Elizabeth engaged a college graduate to serve as a teacher.

As a school-master, Loring Cushing must have been a man of rare talents. He was the eldest son of that leading local citizen, Col. Ezekiel Cushing, and had been born in Provincetown, Massachusetts in 1721. Entering Harvard College at the age of sixteen to study law, he was rated, according to the social standards of the institution, sixteenth in his class. Judging from the college records, young Cushing was not initially a dedicated student. During his freshman year, he was banished from the college for not attending religious services on a fast day in order to entertain a group of upper classmen in his rooms, No. 17 Massachusetts Hall, with a "Rost of Fowls and Revelling together with prohibited Liquors." In addition, his classmate, Thomas Amory, destined to be one of Boston's leading merchants, was "convicted of gross Lying" trying to protect Cushing, and severely punished. After a period of enforced rustication, he returned to Harvard, apparently unenlightened. At the end of his junior year, the Faculty were again forced to take action. As noted in records of the college, they "voted that Cushing for being intoxicated with Strong Drink, which is greatly aggravated by former scandalous behavior, for which He then incurr'd the Censure of the government of the House by Rustication, be publicly admonished, and degraded ten places in his Class." Either this punishment or the influence of his roommate, William Lawrence, class of 1743, a severe and formal divinity student, had its effect, for thereafter he conducted himself "in a very becoming Manner," and as a reward had his name restored to its original place on the Theses Sheet of the class of 1741.

Upon his return to Purpooduck, he joined his father in business, serving as a supercargo on various West Indian voyages, and as personal secretary. In 1750, he married his stepsister, Mary Parker, settled permanently near his father, and proceeded to raise a family. When the Revolutionary War broke out, he enlisted as a private, 15 May 1775, in Capt. David Bradish's company, 31st Regiment Massachusetts Foot. After a great deal of service, Cushing was mortally wounded at the second battle of Freeman's Farm, Saratoga, 7 October 1777, and died two days later. Like all the other casualties, he was buried in a mass grave at Saratoga, the location of which is currently unknown. It is interesting to note in passing, that his son, Loring Cushing, Jr., served three years in the Continental Army, survived the grim winter of Valley Forge, and returned to Cape Elizabeth.

Each school district was supervised by a committee which had the responsibility of engaging a teacher, furnishing the school, and expending their proportional share of the funds appropriated by the town. Under ideal conditions, an elementary education could be, with some difficulty, obtained in such a district school. Such conditions did not exist in Cape Elizabeth for many years. Until late in the century, the only consideration that apparently motivated the maintaining of a school was to avoid being fined by the state. Typical of the action so often taken is the notation that appears in the minutes of the town meeing held Monday, 2 April, 1787. It was voted to give "Parpudoc twenty pounds of that money that was voted last year for a school and they are to keep such a school the present year as to save the town from a fine." Although these were difficult times, the population sparse and poor, education was nevertheless grievously neglected.

In 1797, the town approved for the first time the creation of a school committee, with jurisdiction over the entire town, to consist of seven members. Their first task was to reorganize the various districts and encourage education. At the town meeting held 22 August, the committee reported that no changes had as yet been instituted relative to the expansion of existing facilities and that the money appropriated had been distributed in proportion to the number of children in each district. The following year, $400 was allocated for the support of education. This amount was not increased until 1805 when it was raised to $600.

Throughout this period, it is quite apparent that one teacher served the entire town, moving from one district school to another. In September, 1800, the town engaged the Rev. William Gregg to be the "publik teacher," prior to his ordination as resident minister. Apparently, his service as schoolmaster was terminated when he assumed his ministerial duties.

Between 1806 and 1821, the town, with few exceptions, appropriated $800 for the maintainance of the school districts. From 1822 to 1842, the annual sum was $650 with no significant changes other than the creation of two more districts.

Throughout the nineteenth century, the district school remained the most common form of education in Cape Elizabeth. Not until late in the century was any special attention lavished upon these schools nor any consideration given to instruction, curriculum, or environment. Drably painted and desolate without, the district schools were equally unattractive within, entirely dependent upon the whim of the district school committee. Generally, they were located with an eye to convenience but not at the expense of valuable acreage. All too often, they occupied a bleak and barren site, swept by winter blasts and scorched by the summer sun.

The interior frequently reflected the parsimonious inclinations of the inhabitants and their skeptical attitude toward education. The furnishings were minimal, with comfort the last consideration. The students were accommodated with rows of desks and backless benches of various heights. Near the front of the room was a desk for the teacher and a few benches for the classes "called up" for recitation. The windows were usually too small and too few to furnish enough light. Until the twentieth century, blackboards were rare, and "teaching aids" were novelties provided by the teacher. Heat was furnished by a fireplace in the early years and by stoves as the nineteenth century advanced. In either case, the children near the source of heat were often severely roasted while ice formed in the water pail in the corner.

The teachers in these district schools were poorly paid and often little educated, at best they might be young men trying to earn enough to continue their own academic training. Two interesting examples of such young men who served in the schools of Cape Elizabeth are Thomas Bracket Reed and William Widgery Thomas. The former, graduated from Bowdoin in 1860, became a prosperous lawyer, and was elected to the U. S. House of Representatives in 1876, ultimately becoming Speaker of the House and earning for himself the title "Tsar Reed." The latter also graduated from Bowdoin College in 1860, was admitted to the bar, and in later years served as the American Minister to Sweden and Norway. Reed taught one session in 1857 at the Pond Cove district school that had been built in 1830. Thomas also taught but one term, in 1857, at the Spurwink district school, erected in 1849.

Such men as Reed and Thomas were obviously exceptional. Under ordinary circumstances, the summer term, attended largely by little children and girls, was taught by a woman whose salary rarely exceeded six dollars a month. A male teacher was customarily provided for the winter term as it was apt to be a bit rough, as the students were usually older boys or young men, demanding a firm and resolute hand. His salary ranged from seven to twelve dollars a month. These sums were not the teacher's only remuneration for both men and women had the dubious pleasure of "boarding around" with the local citizens. Generally, the social standing and influence of the teacher in the community were commensurate with the low salary.

Most of the teachers maintained an iron discipline through constant recourse to the rod or ferule. With few exceptions, textbooks were scarce and dull with no attempt at standardization throughout the school districts. The curriculum was normally restricted to the "three R's", the teacher providing additional instruction in geography, history, and science if he could find the time. Innovations as to subject matter or teaching were not encouraged by parents or the town and district school committees, nor were they actually possible with existing equipment and the heavy teaching loads. For most of the students the monotonous reiteration of a few facts, and constant drill in certain elementary skills, constituted the educational process. Despite this stultifying environment, many students rose above it, and, with extraordinary perseverance, acquired a basic, if somewhat limited, education. It was generally these few who looked back with nostalgia to the day of the "little red schoolhouse" where they gained a rudimentary education failing to notice that it was not because of, but in spite of, the training they received.

From 1800-1880, improvement in the schools of Cape Elizabeth was hardly noticeable. The reports of the school committee are filled with gloomy comments relative to inadequate schools, parental indifference,, and unsuccessful teachers. The situation at Ferry Village school in 1857 was all too typical. In regard to the teacher, it was voted that "there was a great lack of order, and consequently, the evils which usually result therefrom. There seems to have been a great lack of interest in the school, from the fact that there were one hundred and eight registered scholars, and only from fifty to sixty in regular attendance. But this is not wholly attributable to the teacher, as many of the parents seem to consider it as a matter of little or no importance whether their children attend school or not; permitting them to stroll about the streets and remain away from school upon the most frivolous excuse, or even with none at all." Again, that same year, the committee pointed out that the schoolhouse at Pond Cove was "a mere apology, being a great discredit to so wealthy a district."

The following year, the school committee unhesitatingly informed their fellow citizens that "many causes serve to retard the progress of our schools which lie beyond the power of your committee to remove, chief of which exists in a lack of moral culture, and intellectual training at home." This same year, 1858, the cause of education was not entirely a loss. The school at Bowery Beach elicited the following comments of a most encouraging nature. "This district possesses every capacity for the working of wonders. A good school house on one of the most enchanting sites in the state of Maine; scholars having no lack of intellect, and men of abundant means. Let them add to this union of action and they might defy competition."

A reading of mid-century reports reveal all too clearly the fluctuations of success that plagued the system. Seldom was there consistency. It was a constant struggle to find and retain adequate teachers, to keep children in school, to overcome public apathy, indifference, and hostility, to keep the schools in a reasonable state of repair, and to meet the needs of a growing community. On 7 January 1870 the *Eastern Argus* recommended Cape Elizabeth "as a good field for missionary labor. In one of the schools the scholars lock the master out, and in another they have made such strong objections to the opening prayer that the master has been compelled to leave."

By 1875, there were fourteen school districts within the town of Cape Elizabeth. They were: No. 1 Long Creek, No. 2 Brown's Hill, No. 3 Barren Hill, No. 4 Ridgeway, No. 5 Ferry Village, No. 6 Point Village, No. 7 Pond Cove, No. 8 Spurwink, No. 9 Bowery Beach, No. 10 Running Hill, No. 11 Knightville, No. 12 Turner's Island, No. 13 Rolling Mills, No. 14 Pleasantdale. Some were subdivided into various departments. The Ferry Village school, having the largest student body, had a Grammar Department, a First Primary Department, and a Second Primary Department. Such subdivisions soon became common in the villages.

The diverse difficulties of the school district system prompted the Supervisor of Schools, Edwin A. Harlow to recommend their abolition and consolidation in 1878, after the state had authorized the various towns to exercise a complete and centralized control. The recommendation apparently fell on deaf ears for it was not accomplished prior to the separation of the towns despite the fact that it was again advocated in 1881.

About 1835, S. C. Millett opened a private boarding school for boys at The Bower. According to his prospectus, he offered a program that embraced all the branches of a "good English Education, including Mathematics, Natural and Moral Philosophy, and Chemistry, &c. Particular attention given to the study of the Latin and Greek languages." He also noted that "instruction is given in all the branches usually taught in our Academies."

The boys entrusted to Millett's care were carefully and completely supervised. He informed the parents of prospective students that "strict attention is paid to the moral and physical, as well as intellectual education of those entrusted to him. It is believed that the great object of Education can be more effectively accomplished where there is a constant intercourse between teacher and pupil. For this purpose they will be entirely under the care of the teacher both in their studies and amusements. It will be his object by keeping them thus under his observation to become thoroughly acquainted with their habits and dispositions . . . All the boys with the teachers and their families will constitute one household."

The entire cost of tuition, board, washing, books, and everything except clothing was $125 a year. If the boy was so inclined he could reduce his tuition to $90 by working two hours each day for the school. The school began on 15 October and was divided into four twelve week terms with a vacation of one week between each term. No boy was accepted for any period shorter than a year.

Although Millett continued to run an advertisement in the *Portland Advertiser, Kennebec Journal,* and *Bangor Whig* until 1838, there is little evidence to suggest that the school was a success. The continued use of The Bower as a summer boarding house seems to substantiate such an assumption.

Another interesting educational institution established at Cape Elizabeth in these early years was the first school in the state of Maine for the education of juvenile delinquents. This was the State Reform School established on the north bank of Long Creek near its mouth late in 1850. In December of that year, 164 acres of land were purchased, and construction started early in the following year. The main building was completed and occupied in October of 1853. The institution was immediately placed under the control of a board of five trustees appointed by the governor and council.

Initially, any boy under the age of eighteen years could be sentenced to the school by a court or justice for any crime other than assault and battery or a capital offense. The most common causes for commitment were petty larceny, running away, vagrancy, truancy, common idling, and disturbing the peace. The sentence could not extend beyond the boy's twenty-first birthday, nor could it be for less than one year. If a boy was in residence at the age of twenty-one, he was released and the rest of his sentence expunged from the record.

The method of rehabilitation generally consisted of instruction "in such branches of useful knowledge as shall be adapted to their ability so that they might obtain the rudiments of a trade." Occasionally some were "bound out" to work for men approved by the trustees, thereby enabling the boys to obtain a practical education.

After the first two boys were admitted in November 1853, the number increased so rapidly that, three years later, the trustees requested a sharp increase in the annual appropriation. Between 1853 and 1895 the number of boys varied from a low of ninety-three to a high of two hundred and forty.

A routine day in the life of a boy at the State Reform School usually included four hours of school, six hours of manual labor, eight and one half hours of sleep, and five and a half of moral instruction, eating, and recreation. The boys received basic instruction in reading, grammar, spelling, penmanship, arithmetic, and geography. The task of the teacher was difficult indeed, as many of the boys were not only illiterate, but completely indifferent to education, and often of limited intelligence. In 1865, a gymnastics teacher was added much to the delight of the boys. Another source of enjoyment was the very adequate library that grew with each passing year.

There were three major areas of practical work experience open to the boys: agricultural, mechanical, and domestic. Of the three, farming was by far the most popular from the start. The work hours were from seven to ten in the forenoon and from three to six in the afternoon. Upon occasion, some of the more reliable boys were indentured to farmers, carpenters, shoemakers, brick-makers, and mechanics of various kinds. In 1882, a mechanic arts shop was built at the school, greatly expanding the opportunities for learning a trade.

In 1876, many needed reforms were instituted. The school was graded for the first time; cells were replaced by dormitories, and a generous program of privileges to be earned by good behavior was established. Despite these good beginnings much could still be done from the standpoint of humanity. The state was deeply shocked by a series of investigations in the early eighties that revealed practices and punishments that were unncessarily cruel. Additional reforms were immediately carried out that ended the brutal and abusive treatment meted out to some of the more recalcitrant boys.

After several years of agitation by the trustees, a "Cottage System" was instituted at the school whereby the boys were organized into "families." In such a situation it was soon evident that the boys greatly benefitted from the more personal treatment they received. In conjunction with the new program the age limit was reduced to sixteen. In 1889 the first "cottage" was built to accommodate fifty boys, and in 1891, another was constructed, only to be destroyed by fire within a year. Other cottages were erected in the years that followed. To accommodate this expansion of the facilities, twenty more acres of land were added to the school. By 1900 it was more than fulfilling its intended purpose to serve "rather as a refuge for misfortune than a receptacle for criminals."

Although its need had been evident for some years the town of Cape Elizabeth offered nothing more than a grammar school education until 1853. On 13 August of that year S. C. Knights announced in the *Eastern Argus* that he would open a high school at the Town House on 22 August. He offered instruction "in the higher English, Latin, and French." Just how successful this private high school was it is impossible to say. Apparently Mr. Knights was an experienced teacher, judging from his prospectus, and maintained his school for at least three years.

It was not until the meeting of 26 March 1874 that the town voted to establish its first public high school. On this occasion $500 was appropriated to bring such a school into being. Actually, the incentive for creating a high school had been supplied by a state law passed the year before providing for grants to the towns equal to half the sum they appropriated for a free high school. Among the more active and persistent supporters of this educational improvement were Joseph S. Fickett and Edward F. Hill, both closely associated with the teaching profession for many years.

As there was no suitable structure to house the high school when instruction began in the fall of 1874, it was decided to have the first term at district school No. 12, Turner's Island, and the second term at No. 6, Point Village. However, when the new Town House was completed late in 1874, two rooms were finished off on the second floor to house the high school. One served as a school room and the other as a recitation room.

When the third term began in the spring of 1875 at the Town House, there were ninety-eight students in attendance. There to greet them were two very able teachers, D. Winslow Hawkes and Josephine Gerry. Also serving as the first principal, Mr. Hawkes was an experienced educator. He attended Westbrook Seminary, and, upon graduation, stayed on briefly as an instructor. His term of service at Cape Elizabeth High School was destined to continue, with the exception of two terms in 1887, until his retirement in 1895. He died 7 July, 1910, at the age of seventy-two.

Public support of the new high school was not unqualified. For the first four years, it was a constant and often bitter struggle to preserve its existence. Many of the citizens felt that the high school injured the district schools by removing the older, more advanced students, who were a steadying influence and an inspiration to the younger pupils. The rather casual approach to the desirability of a high school education is discernible in the attendance figures for the first four years. Of the ninety-eight students who entered, only four were prepared to graduate in June of 1877, with the figure rising to thirteen the following year.

Two factors that cut down the early graduating classes were inadequate preparation and the necessity of gainful employment at an early age. In the first few years of educational endeavor at the high school, many improvements were made. The curriculum was broadened to include two courses of study, Classical as well as English. Also, in 1875 the students organized a debating society that continued with some success for several years. Three years later, an alumni association was organized with Edward C. Reynolds, '77, as its first president. In 1881, the association was instrumental in obtaining a contribution of $100 from Dr. John Buzzell for the establishment of a high school library known as the Buzzell Library.

The establishment of the high school worked many changes within the educational system. Not only did it lighten the student load at many of the more populous district schools, but it also made possible an expansion of the grammar school program in these schools. This improvement in facilities was reflected in the creation of examinations for admittance to the high school. A sample examination was published in the town report of 1882 and was broken down into five equal parts: arithmetic, grammar, geography, history, and bookkeeping, with ten questions in each. They certainly reflect a much improved educational situation and a curriculum of greater academic respectability.

When the separation of the town occurred in 1895, the new town of Cape Elizabeth was devoid of any high school. As a result, between 1895 and 1902, pupils from Cape Elizabeth continued to attend what was now South Portland High School with the town paying their tuition. In 1902, $500 was appropriated to establish a high school in two rooms set aside for that purpose at the new Cape Elizabeth Town Hall. The first class, of twenty-one pupils, entered in September of 1902, and at that time, Ernest L. Jordan was the entire teaching staff. On 20 June, 1905, the new Cape Elizabeth High School had its first graduation. Six students, Harvard M. Armstrong, Hazel C. Hannaford, Albert F. Jones, Emma I. Peabbles, Ethel A. Staples, and Charles S. Strout, received their diplomas at exercises held in the town hall.

Although the town had at least a rudimentary high school, many students continued to attend the schools of South Portland and Portland. As transportation was still something of a problem, the town continued to pay tuition for some students living in close proximity to South Portland High School until 1913. The gradual increase in the number of students brought significant improvements, however, with a second teacher added and the curriculum expanded in 1906. A well planned program relative to the meeting of rigid state requirements resulted in a classification by the state of Cape Elizabeth High School as a Class A institution in July of 1910, much to the satisfaction of the town. Under this system, it was necessary to maintain an annual school session of thirty-six weeks, employ two teachers, provide an approved laboratory, and have the curriculum certified by the State Superintendent of Schools. At this time the curriculum consisted of two programs, classical and general. The Class "A" rating was doubly appreciated as it provided for an annual $500 stipend from the state.

In an effort to improve the effectiveness of the high school, an agricultural course was added to the curriculum in 1913, with special emphasis on field work. Thus encouraged by the new course, the boys involved proceeded to organize a Potato Club. The course of study provided much-needed instruction in a variety of skills such as the planting, pruning, grafting, and spraying of trees. Although the agricultural course was moderately successful, it did not receive enough encouragement and was discontinued at the end of the 1915-16 school year.

Extra-curricular activities at the high school were practically non-existent in this era. A glee-club had been organized in 1913 but no organized recreation was available to the students except dancing. As yet, there was no athletic program. A prize-speaking contest was initiated during the school year 1916-17 and involved students from the high schools of neighboring towns.

The need to expand the curriculum and facilities of the high school created quite a debate during the winter of 1923-24. One faction favored expansion and another group advocated closing the high school as an unnecessary frill. The fact that many residents in the northeast corner of the town chose to send their children to the high schools of Portland and South Portland greatly aggravated the situation. Fortunately, those favoring the expansion of existing facilities were successful, and, at the March meeting in 1923, a resolution calling for such an undertaking was passed. A committee, consisting of the Selectmen, the School Board, plus Dr. Sylvester J. Beach, Stewart M. Taylor, and Philip N. Jordan, was given the task of preparing a suitable plan. After a great deal of careful investigation, the committee decided that the most feasible plan would be to construct an addition to the town hall.

Subsequently, at a special town meeting held 3 September,

1924, James E. Marriner, Fred H. Peabbles, Howard Hannaford, the Selectmen, and the School Board were constituted a building committee with Edward E. Chase as chairman. The town appropriated $40,000 for this purpose, to be raised by a bond issue. The new high school was completed and occupied in the fall of 1925. At this point, there were fifty students in attendance and four teachers.

The new facilities eliminated the congestion that had been recently experienced and provided an opportunity to expand the curriculum further. Another valuable addition was the gift of an adjoining lot of land from Charles H. Robinson which the town voted to accept as a playground in March, 1926, and promptly named Robinson Field.

Despite these improvements and a physical capacity of 120, the attendance rarely exceeded fifty throughout the late twenties and early thirties. One primary problem that did much to eliminate students from the northeast section of the town was transportation. Another consideration that contributed to this rather poor attendance was the erroneous idea that a better high school education could be obtained in Portland or South Portland. However, what Cape Elizabeth High School lacked in "snob-appeal," it more than made up for in enthusiasm and seriousness of purpose.

As the town was developing rapidly as a "sleeper-community" the school population began to grow despite the lack of support evident in some quarters. On 1 July, 1930, the school union that bound South Portland and Cape Elizabeth together was dissolved, and a new union, No. 13, was formed, consisting of Falmouth, Cumberland, North Yarmouth, and Cape Elizabeth. This new arrangement made for a more economical operation of the school system as well as an improvement in existing facilities. Two such improvements were the addition of a manual training course and a home economics course. In addition, a gymnasium was fitted up in the town hall thus providing basketball facilities for the first time. These additions to the high school program brought an increase of fifty-one per cent in enrollment whereby there were sixty pupils in attendance by the spring of 1930.

As was to be expected, the high school soon outgrew its quarters in the town hall building. The Superintending School Committee accordingly noted in their annual report of 1932 that a new high school should be of "paramount concern." At this time, there were eighty-three high school students and forty-nine junior high pupils using the town hall facilities. To meet this need, the town voted to construct a new high school at the March meeting in 1932 and authorized a bond issue to raise the $65,000 needed to cover the cost of land and building. At a special meeting held 16 April, it was voted to place the new high school at the juncture of the Ocean House Road and the Scott Dyer Road.

The new high school was completed late in the summer of 1933. An imposing two story brick structure, with a prominently colonnaded entry facing the highway, it was in every way a testimonial to the foresightedness that now characterized educational planning in Cape Elizabeth. The building was dedicated with appropriate ceremony on 3 November, with the State Commissioner of Education, Dr. Bertram E. Packard, and Prof. Wilmot B. Mitchell of Bowdoin College delivering the keynote addresses. Improvements in transportation facilities and continued suburban expansion resulted in a heavy growth throughout the next decade.

Symptomatic of this rapid expansion in the school population, not only in the high school but in the lower grades as well, were many changes. On 1 July, 1946, Cape Elizabeth was separated from School Union No. 13 and united with Scarborough to form School Union No. 10. Also, in the fall of 1946 congestion in the lower grades prompted the creation of a five year high school. Two years later, in September, 1948, a double session was instituted to alleviate the now overcrowded conditions that existted in the high school. The remodeling of the gymnasium into classrooms late in 1955 reduced the congestion for a short time. Finally, in 1960, further expansion was approved at a special town meeting held 29 February whereby the construction of an addition to the high school was authorized. The continued growth of the town as a suburban community will undoubtedly in the future be accompanied by a periodic enlargement of this currently superior high-school complex.

The development of an adequate program of secondary education would have been impossible had it not been preceded by a successful elementary and intermediate school system. After the separation of the towns, Cape Elizabeth was left with four district schools. Although their distinctive names were retained, their numerical designation was of necessity changed. Henceforth, Bowery Beach would be No. 1, Spurwink No. 2, Pond Cove No. 3, and Ridgeway (Sawyer Street) No. 4. The Bowery Beach school had been built in 1849, the Spurwink school also erected in 1849, but substantially rebuilt in 1877, the Pond Cove school built in 1859, and the Ridgeway school in 1875. For over a decade, there was very little change in the form or method of instruction. In this same period, some students living too great a distance from one of the four district schools were forced to attend the schools of South Portland. The tuition that the town of Cape Elizabeth was forced to pay was a source of dispute for some years. On one occasion, in 1900, civil action by South Portland involving the tuition of four students was narrowly avoided by an out-of-court settlement.

A major change in this educational system was forced upon the town in 1901 when South Portland established a consolidated grammar school in Pleasantdale. By so doing, the grammar grades at the South Portland Heights and Willard schools were discontinued. This left the Cape Elizabeth children who lived in what was known as the "tuition belt" without a grammar school within a suitable commuting distance. At this time, there were twenty-three children in the Ocean House Road area and ten on Cottage Road who must now attend the school at Pond Cove. This school was already the largest in the town, with an enrollment of forty students. As the building would not adequately house thirty-three additional pupils, it was quite apparent that some program of expansion was imminent.

At the annual town meeting in March of 1910, Howard C. Hannaford, Gilbert C. Jordan, John M. Taylor, the Selectmen, and the School Board were empowered as a committee to investigate the possibilities of establishing a consolidated and centralized school system. Initially, the committee favored a program patterned after one adopted at Brookline, Massachusetts. Of primary importance was the establishment of a consolidated grade school at Pond Cove. The advent of the electric trolley had so improved transportation facilities in the northeastern section of the town that the problem of traveling to Pond Cove had been greatly diminished. Despite the inexorable growth of the student population, no action was taken by the town until the annual meeting in March of 1912. At that time, it was voted to appropriate $7,500 for the building of a consolidated grammar school on a lot adjoining the Pond Cove district school to be purchased from George H. Hannaford at a cost of $2,500, the total sum to be raised by a bond issue. As was so often the case, there was determined opposition to these desperately needed changes. They were adopted only after the "hottest kind of a town meeting," to quote the *Eastern Argus*.

Construction of the new Pond Cove grammar school began in the summer of 1912 but was not finished in time for the opening of school in September. The old district school was annexed to the rear of the new building, thereby providing a total of three classrooms. Finished early in October, the Pond Cove School was formally dedicated on the 12th with appropriate remarks delivered by State Superintendent of Schools Payson Smith, Nathan Clifford, and James Otis Kaler. The first classes moved in on Monday, the 14th.

Utilizing the talents of the South Portland journalist, educator and author, James Otis Kaler, a general reorganization of the school system was undertaken by the School Board and the Superintendent of Schools, Simon M. Hamlin. Beginning in September of 1913, district school No. 2 was discontinued and the pupils transferred to the Pond Cove School. As of the academic year 1913-14, there were eighty-two students in attendance, spread throughout nine grades with each room housing three grades. The following year, a collection of 200 books, a piano, and assorted pictures were added to the new school. In addition, the town purchased a suitable horse-drawn wagon from Ira C. Foss for $85 to be used for transporting pupils to and from the school. It was altered to travel on either wheels or runners depending on the season. This was the first such conveyance to be purchased by the town.

With improved facilities, it was now possible to close the Ridgeway district school in the spring of 1915. When the school year opened in September, the only other district school still in operation was at Bowery Beach where five grades were still being taught. The adequacy of school facilities was, as might be expected, only temporary, for the rapid growth of the town brought a large influx of new students with each passing year.

In conjunction with increased activities at Fort Williams, the suburban community that was burgeoning with some intensity along the northeast shore had developed a rather sizeable school population by 1917. As a result, a temporary school of three grades was established in the gymnasium building on the Fort Williams military reservation. The first year of its existance it accommodated twenty-two students from the surrounding area in grades one through three. As the population of this region exhibited no signs of lessening, the need of a new school in this section of the town was soon broached by the School Board.

Thus it was that Nathan Clifford, Ralph M. Howe, Will Hay, the Selectmen, and the School Board were designated a committee at the March meeting in 1919 to carry out the necessary preparations for the construction of a new school. After fourteen meetings and protracted investigation, a site was chosen at the juncture of what is now Woodland Road and Cottage Farms Road. As of 23 August, the town had appropriated $26,000 for the building of this new school. Although $1,000 had been voted for the purchase of a suitable lot, Edwin Files donated a parcel of suitable land and this was accepted as the site noted above.

Construction of what was soon to be known as the Cottage Farms School began early in September. The building was finished, and three rooms were ready for occupancy on 13 September 1920. Seventy pupils were immediately enrolled in a total of seven grades and by spring the number of students had increased to eighty-five.

Despite the enlargement of school facilities, as embodied in the consolidated schools at Pond Cove and Cottage Farms, the number of students continued to increase so rapidly that on 11 September, 1922, the little Ridgeway district school was reopened. With one teacher providing the instruction, grades one through five were taught as at the still active Bowery Beach district school. Finally, in 1929, the town purchased a school bus to transport the widely dispersed students in the northern area to the Pond Cove School. This made it possible to permanently close the Ridgeway School as of September, 1929. The following spring, the Bowery Beach district school was also closed for good and its students transferred to Pond Cove. The closing of this school ended forever the long and not always successful district school era in the history of public education in the town of Cape Elizabeth. The Ridgeway school was subsequently moved to the site of the present town dump and utilized as a tool house. The Bowery Beach school remains on its original site and is now known as Crescent Lodge, used on various occasions for social functions.

The steady population growth, especially noticeable in the northeast section of the town, precipitated a continuous expansion of educational facilities from the early thirties onward. Among the more significant was the enlarging of the Cottage Farms School in 1931. At the March meeting that year, $2,000 was appropriated for the addition of two class rooms and an auditorium.

In 1948, the town found it absolutely imperative that a new elementary school be built, and a site just east of the high school was selected. At a special town meeting held 26 July $102,000 was appropriated, to be raised by a bond issue, to defray the cost of construction. An additional $32,000 was voted 8 November to finish and equip what was officially designated as the Pond Cove Primary School. It was occupied for the first time in September of the following year.

Three years later the now perennial problem of congestion and overcrowding was again accute. At a special meeting held 29 May 1952, $99,000 was raised, again by bond issue, to build and equip an addition to the Pond Cove Primary School. This expansion of facilities was followed by the construction of a new junior high school immediately adjacent to the senior high school. Work was initiated in the summer of 1955 and included, besides classrooms, a gymnasium and auditorium. Completed late in 1956, the first classes were admitted when school reconvened in September. The total cost of this project was approximately $410,-000.

Although these improvements represented a remarkable achievement in meeting the educational needs of the town, further improvements were forthcoming. Once again, the "Pond Cove Campus" was the scene of construction activity. In February 1960, $881,000 was allocated for the building of four additional units, thereby providing badly needed space at the Pond Cove Elementary School, the junior high school and the senior high school. The completion of these projects in 1960-61, opened the way for the erection of a new twelve-room elementary school. Authorized at a special town meeting 3 May, 1962, $183,000 was raised with the customary bond issue. This building was occupied for the first time on 28 January 1963 by six classes, thereby leaving six classrooms available for growth. Shortly thereafter, the new addition to the campus was named the Robert B. Lunt School in honor of the Superintendent of Schools.

Currently, the only educational activity not located on the "Pond Cove Campus" are five grades (1-5) at the Cottage Farms School, and a sixth grade that is located at the Town Hall. With no foreseeable decrease in the school population, the town of Cape Elizabeth has now embarked upon a study relative to the erection of a new elementary school in the northeast sector of the town. An eighteen-acre parcel of land south of Cape Cottage Woods situated between Mitchell Road and Shore Road has been suggested but no definite action taken thereon. Regardless of the fact that approximately $1,707,000 has been spent since 1948 in constructing new educational facilities, the constant population increase associated with suburban growth seems to indicate a continuation rather than a curtailment of this extraordinary situation.

II.

In tracing the course of organized religion, as it affected the inhabitants of Cape Elizabeth, various generalizations may easily be made and substantiated. Basically the people were Anglo-Saxon Protestants who viewed religious convictions as a purely personal matter. Although the Anglican Church, and later the Congregational Church, were established institutions protected by laws and ordinances for many years, the spirit of dissent was always present. Once the inviolability of these governmental regulations was ended, nonparticipation and freedom of choice became a right cherished by a majority of the citizens. Despite the fact that many clergymen railed, ranted, cajoled, or pleaded, the great bulk of the population held firmly to religious individualism. The fires of revivalism and evangelism seldom scorched the earth of Cape Elizabeth. Fulminations and dire predictions of eternal damnation fell for the most part on unresponsive ears. This is not to say that the people were irreligious, for this was not the case. It was not a part of their nature to be demonstrative or effusive in their religious activities. The people of Cape Elizabeth consistently exhibited most of the Christian virtues but rejected the cant and dogma of any authoritarian Church.

The first organized Christian church to include Cape Elizabeth within its sphere of influence was the Anglican. In the latter part of the reign of Queen Elizabeth I, a royal patent was granted to Sir Humphrey Gilbert, authorizing him to take possession of any area in North America, "remote and barbarous," not occupied by Christian people, and to establish laws and ordinances consistent with the government of England, and in harmony with the "true Christian faith or religion professed by the Church of England." During his second voyage Gilbert landed on the shores of Newfoundland in 1583, and took possession of the territory, extending two hundred leagues in every direction. Acting in the name of his sovereign, he proclaimed the Church of England as the established church of this new domain, which by the terms of the grant, embraced what is now Cape Elizabeth. This was the first formal religious act, of which there is any record, to occur on this section of the North Atlantic coast. It was most certainly intended to dictate the religious character of its future population and proved to be of some significance in awarding subsequent grants of land.

Twenty two years later, another voyage of exploration was undertaken by George Weymouth. Landing on the coast of Maine in 1605, he cruised up "the most excellent, and beneficial river of Sachadehoc," and on one occasion, had two Indians "in presence at service, who behaved themselves very civily, neither laughing nor talking all the time." Although there may have been earlier services, this is the earliest specific reference with regard to the Maine Coast.

In the spring of 1629 Sir Ferdinando Gorges, under the sanction of a royal grant, organized the first permanent government to be established within the present limits of the state of Maine. The rights bestowed upon the grantee included an obligation to provide the services of the Church of England for any and all settlers. In this instance Gorges was given the authority to select appropriate ministers for all Anglican churches and chapels which might be built within his domain.

Subsequently, in 1631, Gorges granted to Robert Trelawny and Moses Goodyear, prominent merchants of Plymouth, England, all of the area now comprising Cape Elizabeth, for the establishment of a fishing and trading station. In the following spring, John Winter arrived at Richmond's Island with a sizeable work force and immediately began erecting suitable structures for the projected enterprise.

By the summer of 1635, the plantation having attained a substantial degree of prosperity, Winter returned to England to confer with his employers. During his absence Edward Trelawny, brother to Robert, visited Richmond's Island. The reports he forwarded to his brother deal rather largely with business matters. He did however, recommend that Robert engage a "religious, able minister for the plantation." Consequently, when Winter arrived at the Island on 24 May 1636, he was accompanied by the Anglican clergyman Richard Gibson.

As far as can be ascertained, Gibson was the first clergyman of the Church of England to preach in Cape Elizabeth. Although nothing is known about his background, it is assumed that he had a university education. According to his Puritan opponents in Massachusetts, Gibson was a man of superior ability and scholarship. His ideas of church polity were exclusively Anglican, and he was deeply devoted to the English hierarchy. He was apparently furnished with the appropriate altar and sacramental pieces, for they appear in the plantation inventories.

Early in the summer of 1639, the Reverend Gibson terminated his services at Richmond's Island as his three year contract with Robert Trelawny was expiring. His relations with Winter had become somewhat strained due to the fact that the inhabitants had not consulted him about a projected raise in Gibson's wages. Shortly thereafter, Gibson departed for "Piscattaqua" to minister to the needs of a fishing settlement at the Isle of Shoals and ultimately returned to England.

During the summer of 1641, Gibson's successor arrived at Richmond's Island and became the first settled minister in Maine as well as Cape Elizabeth. This was the Reverend Robert Jordan, an Anglican clergyman, who had previously resided for two years at Pejepscot with Thomas Purchase, a relative. He graduated from Balliol College, Oxford University, in 1634 at the age of twenty-one. His father Edward Jordan, a bookseller in Worcester, apparently could not meet the cost of his son's education, for Robert was granted a scholarship, provided by a Dr. John Bell, as well as employment by the University. It is assumed that he was ordained prior to his departure from England.

From the very beginning, Jordan allied himself closely with Winter in a variety of secular matters. In January 1643 he married Sarah, the only daughter of his employer. There is no doubt but that he discharged his ministerial duties to the satisfaction of his father-in-law, for no reports of censure were forthcoming from that quarter despite the fact that Winter was very critical in his judgment of others. When the factor died in 1645, Jordan was named executor of the estate. As such he immediately became involved in territorial, jurisdictional, and ecclesiastical disputes that were as acrimonious as they were protracted.

It was soon apparent to the Reverend Jordan that the unsettled conditions prevailing in England precluded any possibility that Winter's estate would be properly compensated for unpaid wages and personal funds disbursed to meet operational expenses at Richmond's Island. Therefore, as executor, he instituted a suit and seized most of the plantation's land holdings, in his wife's behalf, as a compensatory settlement.

These bold activities were viewed with open hostility by the Puritan authorities in Massachusetts who made no attempt to disguise the avaricious designs they entertained relative to Gorges' holdings in Maine. In 1653 and 1654, when Massachusetts, after re-appraising her charter rights, laid claim to these lands, Robert Jordan's vigorous opposition and disdainful attitude outraged the Puritan divines. Threats were repeatedly ignored or treated with contempt until finally, in 1657, this doughty clergyman was arrested and taken to Boston for trial. He was charged with flagrantly disregarding the laws of Massachusetts, especially in carrying on his ministerial duties. After a brief imprisonment and a severe rebuke he was set at liberty.

Upon his return to the banks of the Spurwink, Jordan was elected to the office of Associate in the county court. Even though the authority of Massachusetts was predominent, until the return of a Royalist government in England in 1663, he was quite obviously unrepentant and most certainly unawed. Between 1657 and 1663 he was continuously harassed and persecuted without success by Puritan officialdom never once acknowledging their jurisdiction over him.

One incident that occurred in this period and involved Robert Jordan in a matter frought with potential horror must of needs be noted for it reveals much of the courage and enlightened thinking that was his nature. Early in the summer of 1659, the Reverend John Thorpe settled at Black Point as the resident Puritan divine. As this was a poor parish without a parsonage, he found it necessary to lodge with the family of Goodman Bayley. In a short period of time, Thorpe revealed himself to be something less than saintly. His most distressing shortcomings were addiction to strong drink, extreme profanity, and a foul disposition. When Christian charity and forebearance could stand no more, he was severely criticized by Mrs. Bayley for abusing their hospitality. He was told either to reform or leave the house. Not being kindly disposed toward his hostess for thus rebuking him, Thorpe moved out.

Shortly after this incident the minister journeyed to Spurwink, and, while there, discovered that one of Jordan's cows had died. Seizing this as an opportunity for revenge, Thorpe immediately informed two of Jordan's men that the beast had been killed by witchcraft. He directed them to haul the carcass to a spot near the main road to Casco and burn it. By so doing, Thorpe informed them, the witch would be drawn to the scene. Prior to his departure from Black Point, on that day, he had learned that Mrs. Bayley was also planning a trip to Casco. By coincidence, he passed her on the road, thereby anticipating her arrival at Spurwink.

Coincident could not have worked more advantageously for Thorpe. Just as the fire was beginning to consume the carcass of the cow, Mrs. Bayley came upon the scene. She was immediately denounced by the cleric as a witch and her arrest occurred shortly thereafter. In that age, with the Salem witchcraft trials just thirty-three years in the future, this was a serious, and potentially a capital crime. Upon learning of these proceedings, Robert Jordan appeared and gave testimony that precluded any possibility of a trial. He stated that the cow had died as a result of being neglected by the two men now appearing as witnesses against the accused. With some measure of personal courage, he pointed out that the two men in question accepted Thorpe's story as a convenient explanation of the cow's death that would absolve them of blame. He also pointed out the fact that Thorpe had passed Mrs. Bayley on the road and therefore had reason to anticipate her arrival. Under the circumstances, the case was dismissed and Mrs. Bayley was allowed to return home.

If Robert Jordan had not interceded, the possibility of a grave injustice was not remote. In the light of subsequent activities at Salem, the consequences of a conviction in this case might have been far-reaching indeed. As it was, Jordan earned the bitter emnity of Thorpe. Apparently the Puritan divine tried to intimidate him, for on 4 July 1659 Thorpe was hailed into court "for abusing Rev. Robert Jordan and preaching unsound doctrine." Two years later, he was convicted of drunkeness and forbidden to preach. Under the circumstances it is very doubtful if Jordan experienced any improvement in his estimation of Puritan leadership.

When Massachusetts re-established its authority over Maine in 1668, the influence and activities of Robert Jordan were soon curtailed. He was arrested in 1669 and again in 1671 for refusing to abide by the edicts of Puritan magistrates to desist from exercising the duties of his ecclesiastical office. Needless to say, they found him neither yielding nor obedient to their pronouncements.

With the outbreak of King Philip's War in 1675, Jordan was forced to abandon all he held dear on the banks of the Spurwink. Fleeing literally minutes before the Indians struck, he watched from a small vessel the burning of his home. He settled at Great Island, now New Castle, New Hampshire and helped to organize an Anglican church there. Although he was still defiant in spirit, his days of active resistance to Puritan authority were now forever past. The details of these final years are lost, but it is known that he died in 1679 at the age of sixty-eight, attended by his wife and family. He was buried close by his final residence, within what is now Fort Constitution. The exact site of his grave is unknown, and no stone or marker exists to commemorate his extraordinary life. Although Jordan's memory has been perpetuated by many legal documents, the only tangible relic of his ministry known to exist, is his beautifully-wrought brass baptismal font that is now the property of the Maine Historical Society. It is significant to note that in the resettlement that followed the Indian Wars no attempt was apparently made to reestablish the Anglican church in Cape Elizabeth.

In the era of the Indian Wars the area that became the town

of Falmouth was only fitfully occupied in the forty-three year period between 1675 and 1718. The settlers who tried to hold, reclaim, or reestablish their land grants experienced all the hazards and privations of a frontier existence. Under the best of conditions the services of a minister were difficult and frequently impossible to obtain. According to William Willis, "the want of a regular government east of the Piscataqua for many years, encouraged a laxity of morals which did not prevail in any other part of New England." As early as 1661 the Massachusetts General Court upon learning that divine services were lacking at Falmouth issued an order whereby:

> ... all the inhabitants of the said place from time to time in one or more convenient place or places to meet together on the Lord's Day, for their mutual edification and furtherance in the knowledge and fear of the Lord, by reading of God's word and of the labors of known and orthodox divines, singing of psalms, and praying together, or such other ways as the Lord shall enable them, till the favor of God shall so far smile upon them as to give them better and more public means for their edification.

Despite the obvious need, few Puritan ministers responded to any call from Falmouth. The earliest non-Anglican minister to be mentioned who frequented the region was the soon discredited Reverend John Thorpe. The next Puritan, of which there is any record, arrived about 1674, apparently with the intention of settling. This was that enigmatic and tragic figure, the Reverend George Burroughs.

A man of uncommon ability, Burroughs had graduated from Harvard College in 1670. Where or when he was ordained it is impossible to determine; however, his earliest ministrations were in all probability at Falmouth where he received a large grant of land. This first period of residence was rather brief for shortly after King Philip's War broke out, the area was evacuated. With ten men, six women, and sixteen children, Burroughs took refuge on Bang's Island in August 1676. In response to an appeal for assistance Henry Jocelyn took them off by boat and carried them to his garrison at Black Point. From there, many of the refugees, Burroughs among them, journeyed to Boston.

On 25 November 1680 he accepted a call to preach at Salem Village, now Danvers, Massachusetts. This settlement had a reputation of being one of the most faction ridden communities in the Massachusetts Bay Colony. Although such a situation was hardly uncommon throughout the Puritan commonwealth, Salem Village harbored quarrels that were in reality bloodless feuds. The ecclesiastical environment engendered an atmosphere of suspicion and fear that was as vexatious as it was harrowing. Under the best of circumstances the villagers were prone to harass and badger a minister unmercifully. Since its founding in 1672 as a separate parish the only settled minister, the Reverend James Bayley, had been hounded out of his church by the bitter disputes, constant snooping, and the almost total absence of remuneration. This was the situation when the Reverend George Burroughs arrived as Bayley's successor.

This new Puritan divine was immediately beset with the same problems. His efforts to avoid any involvement in the long standing doctrinal disputes earned him the condemnation of all factions. As was to be expected, his salary was soon in arrears, and his debts were mounting rapidly, especially after the funeral expenses of his wife who died in September, 1681. By the spring of 1683, his endurance had been exhausted, and, on 14 April, he resigned, abandoning all claims he had against Salem Village. Unfortunately he left behind a host of enemies who would not overlook any opportunity for revenue.

By the spring of 1685, he was again serving the Falmouth area and resided at Black Point. It is generally assumed that Burroughs relished the rough, precarious life of this frontier region rather than the frustrations and disputes that so often characterized secure little hamlets like Salem Village. From the descriptions that have survived, he was well fitted physically for this arduous existence. Although somewhat short of stature, he was solidly built, very agile, and gifted with an extraordinary strength. While a student at Harvard, his prowess as an athlete had been a matter of some amazement throughout the college. In addition, he was very swarthy in complexion and had jet black hair which he wore very long, even by the standards of that age. The Indians who saw him frequently remarked that he closely resembled Canadian "coureur de bois." Lastly, he was apparently somewhat irascible in temperament with a dark and brooding nature.

As before, the outbreak of an Indian War ended his ministry in the Falmouth area. Early in May 1690 he fled to Wells with his third wife, her daughter, and his own seven children, the oldest a boy of seventeen. Here he attempted to resume his ministrations, preaching on Sunday and Lecture Day, planting a crop, and caring for his large family. It was during his residence at Wells that tragedy struck him down.

In 1692 Salem Village became the scene of one of the strangest and most remarkable perversions of justice ever to occur on this continent. Early in the year, a group of young girls developed symptoms that were attributed to the malevolent activities of a witch. Prominent among the girls were Elizabeth Parris, Abigail Williams, Ann Putnam, Mercy Lewis, Elizabeth Hubbard, Mary Warren, Mary Walcott, and Susanna Sheldon. All had been relentlessly catechized in such Calvinistic realities as predestination and damnation. Inherent to their religious education was a deep and abiding belief in the devil and his earthly disciples. To doubt the existence of the devil was a blasphemy equal to that of doubting God himself, and to reject acts of malefic witchcraft was to deny the devil. In due course, these girls revealed by divers means the names of the witches who had so afflicted them, beginning with the half Carib, half Negro slave Tituba, then Sarah Good and Sarah Osburne. Indugling in a Dionysiac frenzy, these paranoid schizophrenic girls quickly expanded their list of witches.

As the devil's conspiracy against Salem Village began to unfold before the eyes of such Puritan magistrates as John Hathorne, Samuel Sewall, and William Stoughton, the presence of a missionary from the devil was "detected." With some prompting, the possessed girls, and a few of the confessed witches, revealed the existence of a "small Black minister" who had been in Salem Village, as the devil's advocate who presided over unholy rites in the capacity of grand wizard of all Massachusetts.

The identity of this "small Black minister" was subsequently furnished via an appropriate "shape" or apparition. Corroborating evidence was also supplied by Abigail Williams from the same "unimpeachable" source. As the Puritan divines believed that the devil could not assume the "shape" of an innocent individual, the validity of such "spectral evidence" was beyond doubt. Thus it was that figments of the imagination, hallucinations and flights of fancy were accepted by the court as absolute proof, not of the mental instability of the accuser, but of the guilt of the accused. In the face of such proof there was absolutely no defense.

On 20 April 1692 a warrant was issued for the arrest of Burroughs in which it was stated that he was ". . . suspected for a confederacy with the Devil, in oppressing sundry about Salem . . ." Shortly thereafter John Partridge, Field-Marshall of New Hampshire and Maine, seized him at Wells, literally hauling him from the dinner table without an opportunity to bid his family farewell or to pack any personal belongings.

The task of conducting Burroughs to Salem proved to be an unsettling experience for Partridge and his two deputized constables. In traveling from Wells to Newichawannock (South Berwick) they followed a rude trail through the woods. On the edge of darkness a thunderstorm of some violence overtook them. With Burroughs riding in the lead, they came out upon a rather bare ridge of land where they were subjected to the full force of the storm. The figure of their prisoner hunched low in the saddle his cape billowing in the gale, bolts of lightning flashing around them, his form aglow with Saint Elmo's fire, and thunder crashing in the background, rendered them speechless with fright. This incident convinced them that surely here was a man in league with the powers of darkness. Henceforth this stretch of road would be known among the local citizens as the "Witch Trot Road." Great was Partridge's relief when he delivered Burroughs to the authorities of Salem Village on 4 May.

Upon his return to this affrighted community, Burroughs was confined, in an upper chamber of Thomas Beadle's house where he received a few friends willing to brave the suspicious stares of the villagers. On 9 May, he faced a private preliminary examination by a group of magistrates and ministers. They accused him of neglecting the communion service and the baptism of his children with the exception of his eldest son. His admission that this was true, led his examiners to view him as tainted with Anabatist teachings, a heresy attributable to the devil. Despite constant badgering, he refused to admit the truth of the witchcraft charges lodged against him. Lastly, the examiners stripped Burroughs naked but were unable to find any damning "witch-marks."

Next, the accused was conducted into the presence of the "afflicted" girls who immediately exhibited frenzied convulsions and howlings appropriate to the occasion. One of the girls, Ann Putnam, regained sufficient composure to testify that the soldiers from Salem Village who had perished fighting Indians in the "eastward country" had not been killed but had been bewitched to death by Burroughs. In addition, Susanna Sheldon revealed that his two deceased wives were present and had informed her that they had been murdered by the accused. Another of the girls, Mercy Lewis, who had lived with the Burroughs family at Falmouth and later at Salem Village, testified that he had urged her to join his unholy congregation. All claimed that they had been visited and tormented by the minister's "shape" on several occasions.

Just as damning as the "spectral evidence" was the testimony given relative to his unnatural strength. A former parishioner from Cape Elizabeth, Samuel Webber, who had built the first saw mill on Long Creek in 1681, related how Burroughs had lifted a barrel of molasses by inserting a few of his fingers in the bung. Another witness was Capt. Simon Willard, formerly stationed at the Purpooduck Garrison, who testified as to the ease with which the minister carried barrels of cider and molasses from a boat to the shore. He did note however, that on one occasion Burroughs missed his footing while heavy laden and sprained his leg. Still others revealed that the minister had displayed his strength in more spectacular ways, some quite difficult to believe. In one instance, he is reputed to have held a seven foot musket with his outstretched arm, like a horse-pistol, by grasping it just behind the lock. On another occasion he supposedly inserted his forefinger into the muzzle of a six-foot musket and held it straight out at arms length.

Finally, one Hannah Harris who had lived with the Burroughs family at Falmouth testified that the minister was an unusually severe husband. Frequently, when he returned home after a lengthly absence, he would berate his wife for conversations held while he was away and would relate to her much of what had been said. It was the considered opinion of this witness that Mrs. Burroughs lived a life of virtual slavery.

Despite his protestations of innocence the Reverend George Burroughs was placed in the Boston gaol to await trial. As in the case of the other victims, he was denied the right of counsel. Unlike some of the accused, the prelate refused to declare that he was a witch, an admission that would perhaps have spared him the agonies of a trial.

On the 5th of August he was tried with two women and three other men. The evidence presented at the examination of 9 May was heard again, elaborated upon, and expanded more fully. In defending himself, Burroughs spent little time trying to disprove the established facts of his guilt. Instead, he attacked the entire concept of witchcraft. The night before his day in court, the afflicted girls were visited by his "shape" and badly bitten. When the bites were examined in court and "compared" to an impression of Burroughs' teeth, along with those of various spectators, the judges ruled that the minister was indeed the guilty party. Although Burroughs tried to continue his disputation, the cause now was hopeless. These developments, and the merciless badgering of Deputy Governor William Stoughton, robbed him of his determination. He and four of his fellow defendants were found guilty and, as expected, sentenced to hang. It is interesting to note that one of the judges who condemned Burroughs was a former friend and classmate at Harvard, the famous Massachusetts jurist Samuel Sewall. On one occasion, Wednesday, 18 November 1685, he had entertained Burroughs in his home as a dinner guest. As one historian noted, relative to Sewall and his part in sentencing this hapless divine, "the spirit of a cruel and relentless creed had overmastered the amiability of its devout disciple."

On 19 August 1692 John Procter, John Willard, George Jacobs, Martha Carrier, and the Reverend George Burroughs were placed in a cart and carried to Gallows Hill in Salem. Prior to the placing of the noose about his neck the prelate was allowed to speak from the ladder to the large crowd of spectators. He proclaimed his innocence with such fervor that many "unthinking people," as Sewall phased it, were moved to tears. At the end of his speech, he slowly and faultlessly repeated the Lord's Prayer, a feat generally accepted as impossible for a witch to perform. As Burroughs mounted the scaffold, the crowd pressed forward as if to rescue him. Just at this moment a man dressed all in black rode his horse into the crowd and began to harangue them. This was that great Puritan divine, the Reverend Cotton Mather. He reminded the crowd that the devil was never more subtly himself than when he was disguised as an "angel of light."

Without further incident the five condemned witches were hanged. At dusk, the bodies were cut down by the sheriff and his deputies. In the case of Burroughs, his body was dragged by the noose to a shallow grave dug in a crevice between outcroppings of felsite ledge. His shirt and breeches were pulled off, and an old pair of trousers taken from a corpse put on to cover his nakedness. He was buried with John Willard and Martha Carrier, the grave being so shallow that his chin and one hand protruded from the soil. Nothing has survived to mark the final resting place of this victim of Puritan piety. Without any doubt, the Reverend George Burroughs was one of the most extraordinary and certainly the most tragic, cleric ever to preach within the confines of Cape Elizabeth. The only relic of his life known to exist in this area is one of his books with his signature on the title page now preserved by the Maine Historical Society. An interesting postscript to his career is his inclusion as a character in an historical novel, *Rachel Dyer: A North American Story*, written by the Portland author John Neal and published in 1828.

The signing of a treaty with the Indians in 1713 ended the local hostilities of Queen Anne's War and brought peace to the deserted acres of Cape Elizabeth. The first settlers returned early in 1715 and grew rapidly in number as the year advanced. Three years later, the town of Falmouth was formerly incorporated by the Massachusetts General Court, thereby providing a suitable local government to supervise the permanent resettling of the area. The extreme poverty of the inhabitants precluded the immediate possibility of settling any minister within the confines of the town.

During this trying period, a ship bearing Scots-Irish immigrants arrived and anchored close by Clark's Point late in October 1718. This was the brig *Robert* with approximately thirty families aboard. They were all devout Presbyterians, descendants of a group who had fled from Argyleshire, Scotland to the north of Ireland in the middle of the seventeenth century to escape the persecution of Charles I. The Reverend William Cornwall from Cloghr, County Tyrone, was their leader when they arrived at Falmouth.

Although they were low on provisions and badly used by their long voyage, they made immediate preparations to seek an area in which to settle. The onset of a very early and severe winter forced them to postpone a continuation of their journey. In a remarkably short time, the brig was immobilized as the harbor became locked in an unbroken sheet of ice. Many of the immigrants erected rude huts at Purpooduck to shelter them until spring while others remained aboard the *Robert*. With starvation looming among them, they forwarded a petition to the Massachusetts General Court for assistance. Action on the petition was taken forthwith, and on 2 December, 1718 the Commonwealth ordered that these destitute colonists be supplied with one hundred bushels of Indian meal.

With the approach of warm weather in the spring of 1719, approximately two thirds of the Presbyterian settlers elected to move on to Londonderry, New Hampshire. They left late in March, sailed to Newburyport, and moved overland via Haverhill, reaching their destination on 11 April. The remainder of the group decided to stay, many of them establishing homes in Cape Elizabeth. Their pastor, the Reverend Cornwall, returned to Ireland, one winter at Purpooduck having been enough. He was soon replaced by a Reverend McGregor whose stay was also brief. Prominent among those who settled locally were the families of James Armstrong, John Barbour, William Jameson, Thomas Bolton, John McLellan, Andrew Simonton, William Simonton, Robert Holmes, Robert Means, and William Slemmons.

Although many of the Scots-Irish became, of necessity, Congregationalists, some refused to abandon the teachings of John Knox. In the years that followed, these surviving Presbyterians were infrequently visited by clerics of their faith. Among them was the Reverend William McClenathan, a vitriolic and argumentative individual, who resided in the area for a brief period late in the thirties. Regardless of their faith, these hardy immigrants from the north of Ireland played many a prominent role in the early history of Cape Elizabeth.

Not the least of their contributions were those they made to the argricultural and domestic life of the region. In the spring of 1719, they planted what may have been the first potato crop in Cape Elizabeth, using the seed potatoes they had carried with them in the brig *Robert*. Also, they introduced the cultivation of flax, the foot propelled spinning wheel, and improved methods for manufacturing linen.

Once the town of Falmouth became a legal entity, the problem of procuring the services of a proper divine became a matter of pressing importance despite the indigenous poverty of the area. Regardless of the need, no minister was settled until 1721 when the Reverend Jonathan Pierpont accepted the call. The inability of the community to pay him brought an end to his ministry the following year.

In 1722, the settlers at Purpooduck constructed a rough log building to serve as a garrison, house of worship, and a school. Extremely crude, it lacked benches and glass for the windows until 1728. It was here that Pierpont conducted infrequent services. This meeting house was not replaced until Cape Elizabeth was set off as the Second Parish in 1733.

The first minister to become a settled member of the community was the Reverend Thomas Smith who arrived 23 June 1725. A graduate of Harvard College in 1720, this was his first independent ministry. However, it was not until 26 April 1726 that he was asked by the community to settle permanently among them. He deliberated for some time, but continued to preach, not giving an affirmative answer until 23 January of the following year. It was undoubtedly a difficult choice for Smith to make. As William Willis so aptly puts it, "for such a man, brought up in Boston, then the largest town on this continent north of Mexico, to fix his destinies on this spot under such circumstances, required almost the zeal of an apostle and the courage of a martyr."

His ordination took place on 8 March with pastors and delegates present from the churches of Berwick, Wells, York and Kittery. It is interesting to note that these groups from the southern parts of the Province were forced by necessity to follow the circuitous thoroughfare, euphuistically known as the "King's Highway," through Cape Elizabeth to the ferry at Purpooduck where they left their horses with the ferryman John Sawyer. Although most of the citizenry could not attend, they contributed "free-will offerings" of provisions. Collections were made at Spurwink by Capt. Dominicus Jordan and at Purpooduck by Jonathan Cobb.

Even though the town of Falmouth struggled along in a poverty stricken and wretched condition, the populace provided for the Reverend Smith in a rather handsome manner. They voted to supply him with fire wood, to pay his annual salary of seventy pounds in two installments, and to give him six acres of land on the neck, cleared and fenced. In addition, they built him a home "forty feet long, twenty feet wide and sixteen feet stud, with a convenient kitchen on the back side," on the north side of Congress Street at the head of India Street. It was the first house in Falmouth to have a wall-papered room, but was destroyed during Mowatt's bombardment and fire 18 October 1775. Until the creation of the Second Parish, Smith preached at the Purpooduck meeting house every third Sunday.

The difficulties of travel that prevented many people south of Fore River from attending religious meetings and services on the Neck, more than anything else, contributed to the setting off of Purpooduck and Spurwink as the Second Parish of Falmouth. Authorized by the Massachusetts General Court 24 August 1733, the people of the Second Parish held their first official meeting 18 September at their rude log meeting house on Spring Point. At this gathering it was voted to extend a call to the Reverend Benjamin Allen of Bridgewater, Massachusetts, and to erect a new meeting house.

The construction of the new meeting house began at once on a site close by the corner of what is now Cottage Road and Pine Street in South Portland and in the southwest corner of the present Mount Pleasant Cemetery. Framed wtih timbers hewn from white-oak trees cut nearby and completed early in the fall of 1734, it reflected the poverty of the Second Parish. Devoid of steeple or architectural embellishments, it closely resembled a large barn. This modest building, its side pierced with two tiers of windows, had three entrances, one on each side as well as one in the end facing the road. Unpainted for most of its existence, it nevertheless exhibited a rustic, sturdy charm that seemed to personify the simple but resolute character of the citizenry.

The interior of the new meeting house was as stark as its exterior. A large gallery extended around three of its sides with a raised pulpit against the northern end. Square or box pews were built and they were sold at a vendue as was customary in most communities. Apparently the only major alteration that occurred during its century of use was a lengthening of the structure, by adding fifteen feet to its northern end, several years after its construction. This provided for an increase in the number of pews and placed the pulpit almost in the center of the building. Throughout its many years of use, no bell, organ, or other embellishments were apparently added, with the exception of stoves. From the day it was finished, the building housed religious services, town meetings, and a variety of other gatherings.

The first minister to preach in this new meeting house was Benjamin Allen who accepted the call of the Second Parish early in 1734. He was formally installed as pastor on 10 November, with the Reverend Samuel Willard of Biddeford preaching the sermon, the Reverend William Thompson of Scarboro giving the charge, and the Reverend Samuel Jeffard of Wells extending the right hand of fellowship. The Reverend Thomas Smith also attended but did not play any official part in the installation services. Immediately thereafter, five parishioners, John Armstrong, William Jameson, Robert Means, Robert Thondike, and Jonathan Cobb, were formally admitted as members of the Second Parish, having been dismissed from the First Parish for that specific purpose. It is interesting to observe that three of these first parishioners were Presbyterians. As was customary, the support of this new parish and its minister involved a financial obligation, imposed by law, on each adult inhabitant, regardless of his personal religious convictions.

The Reverend Benjamin Allen, destined to spend the rest of his life as pastor of the Second Parish, was forty-five when he was installed. He was born at Tisbury, Martha's Vineyard, the seventh son and tenth child of James and Elizabeth Perkins Allen. After graduating from Yale in 1708, he studied theology with the Reverend Noadiah Russell of Barnstable, Massachusetts, the father of a classmate. In 1710, he was preaching at Chatham, on Cape Cod, and helped to re-settle Worcester five years later where he remained until 1717. Later that same year he moved to the South Parish of Bridgewater where he was ordained 9 July 1718. His pastorate here was not an unqualified success. Apparently he was rather negligent in handling his personal finances, for after rescuing him from debt on several occasions the parish reluctantly relieved him of his duties, delivering his last sermon in Bridgewater 11 October 1730.

In 1712, the Reverend Allen had married Elizabeth Crocker of Barnstable. She bore him eleven children, all born prior to 1734. Five of the children died in the space of one week during a throat distemper (diphtheria) epidemic in September 1738. The six surviving children, all girls, were Hannah who married the Rev. Stephen Emery of Chatham, Massachusetts, Reliance who married the Reverend Joseph Crocker of Eastham, Massachusetts, Priscilla who married the Reverend Caleb Upham of Truro, Massachusetts, Elizabeth who married Clement Jordan of Cape Elizabeth, Dorcas who married Tristram Jordan of Saco, and Sarah who never married, living out her life in Cape Elizabeth.

During his ministry in the Second Parish, Allen enjoyed a very close friendship with the Reverend Thomas Smith. In his journal, Smith speaks of entertaining him at dinner, and of taking dinner with him, on many occasions. They also exchanged pulpits rather frequently, besides serving as substitutes when sickness or some crisis called the other away. When Smith's wife died, Allen preached for him and conducted the funeral service on Sunday 3 October 1742. In addition, Allen enjoyed a cordial relationship with ministers in many other neighboring towns.

The ministry of Benjamin Allen was not entirely undisturbed by doctrinal disputes and sectarian controversies. In 1740 a small number of the Scots-Irish families who had not given up their preference for Presbyterianism petitioned the General Court for a division of the Parish. Such a division was vigorously opposed by a majority of the populace, and as the Presbyterians were too few in number to support a minister, the petition was successfully defeated. Unhappily, the ill feeling engendered by this situation persisted for some years and was usually very evident when a liberalizing of the orthodox Calvinism was attempted by some Congregational prelate or partisan.

Yet another controversy centered around Allen's interest in the revivalistic activities of the Reverend George Whitefield, a product of the Great Awakening. When Whitefield ventured into Maine in 1745 the Reverend Allen was eager to have him visit the Second Parish.

However, some rather strong protests were voiced in the First Parish relative to the value of revivals, and as a result Whitefield turned back at Dunstan. Not to be deterred, Allen sent a messenger after him urging him to come to Cape Elizabeth which Whitefield finally consented to do. Although he conducted revival services in Cape Elizabeth and Yarmouth, as well as on the Neck, Whitefield's impact upon the Second Parish would not be immediately apparent.

After close to twenty years of service the Reverend Benjamin Allen died Monday 6 May 1754 at the age of sixty-five. He was buried slightly east of the meeting house in the parish cemetery. The funeral was conducted by the Reverend Thomas Smith on Thursday 9 May 1754. The slate stone marking his grave, badly eroded by the elements, was restored in 1884 on the 150th anniversary of the parish.

Finding a suitable minister to replace Allen proved to be a rather difficult problem. Although submerged for some years, the controversy involving orthodox doctrines blazed anew. In October 1754, a call was extended to the Reverend Eleazer Holyoke, a class of 1750 Harvard graduate, but he declined. The dispute continued unabated for on 15 December Smith noted in his journal that "the Purpooduck parish is in a sad situation, dismally divided and quarreling."

In January of the following year the Reverend Ephraim Clark of Boston was invited to preach. In April he accepted a call extended to him by the church to settle as minister of the Second Parish. His selection and acceptance immediately touched off the most bitter and protracted religious controversy ever to descend upon this community.

The crux of the problem were the doctrinal views held by the Reverend Clark. Of his early life almost nothing is known except that he was born in 1722. From the meager accounts that have survived he apparently was not a college graduate but received a theological education by studying with one of the prelates who embraced the New Light doctrines of the Reverend George Whitefield. As a New Light minister Clark was something of a Calvinistic Methodist rejecting the basic premise of the Old Lights or Old Calvinists that salvation was dependent upon faith alone.

While a majority of both church and parish favored the selection of the Reverend Clark, a small and influential minority of Old Lights, led by Col. Ezekiel Cushing, were adamant in their opposition. Two councils, one consisting of fifteen ministers which convened in May, and another of forty-three ministers and delegates which met in July devoting three days of "close, hot work" to the problem, voted by small majorities not to install him. When a third council was called, the various churches invited refused to send delegates. Despite the arcrimonious dispute raging around him, Clark continued to preach.

In an attempt to discredit Clark, the Cushing faction had him arrested and tried on a charge of lying in August 1755. Their efforts were not successful, for he was quickly acquitted by a Falmouth jury. At the height of this crisis, the Reverend Smith commented in his journal that "things are in a sad toss about Mr. Clark." Never were truer words spoken.

The parishioners who supported Clark and his doctrines finally succeeded in arranging his installation. On 21 May 1756, the ceremony took place despite the fact that the Old Light faction were successful in locking them out of the meeting house. Gathering in William Simonton's orchard they held the installation with the Reverend John Rogers of Kittery preaching the sermon, the Reverend Ebenezer Cleveland of Gloucester giving the charge, and the Reverend John Cleveland of Ipswich extending the right hand of fellowship. This was, interestingly enough, the Reverend Rogers' second "orchard installation." In 1745 he had installed another New Light cleric, the Reverend Dudley Leavitt, at Salem under similar circumstances.

With the Reverend Ephraim Clark formally, albeit irregularly, installed the Cushing faction were outraged at what they considered to be absolutely illegal proceedings. The following year, twenty-four Old Light recalcitrants were convicted and jailed for refusing to pay the parish rates legally assessed against them. Shortly thereafter, acting in behalf of this dissident faction, Col. Cushing petitioned the Massachusetts General Court that they be separated from the Second Parish and allowed to rejoin the First Parish. In the petition he emphasized the contrary ruling of the ecclesiastical councils held in 1755 and the irregularity attending Clark's installation. Using Cushing's words, he stated that "they went to the Meeting-House; where we made a second Demand to be heard, and instead of making us an answer, they quitted the Meeting-House, and in a riotous and tumultuous Manner, went to one Mr. Simonton's Orchard; and there they performed some ceremonies which they called and the people understood to be an installment of the said Clark." Speaking specifically, Cushing objected to the minister because of "his want of liberal and learned education; his separating principles which he set out upon when he was ordained over a separation in Boston; his immoral conduct; and the divisions, contentions and mischiefs that will attend said Parish."

The General Court responded favorably to the petition, and, on 18 January 1760, the Cushing faction were given leave to rejoin the First Parish. As is so often the case, the passage of time proved to be a healing balm to inflamed passions. After Cushing died in 1765, the surviving dissenters petitioned the General Court to be returned to the Second Parish. The request was granted 25 February 1767.

In the years that followed, the Reverend Ephraim Clark presided over his congregation with great charity and forebearance. Gradually his quiet, peaceful disposition and his unfailing devotion to the parish, won the respect and confidence of his fellow citizens as well as that of his colleagues in surrounding communities. In the forty-one years of his pastorate, the longest in the history of the parish, he witnessed and participated in many historically significant events.

When the district of Cape Elizabeth replaced the Second Parish in 1765, he was its only resident minister. In 1772 it was his painful duty to attend a man condemned to hang for murder. The man was a Solomon Goodwin who struck and killed a companion while drunk. He was tried and convicted in a Falmouth court and his date of execution was set for 12 November 1772. The gallows was erected in what is now Bramhall Square in Portland, and, as Goodwin stood upon the trap, the Reverend Clark delivered a long, moralizing sermon. It was subsequently published in Boston the following year as a pamphlet entitled *Sovereign Grace Displayed in the Conversion and Salvation of a Penitent Sinner, set forth in a Sermon Preached before the Execution of Solomon Goodwin, who was executed at Falmouth, November 12, 1772 ... By Ephraim Clark of Cape Elizabeth ....*

During the Revolutionary War Clark was an ardent patriot serving briefly as an army chaplain at Cambridge, Massachusetts in 1776. The troubles and privations of this conflict removed any misgivings that lingered in the minds of his colleagues. In 1776, he participated in an ecclesiastical council at Woolwich and in 1782 at Gray. When the Second Parish of Portland was set off in 1788, he took part in the ordination of its first pastor, the Reverend Elijah Kellogg, that same year, extending the right hand of fellowship.

Probably Clark's most distressing experience of the Revolutionary War era involved the ill-fated Bagaduce Expedition against the British base at Castine in the summer of 1779. He joined Col. Jonathan Mitchell's regiment as chaplain and landed with the troops on 28 July. When it became apparent that the operation was a failure, the minister stayed with Mitchell's regiment during its long and painful march back to Portland. Upon his return to Cape Elizabeth, it was his sorrowful duty to conduct the funeral service of his close friend Dr. Nathaniel Jones, leading physician of the town, who had died of exposure 4 September during the retreat while serving as regimental surgeon.

During his long pastorate at Cape Elizabeth Clark's annual salary of eighty pounds varied very little from year to year. How this compared to the salary his predecessor received it is now impossible to ascertain. The first notice of Clark's annual stipend appears in the 1767 when the town voted what would be henceforth his customary remuneration of eighty pounds. The only departure from this fixed rate occurred during the Revolutionary War. In 1778 it was voted that he be paid 220 pounds and the following year his salary was to be 550 pounds, "lawful money." This substantial increase did not reflect a raise in his income, rather it was occasioned by the inflationary conditions that plagued the country, or as the town records state, "on account of the dearness of Provisions." This generosity on the part of the town was an empty gesture however, for the Reverend Clark received absolutely nothing in either year.

In 1780 and 1781 no such financial settlement was attempted by the town. The lack of cash precluded any monetary expenditure, instead it voted that Clark be paid in produce to the value of seventy pounds, each of the two years. By 1782 the situation must have improved slightly. The notation in the records for 19 March reads "voted Seventy Pounds Ministers Salary which Sum the Rev. Mr. Eph. Clark Accepted as this years Salary, he being Present."

That same year a committee was appointed by the town to negotiate with Clark relative to the stipend he failed to receive in any form in 1778 and 1779. At a meeting held 4 June 1782, the patient cleric announced that he would accept eighty pounds for each year, less twenty pounds as his contribution to the war effort and the value of provisions given him by several thoughtful parishioners. Shortly thereafter, he was voted 105/19/10, to be paid in two installments, the first in 1784 and the second in 1785. For the remainder of his life his salary of eighty pounds was paid without further difficulty.

Hardly had the vicisitudes of the Revolutionary War begun to subside when tragedy again entered Clark's life. On 18 February 1785, his wife Elizabeth died after a long illness at the age of fifty eight. She was buried a short distance from the grave of Benjamin Allen, close by the meeting house, Friday 5 March. With no children to lessen the loneliness of the struggle for survival in this difficult era, Clark apparently remarried in a few years, for in March of 1798 the town voted to pay his salary covering the previous year to his widow Sarah Clark.

Death came suddenly to the Reverend Ephraim Clark at the age of seventy-five on 11 December 1797. He had been pastor for forty-one years but had actually preached close to forty-three. His body was laid to rest next to that of his wife Elizabeth and several feet from his close friend of former years Dr. Nathaniel Jones.

One interesting relic of Clark's ministry is a graceful pewter communion flagon presented to the church by William Simonton in 1760. Of English manufacture the vessel is inscribed: "The Gift of Mr. Willm Simonton to the 2 Church in Falmouth 1760." It is currently exhibited in a display of kitchen pewter at the Tate house in Stroudwater.

The finding of a new minister to replace the humble and dedicated Clark was a problem of long duration. These were years in the midst of a period of spiritual deadness, an era of religious and moral indifference that would last well into the nineteenth century. In August of 1798 a Rev. White agreed to preach at Long Creek, Spurwink, and Purpooduck, for a salary of $100, but he apparently moved on almost immediately.

The meeting house, in this same period, was also in a state of disrepair. Although some rebuilding had been carried out in 1789, with each pew owner paying his alloted share, the structure was still in bad condition. Ten years later, a committee was appointed by the town to draw plans and select a site for a new meeting house. Nothing was done, however, and the old building continued to serve despite its dilapidation.

Finally, early in 1800, the Reverend William Gregg was prevailed upon to accept a call to serve as minister. Actually, it was a dual position, for he was also hired to serve as a "Public Teacher." The town voted to pay him a salary of $333.33 if he would agree to settle permanently. In March of the following year Gregg agreed to settled and plans were made for his ordination the following June. A committee was also appointed to make the necessary arrangements which included replacing the missing and broken panes of glass in the meeting house.

The ordination of the Reverend Gregg took place on 15 July 1801. Little is known of his early history, except that he

295

was born in Londonderry, New Hampshire and graduated from Dartmouth in 1787. From the evidence that survives it is quite clear that he was not a dedicated cleric. A fat, rather jovial man, his lack of "evangelical orthodoxy" was a source of some annoyance to many members of the church. During his ministry, he continued to serve as a full-time teacher. In addition, he was elected to represent the town in the General Court of Massachusetts for the year 1806. After five years, he asked to be relieved of his pastoral duties and was dismissed on 6 December 1806.

During the ministry of the Reverend Gregg, various changes occurred that considerably altered the church. Just before his ordination in 1801, it was reorganized as the First Congregational Church of Cape Elizabeth, a covenant of faith was drafted and signed by the nine members of the governing board.

The following year, the condition of the meeting house again became a matter of some concern to the town. However, instead of spending limited funds for repairs, it was voted to remove sections of benches on the main floor and in the gallery, close off the doors in the eastern and western sides of the meeting house, and construct additional pews. They were sold at two public auctions, and the prices received are an indication of their comparative value. On 5 July 1802 pew No. 20 was sold to Caleb Dyer for $14.50, No. 19 to George Knights for $16.25, No. 33 to Mark Dyer for $17.00, No. 32 to Israel Woodbury for $18.00, No. 35 to Georges Robarts for $18.50, and No. 34 to Lemuel Sawyer for $19.25, all on the main floor. In addition, two pews in what had been the women's gallery was sold, No. 26 to Edward Small for $7.00, and No. 27 to Daniel Sawyer for $6.25. The second vendue occurred 3 November whereby the pew between the parsonage pew and that of George Knights was sold to Robert Dyer for $60.00, the pew built where the western door had been to Isaac Ficket for $28.50, and the pew where the eastern door had been to Nathaniel Dyer for $30.50.

Another important change that had been a subject of agitation and debate for some years was the construction of a meeting house in the Spurwink section of the town. After the creation of the Second Parish in 1733, services were no longer conducted in that area with the possible exception of a few months in 1798-1799. The year that the district of Cape Elizabeth had been formed the matter had been taken up at town meeting but was voted down. The same thing occurred in 1770, 1771, and again in 1773, with the same results. In the trying years of the Revolution and postwar recovery, the agitation was temporarily suspended pending the return of normal conditions.

Finally, in 1801 the town agreed "that Spurwink have their proportional part of the preaching in that part of the town . . . ," but that the construction of a church would be left to them to accomplish. Land for the Spurwink church and a cemetery was quickly donated by Jonathan Mitchell, with other local inhabitants providing timber for the frame in addition to the necessary plank, hardware, and building supplies.

When completed in 1802, the church was a small, unimpressive structure with an entry on the east side and a covered porch along the north side. The windows were very close together and were provided with 7 x 9 inch panes of glass. A pulpit was placed against the north wall and rough plank benches were provided for the congregation. The ceiling was supported by four stout pillars, each a timber approximately fifteen inches square. About the only finished aspect of the interior was that the walls were plastered. As was to be the case for some years, the building was unheated.

At this stage, there was no steeple, and the building was unpainted. To accommodate the women, Jonathan Mitchell and Lieut. Benjamin Jordan each provided a massive granite horse block to make it easier to dismount from horseback. In this period the poverty of the citizenry and condition of the roads made it difficult if not impossible for them to own or maintain a carriage of any kind. Rather than ride to church in a farm wagon or cart, the women generally preferred to travel via pillion, seated behind their husbands on the back of a horse.

Two years later, in 1804, the benches and pulpit were removed. High box pews were installed, with seats hung on butt hinges so that they could be raised when it was necessary to stand for prayers or singing. Two pews against the west wall were set aside for the use of the singers. Shortly after they were completed, the pews were sold at a vendue as was customary. In addition, a new raised pulpit was built and equipped with a short flight of winding stairs. No further changes were forthcoming for the next thirty years.

Another very significant change that occurred in this era was the disestablishment of the "Puritan Church". Two years after the creation of the new First Congregational Church, an act of incorporation was passed by the Massachusetts General Court. On 22 June 1803 the "Proprietors of the Meeting House in Cape Elizabeth" were empowered to choose all such officers as parishes were by law entitled to choose, to raise money for the maintenance and repairs of the meeting house, and to assist the owners of pews to meet the cost of such maintenance and repairs. Thus, the church became responsible for its own upkeep and relatively independent of the town. Complete separation of the church and town would not be accomplished until provided for by law under the Maine constitution of 1820. As long as Massachusetts exercised control, the town was legally responsible for the perpetuation of the church, including the selection of ministers, setting off of dissenting religious groups, and the control of lands granted to the town for the support of the church. Actually, the last official action taken by the town for the settling of a minister occurred in May 1808 when a committee was appointed to seek a replacement for the Reverend Gregg. As to the lands held by the town for the benefit of the church, the town voted 2 November 1818 to sell the land and turn the money thus obtained over to the First Congregational Church. On 18 February 1819, the Massachusetts General Court created as a legal entity the Cape Elizabeth Ministerial Fund with Ebenezer Thrasher, Rishworth Jordan, William Cobb, Ebenezer Webster, Jr., and Daniel Skillings as the first board of trustees. This fund received the money derived from the sale of the ministerial lands and they in turn were authorized by the terms of incorporation to invest it for the benefit of the church. After 1818, the town records are devoid of details relative to the church. The only notations that appear are infrequent appropriations to assist the church in keeping the meeting house in a habitable condition. The town had no such obligation after 1834 when the meeting house was demolished.

In May 1808 a committee appointed by the town obtained the consent of the church to extend a call to the Reverend Richard Briggs to serve as minister. He, however, declined the call and in February the town was forced to deal with charges brought by the Commonwealth relative to the lack of a settled minister. Finally, in August of the same year, the Reverend Benjamin Sawyer accepted a call and was ordained 22 November, 1809.

Apparently Sawyer was found to be lacking in the exercise of his ministerial duties for in April 1812 the church voted to reduce his salary and the following year, voted to suspend it altogether. As no record of his dismissal can be found, the assumption is that he had left the church some time between April and June 1812.

After three years of inactivity, the church decided to ask the Reverend William Gregg to return to the pulpit. Despite some rather bitter criticism of his first period of service, a call was extended to him 10 October 1815. On Wednesday 31 January he was installed and remained until 4 March 1824 when he was dismissed at his own request. The reason for his dismissal was his sudden and rather dramatic conversion to Universalism. He died in Andover, Maine in 1856 at the age of ninety-two.

After 1826 the church was again without a pastor for an extended period of time. One caustic comment upon the state of religion in Cape Elizabeth during this period appeared in a Portland periodical *The Yankee*, Wednesday 2 July 1828, and came from the pen of John Neal. It was certainly food for thought.

> Instead of sending abroad our thousands and our tens of thousands of dollars to build churches within the heart of India or along the shores of Africa, what if we look about us here, and see what may be done for our next-door neighbors? Just over Vaughan's Bridge people may be found who if they are not overgrown with hair, like Peter the wild boy, are at least overgrown with squalor and filth. No differences do they make, none do they know, between the Sabbath and any other day! Why not send missionaries to them?

Later that same year, on 11 November the church offered the pulpit to the Reverend Isaac Esty who immediately accepted with enthusiasm. At the age of thirty-two, he was filled with an extraordinary evangelical zeal which he hoped to impart to his new parishioners. He was ordained 29 January 1829 and began at once to labor among the citizens of Cape Elizabeth. Although nothing is known of his success that first year, it apparently fell far short of his great expectations. An ardent advocate of temperance he also found his success in this area to be a little less than spectacular.

Undoubtedly angered and possibly embarrassed by his lack of noteworthy achievement he bitterly assailed his parishioners for their real and imagined shortcomings. In January 1831 he attended the annual meeting of the Cumberland County Conference of Congregational Churches and addressed the gathering on his findings in Cape Elizabeth. His remarks were undoubtedly the sensation of the conference.

> . . .The religious prospects of Cape Elizabeth are dark and discouraging. The church has become reduced to about twenty members, containing only one man and the rest with one or two exceptions, are aged females; and a number of them too old and infirm to attend public worship. The pastor is not aware that any case of hopeful conversion has occurred the past year. Nor can he at present discover any hopeful tokens of better times as it regards attention to religion. Indeed he observes, that the town exhibits in a moral point

of view, an almost unvaried, dreary, and desolute waste; and what renders the prospect more preeminently dreary, it is the dreadful prevalence of intemperance.
. . .The deplorable state into which we are sunk, may be learnt from the fact, that dram shops are open here on the Sabbath, forming a school of vice that, one would think the prince of darkness himself would hardly desire to improve upon . . . .

Shortly thereafter, he addressed the first annual meeting of the Cumberland County Temperance Society where he greatly elaborated upon his earlier remarks relative to the liquor problem .

The town contains probably about 1700 people, and from a residence of more than two years among them, and after having made many inquiries, I am fully persuaded, that more than three-fourths of the male heads of families through the town are habitually intemperate, and will become intoxicated whenever a favorable opportunity occurs; and to this number must be added many young men, and boys, who are following hard after the steps of their fathers; and now and then a drunken wife and mother. . . . .

When these revelations appeared in the local newspapers the citizens of Cape Elizabeth were quite naturally outraged. On Monday 21 March 1831, at a regular town meeting, a special committee of seven men, William Cummings, Elisha Jordan, Sylvanus Higgins, James Dyer, Charles Staples, Ebenezer Webster, Jr., and Nathaniel Dyer, was appointed to meet with the Reverend Esty to ascertain the truth of these extraordinary charges. A meeting was shortly arranged, and, Thursday 24 March, they met with the cleric at his home. Apparently his comments on church membership were close enough to the truth to be ignored, for the entire conference was concerned only with the liquor problem. When asked why he had made such a report Esty replied that it was not hastily conceived but represented his carefully considered opinion of existing conditions. The committeemen then demanded to know where he found such conditions as would lead him to make such charges. To this question he declined to respond.

According to the report subsequently presented to the selectmen, the members of the committee claimed that Esty offered to retract his charges if one quarter of the male heads of families, or fewer if need by, would join his Temperance Society. Also, they stated that his only specific allusion to intemperance involved the heavy drinking that occurred at the annual town meeting in March 1830. To this, the committee retorted that Esty had hired out his horse to haul the liquor to the meeting house. In conclusion, they stated that the Reverend Esty was quite firm in his convictions and exhibited no intention of either altering or retracting his charges, even though they offered to submit to an examination of the town by impartial observers. To this last suggestion Esty replied that any such reports would not be fact but only opinions and therefore not a refutation of his charges.

After examining the report of these proceedings the selectmen issued a public statement.

> The undersigned, Selectmen of the town of Cape Eilzabeth pursuant to the foregoing report accepted by the town . . . and from an actual and careful examination and inquiry, feel authorized to report that Mr. Esty's representation. . . is entirely without justification, and absolutely false. . .
> We do not hesitate to assert and to stake our individual characters on the truth of the assertion that Mr. Esty has, either through ignorance of the people among whom he has been willing to seek bread and sustenance for himself and family, or from design, reversed the truth in nearly every particular of his representation. .
> . . . It only now remains for the injured inhabitants of Cape Elizabeth, having pronounced Mr. Esty's statement to be false and the man unworthy of their confidence, to ask the members of the Cumberland Country Temperence Society to do them justice, and to deal out justice to Mr. Esty, with an even hand. The result, it is believed, will show that in his own character as a minister and man of professed veracity, has grossly deceived the Society which has adopted him as their tale bearer.
> Cape Elizabeth, April, 1831.
>
> Charles Staples
> Nathaniel Dyer
> Micah Higgins

The findings of the committee and the report of the selectmen were printed in full by the *Eastern Argus* on Tuesday 10 May 1831.

The following Tuesday this same newspaper published a lengthy letter from the Reverend Esty in which he carefully, and not without humor, attempted to answer the published reports of the committee and the selectmen.

> It appears from your paper . . . that I have received a general attack from all the forces of Cape Elizabeth, horse, foot, and dragoons, and that my situation has become nearly as perilous as that of honest Jack Falstaff, when attacked by eleven men in buckram, and three misbegotten knaves in Kendal Green, let drive at his back. No less than three selectman and seven committeeman, have come out in battle array, and have commenced the onset, by publishing

nearly two columns of their effussions, that have been brewing in their breasts for nearly forty days, and forty nights, and which seem to breathe little else but war. Under these circumstances you will not wonder, if I approach these communications with some fear and trembling, and my pulse considerably quickened. . .

Following this introduction Esty commented at some length upon what he considered the most damaging retort contained in the committee's report, that he provided his horse to haul liquor for the town meeting without denying it when questioned by the committeemen. This allegation he absolutely rejected. "Truth bids me declare that the whole of this horse-story is a sheer fabrication. It does not contain one word of truth from beginning to end."

With regard to the committee's comment that his only personal observation of intemperance involved the buying and drinking of liquor at the town meeting in March 1830, Esty insisted that this was not the entire story.

The committee make me say, that I saw the people buying and drinking spirits at the town meeting last season, but why not tell the whole truth. I observed still further that I saw men drunk by scores, not last season only, but on every similar occasion, when I have been present the latter part of the day.

Next, Esty examined other statements contained in the committee's report concluding with the observation that they were distortions of the truth, innuendoes, and prevarications. His assessment of the committee's findings, as they appeared in print, certainly reflects his inflexible and uncompromising stand relative to the validity of his original charges.

There must evidently be some powerful chemical properties in the brain of the author of this report, for it seems completely to decompose everything that passes through it. . .
Now gentlemen of this committee, this is too cruel, to invent such monstrous absurdities to put into my mouth, and then to send them abroad through this enlightened community, as coming from me, it is to abominably cruel, I do solemnly declare that I never did utter one word of such intolerable foolishness, in the presence of this committee. . . .
It has been a mystery with me, what possible object these men could have proposed to themselves, in publishing this violent philippic against me, and my report, when the whole of it does not contain a single particle of evidence, as I can discover, that I have made any erroneous statement.
. . . Gentlemen, where is your proof, and we will listen to you;

but we cannot take bare assertions in this case. . . .
Under these circumstances I shall make no appeal to the sympathies of this community; for I have not an anxious though about any consequences that may result from this attack in reference to my character. My measures have been approved by so many men in all the different professions of life, who have been acquainted with the circumstances in which I have been placed and who will by their talents, weight of character, and moral worth, guide and control the public mind, that I feel perfectly safe as it regards any injury that will result to my reputation.
Cape Elizabeth, May 11, 1831.

I. Esty

Regardless of how this fascinating controversay was viewed by the general public, the church acted before these mutual recriminations had been fully aired. At its annual meeting early in April, it had been voted "that the pastoral cares of Rev. I. Esty be discontinued." He was then dismissed an 18 April by a church council that apparently did not share the views held by the selectmen and the special town committee.

Although it is known to the council, that much excitement has been produced among the inhabitants of this town, and that the members of the Parish have become considerably disaffected with Mr. Esty, in consequence of certain statements made by him as to the prevalence of intemperance in the town, yet they cannot regard the course he took in the matter as meriting their censure. They believe he acted from honest motives, and with a view to the high object of promoting the best interests of the place.

One interesting sidelight of the controversy involved a Methodist circuit-riding minister who had visited the town on various occasions. Meeting the Reverend Esty early in May, he sharply criticized him for exaggerating the situation. He said that Esty could not help but observe that not more than a majority of the heads of families were habitually intemperate!

Despite the bitterness of the controversy, the Reverend Esty had no difficulty in finding a new parish. Shortly after his dismissal, he was settled at Freeport where he continued to preach for several years. He died at the age of seventy-nine, in 1875, at Amherst, Massachusetts.

Early in 1832, the Maine Missionary Society sent the Reverend Josiah G. Merrill to the First Congregational Church and on 6 February 1833 he was installed as pastor. Under his leadership, the church experienced a remarkable improvement in its fortunes that included several baptisms and accessions. The office of Deacon was created, and Ebenezer Webster, Jr. was the first to be elected to that post. In the spring of 1834 Merrill conducted a very spirited and successful series of revival meetings that significantly increased church membership. Shortly thereafter, he organized a temperance society the need for which must have been a little more than obvious. As the society included the entire congregation, the church adopted a resolution whereby they agreed "not to admit persons to membership who will not abstain from the intemperate use of ardent spirits."

The year 1834 also witnessed the demolition of the old meeting house. A century of use and only occasional repair had taken its toll. The process of tearing down the old building and erecting the new church continued through the fall and winter. The usable material salvaged from the structure was sold at public auction Tuesday 31 March 1835 by John Armstrong the Parish Clerk. When the debris had been cleared away, the stumps of white oak trees were found, protected from the elements for a century, beneath the meeting house.

Completed early in the summer, on the site of its predecessor, the new church was formally dedicated Wednesday 15 July 1835. Structurally, it was plain and unimpressive with a bell-tower and spire on the end that faced Shore Road. This same end served as the front of the church and was pierced with two entry ways. The interior was as plain as the exterior with slip pews along the east and west walls, and the pulpit against the north end.

The evangelistic fervor of the Reverend Merrill continued to strengthen the membership of the church. In this period he wrote a little book that enjoyed a wide circulation, entitled *Sermons for Children,* that was published in 1837. The following year he requested that he be permitted to resign and reluctantly the church council voted to gratify his wish, dismissing him 12 August 1838. He died at the age of eighty-five in 1872 at Lynn, Massachusetts.

Changes were also being made in this era at the Spurwink Church. In 1834, Capt. Clement Jordan, Capt. Elisha Jordan, and Rufus Jordan, Jr., were designated a committee to supervise its rebuilding and repair. The building was stripped to its frame and entirely reconstructed. New windows were installed, a vestibule with two doors was built onto the end toward the road, and a belfry with a steeple, added at the same time. The steeple was surmounted by a weather vane that cost the then extravagant sum of forty dollars.

The interior of the little church was also drastically altered.

The box pews were replaced by new ones that were sold late in 1835 at a vendue. One very desirable change was the addition of stoves for the first time. They were salvaged from the old meeting house of 1734 and transported to the Spurwink Church by Ebenezer Webster, Jr. The porch that had been attached to the east wall was also removed and added to the residence of George Doughty. In addition, the massive horse blocks fell into disuse and eventually vanished from the scene. Lastly, the rebuilt church, externally almost the same as it is today, was given its first coat of white paint. Henceforth, the Spurwink Church would stand out as one of the most charming and picturesque structures in the town, rivaling Portland Head Light as a subject of interest to the artist.

In the spring of 1840 a replacement for the Reverend Merrill was found at last but only on a temporary basis. On 17 May the Reverend John C. Hurd was installed and agreed to remain a year. Leaving early in 1841 he was succeeded by the Reverend William Pierce, a Methodist by inclination, who was duly installed 21 July 1842. During his ministry the church lost one of its most highly respected and able champions, Deacon Ebenezer Webster, Jr. He died March 1844 at the age of forty-eight. A glowing testimonial to his devotion was suitably inscribed in the records of the church. Later that same year, the Reverend Pierce requested a release from his duties and on 21 October he was dismissed. According to the records of the church "his main reason appeared to be want of an adequate support and an inability, arising from his ill health, to perform all the labor required of him in this place, obliged as he had been by the small salary given him to labor on his farm at a great distance from both houses of worship."

For the next three years the church was without a settled minister. However, the Reverend David M. Mitchell of Portland preached to the congregation on infrequent occasions. It was during this era that the church was quite violently affected by the Millerite excitement. In 1831, a former Baptist in western Massachusetts, one William Miller, after studying certain selected passages in the books of Daniel and Revelation became convinced that the second coming of Christ was imminent. Unlike other millennialists of the period, he was able to establish a specific date from his investigations. He created a sensation among the credulous by proclaiming 21 March 1843 as the day of final judgment. As this date approached, the excitement was intense, many converts divesting themselves of all their worldly goods in preparation for the end. When the expected end failed to materialize Miller set a new date, 22 October 1844, but once again Christ failed to appear and the day passed into history.

A significant number of people in Cape Elizabeth embraced the doctrines of Miller, and, although many quickly abandoned the Millerite cause, others remained true to the Adventist Church. One of the earliest converts to leave the First Congregational Church was Morris Cobb. When he became convinced that Miller possessed the truth, he disposed of his prosperous farm and awaited the end, devoid of any doubts. After the disappointment of 22 October 1844 he resigned himself to the task of awaiting what he considered to be the inevitable second coming of Christ. Building a small shack as a shelter, he lived from day to day on a diet of bread and fish in the belief that this was the only food of which Christ partook. Living primarily the life of a hermit, he preached Adventist doctrines whenever the opportunity presented itself. With extraordinary fortitude he managed to survive until Saturday 2 July 1887 when he died of a stroke at the age of ninety.

Yet another group that added some excitement to this period was the Church of Latter Day Saints. Practically nothing is known of their activity but apparently a few converts were made in 1841 or 1842. Early in 1843 a shadowy figure by the name of "Cincinnatus" Jordan led a tiny band of Cape Elizabeth Mormons in a very difficult pilgrimage to a new home at Nauvoo, Illinois, the "New Jerusalem" of this faith. Almost nothing is known about this man except that his real name was James Payson Jordan and that he was born in Ellsworth. In his early years he sailed from Portland as a crewman aboard the locally owned whaling ship, *Science*. How he acquired the pseudonym "Cincinnatus," or what his ultimate fate was, has not survived in any existing records.

The years 1845-1847 inclusive are something of a hiatus in the history of the church. Apparently the Reverend Royal Parkinson was sent to the church in September of 1847 by the Maine Missionary Society. He was not ordained and installed as pastor, however, until 18 October of the following year. A recent graduate of the Andover Theological Seminary, he was filled with a proselytizing zeal that was soon lost in the emptiness of his church.

During his ministry, the Reverend Parkinson became quite interested in the history of the town and spent much of his leisure time in research. As a result of his investigations, he succeeded in writing what must have been the first attempt at a history of Cape Elizabeth. Regardless of its brevity and sketchiness, it does represent a carefully executed beginning. After his three years as the resident minister, the results of his preaching "not being equal to his lofty ideals, he felt it his duty to resign." The notation in the church records that Parkinson ". . . felt that God will not prosper religion in this church, as such, until its few male members, when not prevented by sickness, infirmities, or other providential hindrances, feel free to become co-workers with their Pastor in sustaining the prayer meeting and the Sabbath School . . .and He will not prosper this Parish until those who constitute it manifest a degree of interest and care." On 13 October 1851 he was dismissed and moved away. He died 22 December 1882 in Washington, D. C. at the age of sixty seven.

For the next nine years, no church records were kept, or, if they were, they have disappeared. In these years, the church was served by a succession of ministers who preached with great irregularity and quickly moved somewhere else. The pulpit was filled in 1852-1853 by the Reverend C. E. Lord, in 1855-1858 by the Reverend Horatio Merrill, in 1860-1862 by the Reverend A. F. Beard, and in 1865-1871 by the Reverend Henry M. Vaill. The last named individual was engaged on a per annum basis, finally leaving for reasons of ill health.

Not until 1871 was a candidate found who would accept a call to become a settled minister. Arriving in October, the Reverend Edwin A. Harlow was installed 21 November. A man of great fortitude and enthusiasm, he overcame the lassitude of previous years thereby significantly increasing the congregation. During his ministry the church celebrated its 150th anniversary with appropriate ceremonies, Wednesday 10, September 1884. One very interesting aspect of the celebration was the publication of a pamphlet, prepared by the Reverend Harlow, that included an extraordinarily informative historical sketch of the church. Also at this time, the name of the church was changed to the First Church of Christ.

The Reverend Harlow resigned his pastorate and was reluctantly dismissed 1 October 1884. He was succeeded the following May by the Reverend James E. Aikins who was installed 11 November 1885. Remaining but six months, he was replaced in May 1886 by the Reverend Benjamin P. Snow. Four years later he was dismissed and his place was taken by the Reverend George W. Kelley.

During the ministry of the Reverend Kelley three significant changes occurred that were to have a lasting influence upon the church. In the summer of 1891 the building was moved to a new site, donated by David Boyd, located near the juncture of Cottage Road and Mitchell Road. On this occasion the church was thoroughly renovated with new lights installed, central heating provided, and a new vestry constructed. Five stained glass windows were also added. One presented by the Sunday School in memory of Tristram J. Prince, a deacon for fifty years, and another given by Winthrop S. Jordan in memory of his sister Caroline Fox Jordan. The church was re-dedicated Thursday 10 September 1891.

In 1892 the church voted to build its first parsonage. The sum of $1,800 was appropriated and a lot of land at the corner of Chase and Sawyer Streets was donated by Martin P. Walls of Marietta, Ohio a former Cape Elizabeth resident. Completed the following year at a cost of $1,757.40, it was occupied for the first time by the Reverend Kelley and his sister.

Three years later, the separation of the towns occurred and although the church continued to serve many citizens in both towns it left Cape Elizabeth with but one resident Congregational Church. Its popular designation as the "North Church" soon fell into disuse and the "South Church," now in Cape Elizabeth, became simply the Spurwink Church.

Despite the separation of the towns, the resident minister of the First Church continued to occupy, upon occasion, the pulpit of the church at Spurwink. In the summer of 1909, during the ministry of the Reverend John A. Waterworth, the interior of the Spurwink Church was again extensively altered. The old box pews were removed and more modern settles replaced them. A raised platform for the pulpit, organ, and singers was built against the northern end. Since that time, no important structural changes have occurred.

As the twentieth century advanced, the South Congregational Church grew apart from the parent First Church in South Portland. On Tuesday 28 May 1935, it was formally separated and became an independent entity known as the Spurwink Congregational Church. Unfortunately, the period that followed did not witness a continuation of ecclesiastical activity. The care and preservation of the church soon became the responsibility of the town.

Finally, in March 1945, the town voted to assume control of the cemetery, adjacent to the church with an adjoining tract of land of approximately twenty-six acres. Originally designated as Riverside Cemetery it had been incorporated by twelve Jordans and a Brown, all members of the Spurwink Church, in February 1882. The cemetery was now expanded to include Riverside Memorial Park, and a three-man board of trustees was created to supervise its use. Two years later, a set of by-laws were adopted for the park whereby the selectmen were authorized to establish regulations for its operation and maintenance.

In 1953, the Sprague Corporation donated a lot of land adjacent to the cemetery to expand its facilities further. Three years later, the Spurwink Congregational Church, as per vote of the trustees, was transferred to the town with the provision that it be maintained as a cemetery chapel, a community chapel, and as a "house of God." The town accepted the building in April of 1957, thereby ensuring the preservation of this venerable church for future generations. Other than this chapel, the town of Cape Elizabeth does not now contain an active Congregational Church.

III

Despite the sanctity of the established Congregational Church other sects were not hesitant about conducting missionary activities in Cape Elizabeth. In 1794 the Methodist Elder Jesse Lee of Virginia preached on several occasions with some success in the northern areas of the town. The Portland Circuit was formed that same year with an Elder Wager appointed as the first cleric to travel this circuit which included Cape Elizabeth. By 1800, a small group of Methodists had been formed in the northwestern reaches of the town served by the first settled Methodist cleric in Portland the Reverend Joshua Taylor. The first minister to settle among the Cape Elizabeth Methodists was the Reverend Samuel Snowden, a Negro preacher of superior intellect and great evangelical fervor. He was assisted on occasion by the Reverend Asa Heath, the Reverend Samuel Barnes, and the Reverend Reuben Hubbard. In June of 1803, the Reverend Daniel Perry formally organized the first resident Methodist Church in Cape Elizabeth.

That same year, 1803 the members of this church petitioned the town to be allowed to legally separate from the established church and form their own society. Their request was denied, however, leaving them no alternative but to petition the Massachusetts General Court for leave to secede. As the General Court responded favorably to this request, the town reluctantly consented in November of 1806. The following February an act was passed by the General Court incorporating the Methodist Society in Cape Elizabeth with forty men specifically mentioned as the members of this church. This was the first incorporated religious society within the limits of the town.

In 1808, under the leadership of the Reverend Joshua Taylor, a plain and roughly finished church was built at Barren Hill. Here it remained until 1824 when it was moved to Brown's Hill and placed on a lot donated to the society by Elisha Brown. During this era, many fruitful prayer meetings were conducted at Long Creek by Jennie, Annie and Rebecca Skillings. In addition an extremely active Sunday School was established by several ladies of the society.

The church built its first parsonage in 1848 when a suitable dwelling was erected on the corner of Brown and Lincoln Streets. The first pastor to reside here was the Reverend James Harrington. Although the church could now offer its minister a suitable residence few of them remained any longer than two years. In the first century of its existence, this Methodist society had eighty-three different pastors.

In 1858, another Methodist church was established on what is now Elm Street in Pleasantdale and was served by the same circuit ministers who preached at Brown's Hill. This was a small building that was erected at Point Village to house another Methodist society and sold by them in 1851. It was moved to the Elm Street site to serve the large number of methodists who resided in that area. This building was not replaced until 1891 when the present Elm Street Church was constructed.

By the early 1860's the Brown's Hill Church was badly in need of rebuilding despite extensive alterations and repairs carried out in 1836. The society decided in 1865 to erect a new church on land contributed for that purpose by Samuel Haskell.

The following year, the Reverend Frank C. Ayers was appointed to the circuit, and, largely through his influence, the construction of this new church was undertaken. At a cost of $13,000 this new church was finished late in 1867 and dedicated on Wednesday, 29 January 1868, with the presiding Elder Joseph Colby preaching the dedication sermon. The completion of this church was due primarily to the generosity of two local men. When it was discovered that contributions and the sale of pews would only produce $8,000 the balance of $5,000 was donated by two brothers, Eben T. Nutter and Henry Nutter.

Three years later in 1871, Eben Nutter purchased a large bell to be installed in the belfry. That same year, the old parsonage was sold and a new one erected on Evans Street, on land donated by Mrs. Elmira Fickett and Mrs. Martha Dyer.

The second Methodist society to be formed in Cape Elizabeth was gathered at Point Village in 1839 by the Reverend Jesse Stone. The following year, a small church was erected in this village and completed in 1842. Despite the efforts of a new pastor, the Reverend George D. Strout who was appointed in 1843, this church was temporarily eclipsed by the intense excitement among its parishioners engendered by the revelations of the Reverend William Miller. However, by 1850 this frenzy had subsided and the congregation began to increase.

On 6 November 1851 the trustees of this church voted to sell the building and erect a new one at Ferry Village. A lot of land on Dyer Street was donated for this purpose by Dr. Eliphalet Clark of Portland. However, the society thought the site unsuitable and sold the land. Shortly thereafter, the local firm of Turner and Cahoon contributed a lot approximately ninety feet square on the west side of Sawyer Street in Ferry Village. Construction was started early in 1852, and on 26 January 1853 the new church, measuring 56 x 42 feet, was dedicated. The total cost of $2,300 was met by the sale of fifty-six pews. The first minister to preach in this building was the Reverend Uriel Rideout.

The rapid growth of this society demanded an enlargement of the building. This was carried out in 1862 at a cost of $2,000 raised by popular subscription. No further expansion occurred until 1874 when a combined parsonage and vestry was constructed at an expense of $1,500 which temporarily exceeded available capital.

Throughout the seventies the Ferry Village society was extremely active and several successful revivals were carried out. In 1882 various improvements, that included an organ, were instituted, culminating in 1884 with the purchase of a fine-toned "centennial bell" of 1,021 pounds. Unfortunately, the activity that was so pronounced late in the nineteen century experienced a sharp decline before the twentieth century was very far advanced.

A small society was also active in Knightville, and, in 1880, a chapel was erected on land given by Dr. Eliphalet Clark for that purpose. Completed at a cost of $3,000, it served the village for many years and was ministered to generally by the pastor at Brown's Hill.

Yet another Methodist society that was formed within the town of Cape Elizabeth was gathered at Bowery Beach. Organized in 1839 by the Reverend Jesse Stone a church was constructed the following year on the Shore Road immediately east of Great Pond. Although this church was small in membership, it did exhibit a rather enthusiastic spirit and several successful revivals occurred under the leadership of the Reverend George D. Strout.

The first Bowery Beach Church was demolished in 1857 and replaced by the current structure in 1859. Very few external alterations have occurred since its construction. The spire that once adorned the belfry was blown down in the gale of November 1898 and never restored. Also, the two doors that once graced the front have been replaced by one entrance. In 1956, the building was raised from its old foundation and a new basement built to house a kitchen, classroom space, as well as a new heating plant. Currently the interior is separated into two equal sections, one serving as the church proper and the other providing space for meetings and classes. This society was significantly expanded about 1945 and in the spring of 1964 a "Crusade of Progress" was launched to replace what is now the only Methodist Church in Cape Elizabeth.

Shortly after the Methodist society had been organized early in the nineteenth century, the Baptists became quite active. The Reverend Thomas B. Ripley, who had settled in Portland in 1815, was very successful in gathering a Baptist society in the northern area of Cape Elizabeth, baptizing about twenty people in the summer of the following year. It was not until 1819, however, that any Baptist minister was settled to organize a church. In December 1819, the Reverend Noah Hooper was ordained at the Cape Elizabeth meeting house and the same year established a Calvinist Baptist church with twenty-four members.

After the departure of the Reverend Hooper early in the twenties this society was visited occasionally by Baptist missionaries. One who was very active over a period of years was the Elder Robert Mitchell of Freeport. He conducted his first service at the Bowery Beach district school house in 1822. His visits to the town were frequent throughout the next two years. Without a church building at his disposal, it was customary for Mitchell to use a district school as a house of worship. Despite such efforts, the society apparently languished after Mitchell suspended his visits in 1824. Enough enthusiasm survived late in the thirties for them to construct a small, exceedingly plain, chapel like building on the north side of Sawyer Street, slightly west of the Ocean House Road.

In this same period, a small group of citizens led by William Cummings, James Johnson, Sargent Shaw, Andrew Hobson, and

Elder Joseph White organized a society of Free Will Baptists. They were formally organized as a church 24 December 1831 and separated from the existing Calvinist Baptist society. Evidently this group flourished, and, by 1840, were sufficiently numerous to purchase the small church on Sawyer Street. In March of that year, a revival created some excitement, and, as a result thereof, the Elder Almon Libby baptised fifty-five new Free Will Baptists. The following year, the Calvinist Baptists combined with a group of similar persuasion in Scarborough, and a suitable church was built at what is now called "Eight Corners" in that town. These two groups, regardless of their doctrinal differences, technically continued to function as one society.

With the passage of time, the two groups persisted in their separate activities. Finally, in January 1853, they were permanently divided into an Eastern Branch (Free Will Baptist) and a Western Branch (Calvinist Baptist) but were still known simply as "The Cape Elizabeth Church."

The era of the fifties must have been somewhat lacking in a vigorous manifestation of Baptist activities, despite the fact that the church on Sawyer Street was expanded in 1858. In this same decade the Elder Robert Mitchell returned frequently to the town. The rather terse comments in his journal do not bespeak the presence of an active society.

> October, 1851, visited Cape Elizabeth, and visited the most of the church there; preached twice, with freedom of the soul.
> November, 1852, first Lord's day at Cape Elizabeth and spent about four days in visiting from house to house. Professors much as they were.
> . . . My grief to hear an old sister of Cape Elizabeth Church say in 1858 she thought she had not seen a Baptist minister there for fifteen years, except an unworthy one.
> January, 1859, I spent three first days of the week in three meeting houses at Cape Elizabeth, and preached one discourse in two of the three, with the Methodists. . .

In 1865 the Free Will Baptist society purchased as its first parsonage a house at what is now 51 Ocean House Road. The first pastor to reside therein was the Reverend Almon Libby. Nine years later, the church was extensively altered and repaired. The foundation was restored; a new entry way, six new windows, and a steeple were added. A new pulpit and platform were installed, and the walls were replastered. In addition, the building was clapboarded and painted.

No further changes were made until 1883 when the "Eastern

Branch" and the "Western Branch" were completely disassociated. When the town of South Portland was created in 1895, the society on Sawyer Street was known as the Free Baptist Church in Cape Elizabeth. Henceforth, although it was now in a neighboring town, many Cape Elizabeth citizens continued as members. As of 1965, the present town of Cape Elizabeth does not have a Baptist church within its borders.

One sect that flourished very briefly in the early decades of the nineteenth century was the Society of Friends. Although they were few, they built a small, plain, unpainted meeting house in what is now Bay View Cemetery on Sawyer Street about 1828. This building was used for town meetings in the years 1835-1837. Two prominent members of this tiny band of Quakers were Nathaniel Dyer and Greely Hannaford. The society was quite inactive toward the middle of the century and about 1865 they sold their meeting house to Captain John W. Burke of Portland who moved it to a new location. The old section of Bay View Cemetery was the original Quaker burying ground and is the final resting place of many members of this now vanished society.

With the establishment of various industries in the northern area of the town just before the Civil War, many families from Ireland and a few from southern Europe found suitable employment that prompted them to settle. Quite a number were members of the Roman Catholic Church. In 1861, Calvary Cemetery was established in the immediate vicinity of Ligonia to serve as a Catholic burial ground for the Greater Portland area and replaced the southeast corner of the Western Cemetery that had previously been used. That same year, Calvary Chapel was constructed, thus becoming the first Roman Catholic Church to be located within the town of Cape Elizabeth and served as a place of worship for local members of that faith. None has existed in the town, however, since separation.

The most recent sect to build within the town of Cape Elizabeth is the Protestant Episcopal Church. On St. Alban's Day in 1914, a mission was established in South Portland by the Reverend Canon Philip Schuyler, A chapel was constructed that same year on the corner of the Shore Road and Woodbury Street. In 1938 the chapel was replaced by a modest church and eleven years later became St. Alban's Parish with the Reverend John E. Gulick as rector.

By 1954, the St. Alban's congregation had outgrown the church that had been built sixteen years earlier. In April, plans for a new church to be erected on the corner of Oakhurst Road and the Shore Road were well advanced. The site for the new St. Alban's Episcopal Church was dedicated by the Right Reverend Oliver L. Loring, Bishop of the Maine diocese, on Sunday, 15 August 1954. Among those participating in the ceremony was the Right Reverend Edward M. G. Jones, Bishop of St. Alban's Parish in England, who presented a stone from the 1,200 year old abbey to be built into the altar of the new church. This was the first service of the Anglican or Episcopal Church to be celebrated since the departure of the Reverend Robert Jordan 279 years earlier.

The cornerstone was laid with appropriate ceremonies on Sunday, 30 October, 1955, conducted by the Right Reverend Oliver L. Loring and the Reverend John E. Gulick. When finished early in 1956, the new St. Alban's Church exhibited most of the essential features of an English parish church, but utilized a modern treatment of windows and lighting. The nave of the church provides seating for 145 people and the chancel has sufficient space to accommodate the choir as well as the clergy.

Although no new churches are currently being formed, it is certainly to be expected that the population growth will eventually bring them forward. The new "suburbia-by-the-sea," while utilizing the churches of the Greater Portland area, will undoubtedly initiate suitable sectarian activities in future years.

Although the average Cape Elizabeth Yankee of the past was generally an irregular churchgoer, religion was often a deeply felt, soulsearching experience. The Protestant churches for many years drew their congregations from almost the entire town. When a new citizen took up residence he usually chose the church that came closest to harmonizing with his own doctrinal viewpoints. Not infrequently such doctrinal viewpoints were passionately felt and held.

The suburbanite of the modern era may still exhibit similar characteristics but he is often motivated by more complex considerations. He is all too frequently concerned with the thought that going to church is the nice thing that proper people do on Sundays. It advertises his respectability, gives him a warm feeling that he is behaving as his God-fearing forebearers did, and adds, he hopes, to his social stature by placing him in the social group with which he wants to be identified. Even when he takes his worship seriously he usually prefers to do so while surrounded by his own kind of people. In joining a particular church he is far less concerned with doctrinal details than he is with the implications of status.

Thus the suburban church of the future will resemble but slightly the church of Robert Jordan or Ephraim Clark of Joshua Taylor. In all probability it will reflect the national trend common to communities of this type. Such churches are customarily viewed as community facilities, like the school, the drug store, the town government, and the neighborhood bowling alley. Hopefully they might also reflect the traditional concepts of brotherhood and social responsibility that consistently motivated the less sophisicated citizenry of the not too distant past.

CHAPTER IX

SUBURBIA-BY-THE-SEA

The inhabitants of the "new" town of Cape Elizabeth quickly set about the task of reorganization, and a town meeting was held in the Grange Hall at Spurwink on Saturday, 20 April, 1895. The various offices were filled, necessary appropriations made, and a committee of eight, (Charles Peabbles, Nathaniel Dyer, Clement E. Staples, Michael J. Peabbles, Charles E. Jordan, Albert F. Hannaford, Edward F. Hill, and William C. Robinson,) was appointed to confer with the town of South Portland relative to the financial settlement. It was voted to meet with the Grange Hall Committee in relation to renting office space necessary for the transaction of town affairs. Of the town's 225 registered voters, 149 attended this first meeting.

At the end of the first post-separation year, the town officers were able to report favorably on the results of the division. They pointed out a fact that must have been gratifying by stating that:

> . . . the expenditures for the past year are greatly reduced from what you have been accustomed to examine, it is equally true that your public needs have been as fully met as in former years of high taxes and large expenditures in enterprises wherein your interests have been too remote for recognition . . . Your present town is now of a compact and homogeneous character and the reduction of your expenditures to your own public needs. . . has reduced your rate of taxation by about one-third of your former assessments.

From the point of view of financial saving, this first year was more than satisfactory to the frugally inclined inhabitants of Cape Elizabeth.

The settlement of financial affairs relative to the partitioning of the town was still uncompleted when the annual meeting was held 14 March 1898. The selectmen reported that during the previous year they had been in constant readiness to meet any legitimate demand made upon the town for full payment of Cape Elizabeth's portion of the old town's debt. Despite repeated requests by the town of South Portland, Cape Elizabeth refused to institute a system of partial payments on an unknown sum for an unknown time. It was also announced that experience had proven that the "division line" had been correctly placed and that the condition of the town warranted a vote of thanks to the "divisionites" (sic). Apparently the benefits derived from the separation were making themselves felt. The Cape Elizabeth tax rate of $13 per thousand, for example, was about half that prevailing in the pre-separation town.

The final reckoning of the financial settlement was not achieved until 25 April 1899, after weeks of discussions that were often acrimonious. On that date, the Cape Elizabeth committee met with the South Portland authorities and paid $12,362, the sum constituting that portion of the debt agreed upon as due from the new town of Cape Elizabeth.

Although South Portland realized its ambition of becoming a distinct and separate entity, a certain amount of dissension involving various individuals soon became evident. Some were dissatisfied with the name, and one critic disdainfully wrote, "South Portland indeed, why not East Scarboro or Westbrook Supplement, if we must merge our identity in that of our neighbors?" Others, with facetious inclinations, suggested Mudville and Clamville. Annoying comments of this type were naturally ignored and the chosen name remained unaltered.

The first serious expressions of dissatisfaction were heard in Willard. Many of the taxpayers and property holders in that locality were anxious to obtain a city charter and early in 1897 circulated a petition with this objective in mind. Lack of municipal improvements and an unsatisfactory rate of taxation apparently provided the basis for this sentiment.

This dissenting element in Willard persisted in its efforts to secede from South Portland. These activities once again attracted attention when in August 1898, they engaged a prominent Portland attorney to present their case before the state legislature. Not satisfied with these developments, this same group, later in the year, sought annexation to Cape Elizabeth and drafted a petition with this in mind for presentation to the legislature. On Wednesday, 14 December, 1898, some of the more enthusiastic Willard dissenters held a meeting at Bowery Beach to explain their case to any interested Cape Elizabeth citizens. The loyal supporters of South Portland immediately instituted measures to counteract his disaffecion in their midst and in January of 1899, set in motion a counter-petition opposing any division either by annexation to the Cape or by the creation of a new town. Another group within the town created further confusion by presenting a petition to the legislature with the representatives from the various factions given time to present their respective cases. As no change occurred, it is safe to assume that the findings of the legislative committee were not favorable to the Willard secessionists. Undaunted by a lack of success, the group seeking the annexation of South Portland to Portland assumed a die-hard attitude and continued their agitation in October 1900. The usual campaign involving petitions, demonstration, and hearings once again made its appearance but achieved no results. This can also be said for the campaigns waged in 1902, 1903, and 1904. In 1905, the City of Portland was finally inveigled into obtaining a popular vote on the question. The results were not encouraging to the pro-annexationists, for the good citizens of Portland, with barely one-quarter of the electorate participating, rejected the proposal by a vote of 1,735 to 1,360. Undismayed, these same inhabitants of South Portland once again brought the question before the voters of Portland in December 1906. This time the projected union was soundly defeated by a large majority. Other than an attempt in 1907 to change the name of South Portland to Elizabeth City, as it read in the original charter, no further annexation agitation was discernable until 1919 when parties from both cities met to discuss, for the last time, the merits of uniting the two areas. The results were the same, and with this, apparently resigned to its fate, South Portland ceased to actively promote a union with Portland, pursuing an independent course to the present time.

Although the new town of Cape Elizabeth was momentarily untroubled by the more pressing problems of urbanization, the inexorable growth of "Suburbia-by-the-Sea" continued unabated. Within a decade, the citizenry would be forced again to come to grips with the troublesome issues inherent in a residential community. The division of the old town had at best, provided nothing more than a brief respite in the development of Cape Elizabeth as a section of the metropolitan area known as Greater Portland.

Indicative of this change was the gradual construction of Fort Williams, near Portland Head, as the most formidable military installation among the harbor defenses of Portland. The selection of this site reflected its great strategic value. During the Revolutionary War an observation post was located there to warn the inhabitants of Falmouth should an enemy vessel be sighted. Although unfortified throughout the Neutral-Profits era and the War of 1812, it was occasionally mentioned in military surveys of the port of Portland conducted by the Federal government. Peacetime budgets, however, prevented any utilization of the site. The *Caleb Cushing* incident during the Civil War brought a renewal of interest in the advisability of constructing some type of fortification. In the summer of 1864, plans were prepared for building a series of earthworks and emplacing fifteen-inch Rodman smoothbore guns. The end of the war the following April halted the project before any action could be taken on it.

This cessation was only temporary, however, for in 1871, the War Department was authorized to construct a barbette battery for twenty-nine heavy guns close by Portland Head. The following year, fourteen acres were purchased from Asa T. Webster, George C. Thompson, William M. Pennell, Benjamin B. Dyer, and Green Walden, for $200 an acre. Although work was started in 1873, it proceeded so slowly as to go almost unnoticed. When the project was abruptly terminated for lack of funds in 1876, The Battery at Portland Head as it was called, consisted of nothing but partially completed earthwork emplacements and no guns.

Nothing further was done until the spring of 1891 when an entirely new and more modern system of fortifications was laid out by the War Department. Construction began early in the summer on a series of formidable works that would include a number of heavy coast-artillery pieces. As usual, the work progressed quite slowly. A force of about twenty men was employed until early winter, blasting ledges and excavating sites for the gun emplacements. For the next five years, the work continued with great irregularity but with noticeable progress.

In constructing this first group of batteries it was necessary to make elaborate preparations. A large stone-crusher and a huge cement mixer were built to provide the vast quantities of concrete that were needed for the gun emplacements and magazines. To transport these materials to the construction sites, a narrow gauge railway was built, using gondola cars and donkey engines.

The first installation to be completed was a mine casement and underground gallery on the south side of Ship Cove. Despite a labor dispute, the work was finished late in July 1891. Consisting of a long tunnel cut into the ledge, with an entry facing the cove, the casement housed the equipment necessary for exploding mines placed in the channel. If a vessel tried to enter the harbor through the mine field, the mines would be detonated via the cables that linked them to the underground casement. The signal for firing them would be given by an observer stationed in a bunker on the bluff directly above.

First of the emplacements to be built, was Battery Sullivan, named for Major General John Sullivan of the Continental Army, and completed in 1896. Next was Battery De Hart, finished the following year, and named for Captain Henry V. DeHart, Fifth U.S. Artillery, mortally wounded at the battle of Gaines Mill, Virginia, 13 July 1862. The last in this initial series was Battery Hobart, completed in 1898, honoring First Lieutenant Henry A. Hobart, U.S. Light Artillery, who was killed in action 27 May 1813 at Fort George, Upper Canada. As to armament, Battery Sullivan was designed to accommodate three ten-inch disappearing guns; Battery DeHart, two more ten-inch disappearing guns, and Battery Hobart one 4.2 inch mine defense gun of British manufacture, on a pedestal mount. The five disappearing guns were emplaced on a height of land between the lighthouse and Ship Cove with Battery DeHart on the lighthouse end and Battery Sullivan on the other. Between Battery Sullivan and the Cove, with a commanding view of the channel, was Battery Hobart.

As the emplacements neared completion, the government began the laborious process of transporting the five massive guns and carriages destined for Batteries Sullivan and DeHart. The guns were late-model ten-inch breech-loading, disappearing types, mounted on Crozier-Buffington carriages. Moved by ship from the Watervliet Arsenal at Troy, New York, where they were made, the guns were landed at Fort Preble. Since they weighed approximately five tons and had an overall length of thirty-five feet, the task of moving them overland to Portland Head was formidable. The guns were inched along by teams of oxen and draft horses, sometimes on sledges when ice and snow permitted it, and sometimes on ponderous low-beds. If no accidents occurred enroute, the trip could be usually accomplished in a week. By the spring of 1898, three of the five emplacements had received their guns. The last ten-inch piece was installed early in April, and the 4.2 mine defense gun, (transported to the site on a special flat car over the tracks of the trolley company), was emplaced on the sixteenth.

The installation of these heavy guns occurred none too soon for on 21 April the United States declared war on Spain. This war, one of the most unnecessary that this nation has ever waged and heavy with comic opera overtones, immediately transformed The Battery at Portland Head into an active military installation.

When the news had arrived that hostilities with Spain were imminent, a detachment from the 2nd Regiment, U. S. Artillery, stationed at Fort Preble, was moved to Portland Head. They also had the dubious pleasure of moving and storing 33,000 pounds of projectiles and powder for the disappearing guns. Although none of the guns had as yet been test fired, they were, nevertheless, loaded and kept in a constant state of readiness.

When it was learned locally that a Spanish fleet under Admiral Pasqual Cervera had left the Cape Verde Islands 28 April and that its whereabouts was unknown, a tremor of consternation swept through Greater Portland. The channel between Cushing's Island and Portland Head was sewn with mines to be exploded from the casement if the need arose. On 13 May, batteries D and E of the 7th Regiment U. S. Artillery, under the command of Captain F. E. Harrison, arrived on the New York boat from Fort Slocum, New York and quickly relieved the men of the 2nd Regiment at Portland Head. Close on the heels of this detachment, further protection for the Portland area arrived in the form of the monitor *U. S. S. Montauk*. This relic of the Civil War, with its smoothbore, muzzle-loading cannons, could never have repulsed a Spanish warship, but it was a morale booster to the apprehensive citizenry. Later the same month, a detachment of the 1st Regiment Connecticut Volunteer Infantry arrived to lend their support as riflemen at The Battery. All the troops stationed at Portland Head were forced, by the absence of suitable barracks, to live in tents for the duration of the war. Additional fire-power was added late in June when three Gatling guns were added to The Battery.

To prevent the Spanish fleet from slipping undetected into the harbor, a large searchlight was installed on a promontory slightly north of the batteries. It was tested for the first time the evening of Monday, 18 July, sending forth a blinding ray of light that illuminated objects as far to the eastward as Jewell's Island.

With the defeat of Admiral Cervera's fleet in the Caribbean on 3 July and the surrender of Santiago, Cuba on the 17th, the end of the war was in sight. Although the possibility of local hostilities was extremely unlikely, the mine fields were not removed, and navigational buoys replaced, until the middle of August. Also, despite the fact that a general surrender by Spanish forces was imminent, arrangements were made for test firings of the disappearing guns at The Battery.

After several cancellations, Tuesday 26 August 1898 was chosen as the test date. Under the supervision of various officials from the War Department, elaborate preparations were made. A target ten feet square was anchored approximately three miles at sea east-south-east of The Battery. The people living in the vicinity were advised to be prepared for some shaking-up from the concussion of the guns. The greatest concern was for venerable Portland Head Light. Since it was situated almost directly beneath the line of fire, some anxiety was felt relative to the ability of the tower to withstand the blast effect when the guns were fired. On the day of the test, the families of the keepers were evacuated and officials of the Lighthouse Service joined the keepers in an on-the-spot vigil to ascertain the extent of damage if any occurred.

In firing the five disappearing guns a quarter charge, followed by a half charge, and finally a service charge of two hundred and seventy-five pounds of smokeless powder, with a sand-filled shell weighing five hundred and seventy-five pounds, would be used. The loading and sighting of the guns was carried out with the pieces depressed behind the parapet edge of the emplacements. Once loading had been accomplished, the guns were elevated, by the use of gigantic counterweights, above the edge of the parapets, and fired. The recoil of the pieces provided the necessary force to return them to their depressed condition to be loaded and sighted again. In this manner, the guns were not directly exposed to enemy fire except at the instant of firing. As the pieces disappeared from view after each round the gun crews were seldom required to leave the relative safety of the emplacements.

Promptly at 10:00 a.m. on 26 August, the firing began. The first piece to be test fired was the gun at the southern end of The Battery. As it was the closest of the five to the lighthouse, it was anticipated that its discharge would be the most damaging. The fears of injury to the tower were groundless. Although the concussions were tremendous, not a fleck of whitewash was dislodged. One of the lighthouse inspectors standing inside the tower distinctly heard the rumble of the shells as they passed overhead. In due course, the other pieces were fired with a corresponding lack of damage. The only sign of breakage to be found, was in a store room where several boxes of lamp chimneys were dislodged from a shelf and several cans of paint that burst.

As to the accuracy of the service rounds, no hits were scored on the target. The nearest miss was off by approximately ten feet. Three other shells fell within fifty feet of the target, and one landed about seven hundred feet beyond. From the standpoint of performance, the War Department observers were pleased with the results.

Although the war ended 12 August, work continued at The Battery. On 21 October, a contract was awarded to John Burrows of Portland for the construction of several wooden, two story, buildings to serve as barracks, officers' quarters and battery headquarters. With the barracks completed early in December the soldiers struck their tents with enthusiasm and took up residence in their new quarters. Contemporary reports seem to indicate that these buildings left much to be desired, for during the winter of 1898-99, the men, "by keeping the stoves red hot night and day . . . managed to get along fairly well," according to the *Eastern Argus*. In February, another building was added to The Battery. On the 6th a contract was granted to Jeremiah Philbrook and Son to erect a 28' x 42' guard house at a cost of $1,298.

In the spring of 1899, the War Department established The Battery at Portland Head as a permanent and active military reservation. On 13 April, General Order No. 17 was issued, changing the name of this installation to Fort Williams. It was named for a native of Augusta, Maine, Major-General Seth Williams. Born 22 March 1822, son of Daniel and Mary Sawtelle Williams, and nephew of U. S. Senator Reuel Williams, he graduated from West Point in 1842. Commissioned as 2nd Lieutenant of artillery 31 August 1844 and as 1st Lieutenant 3 March 1847, he served in the Mexican War as aide-de-camp to General Robert Patterson, participating in all the principal battles, and brevetted captain for gallantry at Cerro Gordo. He was adjutant of the U. S. Military Academy from 1850 to 1853, and subsequently served in the adjutant-general's department the rest of his life. He became a Major 11 May, 1861, and was appointed brigadier-general of volunteers 23 September. From then until March 1864, General Williams was adjutant-general of the Army of the Potomac, serving under Generals McClellan, Burnside, Hooker, and Meade. When General Ulysses S. Grant, as general-in-chief, chose to make his headquarters with the Army of the Potomac, he selected Williams, in November, 1864, to be his inspector general, a post he continued to hold until 9 February 1866. He was then assigned as adjutant general of the Military District of the Atlantic with headquarters in Philadelphia. Williams took part in nearly every important engagement that involved the Army of the Potomac. He received the brevet of major-general in th U. S. Army 13 March 1865 for gallantry in the final campaign near Richmond, and brevet of major-general in the regular army on the same date for gallant and meritorious services throughout the war. Toward the end of February 1866, he fell ill and went to his sister's home in Boston where he died of a stroke 23 March. Although General Grant requested that General Williams be buried at West Point, his family chose to inter him beside his parents in Forest Grove Cemetery, Augusta.

In September 1899, the five disappearing guns were again fired in practice by resident companies of the Coast artillery Corps who had replaced the batteries of the 7th Artillery. On Friday the 22nd, a series of rounds were loosed at a white buoy anchored 4,100 yards from Portland Head and slightly eastward of Ram Island Ledge. The following day, another series were fired at a ten foot canvass pyramid anchored on a raft 7,050 yards from the same promontory. The men proved to be proficient in working the guns but the accuracy of the pieces was something of a disappointment. Over the years, additional practice would reveal that the Crozier-Buffington carriages not only limited the range of the guns by restricting their elevation but were also liable to enough movement at the instant of firing to cause deflection. The problem of accuracy grew greater as the carriages began to wear.

Late in the spring of 1900, contracts were awarded for an ambitious program of new construction. The wooden buildings were to be replaced by a large number of more substantial structures. Included in the project were an administration building, a group of barracks, commissioned and non-commissioned officers' quarters, a hospital, guard house, bakery, gymnasium canteen, and other specialized structures, all built of brick. To increase the size of the fort, additional land was purchased. The old Goddard mansion was sold by Judge Joseph D. Symonds. Another large tract was acquired from Georgiana Thompson. These purchases ended the expansion of the fort in the direction of Cape Cottage Park.

Plans were also made for the construction of additional batteries and mine storage facilities. In September, preliminary surveys were carried out for locating twelve-inch and six-inch disappearing gun batteries as well as a three-inch mine-defense battery. Work was started in May 1901 on the twelve-inch battery, just south of the lighthouse, and a year later it was ready to receive its guns and carriages. This emplacement would have two pieces and would be known as Battery Blair. It was named for Major-General Francis P. Blair, Jr., a veteran of the Mexican War and the Civil War, and a U. S. Congressman from Missouri. A staunch Unionist, he exhausted his financial assets in supporting the war effort in his home state, of Missouri. After several arduous military campaigns he returned to Washington and worked against tremendous odds for a fair and just reconstruction program in the south. He died 9 July 1875 at St. Louis, Missouri.

The task of moving the first twelve inch gun, after it had been landed at Fort Preble, began in the summer of 1902. Resting on a heavy cradle, it was dragged along very slowly on skids. This gun began its tedious journey early in July but did not reach Fort Williams until the middle of October. In the meantime, the second twelve-inch gun arrived. Instead of coming by water, it was transported by rail and unloaded at the old Cape Elizabeth Depot in Pleasantdale, South Portland.

This second twelve-inch gun was an exact duplicate of the first but the methods employed in moving it were far more elaborate. Measuring forty feet in length and weighing approximately 12,000 pounds it was cumbersome in the extreme. Under the direction of William W. Webster of Portland, a special railway type flat-car was built designed to move on rails. This flat-car would travel on three, thirty-foot section of track that were laid on specially constructed low-beds. Thus the gun, on its flat-car, would travel along the track sections as they were laid down ahead and taken up behind.

Beginning its journey early in November, 1902, it did not reach Fort Williams until March 1903. Bad weather forced the contractor, Webster, to park it for most of January and February on Thomas Street. Once it reached Battery Blair, the problem of moving it was taken over by another contractor. The Crozier-Buffington carriages were also moved by Webster. They were transported on heavy trucks drawn by twenty horses.

While these operations were in progress, work was also started on another battery, located between the Delano Park line and Battery Blair. To facilitate construction, additional land was purchased in September, 1902, from Belle Dyer, thereby establishing what was to be the southern boundary of Fort Williams. This new battery, designed to accommodate two six-inch disappearing guns, was completed in 1903. It was named Battery Garesche in honor of Lieutenant Colonel Julius P. Garesche, chief-of-staff, Army of the Cumberland, who was killed in action during the Civil War, 31 December 1862, at the battle of Stone's River, Tennessee.

Early in September 1903, Fort Williams participated in some rather extensive war games held in the vicinity of Casco Bay. The regular garrison was considerably strengthened by a detachment from the 1st Regiment Massachusetts Heavy Artillery who camped on the point of land at the northern edge of Ship Cove.

They manned a battery of rapid-fire mine defense guns temporarily emplaced at the tip of this same point of land. During the war games, 120 rounds were fired by the guns of Fort Williams with the disappearing pieces expending about twenty of them. Much to the embarrassment of the garrison they were easily overwhelmed by the "enemy." Close to 2,000 sailors, marines, and soldiers, were landed undetected at Bowery Beach and succeeded in capturing the fort by a surprise attack on its undefended rear.

One of the lessons learned from the war games was the need for a permanent battery of light guns on the point of land recently held by the Massachusetts artillerymen. Construction began early in 1904 on a small battery designed to accommodate a pair of three-inch mine defense guns on pedestal mounts. Completed late in 1906, it was named Battery Keyes in memory of Major-General Erasmus D. Keyes who had spent his childhood in the Augusta area. A graduate of West Point in 1832, he served as an instructor there for many years. He served in the Civil War as commander of the IV Corps in the Peninsular Campaign and the Department of Virginia. Resigning from the service in May 1864, he moved to San Francisco, California, where he became very wealthy in mining, banking, and grape culture. He died suddenly 14 October 1895 at Nice, France, and was subsequently buried at West Point.

This was the last permanent battery to be built at Fort Williams. Changes in armament of a minor nature would occur infrequently down to World War II. The first alteration in the series of batteries took place in 1907 when Battery Hobart was abandoned and its 4.2 mine defense gun removed, having been superceded by Battery Keyes.

One very popular feature of garrison life at Fort Williams was the superb band of the 2nd Regiment U. S. Artillery that remained at the post after the regiment departed in April 1898. Organized 21 March, 1821, it became a separate unit in 1901 and was subsequently known as the 2nd Band, Coast Artillery Corps. In the summer of 1905, a separate brick barracks was constructed for the exclusive use of the bandsmen. Their weekly concerts on Sunday afternoons, during the warmer months, became a musical treat heavily patronized by the citizens of Greater Portland.

The construction of new facilities continued at the fort in this first decade of the twentieth century. One of the most ambitious projects was the building of a dock and causeway for the handling of mines and mine equipment. Late in 1907, surveys were conducted on the south side of of Ship Cove for a suitable site. Previous attempts to establish permanent docking facilities in the same area had been nullified by winter storms; therefore, a formidable concrete wharf and causeway was contemplated.

The contract was awarded to McHale & Perkins of Boston and work began early in June 1908. After clearing away rubble stone and boulders, existing ledges were blasted to provide a level surface. The pier, resting upon solid ledge, was built outward a distance of sixty feet and measured fifty feet across its seaward end. The outer edges of the dock were constructed of 206 reinforced concrete blocks weighing close to nine tons apiece. The center was filled with solid concrete. Built into the sides of the pier were two boat landings, and piling was driven across the face as fenders for the larger vessels. Its surface was fourteen and a half feet above mean low water mark. Extending out to the dock, along the shore, just above high water mark was a granite and concrete causeway. To prevent erosion on its seaward side, granite blocks from House Island, left over from the construction of Fort Scammel, were used as facing. Running along the surface of the causeway, from the pier, was a narrow-gauge railway for the transporting of mines and mine equipment. Although completed late in 1908 at a total cost of $45,000, this installation had been almost totally obliterated by the action of the seas forty years later.

In the years before World War I, military life at Fort Williams was quiet, unhurried, and very routine. The band concerts and colorful parades were weekly highlights. Once each year, usually in the later summer or early fall, national guard units were encamped for their annual training, and firing practice with the heavy guns. Few major changes were instituted; however, in October 1911 the old wooden administration building erected in 1898 was torn down. Much of the material was salvaged and purchased by Joseph W. Strout who used it in building a three-story apartment house at Cape Cottage Park. Typical of the rapport that existed between the Coast Artillery Corps garrison and the local citizenry was the testimonial dinner given by the Cape Shore Civic Association in honor of Captain George A. Hubbard when he was transferred to Washington, D.C. In his official capacity as quartermaster at Fort Williams he had been most cooperative in forming his men into fire brigades to assist local residents in time of need. He was also instrumental in constructing one of the finest stretches of highway in the town by grading and paving the section from Cape Cottage Park to Delano Park.

It was this civic-minded attitude that greatly endeared him to his civilian neighbors and prompted the testimonial dinner at the Congress Square Hotel, Wednesday 11, December, 1912.

The war years, 1914-1918, brought few changes to Fort Williams. The companies of the Coast Artillery Corps were reinforced with various National Guard detachments. Instead of strengthening the fortifications, just the opposite occurred in 1917 when three of the ten-inch disappearing guns were removed from their carriages and sent to France. They were not replaced until December of 1919. At the end of the war, the National Guardsmen were withdrawn, and the garrison was reduced to a Coast Artillery Corps battalion a few years later.

Despite the inactivity of the immediate postwar period, one major project of military significance was undertaken at Fort Williams. In the spring of 1921, an attempt was made to expand the fire control facilties for the disappearing guns by using observation balloons. To house them, a balloon hanger was erected during the summer in a small valley between the row of non-commissioned officers' residences on the northern edge of the reservation and barracks row. Constructed, on a concrete slab, of steel girders, the exterior was covered with sheets of asbestos and an outer sheathing of heavy corrugated steel plates. When completed, the hanger measured one hundred and twenty feet long, seventy-six feet wide and was fifty-eight feet high at the peak. The entrance faced the sea and was forty-five feet in height. There were, in addition, three auxiliary buildings; a generator house, a garage, and a storehouse.

A peace time budget, however, forced the army to suspend the use of this new facility. Before the necessary personnel and equipment could be assigned, the value of observation balloons was drastically compromised by the development of the airplane. Not once in the twenty two years of its existence was the hanger used to house a balloon nor was there ever a balloon company assigned to Fort Williams. The entire structure was torn down in 1943 without ever fulfilling the need it was designed to meet.

In April 1923, the garrison was greatly expanded by the addition of one of the most famous military units in the United States Army, the 5th Regiment U. S. Infantry. First formed in 1798 it served with distinction in several Indian Wars, from Indiana and Michigan to the Pacific northwest and the deserts of the southwest. It had formed the main line of battle in Scott's Brigade at the battle of Lundy's Lane in the War of 1812, and served with distinction in the Mexican War, the Civil War, the Spanish-American War, and the Philippine Insurrection. After World War I, the regiment participated in the occupation of the Rhineland in Germany until its return to the United States for duty at Fort Williams. The following year, the 8th Regiment U. S. Coast Artillery was organized and assigned to the harbor defenses of Portland with a large detachment stationed at Fort Williams, now designated as harbor defense headquarters. No further changes of any significance occurred for the next fifteen years. The eighty piece 5th Infantry Band replaced the Coast Artillery Corps Band as a major musical attraction and military reviews were as popular as before.

In the fall of 1939, as war clouds began to gather in Europe, the 5th Infantry was transferred to the Panama Canal Zone. No attempt was made to replace the regiment at Fort Williams until after the U. S. entered the war. Early in 1942, the 240th Regiment Coast Artillery was stationed at the fort, remaining for the duration. In conjunction with the 8th Regiment Coast Artillery, they manned the 90mm dual-purpose guns and coordinated the harbor defense system.

During the war, the now obsolete disappearing guns were condemned. In the summer of 1943, they were dismantled and, with the carriages, were cut up for junk. After approximately forty years of service they were beginning to show their age. Some were in rather poor shape, with No. 1 gun in Battery Sullivan abandoned as unservicable even before the war began. All the disappearing guns and the two mine defense guns in Battery Keyes were gone by early fall.

After the war, the garrison was quickly reduced to a caretaker force, being used during the 1950's as a center for logistical and administrative assistance to various military units throughout the state. In addition, units of the U. S. Army Reserves, Air National Guard, and the Civil Air Patrol made use of the facilities for periodic meetings. As the decade advanced, the various activities carried on at Fort Williams were transferred or gradually phased out. By 1960, nothing but a token force remained, and shortly thereafter the installation was classified as no longer serviceable. Three years later, the fort was turned over to the General Services Administration to be sold. The town of Cape Elizabeth was given the opportunity to buy the property before it was offered to the public. After lengthy negotiations, the G.S.A. accepted the town's offer of $200,000 on 17 October 1964. Although no definite plans had as yet been formulated for its use, the town, in purchasing Fort Williams, acquired 90.45 acres of valuable land and about ninety buildings in various stages of preservation, including the Goddard Mansion.

Much more prosaic than the establishment and growth of Fort Williams was the gradual transformation of the town into a suburban community. Of primary importance in guiding the municipal activities of Cape Elizabeth was the erection of a suitable town hall. From the first meeting of the new town 20 April 1895 to the annual meeting 11 March 1901 the Grange Hall at Spurwink served as a temporary town hall and municipal office.

At their second annual meeting, 9 March 1896, the voters of the new town authorized the selectmen to seek a suitable lot at Pond Cove Corner on which to build a town hall. Two years later an acre lot was purchased for $100 from W. J. Dyer of Ashland, Massachusetts. Abutting the southern edge of the William D. Murray property and located on the easterly side of Ocean House Road, a short distance south of Pond Cove Corner, the site was ideally situated in the center of the town.

Actual construction did not start until early in the summer of 1900. At the annual meeting in March, the town appropriated the sum of $4,000 to be raised by a bond issue to pay for the building. A committee consisting of Albert P. Hannaford, Michael J. Peabbles, and the selectmen, was appointed to draw up suitable plans and supervise construction. Plans were drawn up by Frederick A. Thompson, and the contract was awarded to William D. Murray and Son. The *Eastern Argus* noted on 9 May that ". . . reports have it the building committee of the new town are making haste slowly, but it is hoped surely, in their deliberations concerning the proposed new town building. By August the work was well advanced, for on the 14th the *Eastern Argus* again commented that ". . . the new town building is raising itself aloft. It seems to be a large building for a moderately small rural town. . ."

The building having been completed early in February 1901, the town appropriated $250 for furnishings at the March meeting. The building was occupied for the first time on Monday 8 April when the town records, a safe, and some old furniture, were moved into the new offices. The first meeting held in the new hall occurred on 6 May. At this meeting, the citizenry voted to fence the "Town House lot," build suitable outbuildings, and to appropriate another $50 for furnishings. Finally, on Wednesday 19 June, the new Cape Elizabeth Town Hall was dedicated with fitting ceremonies attended by a large and festive throng.

Another improvement enjoyed by the townspeople of this era was the inauguration of the Rural Free Delivery mail system. After separation, only three post offices were available to serve the town; Bowery Beach established in 1896, Cape Cottage established in 1899, and Pond Cove established in 1900. On 1 October, 1901 the Bowery Beach and Pond Cove post offices were discontinued and replaced by R.F.D. No. 7, South Portland.

The first man to serve as the mail carrier on this new route was Alliston F. Gardner. A native of Nantucket, Massachusetts, he moved to South Portland in 1897 at the age of thirty two and there pursued his trade of carpenter until his appointment in 1901. For many years Gardner covered the twenty eight miles of his route, six days a week, using a small, completely enclosed, horse-drawn wagon. By keeping two horses and driving them on alternate days, their survival rate was fairly good. During one very severe winter, however, he lost three horses in seven months. In the summer, weather permitting, Gardner often covered his route on a bicycle.

Greatly appreciating his devoted sense of duty, the townsfolk frequently provided him with hot food and coffee, as well as shelter and feed for his horse, when winter storms and bitter cold made travel difficult. On three different occasions they collected money to replace a horse Gardner lost in the line of duty. Sometimes, when blizzards raged across the Cape, he would have to lead his horse through the drifts and deep snow. Not infrequently his heavy, fleece-lined coat would be so sheathed with ice when he arrived home that his wife would have to beat it with a poker to loosen it enough for him to take it off.

In 1920, Gardner purchased his first automobile and in the remaining eleven years of his service he wore out five, two open cars and three sedans, that he altered to suit his needs. After thirty years of dedicated duty, he retired 1 October, 1931 at the age of sixty-six. During that thirty year period, few major changes were made except a drastic increase in the volume of mail and redesignation of the route as R.F.D. No. 1. Today four "foot delivery men," one "mounted route man," in addition to R.F.D. No. 1 and No. 2, serve the town. Also, two post offices function as branches of Portland, the old Cape Cottage Post Office and the recently created Cape Elizabeth Post Office at Pond Cove Corner.

Socially, life among the citizenry of the Outer Cape reflected the same activities that were discernible before separation. The Grange and various fraternal organizations still flourished in a perfunctory fashion. One distinguished group that was very much alive in these years was the Cape Elizabeth Veteran Soldiers' and Sailors' Association. Organized in 1896, its membership was made up entirely of men who had served in the Civil War. Most of the members were also Grand Army of the Republic men, affiliated with Bosworth Post No. 2 and Thatcher Post No. 111, of Portland. They were primarily concerned with the perpetuation of appropriate ceremonies and commemorative activities on Memorial Day. A typical observance is described in the town report of 1901.

> On the morning of Memorial Day the veterans assembled at the school house in Bowery Beach, and, accompanied by the Rev. John H. Roberts, Rev. W. L. Nickerson and a local quartette, proceeded to the different cemeteries and private burying places in the town, marking and decorating the graves of departed veterans, with appropriate services at each place. The veterans then returned to the church at Bowery Beach where quite a large number of appreciative friends had gathered to witness the decoration of graves in Seaside Cemetery, and to listen to some very able and impressive remarks from the reverend gentlemen in attendance, also to very excellent and appropriate music rendered by local talent. . . . .Directly after the services in the church the veterans took conveyances for Masonic Hall at Knightville. After partaking of a collation very kindly tendered by the veterans of South Portland, they proceeded with them to the Cape Elizabeth Soldiers' and Sailors' Monument, located near Mount Pleasant Cemetery which it is our duty as well as pleasure to assist in decorating.

Never a very large organization, it gradually declined as the men "fell out of the march of life." Among the more prominent members were Samuel R. Bishop, 17th Maine Infantry; James L. Brown, 15th Maine Infantry; John N. Brown, 17th Maine Infantry; Leonard Brown, U. S. Navy; Walter G. Johnson, U. S. Navy; Scott D. Jordan, U. S. Navy; Nathan I. Sawyer, 25th Maine Infantry; Asbury F. Staples, 1st Maine Battery Light Artillery; Clement E. Staples, 25th Maine Infantry; William D. Staples, Coast Guard Heavy Artillery; Albert Stevens, 1st Maine Cavalry; Benjamin L. Sweetsir, 25th Maine Infantry; and Edward I. Woodbury, Coast Guard Heavy Artillery. The final entry to appear in a town report was made in 1918, and before the next decade was past the association ceased to function. The last member to join the "bivouac of the dead" was Sergeant Asbury F. Staples who died 11 October 1928 at the age of eighty five.

With the dawn of the twentieth century the first residential community was established in the town of Cape Elizabeth. This real estate development elevated to local prominence one of the most flamboyant business men of the era. Few of the later real estate promoters would ever equal the spectacular activities of George Washington Brown.

Born in Brooklyn, New York, Brown spent his early years in Damariscotta, Maine. A lack of success in business prompted his moving to Portland in 1888 at the age of thirty-seven. The following year, he established the Belknap Water Motor Company at 22 Exchange Street acting as president and general manager. Apparently possessed by an insatiable scientific curosity and a mania for inventive experimentation, he was soon fascinated by recent discoveries in electricity. In 1892 he accordingly reorganized his firm as the Belknap Motor Company specializing in electric motors and dynamos. Seven years later, Brown founded the Portland Electric Light Company. Located at 12 Monument Square, this was a pioneer effort in the field of electric illumination. In conjunction with this firm, he also established a water power plant at Great Falls on the Presumpscot River. Shortly thereafter, he sold the business to a large local competitor the Consolidated Electric Light Company.

Using the proceeds from this sale, Brown founded the Suburban Realty Company in the fall of 1900 and purchased a large tract of land on the west side of Shore Road just south of the Cliff House. Much of the acreage had been used as a pasture by a nearby summer resident, Frederick Walker. On Thursday 18 October Brown placed a large advertisement in the *Eastern Argus* that was most certainly a pioneer effort in the promotion of suburban real estate in the town of Cape Elizabeth.

Claiming a view of the White Mountains from its most prominent height of land, he named the development Mountain View Park. Dividing it into thirty-nine lots Brown offered them for sale at ten to fifteen cents a square foot, according to the location. As to the construction of suitable homes, he stipulated that none could be built at a value of less than $1,500 and that the plans had to be approved in advance by the Suburban Realty Company. Under his direction, Ocean View, Island, Mountain View, Bay View, Ridge, and Summit Roads were laid out as per a survey made by the civil engineer Charles W. Fenn.

As an inducement to potential customers, Brown emphasized the availability of trolley service on Cottage Road and a variety of special benefits to be supplied by his firm. Foremost were electric street lights, Sebago water, free mail delivery, telephones, free rubbish removal, as well as perpetual care of the streets and public grounds. In addition, he offered to supply electricity for the illumination of any home free of charge, if it was built before 1 July 1901, until 1 January 1905. Furthermore, if anyone purchased a minimum of ten, but not more than one hundred, shares of stock in the Suburban Realty Company, a ten per cent reduction would be made in the price of a lot. Finally, Brown offered "to pay every owner of a lot that may be purchased for cash this year from ten per cent to twenty per cent margin over and above the purchase of the land at the expiration of two years, if the price has not actually advanced to that extent, but the owner must agree to allow the company the privilege to purchase at the advance if it so desires."

The first house to be built was a residence for Brown closely followed by another for Daniel W. Hoegg, a third for the architect Austin W. Pease, and a fourth for R. A. Sylvester of Boston. By the spring of 1901, a total of nine houses were in various stages of completion. In addition to the homes, Brown soon completed a thirty-foot observation tower on a ridge of land close by Summit Road. Reaching a height of 165 feet above sea level it offered an extraordinary view. Using it for promotional purposes, he placed a brilliant electric beacon at the top but soon extinguished it at the insistence of the Coast Guard who regarded it as a navigational menace. However, during fair weather Brown flew a series of signal flags from the tower that spelled out Mountain View Park.

Late in May 1901, Brown announced plans for a new residential development in the neighboring community of South Portland. Located in the vicinity of Cedar and Sawyer Streets on Meeting House Hill, he named this project Brooklyn Heights. Yet another development was planned the following year and involved a large tract between Pine and Sawyer Streets, Cottage Road and Broadway. This third residential community would be known as Emery Highlands. Incidental to these activities was an independent firm, the Portland Sand and Gravel Company, organized by Brown as an integral part of his real estate promotions.

The culmination of this extraordinary and flamboyant series of business ventures occurred early in 1903. Spread over two full pages of the *Eastern Argus* on Tuesday, 1 January, was a huge advertisement that unveiled Brown's view of the future. It was his considered opinion that Portland would become the winter port of Canada and that this would stimulate the economy to a fantastic degree. This activity would immediately spread to the South Portland side of the harbor with wharfs, railway yards, and a variety of maritime businesses quickly taking shape. As this commercial growth continued, the annexation of South Portland to Portland would be only a matter of time. Under the circumstances, the future of Cape Elizabeth was understandably bright. In a decade, according to Brown, it would be the Brooklyn of Portland. For the next few years, the Mountain View Park development continued to expand with the construction of substantial homes proceeding at a steady rate. Several houses were built on speculation and most were soon rented or sold. With his real estate promotions producing a very adequate return on his investment, Brown had become a rather affluent member of the business community. Now that his financial situation was exhibiting a steady upward growth, he turned his attention to an earlier and less successful period in his life.

As a very young man, George Washington Brown had owned and operated a grocery store in his ancestral town of Damariscotta. Here his promotional talents were first revealed as well as his preoccupation with inventing. On one occasion, he built a windmill on the ridgepole of his store and used it to drive a coffee grinder. In addition, he staged balloon ascensions, band concerts, and other gala events to advertise his business. His ardor for showmanship, however, exceeded his ability as a grocer, and he went bankrupt. He was accordingly declared insolvent and discharged from his debts.

Having accumulated a modest fortune in his real estate dealings, he returned to Damariscotta and sought out all his former creditors. Not only did he pay them dollar for dollar but in many instances he paid them interest as well. Having thus squared himself with his former neighbors and customers, he now turned his talents to a new venture.

After a great deal of experimentation, Brown developed a large and complicated machine to stamp out, print, affix with a string, and impregnate with wax, a cardboard disk to be known as "The Dairyman's Sanitary Milk Bottle Cap." He established a small factory on Elm Street in Portland and went into production. For reasons now unknown, the cap did not sell and in a short time the business failed. This unsuccessful venture again brought financial disaster to Brown.

As of 18 September 1907 his assets were turned over to a receivership under the direction of Jed F. Fanning of Portland. Undaunted by this setback, Brown continued to actively indulge in real estate promotions. The following year, he established the Maine Coast Realty Company to develop Little Diamond Island as a summer colony. With this project, he was able gradually to gain back a degree of financial success. Undetered by earlier failures, he once again hit upon an invention that seemed to have great possibilities. The women of this era wore large and cumbersome hats which they firmly anchored with a series of long hatpins. As these pins extended outward for some distance from the hat, their sharp ends were dangerous, especially in crowded places such as a streetcar. With many people stabbed, skewered, impaled, and raked each year by these hatpins, Brown felt that there was room for improvement. Thus it was that he produced the "Happy Thought Hat Pin," guaranteed to be absolutely free from sharp protruding ends. Unfortunately, it was even less successful than the milk bottle cap. He lost almost all that he had been able to extract from the Maine Coast Realty Company as treasurer and general manager.

With great perseverance he returned to the real estate business and managed to survive. Although he never was able to regain the affluence of earlier days he did continue to enjoy some limited success in this field. In 1928, he tried yet again, but this time the project must have been very obscure, for nothing now remains except the name he applied to the firm, the Anti-Skid Manufacturing Company. About this time, he sold his home at 9 High Ridge Road in Mountain View Park and moved to 35 Everett Avenue in South Portland. It was here that he quietly died 12 January 1933 at the age of eighty-two.

Truly, George Washington Brown was a farsighted pioneer in the development of suburban real estate in Cape Elizabeth. His was the first major effort in a business that would soon bring a proliferation of residential communities within the town. Mountain View Park survives as a monument to this remarkable man, regardless of his ephemeral success in other areas.

One immediate result of the development at Mountain View Park was the introduction of Sebago water. After some negotiation, the town entered into an agreement with the Standish Water and Construction Company 22 June 1903. Under the terms of the contract, the water company would "construct, maintain and operate a system of water works" in the new town whereby Sebago water would be supplied "for domestic purposes and the extinguishment of fires." This initially entailed laying an eight inch cast iron pipe along what is now Shore Road from Angell Avenue in South Portland to Cape Cottage Park. It is interesting to note that the introduction of Sebago water into the new town failed to awaken even a fraction of the excitement that accompanied the same project in the old town. Apparently the rural citizens were reconciled to the fact that the suburban trend could not now be reversed.

The process of urbanization, however, was not carried on without some bitter clashes between residents of long standing and recent arrivals. One of the earliest, and certainly one of the most spectacular confrontations, involved Great Pond.

About 1902, a group of sportsmen from Portland organized the Great Pond Gun Club. One of the charter members, Frederick O. Conant, proceeded to buy or lease the land that surrounded the pond in the name of the Club. In addition, he purchased the rights and holdings of the moribund Great Pond Mining and Agricultural Company, thereby gaining, he believed, complete control of the pond.

The club soon constructed an elaborate duck blind on the southwestern shore of the pond, well concealed, comfortably appointed, and equipped with a four-gauge punt-gun. Next, they built a bunk house, complete with kitchen and dining room for the members, and hired Goold Johnson, who had a small farm on the southern edge of the club's property, as the resident game keeper. He was also responsible for the wooden decoys and the live "tollers" used at the blind. To maintain this private game preserve, each member paid $150 a year. The first president of the club was Fred H. Thompson of Portland, succeeded in a few years by Fred O. Conant. Among the early members were George F. Thompson, Fred W. Huntington, Charles S. Foss, Edward J. Chenery, Dr. William Lord, John H. Pierce, Fred B. Gage, Silas B. Adams, and Fred M. Thompson.

As this club became better organized and began to insist that Great Pond was their exclusive property, friction developed between the townspeople and the "sports." From the earliest days, fowling on this pond had been open to all, a zealously guarded right shared by all inhabitants of the town. The view that this body of water was open to the public was based on a law enacted by the Massachusetts General Court in 1641. This law stipulated that "ponds containing more than ten acres of water are free for any man to fish and fowl there and he may pass and repass on foot through any man's property for that end so that he trespass not upon any man's corn or meadow."

In an attempt to prevent the closing of the pond to the public, and to guarantee easy access, the desirability of constructing a thoroughfare from the Fowler Road to its northern edge was advocated by the selectmen. To accomplish this objective an appropriate article was included in the warrant for a special town meeting, 7 December, 1903. As might be expected, the town voted to accept the road as laid out by the town fathers. Also, at the annual March meeting the following year, funds were appropriated to pay land damages to the Great Pond Mining and Agricultural Company and to cover the cost of constructing the new road.

Acting in behalf of the Great Pond Mining and Agricultural Company, now controlled by Frederick O. Conant of the Great Pond Gun Club, two Portland lawyers Harry R. Virgin and Frank C. Payson petitioned the County Commissioners to disallow construction of this road. On Tuesday, 10 May, 1904, the commissioners conducted a hearing in the town hall and shortly thereafter rendered a decision in favor of the town. However, before any work could be initiated, the Conant faction made a new appeal, this time to the Supreme Judicial Court. The court then appointed a three-man commission, Scott Wilson, Ardon W. Coombs, and Barret Potter, to prepare and submit a report relative to the controversy.

Early in May 1907, the court made its decision, reversing the ruling of the County Commissioners, and forbade the opening of a road to Great Pond. Although bitterly disappointed, the townsfolk were not yet ready to acknowledge the validity of this private game preserve. Hence, they organized the Bowery Beach Association to continue the fight. The officers of the association were Pomeroy W. Jordan, President; Harry S. Jordan, Secretary; Freeman H. Brown, Treasurer; plus an executive committee consisting of Edward D. Jordan, Gilbert C. Jordan, Henry G. Trundy, William L. Trundy, Charles H. A. Peabbles, and Walter Maxwell. To bring the case once again to the courts, a resolute partisan, George A. Jordan, disregarding the "No Trespassing" signs, invaded the bull-rushes of Great Pond in a quest for ducks early in October and was promptly arrested.

Before this case could progress very far through the courts, two more citizens were apprehended upon these forbidden waters. The Bowery Beach Association came to their assistance with legal aid and funds as it did in the case of George Jordan. The two men involved were Edward D. Jordan and Benjamin F. Brown. Both had constructed blinds at some distance from the luxurious encampment of the Great Pond Gun Club.

To forstall such unwelcome incursions, the club had hired Thomas D. Conley and Milo Bumps to serve as guards. On this occasion, late in September, 1909, they received a rather hostile reception when they tried to dislodge Jordan and Brown. Using a small punt, the guards rowed to the vicinity of Brown's blind and called upon him to leave at once. Much to their sorrow they had strayed into the field of fire. As a bird passed between them and the blind, Brown let drive with both barrels of his shotgun. Although they were just out of range, the two watchmen were so showered with spent shot that they immediately withdrew.

Leaving Brown, they rowed to the northern edge of the pond to dislodge Jordan. Here they again entered the field of fire, but this time at shorter range. The results were the same except that in this case they were well stung by bird-shot. Not wishing to press the matter further, Conley and Bumps hastily withdrew, realizing that in this instance discretion was the better part of valor.

In due course Jordan and Brown were arrested on a charge of assault with a deadly weapon. As might be expected, the case actually involved the validity of the 1641 Great Pond Law. As the charges against George A. Jordan, Edward D. Jordan, and Benjamin F. Brown, were soon nol prossed the legal battle centered upon a bill in equity brought by the Conant faction to restrain the citizenry from poaching on their private pond.

Seeking to disprove the possible applicability of the 1641 Great Pond Law, the attorney for the club, Harry R. Virgin, claimed that when the Great Pond Mining and Agricultural Company drained away the water for the cultivation of cranberries, its status as a pond permanently ceased to exist. In reply, counsel for the Bowery Beach Association, Scott Wilson, contended that when the company abandoned its activities and discontinued its drainage system, the subsequent reflooding of the pond restored its legal status as a great pond. Ultimately, the case was heard by the Maine Supreme Court.

Finally, on Tuesday, 27 October, 1910, the court rendered a decision sustaining the views of the townspeople.

> Under the common law of this state, based in part on the Colonial ordinance of 1641 of Massachusetts and in part on the usages and customs of the early inhabitants, the title to all great ponds containing more than ten acres is in the state for the use of the public.
> The public has the right of free fishing and fowling on Great Pond in Cape Elizabeth which contain more than ten acres, although the territory in which the pond is situated was held under private ownership as early as 1831 and has so continued until the present time.
> The common law of England has never been enforced in this State except so far as has been adopted in the usages and customs of the people.
> The doctrine of the English common law regarding the private ownership of ponds has never been recognized and adopted in this

state so far as ponds or more than ten acres are concerned and fishing and fowling on them has been free and equal.

From this decision there was no further appeal, and the contest was resolved. To celebrate their vindication the members of the Bowery Beach Association and the Cape Elizabeth Gun Club, with their friends and families, held a victory dinner at the Wayland House, Dunstan Corner, Scarborough, Thursday evening, 11 November, 1910. The weekly newspaper, *Coast Watch*, caught the spirit of the occasion with a few well chosen words.

> The descendants of Rev. Robert Jordan and of other early settlers of . . . Cape Elizabeth assembled last evening . . . to celebrate the victory by which their ancient rights of fowling and fishing in Great Pond have been forever confirmed by the highest court of the State of Maine. . .
> They assembled around the tables. . .and regaled themselves on the food of their ancestors, the vivacious clan and the stately lobster; they sang and danced, and listened to good speaking. . . .Great was the rejoicing . . . .The ancient rights of the original settlers were restored; the usurpers were routed, and the event at the Wayland was the outward and visible sign of an inward and general satisfaction. . . .

After dinner Harry S. Jordan, master of ceremonies, delivered a short address in which he reviewed the major skirmishes in the eight-year battle of Great Pond. He praised at some length the legal talents of their counsel, Scott Wilson, the man to whom they all owed a great debt of gratitude. As a small token of their appreciation, Jordan presented him with a suitably inscribed trophy.

In response, Wilson noted that the need for speeches on the subject of Great Pond was past, that the case had been settled and justice done. However, he did express some doubts about the present generation of Jordans, and of other settlers, inheriting the marksmanship of their ancestors, inasmuch as one occasion during the conflict they had not been able to disable two watchmen sent against them. Despite such shortcomings, he was honored by their thoughtful gift. The evening was concluded with a concert by Chandler's Band, whist, and dancing.

This first decade of the twentieth century also witnessed unmistakable signs of suburban growth. In 1906 the Shores Acres Land Company began a residential development of approximately 125 acres in the area between Trundy's Reef and Broad Cove. The first few homes to be built were primarily for summer occupancy, but by 1909, the construction of year-round dwellings was undertaken.

Another development initiated in 1906 involved an area immediately adjacent to Bowery Beach. Renaming it Crescent Beach, Charles B. Dalton, Portland real estate promoter and owner of the Cliff House, began his advertising campaign in May. Although he erected a small casino-like club house close by the beach on Ocean House Road, the development enjoyed but a moderate degree of success. The lack of immediate patronage was due largely to the fact that an anticipated trolley line connecting Pond Cove Corner and Bowery Beach failed to materialize.

The rapidly growing residential community in the vicinity of Mountain View Park created problems that were reminiscent of those that plagued the old town prior to separation. The need for a variety of municipal services such as an expanded water and sewage system, fire protection, and better roads in this section, was neither supported nor appreciated by a majority of the citizens. Feeling that a unified effort might be fruitful in overcoming existing inadequacies, these suburbanites organized the Cape Shore Civic Association at a public meeting held in the hall over Joseph W. Armstrong's store near Cape Cottage Park on Tuesday, 25 August, 1908. With Nathan Clifford acting as chairman, a slate of officers was elected: Judge Joseph W. Symonds, President; Nathan Clifford, Henry G. Beyer, Jr., Frederick E. Gignoux, Amos Millett, Daniel W. Hoegg, Vice Presidents; Leon V. Walker, Treasurer; Roscoe T. Holt, Secretary; and Mrs. Jacob S. Winslow, Mrs. Henry St. John Smith, Dr. E. Eugene Holt, Dr. George B. Swasey, Joseph W. Armstrong, Andrew S. MacCreadie, and Fred L. Jones, Directors. As a statement of purpose, Judge Symonds noted that the association had been formed with no intent of hostility to any interests but rather "to cooperate with the Cape Elizabeth people in improvements of lasting benefits."

The first major appropriation sought by the association was the sum of $20,000 for the purpose of macadamizing Shore Road. At a special town meeting held 12 November, 1908, this projected expenditure was soundly defeated. A motion to reduce the appropriation to $10,000 enjoyed the same lack of success. Deeply chagrined, the suburbanite faction contemplated submitting a petition to the state legislature seeking the incorporation of the region as a village. Such a project, however, was never carried through.

This resounding defeat produced a brief lull in the drive for other necessary adjuncts to a suburban community. The agitation broke out again early in 1913 more vigorously than ever. This renewal of the struggle was precipitated by a disastrous fire.

On Saturday, 4 January, 1913, "Channelside," the beautiful summer home of Frederick Walker that had been built across the road from Mountain View Park in 1886, was burned to the ground. The following Friday, a meeting of the Cape Shore Civic Association was held in the library of the *Portland Evening Express*. Prior commitments prevented many members from attending, so the meeting was adjourned to reconvene Monday evening, 3 February, at the Owl's Nest, near Cape Cottage Park, to discuss the appalling lack of fire-fighting equipment in the town of Cape Elizabeth.

At this meeting, with David A. Calhoun acting as chairman and Daniel W. Hoegg, Jr., as secretary, the matter of obtaining fire protection was fully explored. It was the consensus that a hose truck would be too expensive in the light of recent experiences. Therefore, it was voted to seek the purchase of a chemical truck by inserting an article in the warrant for the next town meeting. A committee of three, consisting of Nathan Clifford, Daniel W. Hoegg, Jr., and Albert L. Merry, was given the task of drafting and presenting the warrant.

The article, asking that the town appropriate $500 for the purchase of a chemical truck and incidental equipment, to be stationed in the vicinity of Mountain View Park, was voted down at the annual town meeting Monday 3 March 1913. For the time being it would be necessary to rely upon the fire companies of South Portland and Fort Williams.

Despite the defeat of this desperately needed appropriation, other municipal improvements were forthcoming. At this same meeting it was voted to expend $2,500 to repair Shore Road, $500 for sidewalks on Shore Road, and $500 for street lights in Mountain View Park and adjacent areas.

In the same era, a man destined to be one of the largest land owners in twentieth century Cape Elizabeth was quietly purchasing extensive holdings in the southwestern reaches of the town. This individual was Phineas Warren Sprague of Boston, Massachusetts. Born in Malden, Massachusetts, 4 August, 1860, he became his father's partner in the firm of Charles H. Sprague & Son, wholesale coal dealers, 70 Kilby Street, Boston, at the age of twenty-two.

Within a remarkably short period of time Phineas Sprague became a very successful businessman. He was instrumental in establishing the Sprague Steamship Company, with a fleet of colliers. To further expand his coal interests he opened mines in West Virginia, founding the town of Sprague as well as the New

River Coal Company, in that state. In addition, he was a founder of the Malden Trust Company, Malden, Massachusetts.

The first land to be purchased by Sprague, in the town of Cape Elizabeth, was the farm of Edwin C. Jordan a short distance east of the mouth of the Spurwink River. This property, acquired in 1910, Sprague renamed Ram Island Farm, and it soon became his primary residence within the town. In the next few years, he purchased other large tracts that included Richmond's Island and the holdings of the Great Pond Gun Club. In 1915, he set aside Richmond's Island and a large area near the breakwater, as a game preserve. Using a small number of deer purchased from Riverton Park in Portland, he stocked the preserve with a herd that now numbers thirty head. By 1940, Sprague's land holdings in Cape Elizabeth had reached a total of approximately 2,250 acres.

Throughout most of his life Sprague was deeply interested in conservation and the preservation of what he considered to be historic American principles. In furthering these ideals he was an active member of the General Society of Colonial Wars, Sons of the American Revolution, Old Planters Society of Massachusetts, Bostonian Society, New England Historic Genealogical Society, and the Massachusetts Volunteer Militia.

After Sprague's death, 29 June, 1943, at the age of seventy-nine, few changes were made relative to the use of his acreage. At the present time, much of the property is owned by the Sprague Corporation and the Black Point Corporation with no apparent attempts being made to alter the character of the land.

Early in 1913, a very discordant note was heard by the suburbanite planners of Cape Elizabeth. The residential community was deeply distressed to learn that the County Commissioners contemplated the establishment of a home for alcoholics in the northwestern section of the town. Known officially as the Home for Inebriates, it was intended to be a pioneer effort in rehabilitation. The site under consideration was the farm of Solomon A. Hannaford on Spurwink Avenue approximately where the Purpoodock Club is now located.

When it became apparent that the County Commissioners were prepared to purchase the property immediately, petitions were circulated among the townsfolk seeking a cancellation of the project. Under the leadership of Henry G. Beyer and Dr. Samuel D. Thombs plans were made to purchase the tract of land under consideration to forestall acquisition by the county. In response to this display of hostility, the County Commissioners held a public hearing to ascertain the magnitude of this opposition. Apparently impressed by the vehemence of the citizenry, the Cape Elizabeth site was abandoned, and the Joseph L. Robinson farm at South Windham was purchased in its place.

Although the suburban population continued to increase, many improvements generally associated with residential communities, were stubbornly resisted by the citizens of the "Outer Cape." Some minor additions were provided by the suburbanites through neighborhood organizations. A typical example was the purchase, for the first time, of suitable lifesaving equipment for Cape Cottage Beach by the Maiden Cove Improvement Association in the summer of 1915.

The larger projects, however, were forced to await more widespread support. One very annoying and exasperating problem was the deplorable condition of Shore Road. Its seasonal manifestations, alternating between frozen ruts, clouds of dust, and seas of mud, filled many a resident with impotent rage. As automobiles became more common, the traffic on Shore Road became greater, and acrimonious comments on its condition more widespread. Some of these remarks appeared in the local newspapers with pithy editorial embellishment. The *Eastern Argus*, on Thursday 9 March 1916 expressed the sentiments of many.

> Nothing seems to be of any avail in carrying conviction to the minds of some of the back number clam diggers, cabbage raisers and wood choppers on the Cape that good roads would be of immense benefit to them. To these nonprogressive people roads are just what nature made them and any attempt to improve them would be flying in the face of Providence. They may sometimes think it would be kind of nice if the roads were so they could travel from place to place at any season of the year, but the habit of inertia has made them resigned to making their little journeys abroad depend upon wheither it is "settled going" or not.
>
> The beauties of the scenery along the famous Shore Road do not seem to them any particular reason why they should pay out money, or go to work themselves, to make a respectable highway out of it. It was good enough for their fathers when horseback riding was the mode of traveling from Boston to Portland and it is good for them. Sure enough a slick road would be handy about carrying truck to the Portland market, but they'll risk but what they can get it there somehow.
>
> If we built a good road who would get the benefit of it they argue. Why those automobile fellows. We can't afford to go to all that trouble and expense to please them. They can come here in summer if they want to and pay us big prices for clams, fish, and produce, but we don't propose to make nice and shiny roads for them to ride on. No siree!

This is the narrow view taken by too many Maine people. They are too short-sighted to see the immense profits that would come from increased summer travel, and let things go in the old shiftless way. Millions of dollars are sacrificed every year out of the fatuous, hoggish spirit.

Such views and strictures were quite unavailing. It was several years before Shore Road and other such thoroughfares were paved. As State Aid roads, they eventually received bituminous black-top surfacing.

Much more serious than the absence of paved roads was the lack of fire companies and equipment. The burning of the Cliff House, Saturday, 13 June, 1914, helped to make that year a banner one for fires. Thirteen buildings, with an aggregate value of $46,070, were destroyed. In addition, several serious forest and grass fires brought extensive losses to various individuals.

Realizing that the town was not inclined to take immediate action the Cape Shore Civic Association took the initiative early in 1916 by raising funds to purchase fire-fighting equipment. Assistance was forthcoming, however, from the town for at the annual March meeting, $250 was appropriated to buy fire hose and equipment for the use of the Shore Road citizenry. On Friday, 5 May, a meeting was held at the grocery store of White Bros. & Curtis on the Shore Road to organize a volunteer fire company. At this gathering, Cape Elizabeth Hose Company No. 1 was established with Charles E. Hill, Captain; William White, First Lieutenant; and Willis B. Hay, Treasurer. A purchasing committee was also named and consisted of Albert L. Merry, Emil P. Anderson, and Charles E. Hill.

Meeting on Friday, 21 July, at Armstrong's Hall the Civic Association heard a progress report submitted by Frederick E. Gignoux, the finance committee chairman. He stated that 1,000 feet of hose, three nozzles, spanners, and other equipment had been bought at a cost of $540 and that the town had paid its $250 contribution to Willis B. Hay, the Hose Company treasurer. In addition, a serviceable hose truck had been obtained and was kept in a small shed adjoining the store of Joseph W. Armstrong.

The following year, the town contributed another $250 to the fire company for hose and equipment plus $50 for maintenance. Initially, the area served by this company extended from the town line along Shore Road to Delano Park. It was also determined that the town would pay the volunteer firemen one dollar per hour the same rate previously paid the Willard Hose Company when they had responded to Cape Elizabeth calls.

As the hose truck was soon found to be in a badly deteriorated condition, an old six-cylinder Packard car of forty-eight horsepower was purchased in 1918 and rebuilt to carry 1,000 feet of hose, chemical extinguishers, as well as other equipment. With the new hose truck, the firemen were prepared to respond to any call within the town. Despite their willingness, they were badly hampered by the small number of hydrants available. At the March meeting, the town appropriated $500 for 500 feet of hose, $500 for maintenance purposes, and $1,000 for two more hydrants on Shore Road. This brought the total number of hydrants to seventeen all in the northeast section of the town.

Finally, in 1923, Cape Elizabeth acquired its first municipal fire department. On 5 March the Cape Shore Civic Association voted to present the hose truck, hose, and all incidental equipment to the town as a gift. At a special meeting held the following day, the citizenry voted to accept the offer.

After six years of constant agitation, another fire company was organized in 1924. Located at the Town Hall, Cape Elizabeth Hose Company No. 2 was created, with a chemical truck built and equipped with 800 feet of 2.5 inch hose, a 40 gallon chemical tank, and 200 feet of chemical hose. The following year the town appropriated $2,000 for its volunteer fire department. As a result truck No. 1 was rebuilt and a thirty-five gallon chemical tank mounted on it. In addition, a five horse-power coding siren was mounted on the roof of the Cape Shore Community Club near the junction of Preble Street and the Shore Road, and a fire alarm system instituted, with funds raised by popular subscription. Despite the presence of such equipment, the Willard Hose Company and the troops at Fort Williams were still pressed into emergency service upon occasion.

Over the next forty-five years, improvements were constantly made to the fire department in keeping with its ever expanding responsibilities. Telephone contact and a system of tappers were installed in 1925 to coordinate the two volunteer companies. Three years later, a Seagraves 500 gallon triple combination pumper, equipped with an eighty gallon booster tank and ladders, was purchased to replace the old Packard truck of Hose Company No. 1. At the same time, a tower for drying hose was erected at the rear of the Town Hall.

In 1930, a second Seagraves pumper was purchased for Hose Company No. 2 to replace their aged fire truck. To further improve facilities, the town erected a brick fire station on the east side of Shore Road near the South Portland line in the summer of 1934. Construction was classified as a Federal project, with thirty per cent of the cost of labor and material being furnished by the government. Preparations having been carried out by members of Hose Company No. 1, James W. Rowse, Norman M. Parrott, William Clifford 3rd, Ralph T. Gould, and Joseph Pierce, the new station was dedicated Saturday, 20 October, with the pumper moved from Charles E. Hill's Cape Shore garage across the street and formally installed in its new quarters.

A 550 gallon tank truck was added to the department in 1951 and a year later a new Seagraves pumper replaced the old one used by Hose Company No. 1, at a cost of $15,000. This addition was followed by the construction of a new station for Hose Company No. 2 at Pond Cove Corner in the summer of 1954. The building was dedicated Thursday evening, 26 August, with a dinner and appropriate ceremonies. Two years afterwards, a new Seagraves pumper was purchased as a new replacement for the Pond Cove Company.

By 1958, the Cape Elizabeth Fire Department consisted of two Seagrave 750 gallon pumpers, a Chevrolet pumper, a Seagrave ladder truck, and a 500 gallon tank truck with one 500 gallon Seagrave pumper in reserve. An addition was built on to Fire Station No. 1 and a rescue unit organized that same year. In 1959, a new tank truck was added to the department, and on 10 March, the rescue truck, built and equipped by the department members, was presented to the town. After three years of service a new rescue truck was purchased by public donations. To date, no further addition or changes of any magnitude have been instituted.

A valuable service carried out over a period of years by the fire department was the establishment of friendly relations between the suburban and native populations of Cape Elizabeth. The ice was permanently broken through the efforts of a volunteer fireman associated with Hose Company No. 1, Ralph T. Gould. Taking the initiative, he brought into being the Cape Elizabeth Fire Department Band. It was organized 20 August, 1932, and shortly thereafter, weekly practice sessions were held under the guidance of Clarence Rowe, a cornet player in the 240th Coast Artillery Band. The following year, the town gave the group permission to use a room in the town hall for practice sessions.

By bringing together men from all sections of the town, the band was soon responsible for a vast improvement in social rapport among the citizenry. Although its period of activity was brief the band gave many concerts throughout the town. Its presence was a source of universal satisfaction, and, regardless of whether it was a town meeting, a basketball game, Memorial Day exercises, or a social gathering, the band's contribution was long remembered.

The town had also lacked a public library for many years. This deficiency was finally overcome in 1917 through the philanthropic activities of William Widgery Thomas, a native of Portland. Early in the year, he purchased the old Spurwink district schoolhouse that had been built about 1845. Having taught there the winter term of 1857-1858, his motivation was partially a matter of nostalgia.

The little building was sold to Phineas W. Sprague for $150 in 1916 and moved to a vacant lot near the farm of Pomeroy W. Jordan. After its purchase by Thomas, it was moved back to its former location and completely renovated. The land that comprised its original site had been bought by Pomeroy Jordan and he, in sympathy with Thomas' objectives, donated the land for the projected library.

Completed early in 1919, the Thomas Memorial Library, with a collection of 2,300 volumes, was accepted by the town at its annual meeting, 3 March. The library was immediately incorporated and a board of trustees chosen to govern its activities. Formal dedication ceremonies were carried out Tuesday, 22, April, at the library with the principal address delivered by Willian W. Thomas, and speeches by Mayor Charles B. Clarke of Portland, Mayor Frederick W. Hinckley of South Portland, Percival P. Baxter, Nathan Clifford, John S. Lockwood, and the Rev. Leonard B. Tenney. A speech of acceptance was delivered by Everett R. Josselyn, chairman of the Cape Elizabeth board of selectmen and musical selections for the occasion were played by the Cape Elizabeth Band.

In the early years of its existance, the library was open one afternoon a week for four hours. Despite an increase in the population of the town, the remote location of the library prevented its fullest possible use. Therefore, at the annual town meeting 1 March 1943, it was voted to move it, building and all, to a new site close by the Pond Cove School. The wartime situation made alterations rather difficult to carry out, but on 17 October 1944, it was opened to the public. The town also began a program designed to increase its collection of books and its availability to the school children as well as adults. A year later, the Thomas Memorial Library Association was created and a set of by-laws adopted to further enhance its value to the town.

The library soon outgrew its quarters. To meet constantly expanding patronage, in 1957 the town appropriated $9,250 for a 46' x 30' addition at the rear of the building. To assist the town in its program of expansion the Phineas W. Sprague Memorial Foundation donated $2,000 with a like amount contributed by the family of William W. Thomas. The following year, the town appropriated an additional $5,000 to complete the project. Finished late in the fall, the new addition was officially opened 10 November, 1958. Since that time the library has continued to be an invaluable adjunct to the educational and cultural facilities of the town, with a constant increase in its excellent collection of books.

As the suburban population continued to grow, a logical result was the formation of various social organizations. After the burning of the Portland Country Club at Thornton Heights, South Portland, 26 April, 1913, the members contemplated the selection of a new site at Pond Cove. These plans failed to materialize, however, and a more suitable site was chosen at Falmouth Foreside.

A more successful venture, from the standpoint of its availability, was the Cape Shore Community Club. In 1920, a cottage near the junction of Preble Street and the Shore Road, (formerly the property of Charles F. Libby), was purchased and remodeled as a club house. It was opened with appropriate festivities on Saturday evening, 11 September.

Two years later, a much more ambitious social club was organized. On 21 June, 1922, Clinton W. Davis, Walter G. Davis, Robert Payson, Donald M. Payson, Harold B. Robinson, Dean B. Small, Henry G. Beyer, Henry Lewis, Dr. Talcott O. Vanamee, and Arthur S. Bosworth, met at the home of Walter B. Parker, and created the Purpoodock Club. Shortly thereafter, they acquired a 178 acre tract, between Spurwink Avenue and Ocean House Road, known as the Sullivan-Hannaford property, from Phineas W. Sprague. The first slate of officers, elected this same year consisted of Henry G. Beyer, President; Willis G. Hay, Treasurer; and Dr. Talcott O. Vanamee, Secretary. These officers, with Walter G. Davis, Robert Payson, Walter B. Parker, Mrs. Frederick E. Gignoux, and Mrs. Arthur S. Bosworth, constituted a board of governors.

Conceived as an "exclusive" country club, it was limited to two hundred members, with no provision for non-resident and family membership. Each member, whether man or woman, was required to purchase a share of stock, two shares being required for a man and his wife. Children were expected to become regular members at the age of twenty-one.

The farmhouse on the property was soon remodeled as a clubhouse, and a large cabbage shed was renovated to serve as a dance hall. The surrounding fields, where until recently cabbages had been growing were transformed into an eighteen hole golf course and tennis courts. Thus was established in this rapidly rising "suburbia-by-the-sea," a new status symbol, that bespoke the current affluent society; a social sanctuary where congenial souls could escape the "churlish natives" of the town.

The decade of the 1920's brought a remarkable increase in the number of residential developments. Immediately south of Mountain View Park George W. Brown produced another popular community which he named Oakhurst Park. Separating it from the park was another project in the process of expansion. This was Pillsbury Bluffs in the vicinity of what is now Stonybrook Road, promoted by Llewellyn Leighton, who had been a successful dealer in Florida real estate.

Cape Cottage Park, now abandoned as a trolley park, had been purchased by Harry E. Baker. After converting the old casino into a private residence, which involved lowering the roof one story, he proceeded to divide the park into house lots and to build a large number of homes in a variety of styles. With imaginative landscaping, Cape Cottage Park was transformed into one of the more attractive suburban communities. At the same time, Baker began to develop Cape Cottage Woods almost directly across Shore Road and extending northward to Oakhurst Park.

One early resident of Cape Cottage Park, who lived there primarily in the summer months, was the famous marine artist, Charles Robert Patterson. When the trolley park was discontinued, he purchased the small gazebo-like refreshment stand and moved it from its site near the theatre to a height of land in the northeast corner of the park immediately adjacent to the old Goddard mansion. He converted it into a small studio with a beautiful view of the sea, and attached to it a small addition as living quarters. In later years this charming residence was expanded and winterized and is now the home of the George Stuyvesant Jacksons. Mr. Jackson is also an artist but paints, not in the "refreshment stand," which is too attractive as a living room, but in the coal cellar that was built when Patterson put in central heating.

Yet another rapidly expanding development was located on the northern edge of Mountain View Park. In this section Edwin R. Files was constructing a residential community which he called

Cottage Farms. Here, the homes differed only slightly from their counterparts at Cape Cottage Park and Oakhurst Park.

In keeping with this building boom there was a steady increase in population. Between 1920 and 1940 the number of residents more than doubled. This was not, however, a situation unique to Cape Elizabeth. Actually it was part of a major national trend whereby the American people were moving from city to suburb at a greater rate than ever before. Symptomatic of the increased mobility and financial strength of the middle class was their desire to settle in housing developments where seashore and country life could be enjoyed with all the municipal services that until recently had been available only to the urban dweller.

Despite the need or desirability some of these services, and attendant municipal reforms, considered vital to a residential community, were slow in coming. The constant increase in expenditures to realize such needs was not matched by a parallel growth in revenue. If they were to be instituted it would be necessary to closely supervise the allocation of funds. Therefore, the town voted 5 March 1917 to create its first Budget Committee. Henceforth, the recommendations of this committee would of needs be viewed by the voters as the carefully considered opinions of fiscal experts.

Somewhat later, in seeking to change the nomination and election of town officers, the spirit of reform faltered. At the annual meeting 6 March, 1933, a committee was created to devise a more formal voting procedure, superior to a show of hands and devoid of political rancor. A year later, at the annual meeting 5 March, they presented their carefully considered recommendations to the voters.

. . .We believe that political parties serve no useful purpose in the conduct of town affairs, and that the political party affiliations of individual candidates for town office should not be considered in the selection of town officials. Therefore, we conclude that the designation of candidates in groups as the "Republican Ticket," or "Democratic Ticket" is undesirable.

We believe that the method of nomination by party caucus, which has prevailed in Cape Elizabeth for many years, is an unsatisfactory and distinctly dangerous system of nomination. . .

The Committee recommends that the town adopt the practice of nomination by petition and use of an official ballot in voting. . .

. . .All candidates for town offices. . . .shall have their names printed upon the ballot without political party designation. . .

The voters rejected this non-partisan arrangement, and since

1934, nothing further has been attempted in this area. Although town officers are now elected by secret ballot, the nominating caucus and political affiliations are still utilized.

One municipal service, of which the suburban areas stood in great need, was the collection of garbage. This service had been viewed for some years by many of the older residents as unnecessary and not sufficiently important to warrant the expense. On one occasion, when the subject was raised at town meeting, a citizen by the name of Jordan stated that it was his belief that pigs could not survive on the offal collected in the suburban sections as it would probably consist of nothing but empty gin bottles and grapefruit rinds. Despite such caustic comments, the town finally inaugurated a program of garbage collection at the annual meeting 4 March 1935.

While these suburban areas were experiencing their growing pains, many of Portland's leading citizens were discovering the pleasures of living in Cape Elizabeth. Throughout the first thirty-five years of this century a few proceeded to build imposing homes surrounded by expansive land holdings. In a majority of cases these substantial residences occupied or overlooked long stretches of ocean frontage. From what is now Glen Avenue to Peabbles Cove the unoccupied parts of the shoreline were gradually engulfed, and disappeared. For the most part, a quiet grandeur and disassociation from the maddening crowd were the predominating characteristics. In a few instances, residences were established that can only be described as magnificent estates. With their formal gardens, strutting peacocks, terraced lawns, and imported deer, they somehow seemed slightly incongrous in a town that a few years before had been a quiet rural community of prosperous farmers and fishermen more accustomed to cabbage cellars and manure piles than to golf scores and lawn parties. The coming of World War II closed this era of muted ostentation, and the prospects of its ever being revived can not be viewed as encouraging.

During the war years, the Greater Portland area underwent a major population explosion largely due to military installations and defense industries. In seeking ways to alleviate the acute housing shortage a number of dwellings were quickly constructed in several areas. One such housing complex was established in Cape Elizabeth a short distance west of the high school on the Scott Dyer Road. Known as Elizabeth Park, it soon contained a large number of single family units that lacked individuality as well as space. Despite the rapidity with which they were constructed they have survived in a rather remarkable state of preservation.

In the immediate post-war era the town quickly expanded its role as a "sleeper-community." The suburbanite had at last, by sheer weight of numbers, seized the initiative. Although, the residents of long standing continued to exercise a great deal of influence, the future of Cape Elizabeth was clearly discernible. The progress of urbanization forced the adoption of a variety of changes in the town government that reflected a significant increase in the complexity of municipal affairs.

Among the more significant changes was the appointment of a Planning Committee at the annual meeting in March 1942. The Committee's stated purpose was to examine existing zoning laws relative to revising or amending them and to prepare a plan for establishing a town cemetery. With regard to the latter, Riverside Cemetery was thus designated and accepted at the March meeting three years later.

As of 4 May, 1946, the town adopted the report of the Planning Committee as a Planning Board Ordinance. The primary duty of the Planning Board, as stated in the ordinance, was to "prepare coordinated plans for the physical development of the town." It was further stated, however, that any plans thus formulated would become effective only if approved by a two-thirds vote at town meeting. In addition, the Planning Board was authorized to encourage the formation of community associations that would have as their objective the improvement of neighborhood areas. Lastly, a Board of Appeals was created, consisting of the Selectmen, to hear complaints relative to any action taken by the Planning Board.

At the annual meeting 3 March 1947 a zoning map, platting proposals, and a program for the preparation of a master plan, were adopted by the town. Through such far-sighted action Cape Elizabeth will in all probability escape the problems associated with a chaotic use of the town's land area that has plagued so many other suburban communities across the nation. Advance planning of this type certainly reveals something of a departure from the traditional concepts that often provided a myopic view of the future.

One link with the past that has survived the modernizing spirit of suburbia is the town poor-farm. The current system of poor relief and social security has resulted in a total absence of indigent residents at the farm. As noted in an earlier chapter, Thomas Jordan bequeathed his ninety acre farm to the town as a refuge for the poor with the stipulation that his wife Mary be allowed to live there until she died. After he died in 1828, his wife continued to reside there until 1832 when she was moved by her guardian, Charles Staples, to a private home. After being substantially repaired that same year, Enos H. Jordan moved in as the first "keeper of the almshouse." For the next forty-two years, the existing farm buildings were used with few changes. Finally, in 1874, the need for extensive repairs prompted the town to tear the house down and replace it with a more suitable structure.

The new poor-house was a two story building, 36' x 40' erected about thirty yards from the site of the old Jordan farm house. Designed by Frederick H. Fassett of Portland, the new structure was built, at a cost of $4,000, by William D. Murray of Cape Elizabeth. Until recent years the acreage of the town farm was extensively cultivated and enabled it to survive with the help of annual appropriations.

An unusual degree of prosperity was achieved, however, under the guidance of Clarence L. Phinney who was keeper for several years. In 1924 this situation prompted the inclusion of the following poem in the town report:

TOWN FARM

> Now list to this and give a cheer
> The old town farm has paid this year;
> Contentment reigns, no sign of strife,
> All praise to Phinney and his wife.
>
> Our poor unfortunate friends out there
> Have every kindness, every care;
> For all their troubles, pains or needs
> Are sympathetic words and deeds.
>
> For many years, as is well known,
> Instead of income, loss was shown;
> So here's a thought to ponder o'er:
> If one farm pays, why not have four?

Unfortunately this prosperity did not last, and at the annual meeting 2 March 1931 the selectmen were authorized to sell the town farm. No sale was ever consummated however, and it has continued as municipal property. Although the farm is now tenantless, some of the acreage is being cultivated on a rental basis by neighboring farmers.

In the years that followed World War II, the municipal government became much more complex, with the result that a professional administrator became a necessity. Thus it was that, at the annual meeting 1 March, 1948, a committee was appointed to "investigate the desirability of employing a town manager . . ." The following year the committee reported that the town would, in their estimation, profit from a town manager form of government. No action was taken, however, until 1949. On 15 September, at a special meeting, the town authorized the selectmen to interview candidates for the position. Despite his auspicious begining, nothing further was done at this time.

The adoption of a Town Manager form of government languished until 1957, when a new committee was appointed to investigate the situation anew. This second committee reported favorably at the annual meeting 3 March 1958. A year later, on 16 November, the town finally voted to accept this first major change in the government of the town, in one hundred and ninety four years. On this occasion the *Portland Press Herald* expressed the feelings of many in an editorial.

> . . .What has happened in Cape Elizabeth is that the relatively young and vigorous element which so heavily populates the typical suburban community has gained and responsibly exercised a very full measure of political control. If you will, a revolution against traditional town government, dominated by traditional thinking, has been calmly and studiously brought. . .to completion with a minimum of fuss. . . .
>
> To our way of thinking this will be to the good, for the same reasons that apply to town government anywhere. It is increasingly a business for specialized talent. In the Cape Elizabeth case it is refreshing to find selectmen in the forefront of efforts in self-improvement.

In December 1959, the Board of Selectmen hired Allen M. Marks to serve as Town Manager. He assumed his duties on 1 February, 1960, functioning as town clerk, tax collector and road commissioner, as well as the administrative head of the town government. With little fanfare, and with hardly a backward glance, the individualism of the past gave way to a new era of professionalism and corporate leadership.

Although the need for such manifestations of modern efficiency as budget committees, planning boards, and town managers is indisputable, they nevertheless remove part of the human element that so characterized the town government of earlier days. Under these conditions it is highly doubtful if the qualities that were found in the personal leadership of such men as Harry S. Jordan, Charles H. A. Peabbles, Pomeroy W. Jordan, Harvey E. Maxwell, and Alonzo S. Murray, are ever seen again.

The town meetings of today more closely resemble the deliberations of a board of directors than the spontaneous democracy that was evident a few decades ago. Efficiency and corporate planning, now so vital to municipal government, lack the drama that once made town meetings a personal challenge instead of a prosaic duty. There can be heated arguments, pithy comments on motivations, and endemic rebellions, but the firey vigor is past.

What the town meetings of old may have lacked in organization was more than made up for in popular participation. Such meetings could bring a citizen close to apoplexy and yet preserve an atmosphere of parliamentary decorum. There was also the tradition that town meetings were covered by a form of legislative immunity. Not infrequently, in a moment of extreme provocation, remarks would be exchanged that would have resulted in immediate court action or personal combat had they been uttered in any other setting.

The changes of recent years have introduced a placidity marked by good government and wise spending. Without a doubt modern methods are the only way to operate a town of any size. The delegation of authority to boards, committees, and professional administrators, is a limitation of the democratic process that cannot be avoided. Be that as it may, we can neverthless remember with nostalgia, those years long past when the earthy, unpretentious, and clannish Yankees of Cape Elizabeth held-sway, beholden to nobody and fiercely defending from "foreign" interference their cherished customs and traditions.

The future is firmly in the grasp of the suburbanite. The construction of residential housing developments progresses at a frantic pace. Continuing the now well-established practice of selecting euphonious names to attract the status conscious, such charming housing projects as Sherwood Forest with its Friar Lane, Little John Road, Bridal Path Way, and Locksley Road; as well as Kings Grant, Brentwood Acres, Eastfield, Broad Cove Shore, Mitchell Highlands, Ledgemere, and Meadowcrest, are already prominent neighborhoods. In viewing these areas, common characteristics are discernible that immediately bring to mind the writings of such current authors as Russell Lynes or Vance Packard, to say nothing of that recent folk-song by Malvina Reynolds entitled *Little Boxes*.

Although Cape Elizabeth has undergone a spectacular transformation in the last fifty years, its growth is essentially part of a national trend. The process of urbanization that has almost totally obliterated what was once a predominantly rural way of life cannot be viewed as peculiar to this area. The absorption of the town as a suburb of the city of Portland has progressed inexorably for well over a century. The natural beauty of the town has lent itself admirably to this role. Despite the fact that the natives tried on various occasions to stem the tide the triumph of suburbia was inevitable.

Time, however, has been kind to Cape Elizabeth. Its transition from a quiet, rural community to its current status has been gradual, with the possible exception of recent years. Regardless of the fact that no significant examples of early architecture have survived, many reminders of the past are present. The land of the Outer Cape retains much of its original character. The banks of the Spurwink and Richmond's Island would yet be familiar ground should an early settler return to these historic acres. The few small cemeteries that have not succumbed to vandalism or neglect testify to a way of life that has vanished. Although these vestiges of the past are meager indeed, their preservation from the ravages of residential subdivisions is for the moment assured. Truly, a land without relics is a land without memories, and a land without memories is a land without history. By preserving the history of Cape Elizabeth, a sense of continuity may be achieved, that will provide the citizen of the future with an understanding of the forces that shaped this town as it kept pace with the growth of state and nation.

Appendix I

SELECTMEN

Jonathan Loveitt	1766-1768	Ezekiel Jordan	1794-1795
Samuel Skillin		Joshua Dyer	
Thomas Maxwell		Barzillai Delano	
Clement Jordan	1769	Mark Dyer	1796-1797
Joseph Cobb Jr.		Ezekiel Jordan	
Samuel Skillin		John Mars	
Clement Jordan	1770	Jacob Waterhouse	1798
John York		Ezekiel Jordan	
Jonathan Loveitt		Robert Dyer	
Joseph Mariner	1771	Ezekiel Jordan	1799
James Strout Jr.		Robert Dyer	
James Dyer		Mark Dyer	
Jonathan Loveitt	1772	George Deake	1800
Joseph Sawyer		Samuel Dunn	
Patrick Maxwell		Seecomb Jordan	
Samuel Skillin	1773	Ezekiel Jordan	1801
Jonathan Loveitt		Elisha Jordan	
David Strout		Zebulon Trickey	
David Strout	1774	Ezekiel Jordan	1802
Clement Jordan		Mark Dyer	
Samuel Skillin		Zebulon Trickey	
Samuel Skillin	1775	Morrill Jordan	1803
David Strout		Lemuel Cobb	
Joseph Mariner		Zebulon Trickey	
Joseph Cobb	1776	Ezekiel Jordan	1804-1806
David Strout		Mark Dyer	
Benjamin Jordan		John Goold	
Benjamin Jordan	1777-1778	Daniel Skillin	1807
Joseph Cobb		Mark Dyer	
James Dyer		Jacob Waterhouse	
Clement Jordan	1779	Daniel Skillin	1808
George Strout		Jacob Waterhouse	
George Deake		Morrell Jordan	
Nathaniel Staples	1780-1781	Mark Dyer	1809
Stephen Randall		Ebenezer Thrasher	
David Strout		Zebulon Trickey	
Benjamin Jordan	1782-1786	Nathaniel Dyer	1810
Stephen Randall		Ebenezer Thrasher	
Barzillai Delano		Samuel Dunn	
George Deake	1787	Ebenezer Thrasher	1811-1813
Joshua Dyer		Nathaniel Dyer	
Barzillai Delano		William Cummings	
Benjamin Jordan	1788-1789	William Cummings	1814-1815
Barzillai Delano		Lemuel Cobb	
Joshua Dyer		Ebenezer Thrasher	
Mathew Simonton	1790	Ebenezer Thrasher	1816
Nathaniel Dyer		Lemuel Cobb	
Barzillai Delano		Ephraim Broad	
Ezekiel Jordan	1791-1792	William Cummings	1817-1818
James Leach		Ebenezer Thrasher	
Barzillai Delano		Lemuel Cobb	
Timothy Jordan	1793	Ebenezer Thrasher	1819
Samuel Calef		William Cummings	
Ezekiel Jordan		James Dyer	

Ebenezer Thrasher	1820		Elliott Wescott	1850
John Armstrong			James M. Robinson	
James Dyer			Alfred Dyer	
Woodbury Jordan	1821		Stephen Hubbard	1851
John Armstrong			James M. Robinson	
James Dyer			Alfred Dyer	
Lemuel Cobb	1822		Charles Hannaford	1852
James Dyer			Stephen Hubbard	
William Cummings			James M. Robinson	
Charles Staples	1823		James Trickey	1853-1854
John Armstrong			Alfred Dyer	
Micah Higgins			Andrew W. Peabbles	
Lemuel Cobb	1824		James Trickey	1855
Charles Staples			Thomas E. Knight	
John Armstrong			Charles Barrell	
Micah Higgins	1825-1826		Charles Barrell	1856
John Armstrong			Thomas E. Knight	
William Cummings			Benjamin W. Pickett	
Micah Higgins	1827		Thomas E. Knight	1857
Woodbury Jordan			James Trickey	
William Cummings			Woodbury Dyer	
Charles Staples	1828		James M. Robinson	1858
William Cummings			Dennis M. Skillin	
Woodbury Jordan			Daniel Pilsbury	
William Cummings	1829		James Trickey	1859
Charles Staples			Samuel Haskell	
Micah Higgins			Andrew W. Peabbles	
Charles Staples	1830-1831		James Trickey	1860
Nathaniel Dyer			Benjamin W. Pickett	
William Cummings			Charles Peabbles	
Charles Staples	1832		Dennis M. Skillin	1861
Charles Hannaford			William R. Dyer	
Randall Skillin			David A. Sawyer	
Elliott Jordan	1833-1837		Dennis M. Skillin	1862
Charles Hannaford			David W. Kincaid	
Randall Skillin			Charles E. Jordan	
Charles Hannaford	1838-1840		James Trickey	1863
Hiram Staples			George W. Libby	
Randall Skillin			Charles Peabbles	
Aaron Bedell	1841		James M. Robinson	1864
Randall Skillin			Cyrus Cole	
Hiram Staples			George F. Henley	
Ebenezer Thrasher	1842		James M. Robinson	1865-1866
Aaron Bedell			George F. Henley	
Randall Skillin			Henry S. Jackson	
Randall Skillin	1843		Henry S. Jackson	1867
Reuben Higgins			Clement E. Staples	
Thomas Hannaford			George F. Henley	
Thomas Hannaford	1844		James Trickey	1868
James Trickey			George W. Libby	
Hiram Staples			Michael J. Peabbles	
Reuben Higgins	1845		James Trickey	1869-1871
James Trickey			Joseph S. Fickett	
Elliott Wescott			Charles A. Tilton	
Thomas Hannaford	1846-1847		Charles A. Tilton	1872
Dennis M. Skillin			Thomas B. Haskell	
Ebenezer Jordan			Michael J. Peabbles	
Thomas Hannaford	1848		Thomas B. Haskell	1873
Reuben Higgins			Nathan R. Dyer	
Milton Dyer			Elisha N. Jordan	
Elliott Wescott	1849		Thomas B. Haskell	1874
Reuben Higgins			Elisha N. Jordan	
Milton Dyer			Frederick Hatch	

Thomas B. Haskell	1875	Frank H. Peabbles	1907
Frederick Hatch		John M. Taylor	
Nathan R. Dyer		Pomeroy W. Jordan	
Thomas B. Haskell	1876-1877	Pomeroy W. Jordan	1908
Stephen Scamman		Charles E. Jordan	
Elisha N. Jordan		Harry S. Jordan	
Thomas B. Haskell	1878-1880	Harry S. Jordan	1909
Stephen Scamman		Pomeroy W. Jordan	
Nathaniel Dyer		Charles H. A. Peabbles	
Thomas B. Haskell	1881-1882	Harry S. Jordan	1910
Stephen Scamman		Charles H. A. Peabbles	
Michael J. Peabbles		Frank H. Peabbles	
Stephen Scamman	1883-1884	Harry S. Jordan	1911
Michael J. Peabbles		Frank H. Peabbles	
Augustus E. Skillin		Charles H. A. Peabbles	
Charles A. Tilton	1885-1887	Howard C. Hannaford	
Michael J. Peabbles		Arthur L. Jordan	
Augustus E. Skillin		Harry S. Jordan	1912
Michael J. Peabbles	1888	Pomeroy W. Jordan	
Augustus E. Skillin		Charles M. Hasty	
James H. Harford		Frank H. Peabbles	1913
Michael J. Peabbles	1889-1890	Charles M. Hasty	
James H. Harford		Andrew S. Macreadie	
George C. Mountfort		Frank H. Peabbles	1914-1915
Michael J. Peabbles	1891	Andrew S. Macredie	
George C. Mountfort		Howard C. Hannaford	
Eliphalet C. Robinson		John M. Taylor	1916
George C. Mountfort	1892	Andrew S. Macreadie	
Eliphalet C. Robinson		Harvey E. Maxwell	
Melville B. Fuller		Andrew S. Macreadie	1917
George C. Mountfort	1893	Harvey E. Maxwell	
Michael J. Peabbles		Philip N. Jordan	
Nathan R. Dyer		Harvey E. Maxwell	1918
Charles E. Jordan	1894	Philip N. Jordan	
Melville B. Fuller		Everett R. Josselyn	
William E. Allen		Harvey E. Maxwell	1919
Clement E. Staples	1895	Everett R. Josselyn	
Nathaniel Dyer		Edgar L. Jordan	
Charles Peabbles		Everett R. Jossleyn	1920
Clement E. Staples	1896	Harvey E. Maxwell	
Charles Peabbles		Philip N. Jordan	
Harry S. Jordan		Everett R. Josselyn	1921
Clement E. Staples	1897	Philip N. Jordan	
Harry S. Jordan		Alonzo S. Murray	
Pomeroy W. Jordan		Alonzo S. Murray	1922-1925
Harry S. Jordan	1898	Harvey E. Maxwell	
Pomeroy W. Jordan		William H. Buxton	
Alvah E. Poland		William H. Buxton	1926
Clement E. Staples	1899-1900	Alonzo S. Murray	
Pomeroy W. Jordan		Fred W. Peabbles	
Alvah E. Poland		William H. Buxton	1927
Harry S. Jordan	1901-1902	Fred W. Peabbles	
Charles E. Jordan		Elmer N. Blackwell	
Frank H. Peabbles		William H. Buxton	1928-1929
Charles E. Jordan	1903	Elmer N. Blackwell	
Frank H. Peabbles		Lloyd W. Jordan	
Pomeroy W. Jordan		William H. Buxton	1930-1933
Pomeroy W. Jordan	1904	Elmer N. Blackwell	
Frank H. Peabbles		Philip N. Jordan	
John M. Taylor		William H. Buxton	1934
Harry S. Jordan	1905-1906	Elmer N. Blackwell	
John M. Taylor		Alonzo S. Murray	
Charles E. Jordan			

William H. Buxton	1935-1937		Carl Beyer	1956
Alonzo S. Murray			Lyman A. Cousens, Jr.	
Fred W. Peabbles			Joseph H. Johnson, Jr.	
Alonzo S. Murray	1938		Lyman A. Cousens, Jr.	1957-1960
Fred W. Peabbles			Joseph H. Johnson, Jr.	
Charles W. Leonard			Donald L. Philbrick	
Alonzo S. Murray	1939-1945		Joseph H. Johnson, Jr.	1961-1962
Charles W. Leonard			Donald L. Philbrick	
Ralph E. Leighton			William H. Jordan	
Alonzo S. Murray	1946-1947		William H. Jordan	1963
Richard K. Gould			Joseph H. Johnson, Jr.	
Harold W. Johnson			Ruth W. Bean	
Carl Beyer	1948		Joseph H. Johnson, Jr.	1964
Alonzo S. Murray			Richard E. Jordan	
Richard K. Gould			Ruth W. Bean	
Alonzo S. Murray	1949-1951		William H. Jordan	
Carl Beyer			Frederick P. Armstrong, Jr.	
James W. Rowse			Richard E. Jordan	1965
Carl Beyer	1952-1955		James E. Murray, Jr.	
Lyman A. Cousens, Jr.			Ruth W. Bean	
Alonzo S. Murray			William H. Jordan	
			Frederick P. Armstrong, Jr.	

Appendix II

CAPE ELIZABETH CENSUS RETURNS

1790

A—Name of head of family.
B—Free white males, 16 years or over, including head of family.
C—Free white males under 16 years.
D—Free white females, including head of family.
E—All other free persons.

Abbot. James	B-1, D-2	Crowley. Jeremiah	B-2, C-2, D-3
Alden, Elisabeth	B-2, D-3	Cummings. Thomas	B-1, C-1, D-2
Allen. David	B-1, C-1, D-1	Cushing. Abigail	C-1, D-2
Amory. John	B-2. C-3, D-4	Cushing. John	B-1, C-1, D-3
Armstrong. John	B-1, C-2, D-2	Cushing. Loring	B-1, C-1, D-4
Atwood. Stephen	B-1, C-2, D-2	Davis. Christopher	B-1, D-2
Avery. Jane	B-1, D-2	Davis. Daniel	B-1, D-4
Babb, James	B-2, D-2	Davis. Simeon	B-1, C-1, D-3
Baley, William	B-3, C-2, D-5	Deakes. George	B-1, C-2, D-6
Barnsbotom, James	B-1, D-1	Delano. Bezilla	B-5, C-1, D-5
Beal. Ebenezer	B-1, C-1, D-2	Dingly. William	B-1, C-2, D-7
Bigford. Joshua	B-1, D-1	Doane. Ebenezer	B-1, C-1, D-1
Blake. John	B-1, C-1, D-1	Doane. Edward	B-4, D-4
Bowa. George	B-1, C-6, D-2	Douglas. Archbald	B-1, D-2
Brown. Jacob	B-3, C-2, D-5	Dunn. Enoch	B-2, C-1, D-3
Bryant. Abraham	B-1, D-2	Dyer. Abigail	C-1, D-1
Bucks. Abraham	B-1, D-1	Dyer. Benjamin	C-1, D-5
Calif. Samuel	B-4, C-2, D-1, E-1	Dyer. Caleb	B-1, C-3, D-4
Cash. Nathaniel	B-1, C-2, D-3	Dyer. Ephraim	B-4, C-1, D-3
Cash. Samuel	B-1, C-2, D-3	Dyer. Hannah	C-4, D-4
Clark. Robert	B-2, C-3, D-2	Dyer. Henry	B-2, C-3, D-5
Clarke. Ephraim	B-3, C-1, D-6	Dyer. Isaac	B-1, C-2, D-2
Clarkes. John R.	B-2, C-2, D-4	Dyer. Isaac	B-1, C-2, D-2
Cobb, Joseph	B-3, C-1, D-3	Dyer. Jabes	B-2, D-2
Crocket. Richard	B-1, C-1, D-5	Dyer. James	B-3, C-6, D-2
Crocket. Samuel	B-1, D-2	Dyer. Joshua	B-1, C-3, D-7
		Dyer. Micael	B-2, C-1, D-4

Dyer. Nathaniel	B-2, C-2, D-6		Marrs. John	B-3, C-3, D-4
Dyer. Paul	B-1, C-1, D-2		Maxwell. Patrick	B-2, C-4, D-1
Dyer. Robert	B-1, C-2, D-6		Maxwell. James	B-2, C-1, D-3
Dyer. Samuel	B-2, C-2, D-4		Maxwell. James	B-2, D-2
Dyer. Samuel	B-1, C-3, D-6		Maxwell. Joseph	B-3, C-3, D-5
Dyer. William	B-1, D-1		Maxwell. Thomas	B-4, C-2, D-4
Elder. Ellis	B-1, D-2		Maxwell. William	B-1, C-2, D-6
Elder. George	B-2, C-1, D-2		Mayew. Whitewood	B-2, C-1, D-2
Elder. John	B-1, D-4		McCaning. Elisabeth	
Elder. Joshua	B-1, C-2, D-1			D-2
Flint. Thomas	B-1, C-2, D-2		McCreat. William	B-1, D-3
Fogg. John	B-1, C-2, D-1		McKenny. Eleazer	B-1, C-3, D-3
Fricket. Benjamin	B-3, D-3		McKenny. Jonathan	
Fricket. John	B-3, D-3			B-1, C-2, D-4
Fricket. John	B-1, C-3, D-4		Miller. David	B-1, D-2
Fricket. Nathaniel	B-1, C-2, D-4		Miller. Hugh	B-1, C-1
Fricket. William	B-1, C-3, D-2		Miller. James	B-2, C-3, D-5
Gammon. William	B-2, D-3		Miller. Joshua	B-1, C-1, D-1
Gent. Ephraim.	B-1, D-1		Millet. Elisha	B-2, C-1, D-2
Hatch. Ezekiel	B-1, D-4		Mitchell. Jonathan	
Hatch. John	B-1, C-2, D-1			B-2, C-1, D-7
Hayes. George	B-2, D-2		Nason. Uriah	B-3, C-2, D-4
Higgins. Massy	B-4, C-1, D-3		Parker. Ebenezer	B-1, D-7
Hoole. William	B-2, C-3, D-3		Pilsberry. Hannah	C-2, D-1
Hunscom. Moses	B-3, D-2		Plummer. Jesse	B-1, C-5, D-2
Irish. Patrick	B-2, C-1, D-4		Plummer. Robert	B-1, D-1
Jackson. Thomas	B-1, C-1, D-2		Pollock. Deliverance	D-1
Johnston. Samuel	B-1, C-2, D-4		Pratt. Zenas	B-4, C-3, D-3
Jorden. Abraham	B-1, C-1, D-3		Randal. Stephen	B-1, C-1, D-2
Jorden. Benjamin	B-3, C-3, D-6		Ray. William	B-1, C-1, D-1
Jorden. Dominicus	B-3, C-2, D-4		Richards. Bezilla	B-1, C-1, D-4
Jorden. Elisha	B-2, D-3		Richards. Humphrey	
Jorden. Elisha	B-1, C-1, D-4			B-1, D-2
Jorden. Ezekiel	B-1, C-4, D-5		Richards. John	B-1, D-1
Jorden. Isaac	B-1, C-2, D-3		Robinson. Samuel	B-1, C-3, D-2
Jorden. Jeremiah	B-2, C-4, D-2		Roberts. Ephraim	B-2, C-5, D-2
Jorden. Jeremiah	B-2, C-1, D-2		Roberts. Hannah	C-2, D-2
Jorden. John	B-1, C-3, D-5		Roberts. Mary	D-2
Jorden. John	B-1, C-1, D-3		Robertson. John	B-1, C-1, D-3
Jorden. Jonathan	B-3, C-1, D-5		Roberston. Joshua	B-3, C-2, D-6
Jorden. Joshua	B-4, C-3, D-2, E-1		Roberston, Samuel	B-2, C-3, D-4
Jorden. Nathaniel	B-1, D-4		Ryon. John	B-1, D-3
Jorden Nathaniel	B-2, C-2, D-4, E-1		Sawyer. Daniel	B-1 D-2
Jorden. Nathaniel	B-1, D-4		Sawyer. Ebenezer	B-2, C-2, D-5
Jorden. Noah	B-1, C-1, D-3		Sawyer, Jeremiah	B-1, D-2
Jorden. Noah	B-1, D-2		Sawyer. Jacob	B-1, D-1
Jorden. Rachel	B-1, D-2		Sawyer, Jonathan	B-1, C-7, D-3
Jorden. Richard	B-1, D-1		Sawyer. Joseph	B-1
Jorden. Samuel	B-1, C-4, D-3		Sawyer. Mary	B-2, D-4
Jorden. Samuel	B-3, C-1, D-5		Sawyer. Peeter	B-2, C-4, D-3
Jorden. Samuel	B-1, C-4, D-3		Sawyer. Reubin	B-1, D-1
Jorden. Secomb	B-1, C-1, D-2		Shillings. John	B-1, C-2, D-3
Jorden. Solomon	B-1, C-2, D-4		Shillings. Joseph	B-1 C-4, D-3
Jorden. Stephen	B-1, C-3, D-5		Shillings. Josiah	B-2, D-3
Jorden. Timothy	B-1, D-2		Shillings. Nehemiah	
Jorden. Trustim	B-2, C-1, D-3			B-1, D-1
Jorden. Thomas	B-1, D-1		Shillings. Samuel	B-2, D-1, E-3
Leach. James	B-3, C-1, D-3		Shillings. Samuel	B-5, C-6, D-7
Leatherby. Jonathan			Shillings. Simeon	B-2, C-3, D-6
	B-2, C-5, D-3		Simonton. Andrew	B-3, C-2, D-2
Libby. Jotham	B-1, C-2, D-4		Simonton. Ebenezer	B-1, C-5 D-2
Lovett. James	B-1, C-1, D-1		Simonton. London	E-2
Mariner. John	B-1, C-4, D-4		Simonton. Mary	B-2, D-3
Mariner. Joseph	B-1, C-4, D-2		Simonton. Matthew	B-1, C-1, D-5
Mariner. Moses	B-1, C-1, D-6		Simonton. Thomas	B-1, C-3, D-2

Simonton. Thomas	B-1, D-2		Thrasher. Benjamin	B-1, D-2
Small. Edward	B-2, C-4, D-5		Thrasher, Ebenezer	
Small. Elisha	B-1, C-3, D-4			B-3, C-1, D-3
Small. Timothy	B-1, C-2, D-3		Trickey. Zebulon	B-3, D-4
Smally. Edward	B-1, D-1		Trundy. George	B-3, C-1, D-3
Stanford. Abigail	D-3		Turner. James	B-2, D-4
Stanford. Benjamin	B-1 C-1, D-3		Wallace. John	B-1, C-1, D-2
Stanford. Christopher	B-1, D-2		Wallace. Jonah	B-1, D-3
Stanford. John	B-2, C-3, D-1		Webb. Sarah	B-2, D-3
Stanford. Joseph	B-1, D-1		Webster. James	B-1
Stanford. Sarah	B-1, D-5		Webster. James	B-2, C-3, D-4
Staples. Nathaniel	B-2, C-1, D-1		Webster. John	B-1, C-2, D-2
Stout. David	B-1, D-2		Welch. James	B-1, C-2, D-1
Stout. Eleazer	B-1, D-5		Welch. Mary	C-2, D-5
Stout. Eleazer	B-1, C-2, D-2		Westcot. Josiah	B-1, C-3, D-3
Stout. George	B-2, D-2		Westcot. Samuel	B-1, C-1, D-4
Stout. George	B-1, D-4		Weston. Beniah	B-1, C-2, D-8
Stout. Levi	B-1, C-1, D-2		Wheeler. John	B-1, C-3, D-9
Stout. Levi	B-2, D-2		Willard. Jesse	B-1, C-2, D-3
Stout. Nathaniel	B-3, C-3, D-4		Woodbury. Israel	B-1, C-3, D-5
Surline. John	B-1, C-1, D-2		Woodbury. John	B-2, C-1, D-6
Thomas. Abigail	B-1, C-2, D-3		Woodbury. Lucy	C-1, D-2
Thombs. Benjamin	B-1, D-1		Woodbury. Peeter	B-1, C-1, D-2
Thompson. Robert	B-1, D-1		Wuman. Valentine	B-1, D-2
Thorndike. Christian	D-3		York. Jacob	B-1, D-1
Thorndike. Ebenezer			York. John	B-2, D-1
	B-3, D-2		York. Joseph	B-1, C-1 ,D-2
			York. Samuel	B-1, D-1

Note: All names are spelled as they appear on the original schedules.

Enumeration of inhabitants as per each census year.

1790:	1,356		1880:	5,302
1800:	1,275		1890:	5,459
1810:	1,415		1900:	887
1820:	1,688		1910:	1,857
1830:	1,695		1920:	1,534
1840:	1,666		1930:	2,376
1850:	2,082		1940:	3,172
1860:	3,278		1950:	3,816
1870:	5,106		1960:	5,505

Estimated number of inhabitants prior to census of 1790 based on number of males listed on tax polls.

1776:	1,469		1781:	1,168
1777:	1,428		1784:	1,228
1778:	1,208			

APPENDIX III

VESSELS BUILT IN CAPE ELIZABETH

Name	Tonnage	Type	Date	Builder
Adelaid	437	bark	1863	unknown
Adonis	538	ship	1850	Turner & Cahoon
Adriana	139	schooner	1852	unknown
Alice D. Cooper	1,392	ship	1875	Daniel Brewer
Artemisia	447	bark	1865	Benjamin W. Pickett
Bamberg	1,119	ship	1856	Joseph W. Dyer

Name	Tonnage	Type	Date	Builder
Black Squall	420	ship	1850	Alford Butler
Caroline Dow	515	ship	1849	Turner & Cahoon
Carrie Heckle	498	barkentine	1877	Daniel Brewer
Carthagena	146	schooner	1862	unknown
Charles Edwin	344	bark	1856	Benjamin W. Pickett
Clara Leavitt	455	schooner	1874	Daniel Brewer
Cordelia	185	brig	1810	Ezekiel Dyer
Corinthian	1,098	ship	1851	Joseph W. Dyer
Cumberland	1,066	ship	1853	Benjamin W. Pickett
Dart	42	schooner	1812	Ezekiel Dyer
Dirigo	941	steamer	1866	Nathan Dyer
Dreadnought	86	schooner	1866	Joseph W. Dyer
E. G. Willard	96	schooner	1859	unknown
Echo	864	ship	1856	Thomas E. Knight
Edith Davis	823	bark	1876	Daniel Brewer
Elizabeth	147	steam ferry	1848	Turner & Cahoon
Ellen Stevens	354	bark	1856	Benjamin W. Pickett
Elton	348	bark	1853	Thomas E. Knight
Eugenie	435	bark	1864	unknown
Ezra F. Lewis	182	schooner	1851	Thomas E. Knight
Faith	300	bark	1853	Joseph W. Dyer
Forest City	492	ship	1852	Benjamin W. Pickett
Fortunio	202	brig	1849	Turner & Cahoon
Frank Johnson	529	ship	1850	Turner & Cahoon
G. W. Carpenter	222	schooner	1861	unknown
General Berry	144	steamer	1863	unknown
General Shepley	134	steamer	1864	unknown
George Turner	518	ship	1849	Turner & Cahoon
Georgia	160	schooner	1851	Turner & Cahoon
Glenisla	549	bark	1849	unknown
Golden Sheaf	453	barkentine	1874	Daniel Brewer
Grace Deering	733	bark	1877	Daniel Brewer
Grecian	1,150	ship	1851	Turner & Cahoon
H. H. Day	49	steamer	1864	unknown
Hound	32	schooner	1813	Ezekiel Dyer
Hunter	396	bark	1862	Benjamin W. Pickett
J. G. Craig	77	schooner	1866	Joseph W. Dyer
Jasper	300	bark	1850	Turner & Cahoon
John C. Brooks	227	schooner	1854	unknown
Julia Newell	128	schooner	1852	unknown
Kate Dyer	1,278	ship	1855	Joseph W. Dyer
Kineo. U. S. S.	507	gunboat-steamer	1861	Joseph W. Dyer
Lady Woodbury	75	schooner	1866	Joseph W. Dyer
Little Eastern	32	steamer	1857	unknown
Lizzie H. Jackson	504	bark	1866	Benjamin W. Pickett
Macon	325	bark	1853	Joseph W. Dyer
Maggie Ellen	217	schooner	1874	Nathan R. Dyer
Mary W. Libby	20	steamer	1874	Nathan R. Dyer
Mary N. Locke	312	brig	1863	Benjamin W. Pickett
Mary C. Mariner	262	brig	1861	unknown
Melody	549	bark	1849	unknown
Merrimac	331	bark	1857	unknown
Orient	262	steamer	1865	unknown
Parodi	528	bark	1851	Turner & Cahoon
Phoenix	1,484	ship	1854	Thomas E. Knight
Portland	997	ship	1853	Joseph W. Dyer
Richmond		bark	1637	John Winter
Richmond		ship	1641	John Winter
Rocky Mountain	45	stone sloop	1866	unknown
Scotland	284	brig	1854	Benjamin W. Pickett
Sebago	78	steamer	1871	Nathan Dyer
Snow Squall	742	ship	1851	Alford Butler
Starlight	205	schooner	1857	unknown

Name	Tonnage	Type	Date	Builder
Thomas Owen	289	brig	1860	Benjamin W. Pickett
Triumph	125	schooner	1852	Frederick Hannaford
Uncle Sam	67	steamer	1855	unknown
United States	65	stone sloop	1868	unknown
Wallace	638	bark	1865	Nathan Dyer
Warner	500	ship	1851	Alford Butler
Wave	13	schooner	1847	unknown
White Sea	577	bark	1854	Joseph W. Dyer

APPENDIX IV

CAPE ELIZABETH SHIPWRECKS

Year	Name	Tons	Type	Site
1780	Nancy		schooner	Broad Cove
1798	Grand Turk	564	ship	Cushing's Point
1798	unknown	90	schooner	Portland Head
1798	unknown		schooner	Portland Head
1804	unknown		schooner	Peabble's Cove
1804	Apollo		brig	Trundy's Reef
1807	Charles		schooner	Watt's Ledge
1811	Resolution		sloop	Dyer's Cove
1825	Cero		brig	Alden's Rock
1829	Hannah	30	schooner	Peabble's Cove
1831	North Star		bark	Ship Cove
1832	Nancy		schooner	Spring Point Ledge
1834	United States		brig	Alden's Rock
1836	Concord		schooner	Trundy's Reef
1837	Galen		brig	Simonton's Cove
1837	President		schooner	Portland Head
1838	Macedonia		ship	Portland Head
1841	Traveler		sloop	Simonton's Cove
1843	Clarissa		schooner	Broad Cove
1843	Lighter		schooner	Simonton's Cove
1844	Echo		schooner	Richmond's Island
1844	Isidore		bark	Trundy's Reef
1847	Northerner	235	brig	Trundy's Reef
1848	Syrian		schooner	Portland Head
1848	Temperance		schooner	Portland Head
1848	Hortense		brig	Portland Head
1849	Minerva		schooner	Portland Head
1849	Cygnet		schooner	Ram Island, C. E.
1852	Ann		schooner	Stanford's Ledge
1852	Herald		schooner	Broad Cove
1852	Rose		schooner	Richmond's Island
1854	Louisa	70	schooner	Broad Cove
1854	Mary		schooner	Portland Head
1855	Foster		brig	Broad Cove
1857	Tasmania	386	bark	Broad Cove
1858	Halcyon		schooner	Broad Cove
1858	Abigail		schooner	Dyer's Cove
1862	Gannet		schooner	McKenney's Point
1863	Reaper	61	schooner	Broad Cove
1864	Bohemian	1,488	iron steamer	Broad Cove
1866	Catherine Beals		schooner	Trundy's Reef
1869	Gipsy Queen		schooner	Trundy's Reef
1869	Mary Alice		schooner	Trundy's Reef
1873	Livonia	41	schooner	Richmond's Island
1874	Oceanica		schooner	Watt's Ledge

Year	Name	Tons	Type	Site
1875	Little Fanny		schooner	Trundy's Reef
1875	Dray	68	schooner	McKenney's Point
1876	Joshua Bates	70	schooner	Stanford's Ledge
1877	Louisa Johnson	226	schooner	Pond Cove
1878	Saladin		schooner	Simonton's Cove
1879	Leesburg		schooner	Broad Cove
1879	Winnie Weston	75	schooner	Broad Cove
1884	Etna		schooner	Cranberry Cove Ledge
1884	G. & B. Morse		schooner	Trundy's Reef
1884	Casco Lodge	115	schooner	Cranberry Cove Ledge
1885	Australia	62	schooner	Dyer's Point
1885	Empire		schooner	Broad Cove
1886	Annie C. Maguire	1,363	bark	Portland Head
1888	Nellie Bowers		schooner	Richmond's Island
1889	L. A. Merryman	45	sloop	Richmond's Island
1891	Helen	120	schooner	Broad Cove
1894	Laura Cox		schooner	Broad Cove
1894	Rosa & Ada		schooner	Trundy's Reef
1894	D. K. Ham	68	schooner	Richmond's Island
1897	Winner	176	schooner	Richmond's Island
1899	Kendrick Fish	143	schooner	Danforth Cove
1901	Wendell Burpee		schooner	Broad Cove
1905	Mary Willey		schooner	Dyer's Cove
1906	Fortuna		schooner	Alden's Rock
1910	John Cadwallader	137	schooner	Watt's Ledge
1912	Empress	120	schooner	Richmond's Island
1916	Bay State	1,555	wooden steamer	McKenney's Point
1916	Go-Get-Em		schooner	Trundy's Reef
1918	Herman F. Kimball	100	schooner	Trundy's Reef
1920	Pochasset	254	schooner	Trundy's Reef
1932	Lochnivar		schooner	Portland Head
1939	Annie Mary		dragger	Richmond's Island
1947	Oakey L. Alexander	5,284	collier	High Head

Appendix V

SELECTED BIBLIOGRAPHY

General Accounts

Abbott, John S. C., & Elwell, Edward H., *The History of Maine*, Portland, 1892.

Acts and Laws of the Commonwealth of Massachusetts, 1780-1805, Boston 1890-1898, 13V.

Acts and Resolves, Public and Private, of the Province of the Massachusetts Bay, 1692-1780, Boston, 1869-1922, 21V.

Adams, Charles F. Jr., *The New English Canaan of Thomas Morton*, Prince Society, Boston, 1883.

Address and Poem Delivered at Cape Elizabeth, Maine, September 10, 1884 at the 150th Anniversary of the First Church of Christ (North Congregational), Portland, 1864.

Akagi, Roy H., *Town Proprietors of the New England Colonies*, Philadelphia, 1924.

Allen, Rev. Stephen & Pilsbury, Rev. W. H., *History of Methodism in Maine, 1793-1886*, Augusta, 1887.
Atwood, Stanley B., *The Length and Breadth of Maine*, Augusta, 1946.
Backus, Isaac, *Church History of New England from 1620-1804*, Philadelphia, 1844.
Barnes, Viola F.,*The Dominion of New England*, New Haven, 1923.
Baxter, James P., *George Cleeve of Casco Bay, 1630-67, with Collateral Documents*, Gorges Society, Portland, 1893.
Baxter, James P., *Christopher Levett of York, the Pioneer Colonist in Casco Bay*, Gorges Society, Portland, 1893.
Beers, F. W., *Atlas of Cumberland Country, Maine*, New York, 1871.
Boardman, Samuel L., *Agricultural Bibliography of Maine, 1850-1892*, Augusta, 1893.
Bodge, George M., *Soldiers in King Philip's War, 1675-77*, Boston, 1891.
Bolton, Charles K., *Scotch Irish Pioneers in Ulster and America*, Boston, 1910.
Bolton, Charles K., *The Real Founders of New England*, Boston, 1929.
Burrage, Henry S., *Beginnings of Colonial Maine, 1602-1658*, Portland, 1914.
Carnes, J. A., *A Trip to Portland*, Boston, 1859.
Census, Bureau of, *Heads of Families, First Census of U. S., 1790, Maine*, Washington, 1908.
Chadbourne, Ava H., *A History of Education in Maine*, Orono, 1936.
Chandler, Alfred N., *Land Title Origins, A Tale of Force and Fraud*, New York, 1945.
Church, Thomas, *History of King Philip's War also of Expeditions Against the French and Indians in the Eastern Parts of the New England, 1689, 1690, 1692, 1696, 1704*, Boston, 1825.
Clark, Arthur H., *The Clipper Ship Era*, New York, 1910.
Clayton W. W., *History of Cumberland County, Maine*, Philadelphia, 1880.
Coggeshall, George, *History of the American Privateers and Letters-of-Marque During Our War with England in the Years of 1812, 13 and 14*, New York, 1856.
Coleman, Emma L., *New England Captives Carried to Canada, 1677-1760*, Portland, 1925, 2V.
Collections of the Maine Historical Society, Portland, 1831-1906, 23V.
Combe, George, *Notes on the United States of North America during A Phrenological Visit in 1838-39-40*, Edinburgh, 1841, 3V.
Coolidge, A. D., & Mansfield, J. B., *History and Descriptions of New England*, Boston, 1860.
Cutler, Carl C., *Greyhounds of the Sea; The Story of the American Clipper Ship*, New York, 1930.
Douglas-Lithgow, R. A., *A Dictionary of American-Indian Place and Proper Names in New England*, Salem, 1909.
Drake, Samuel G., *The Witchcraft Delusion in New England, Its Rise, Progress, and Termination as Exhibited by Dr. Cotton Mather in the Wonders of the Invisible World; and by Mr. Robert Calef in His More Wonders of the Invisible World*, Roxbury, 1866, 3V.
Drake, Samuel G., *The Book of the Indians to 1641*, Boston, 1841.

Dunnack, Henry E., *The Maine Book*, Augusta, 1920.
Dunnack, Henry E., *Maine Forts*, Augusta, 1924.
Eckstorm, Fannie H., "Indian Place-Names of the Penobscot Valley and Maine Coast," *University of Maine Studies, Second Series, No. 55*, Orono, 1941.
Ellis, George E., *The Puritan Age and Rule in the Colony of the Masschusetts Bay, 1629-1685*, Boston, 1886.
Elwell, Edward H., *Portland and Vicinity*, Portland, 1881.
Elwell, Edward H., *The Successful Business Houses of Portland*, Portland, 1875.
Elwell, Edward H., *The Schools of Portland from the Earliest Times to the Centennial Year of the Town*, Portland, 1886.
Fairlie, John A., *Local Government in Counties, Towns, and Villages*, New York, 1906.
Felt, Joseph B., *The Ecclesiastical History of New England*, Boston, 1855, 1862, 2V.
Felt, Joseph B., *The Customs of New England*, Boston, 1853.
Folsom, George, *Catalogue of Original Documents in the English Archives relating to the Early History of the State of Maine*, New York, 1858.
Forbes, Harriette M., *New England Diaries, 1602-1800, A Descriptive Catalogue of Diaries, Orderly Books and Sea Journals*, Topsfield, Massachusetts, 1923.
Freeman, Samuel, *The Town Officer*, Boston, 1802.
Freeman, Samuel, *Extracts from the Journals kept by the Rev. Thomas Smith, late Paster of the First Church of Christ of Falmouth, in the county of York, now Cumberland. From the year 1720 to the year 1788 with an Appendix contaniing a Variety of Other Matters*, Portland, 1821.
Gardiner, Henry, *New England's Vindication*, Charles E. Banks, editor, Gorges Society, Portland, 1884.
Goold, William, *Portland in the Past with Historical Notes of Old Falmouth* Portland, 1886.
Grant, W. L., *Voyages of Samuel De Champlain 1604-1618*, New York, 1907.
Greene, Evarts B. & Harrington, Virginia, *American Population Before the Federal Census of 1790*, New York, 1932.
Greene, Lorenzo J., *The Negro in New England, 1620-1776*, New York, 1942.
Greenleaf, Jonathan, *Sketches of the Ecclesiastical History of the State of Maine, from the Earliest Settlement to the Present Time*, Portsmouth, 1821.
Greenleaf, Moses, *A Survey of the State of Maine*, Portland, 1829.
Greenleaf, Moses, *A Statistical View of the District of Maine*, Boston, 1916.
Handbook of Incorporations, Dissolutions, and Boundary Changes in the Counties, Ctiies, Towns, and Plantations of Maine, Maine Historical Records Survey, unp., 1940.
Hayward, John, *The New England Gazetteer*, Boston, 1839.
Historical Address, Sermon, Poem, and Hymn Read at the One Hundred and Seventy-fifth Anniversary of the First Congregational Church and Parish of South Portland and Cape Elizabeth, 1734-1909, Portland, 1909.

Hosmer, James, *Winthrop's Journal History of New England, 1630-1649*, New York, 1908, 2V.
Hubbard, Rev. William, *History of the Indian Wars in New England from 1607-1677*, Roxbury, 1865, 2V.
Hull, John T., *Hand-Book of Portland, Old Orchard, Cape Elizabeth, and Casco Bay*, Portland, 1888.
Hull, John T., *Directory of the City of Portland and of the Towns of Cape Elizabeth, Deering, Westbrook, and Falmouth for A. D. 1882. Being the 250th Anniversary of the Settlement of those Towns which Comprise the Territory of "Ancient Falmouth"*, Portland, 1882.
Hutchinson, Thomas, *The History of Massachusetts from the First Settlement Thereof in 1628 until the Year 1750*, Boston, 1795, 2V.
Hutchinson, Thomas, *The History of the Province of Massachusetts Bay from the Year 1750 until June, 1774*, London, 1828.
Hutchinson, Thomas, *A Collection of Original Papers Relative to the History of the Colony of Massachusetts Bay*, Boston, 1769.
Index to the Private and Special Laws Enacted by the Legislatures of the State of Maine from 1820 to 1944, Inclusive, Augusta, 1944.
Jackson, Charles T., *First Report on the Geology of the State of Maine*, Augusta, 1837.
Jewell, Margaret H., "The Fair at Scarboro, Maine," *Old Time New England*, Boston, 1933, V.23.
Johnson, Allen, *The Archives of the State of Maine*, Washington, 1910.
Jones, E. Alfred, *The Loyalists of Massachusetts, their Memorials, Petitions, and Claims*, London, 1930.
Jordan, Tristram F., *The Jordan Memorials Family Records of the Rev. Robert Jordan and his Descendants in America*, Boston, 1882.
Josselyn, John, *An Account of Two Voyages to New England, 1636 & 1663*, Boston, 1865.
Kingsbury, Benjamin, *The Maine Townsman*, Portland, 1858.
Libby, Charles T., editor, *Province and Court Records of Maine*, Portland, 1928, 1931, & 1947, 3V.
Lord, John P., *Reference Book of the State of Maine, 1845*, Portland, 1845.
McMurtrie, Douglas C., *Maine Imprints, 1792-1820, An Open Letter to R. Webb Noyes*, Chicago, 1935.
Maclay, Edgar S., *A History of American Privateers*, New York, 1899.
Maine at Valley Forge: Proceedings at the Unveiling of the Maine Marker October 17, 1907; Also Roll of Maine Men at Valley Forge, Augusta, 1910.
Maine Historical and Genealogical Recorder, Portland, 1884-1898, 3V.
Manuscripts in Public and Private Collections in the United States, Washington, 1924.
Mather, Cotton, *Magnalia Christi Americana, or the Ecclesiastical History of New England, 1620-1698*, Hartford, 1820, 2V.
Mather, Increase, *The History of King Philip's War. Also, a History of the Same War by Rev. Cotton Mather*, Samuel G. Drake, editor, Boston, 1862.
Matthews, Frederick C., *American Merchant Ships, 1850-1900*, Salem, 1930 & 1931, 2V.
Maverick, Samuel, *A Brief Description of New England, 1660*, John W. Dean, editor, Boston, 1885.
Millet, Joshua, *A History of the Baptists in Maine*, Portland, 1845.

Moody, Lemuel, *A Chart of the Portland Harbour and Islands and Harbours Adjacent standing from the River Kennebeck to Wood Island and Winter Harbour, drawn from the Survey of DesBarres, with Additions and Corrections,* 1825.
Neal, Daniel, *History of New England, to 1700,* London, 1747, 2V.
Neal, John, *Portland Illustrated,* Portland, 1874.
Noyes, R. Webb, *A Bibliography of Maine Imprints to 1820,* Stonington, Maine, 1930.
Noyes, Sybil; Libby, Charles T., & Davis, Walter G., *Genelogical Dictionary of Maine and New Hampshire,* Portland, 1929.
Palfrey, John G., *History of New England,* Boston, 1876-1890, 4V.
Pearson, Gardner W., *Records of the Massachusetts Militia in the War of 1812-14,* Boston, 1913.
Penhallow, Samuel, *History of the Wars of New England with the Eastern Indians, 1703-1726,* Cincinnati, 1859.
Perry, William S., *The Connection of the Church of England with Early American Discovery and Colonization,* Portland, 1863.
Pope, Charles H., *The Pioneers of Maine and New Hampshire, 1623-1660,* Boston, 1908.
Porter, C. F., *A Brief History of Works Erected for the Defense of Portland, Maine,* Washington, 1905.
Reynolds, Edward C., *The Cape Elizabeth High School: A History,* Portland, 1892.
Ring, Elizabeth, "A Reference List of Manuscripts Relating to the History of Maine," *University of Maine Studies, Second Series, No. 45,* Orono, 1938-1941, 3V.
Robinson, John & Dow, George F., *The Sailing Ships of New England, 1607-1907,* Salem, Massachusetts, 1922, 1924, 1928, 3V.
Rosier's Relation of Weymouth's Voyage to the Coast of Maine, 1605.
Rowe, William H., *Shipbuilding Days in Casco Bay, 1727-1890,* Yarmouth, Maine, 1929.
Rowe, William H., *The Maritime History of Maine,* New York, 1948.
Ryerson, Egerton, *The Loyalists of America and their Times, 1620-1816,* Toronto, 1880.
Sabin, Joseph, *Dictionary of Books Relating to America, from its Discovery to the Present Time,* New York, 1868-1934, 29V.
Sabine, Lorenzo, *Biographical Sketches of Loyalists of the American Revolution,* Boston, 1864.
Sargent, William M., editor, *Maine Wills, 1640-1760,* Portland, 1887.
Scammon, Stephen, *History of Hiram Lodge, No. 180, of Free and Accepted Masons, Cape Elizabeth, Maine,* Portland, 1892.
Sewall, Rufus K., *Ancient Dominions of Maine,* Bath, 1859.
Smith, Captain John, *The General Histories of Virginia, New England, and the Summer Isles, 1584-1626,* Glasgow, 1907, 2V.
Spencer, Wilbur D., *Pioneers on Maine Rivers,* Portland, 1930.
Sprague's Journal of Maine History, Dover-Foxcroft, Maine, 1913-1926, 14V.
Stark, James H., *The Loyalists of Massachusetts,* Boston, 1910.
Sullivan, James, *History of the District of Maine,* Boston, 1795.
Thayer, Henry O., *The Sagadahoc Colony,* Gorges Society, Portland, 1892.
Tuttle, Charles W., *Capt. John Mason,* Prince Society, Boston, 1887.

Upham Charles W., *Lectures on Witchcraft, Comprising a History of the Relusion in Salem in 1692*, Boston, 1831.
Upham, Charles W., *Salem Witchcraft*, Boston, 1867, 2V.
Varney, George J., *A Gazetteer of the State of Maine*, Boston, 1881.
Wade, Herbert T., *Brief History of the Colonial Wars in America, 1607-1775*, New York, 1948.
Weeden, William B., *Economic and Social History of New England, 1620-1789*, New York, 1890, 2V.
Wemyss, Stanley, *General Guide to Rare Americana*, Philadelphia, 1944, 2V.
Whipple, Joseph, *A Geographical View of the District of Maine*, Bangor, 1816.
Whitman, William E. S. & True, Charles H., *Maine in the War for the Union, A History of the Part Borne by Maine Troops in the Suppression of the American Rebellion*, Lewiston, 1865.
Whitmore, William H., *The Massachusetts Civil List for the Colonial and Provincial Periods, 1636-1774*, Albany, 1870.
Willard, Captain Benjamin J., *Life History and Adventures of Capt. B. J. Willard*, Portland, 1895.
Williamson, Joseph, *A Bibliography of the State of Maine from the Earliest Period to 1891*, Portland, 1896, 2V.
Willis, William, *Guide Book for Portland and Vicinity to which is Appended a Summary History of Portland*, Portland, 1859.
Willis, William, *Journals of the Rev. Thomas Smith and the Rev. Samuel Deane, Pastors of the First Church in Portland with Notes and a Summary History of Portland*, Portland, 1849.
Willis, William, "Maine; A Descriptive Catalogue of Books and Pamphlets relating to the History and Statistics of Maine, or Portions of it," *Norton's Literary Letter*, No. 4, New York, 1859.
Willis, William, *History of the Law, the Courts, and the Lawyers of Maine from its First Colonization to the Early Part of the Present Century*, Portland, 1863.
Willis, William, *The History of Portland from 1632 to 1864; with a Notice of Previous Settlements, Colonial Grants, and Changes of Government in Maine*, Portland, 1865.
Willis, William, *Scrap Book*, Maine Historical Society, unp. n.d.
Winship, George P., *Sailors Narratives of Voyages along the New England Coast, 1524-1624*, Boston, 1905.
Winthrop, John, *History of New England from 1630-1649*, James Savage, editor, Boston, 1853, 2V.
Wood, Isaiah, *The Massachusetts Compendium*, Hallowell, 1814.
Wood, William, *New Englands Prospect*, Prince Society, Boston, 1865.
York Deeds, 1641-1737, Portland, 1887-1896, Bethel, 1903-1910, 18V.
Young, Alexander, *Chronicles of the First Planters of the Colonoy of Massachusetts Bay, 1623-1636*, Boston, 1846.

NEWSPAPERS

Cape Elizabeth Sentinel, Cape Elizabeth, 1881-1912, scattered numbers.
Coast Watch, Cape Elizabeth, 1895-1916.
Cumberland Gazette, Falmouth, 1789-1791.

Eastern Argus, Portland, 1803-1921, 249V.
Eastern Herald, Falmouth, 1792-1796.
Eastern Herald and Gazette of Maine, Falmouth, 1796-1800.
Eastern Herald and Maine Gazette, Falmouth, 1801-1803.
Falmouth Gazette and Weekly Advertiser, Falmouth, 1785-1786.
Portland Advertiser, Portland, 1831-1852, 22V.
Portland Daily Press, Portland, 1862-1921, 30V.
Portland Evening Express, Portland, 1885-1965.
Portland Press Herald, Portland, 1921-1965.
Portland Sunday Telegram, Portland, 1920-1965.
Portland Sunday Times, Portland, 1900-1924, 26V.
Portland Transcript, Portland, 1837-1910, 64V.

MANUSCRIPTS

Ancient Records of Cape Elizabeth, 1765-1823, South Portland City Hall.
Baxter, James P., *Transcripts of the Early Records of the Province of Maine, 1636-1686,* Maine Historical Society, n.d.
Cushman, Hosea L., *Diary of Hosea Lewis Cushman, who died at Cape Elizabeth and is buried in the graveyard of the North Meeting House, Journal kept during the Seminole War in Florida, 6 February 1836 to 15 February 1837,* Maine Historical Society, n.d.
Heseltine, Charles D., *History of the Portland Railroad Company,* Maine Historical Society, n.d.
Mayberry, Stephen P., *Miscellaneous Notes and Papers on Cape Elizabeth* Maine Historical Society, n.d.
Meeds, Melvil F., *Early Settlers of Richmond's Island,* Maine Historical Society, n.d.
Noyes, R. Webb, *A Guide to the Study of Maine Local History,* Maine Historical Society, 1951.
Parkinson, Rev. Royal, *History of Cape Elizabeth,* Maine Historical Society, 1846.
Proceedings of the Temperance Watchman Club No. 49 of Cape Elizabeth, Maine, 7 March 1850 — 3 June 1854, Mrs. Fred P. Murray, Cape Elizabeth, Maine.
Smith, F. O. J., *Miscellaneous Notes and Papers,* Maine Historical Society, n.d.
Town Records of Cape Elizabeth, 1823-1895, South Portland City Hall, 4V.
Willis, William, *Miscellaneous Notes and Papers relating to the History of Portland and Vicinity,* Maine Historical Society, n.d., 29V.
Willis, William, *Scotch-Irish Immigration to Maine,* Maine Historical Society, n.d.
Woodbury, Benjamin J., *Miscellaneous Notes and Papers on Cape Elizabeth,* Maine Historical Society, n.d.

INDEX

INDEX

Adonis, ship 203
Agriculture 53, 123-126
  see also: Richmond's Island Plantation
Aiken. Rev. James E. 307
Alden's Rock 237-238, 246
Alewive Brook 40, 53
Alewive fishery 65, 189
Alexander. Charles A. 139, 149
Alice D. Cooper, ship 217
Allen. Rev. Benjamin 35, 38, 288-291
Andros. Sir Edmund 25
Angel Gabriel, ship 166
Anglican Church 12, 16, 275-279
  see also: Episcopal Church
    Gibson. Rev. Richard
    Jordan. Rev. Robert
Annie C. Maguire, bark 228, 251
Anville. Duc de 36
Apollo, brig 245-246
Archibald. George H. 149
Argonaut Association. Portland 155
Armstrong. Joseph W. 160
Artemisia, bark 203
Australia, schooner 249-251

Bagaduce Expedition 49, 293-294
Bagnall. Walter 3-4, 8, 76
Baker. Harry E. 161, 351
Bamberg, ship 211
Band. Cape Elizabeth 349
Band. Cape Elizabeth Fire
  Department 348-349
Band. Knightville 103
Band. Ligonia Cornet 102-103
Band. Merriman's 102, 115
Band. Poppenberg's 78
Band. Town House 102
Band. Union Brass 101-102
Baptists 312-314
Barberry Creek 29, 34
Barren Hill 258, 263, 310
Baxter. James P. 112
Bay State, steamer 251-254
Bay View Cemetery 67
Bayley. Robert 34, 257
Beard. Rev. A.F. 307
Beckett. Sylvester B. 149-150
Beckett's Castle 150
Belfield 151
Bellamy. Samuel 32
Belmont House 154
Bennett. Cornelius 256
Berry. Capt. Charles W. 243
Berry. Jeremiah 231
Black Squall, clipper bark 213

Blanchard. Nathaniel 215-217
Bluff Cottage Club 147-148
Board of Trade. Cape Elizabeth 112
Bohemian, steamer 246-249
Bounty. Fishery 181-182
Bounty. Revolutionary War 48, 50-51
Bower. The 130-131, 263-264
  see also: Bowery House
Bowery Beach 99, 102, 131, 141,
  156, 253, 263, 270, 273, 342
  see also: Cape Cove
    Cape Sands
    Crescent Beach
    Long Sands
    Seal Cove
Bowery Beach Association 339, 340, 341
Bowery Beach Methodist
  Church 311-312
Bowery House 131
Bradshaw. Richard 7-8
Brewer. Daniel 217
Breakwater Light 236
Breakwater. Portland 202, 235-236
Breakwater. Richmond's
  Island 236-237
Brewery 89-90
Brickyard. Dyer's 90
Bridge. Long Creek 55, 64, 69
Bridge, Mill Creek 62
Bridge. Portland 61-63, 72-74,
  93-94, 106, 111, 215, 220
Bridge. Spurwink 65
Bridge. Stroudwater 39
Bridge. Vaughan's 54-55, 62, 65,
  73-74, 95
Briggs. Rev. Richard 298
Brigs. West India 178
Broad Cove Rock 238, 246
Brooklyn, steamer 221
Brooks Arms & Tool Company 111
Broughton. Capt. Billy 153
Brown. George W. 334-337,351
Brown. Harrison B. 150
Brown. John B. 90, 92, 179, 215
Brown's Hill 263
Brown's Hill Methodist Church 310
Bryant. Jonathan 224
Budget Committee 352
Bug Light
  see: Breakwater Light
Bull. Dixie 4
Bulwark. H.M.S. 58, 176
Burgess. John 3
Burrage. Dr. Thomas J. 253
Burroughs. Rev. George 28, 280-285

377

Butler. Alford	213-214
Butler. Cornelius B.	213
Buzzell. Dr. John	267
Cabo de Muchas Isles	1
Cahoon. James B.	72, 107, 202-203
Caleb Cushing Affair	81-83
Calvary Cemetery	249, 314
Calvinists. New Light	291-292
Calvinists. Old Light	291-292
Cameron. John W.	230
Cammock. Thomas	8, 18
Camp Abraham Lincoln	79
Camp Berry	78-81, 88, 248
Camp Ground	89
Campus. Pond Cove	274
Canadian Tourists	142, 144, 152-153
Canal. Cape Elizabeth	63
Cape Cottage. The	132-141
Cape Cottage Beach	345
Cape Cottage Casino	156-157, 160-161
Cape Cottage Company	132
Cape Cottage Hotel	162
Cape Cottage Park	160-161, 337, 342, 351
Cape Cottage Woods	351
Cape Cove	130, 141
see also: Bowery Beach	
Cape Elizabeth, City Charter	121-122
Cape Elizabeth. District of	38-40
Cape Elizabeth Lights	230-235
Cape Elizabeth, Named	2-3
Cape Elizabeth — Portland. Union of	120-121
Cape Elizabeth — South Portland Separation	120, 122-123
Cape Elizabeth. Town of	46, 53, 55-56, 59, 61, 69, 73, 87, 117, 119, 317-318
Cape Sands	141
see also: Bowery Beach	
Cape Shore Civic Association	328-329, 342, 346, 347
Cape Shore Community Club	350
Cape Steam Station	221
Carnes. J.A.	71, 123, 139, 142-143, 181
Caroline Dow, ship	203
Carrie Heckle, barkentine	217
Casco Bay Lines	112
Casco River	13, 30
see also: Fore River	
Cash's Corner	118, 120
Casket. The	104
Casualities. Civil War	80
Catholic Church	314
Cemeteries	
see: Bay View Cemetery	
Calvary Cemetery	
Mount Pleasant Cemetery	
Riverside Cemetery	
Riverside Memorial Park	
Seaside Cemetery	
Central House	162
Chamberlain. Abia	141-142
Chamberlain. Joseph P.	142-144
Chaplain. Samuel de	1-2

Channelside	343
Charles, schooner	246
Charles Edwin, bark	203
Charles I	2, 12, 16, 21
Charles II	23, 24, 25
Chaves. Alonso de	1
Chebacco Boat	184-186
Chipman. Lyman B.	148
Church. Maj. Benjamin	29, 30
Church. North Congregational	114, 288-308
see also: Parish. Second Meeting House (1734)	
Church. Puritan	277-286
Church of England	
see: Anglican Church	
Civil War	77-86, 180-181
see also: **Caleb Cushing** affair	
Camp Berry	
Execution. Military	
Fort Preble	
Clam Fishery	199-200
Clam. Scarborough	153, 199
Clara Leavitt, schooner	217
Clark. Rev. Ephraim	38, 40-41, 46, 53, 291-295
Cleaves. George	7-9, 13, 17-18, 20-24
Cliff Cottage	151, 152
Cliff House	152, 346
Clippers. Mud	176-177
Coal and Railroad Company. Portland and Cape Elizabeth	66
Coal Mines	66-67
Coast Watch. Revolutionary War	45, 47-48, 105
Coast Guard. U.S.	235, 242-243, 254
Cobb. Morris	306
Cod Fishery	182-189, 191-193
Combe. George	131-136
Combe. Cecilia Siddons	134-135
Committees of Correspondence	42-46, 53
Committees of Inspection	45-46
Committee of Safety	46, 53
Commissioners of American Plantations	12
Conant. Frederick O.	339
Congregationalists	38
Continental Army Quota	48, 50-51
Coolidge. John W.	226
Cordelia, brig	202
Corinthean, ship	208-210
Cornelia H., steam ferry	110-112
Cornwall. Rev. William	286
Cottage Farms	351-352
Cottage Farms School	272-274
Council for New England	
see: Plymouth Company	
Country Club. Portland	350
Cragmoor	149
Crescent Beach	141, 342
see also: Bowery Beach	
Cromwell. Oliver	17
Cushing. Col. Ezekiel	35-36, 38, 167-170, 201, 258, 291-293

Cushing. Loring 40-41, 169, 258-259
Cushing's Point 37
Cutter. William 238
Cumberland, ship 203
Cummings. Dr. John M. 143, 236
Cunner Club 145-147
D.W. Hammond, schooner 228
Dalton. Charles B. 152, 342
Danforth. Thomas 25
Dart, privateer 174-175, 202
Davis. Nathan 232
Dearborn. Gen. Henry 61, 225, 230
Decade of Sorrows
  see: King William's War
Declaration of Independence 47
Deering Enterprise 105
Deering, Nathaniel F. 210
Delano. Barzillai 224-225
Delano. James 226
Delano. Thomas 34, 225
Delano Brook 34
Delano Park 150-151
Delano Park Association 150
Depot. Cape Elizabeth 68-69, 76, 88
Diking Corporation. Cape Elizabeth 93
Diking Corporation. Scarborough
  and Cape Elizabeth 61
Diptheria
  see: Throat Distemper
Dirigo, steamer 212
Dog Corner
  see: Willard
Dogbody 184-185
Dory Fishing 191-192
Dow. Neal 111
Down Easter 205
Drail Fishing 189-190
Dreadnought, canal barge 212
Dry Dock and Warehouse Company.
  Portland 219-221
Dudley. Joseph 25
Duke of Richmond 14
Duncan. Dave 225
Dyer. Ezekiel 174, 201-202, 208-209
Dyer. Joseph W. 107, 208-212, 218
Dyer. Lemuel 201, 209-210
Dyer. Mark, Jr. 173-174
Dyer. Nathan 212, 218
Dyer. Nathan R. 211-212, 219
Dyer. Sumner N. 241, 243-244, 252
Dyer's Cove 231, 235, 240, 243
Dyer's Point 242, 250

Eastern Steamship Company 251
Echo, ship 217
Edith Davis, bark 217
Education 256-274
Elementary Schools 270-274
Elizabeth, steam ferry
  107-108, 112, 203, 210
Elizabeth Park 353-354
Elizabeth, Queen of Bohemia 3
Ellen Stevens, bark 203
Elm Street Methodist Church 310

Elton, bark 215
Elwell. Edward H. 150
Embargo Era 172-173
Embargo Forts 57
Emery Highlands 335
Epidemics
  see: Small Pox
     Throat Distemper
Episcopal Church 314-315
  see also: Anglican Church
Esty. Rev. Isaac 299-303
Evergreens. Point Village 113
Execution. Military 83-85
Extracting Company. Portland 98-99
Ezra F. Lewis, schooner 215

Faith, bark 210
Falmouth 24, 27-28, 30-31
Falmouth. Second Parish of
  34-35, 37-39
Falmouth. Town of 32, 34-35, 41-42, 46
Fassett. Francis H. 97, 98
Fellowship, ship 166
Ferry. Cape Elizabeth 107-108, 110-112
Ferry. Nonecusk 29
Ferry. Purpooduck 29, 33, 105-106
  see also: Ferry. Cape Elizabeth
Ferry. Spurwink 28-29
Ferry Company. Cape Elizabeth
  Steam 108
Ferry Company. People's 109-112
Ferry Company. Portland & Cape
  Elizabeth (No. 1) 107
Ferry Company. Portland & Cape
  Elizabeth (No. 2) 108-110, 112
Ferry Village 72, 87, 100-102, 104,
  107-113, 115-116, 118, 120, 170, 174,
  180, 201-204, 208-209, 218-219, 262-263
Fickett. Joseph S. 266
Field. Edwin L. 161-162
Files. Edwin R. 351
Fish Pound 193
Fisheries 165-167, 171, 181-200
  see also: Mariner. John
         Richmond's Is. Plantation
         Simonton. William
Fishing Grounds 182
Fire Protection 115, 343, 346-349
  see also:
  Hose Company No. 1. Volunteer
  Hose Company No. 2. Willard
  Hose Company. Knightville
  Hose Company No. 1. Cape Elizabeth
  Hose Company No. 2. Cape Elizabeth
Five Years War
  see: French and Indian War
Fore River 27, 205, 208
  see also: Casco River
Forest City, ship 203
Forest City Steamboat Company 110
Fort Hancock 47-48, 51, 53, 56
Fort Point 36
Fort Preble 34, 56-59, 77-78, 80, 82-85
  see also: Fort Hancock
Fort Williams 152, 156, 272,
  319-331, 343

Fortune, ship	14
Fortunio, brig	203
Foss. Alexander	138
Frank Johnson, ship	203
Freeman. Daniel	225, 232
Freeman. Joshua	130, 225, 227
French & Indian War	35-36
Friends Meeting House	67
Garbage Collection	353
Gardiner. Alliston F.	332
George Turner, ship	203
Georgia, schooner	203
Gibson, Rev. Richard	12-13, 16, 276-277
Gilbert. Raleigh	2, 5
Gill Nets	190
Glen Cottage	151-152
Glen Cove	149
Goddard. Charles W.	140
Goddard. Henry	107
Goddard. John	139-140
Goddard. Lydia L.	140
Goddard Mansion	139-140
Golden Cross. United Order of the	101
Golden Sheaf, barkentine	217
Good Templars. Independent Order of	99-100
Goodwin. Solomon	293
Goodyear. Moses	8, 13, 165, 276
Gorges. Sir Ferdinando	5-9, 12-13, 16-17, 21, 165, 276
Gorges. Ferdinando, II	24-25
Gorges. John	21
Gorges. Thomas	17
Gorges. Capt. William	12, 17
Governor Dudley's War see: Queen Anne's War	
Governor Dummer's War	33
Governor Shirley's War see: French and Indian War	
Grace Deering, bark	217
Grand Turk, ship	244-245
Grammer School. Pond Cove	271-272
see also: Primary School. Pond Cove	
Grand Banks	181
Grange Hall	317
Graesmere	149
Great Awakening	290-291
Great Pond	63, 127, 130, 338-341
Great Pond Gun Club	338, 344
Great Pond Law	338, 339-340
Great Pond Mining and Agricultural Company	69-71, 338-340
Grecian, schooner	203
Greenleaf. Capt. Joseph	225
Gregg. Rev. William	61, 260, 295-299
Gridiron of Death	74, 93
Gulick. Maj. Gen. John W.	149
Gun Club. Cape Elizabeth	113, 341
Gurry Cove	192-193
see also: Simonton's Cove	
H.H. Day, steam Ferry	108
Haddock Fishery	192
Hanna. Marcus A.	105, 233, 250

Hannaford. Frederick	221
Halibut Fishery	188
Hamlin. Simon M.	272
Harlow. Rev. Edwin A.	263, 307
Hawkes. D. Winslow	266
Hawkins. Narius	11-14, 200
Hercules, ship	13, 15, 19, 166
Herring Fishery	188, 191
High Head	40, 58, 163, 241
High School. Cape Elizabeth	266-270
Hill. Edward F.	266
Hilt. Frank O.	230
Hiram Lodge	101
Hodge. Nicholas	257
Hoke & Farley	193
Holt. Harrison	140
Holycomb Reef	251
Holyoke. Rev. Eleazer	38
Hooper. Rev. Noah	312
Horse Marine	176-177
Hose Company No. 1, Volunteer	115-116
Hose Company No 2, Willard	116, 346, 347
Hose Company. Knightville	116-117
Hose Company No. 1, Cape Elizabeth	346-347, 348
Hose Company No. 2. Cape Elizabeth	347, 348
Hound, schooner	202
House of Correction	65
Hudson. John B.	150
Huntcliffe	149
Hunter, bark	203
Hunter, ship	10, 166
Hurd. Rev. John C.	305
Iberian Trade see: Richmond's Island Plantation	
Indians	12
Indian Killer. The see: Jordan. Dominicus	
Indian trade	10
Indian Wars see: French & Indian War Governor Dummer's War King Philip's War King William's War Queen Anne's War Seven Years War	
Inebriates. Home for	344-345
Impressment	173-174
Ironclad Club	148-149
Isidore, bark	244
Island Mile Track	127
Isle de Bacchus	2
J.G. Craig, canal barge	212
Jackson. George E.B.	92
James I	5
James, ship	11, 166
Jasper, bark	203
Jones. Dr. Nathaniel	294
Jordan. Dominicus	30-31
Jordan. Maj. Dominicus	36
Jordan. Elder	226

Jordan. Elisha	232
Jordan. James P.	306
Jordan. Col. Nathaniel	49, 293-294
Jordan. Rev. Robert	19-20, 22-24, 27-28, 277-279, 315
Jordan. Tristram F.	123
Jordan. William	232
Josephine Hoey, steamer	108, 112
Josselyn. Henry	14, 21-24, 28, 280
Josselyn. John	14-15, 167, 193
Kaler. James Otis	272
Kate Dyer, ship	211
Kelley. Rev. George	307-308
Kellog. Rev. Elijah, Jr.	183-184
Kerosene Works. Portland	90
Kimball. Charles F.	150
Kineo. U.S.S.	211-212
King George's War	
see: French & Indian War	
King Philip's War	27-28
King William's War	29-31
King's Highway	28-29, 33, 37, 288
Knight. Robert W.	215
Knight. Thomas E.	72, 87, 215-217
Knights. S.C.	265-266
Knights of Labor	103
Knights of Maccabees	162
Knights of Pythias	101
Knightville	72, 87, 102-103, 116, 118, 217, 263
Ladies Aid Society. Ferry Village	113
Lady Woodbury, canal barge	212
Laird. William H.	83-85
Launching Print — 1855	210-211
Lawrence's Creek	34
Lee. Richard	225
Ledge House	148
Ledgelawn	149
Leighton. Llewellyn	351
Leverett. Gov. John	25
Levett. Christopher	3
Library Association. Thomas Memorial	349
Library. Jordan	123
Library. Thomas Memorial	349-350
Lighthouse Duty	224
Lighthouses	
see: Breakwater Light	
Cape Elizabeth Lights	
Portland Head Light	
Lifesaving Station. Cape Elizabeth	239-242, 252-253
Lightship, No. 74. Cape Elizabeth	238
Lightship. Portland	239
Ligonia	88-89, 118, 120, 127
Ligonia Irons	89
Lincoln. Benjamin	225
Lion, ship	166
Little Eastern, steam ferry	108
Lizzie H. Jackson, bark	204
Lobster Boats	196
Lobster Canneries	197-198
Lobster Conservation	197-198
Lobster Fishery	189, 193-199
Lobster Pot	194-196, 198
Lobster Smacks	189, 196-197
London Company	5
Long Creek	28-29, 34-36, 40, 258, 263-264, 284
Long Creek Bridge	40
Long Point	146-147
Long Sands	28
see also: Bowery Beach	
Longfellow. Alexander W.	237
Longfellow. Henry W.	130, 228
Lord Palatine	
see: Gorges. Sir Ferdinando	
Lord. Rev. C.E.	307
Loring. Charles	149
Loring. Prentiss	148-149
Losses. Revolutionary War	51-52
Lovell Arms Company. John P.	98
Lunt. Robert B.	274
Lygonia Patent	7, 20
see also: Province of Lygonia	
Machigonne	13, 18, 20, 23
Machine Works. Portland	233
Mackeral Fishery	189-190
Mackworth. Arthur	23
Macon, bark	210
Madockawando	30
Maggie Ellen, schooner	212
Maiden Cove	132-133, 137-138, 161-162
Maiden Cove Improvement Association	345
Margery, ship	166
Mail Delivery. Rural Free	332
Mann. Horace	134
Marine Railway. Cape Elizabeth Wharf and	218
Marine Railway. Portland	218
Marine Railway. Portland Merchants	219
Mariner. John	170
Mariner. Joseph	170
Mariner. Silas	170-171
Marks. Allen M.	356
Mary N. Locke, brig	203
Mary W. Libby, steamer	108, 110, 112, 212
Mason. Capt. John	4, 6
Masonic Lodge	101
Massachusetts Bay Colony	17, 23-25
Massachusetts. Separation from	59-60
Mather. Rev. Richard	11
McClenathan. Rev. William	287
McCullum. Bartley	157-159
McKenney. Freeman	244
McKenney's Point	251
Meeting House. Purpooduck	287-288
Meeting House. Second Parish (1734)	35, 67, 288-289, 295-296
Meeting House. Spurwink	296-297, 304-305, 309
Merrill. Rev. Horatio	307
Merrill. Rev. Josiah G.	303-304
Methodists	309-312
see also: Pierce. Rev. William	

381

Militia. Cape Elizabeth	58-59
Militia Musters	65-66
Mill Creek	92
see also: Lawrence Creek	
Millerites	305-306
Millett. S.C.	263-264
Ministerial Fund. Cape Elizabeth	298
Minute Men. Revolutionary War	43, 45
Mitchell. Rev. David M.	305
Molasses Trade	178-179
Monts. Sieur de	1
Mormons	306
Morton. Thomas	3
Mount Pleasant Cemetery	35, 63, 113, 169, 288
Mountain View Park	334-337, 342-343, 351
Movie Companies	162-163
Mowatt. Capt. Henry	46, 171
Murray. Alonzo S.	40, 357
Murray. William D.	355
Nancy, schooner	50-51, 244
Nativism	
see: Golden Cross. United Order of the Sons of America. Patriotic Order of the	
Neal. John	132-134, 137, 139, 231, 285, 299
Neale. Francis	24
Neale. Capt. Walter	4, 7, 9
Negro Slaves	168, 169
Neutral Profits Trade	171-172
New England Company	
see: Plymouth Company	
New Proprietors	32-33
New Somersetshire	12, 17
Nichols. Col. Andrew J.	144-145
Nichols. John	224
Oakey L. Alexander, collier	226, 254-255
Oakhurst Park	351
Ocean House	141-145, 247
Old Proprietors	32-33
Ottawa Park	152
Owl's Nest	162, 343
Palatine of Maine	
see: Province of Maine	
Parish. Second	
see: Falmouth. Second Parish of	
Park. Crescent Beach State	163
Park. Two Lights State	163
Parkinson. Rev. Royal	306-307
Parodi, bark	203
Passamaquoddy Trade	173, 174
Patterson. Charles R.	351
Patrons of Husbandry	103-104
Peabbles Cove	147, 162
Peverly. John	3-4
Phoenix, clipper ship	216
Pickett. Benjamin W.	107, 202-204, 211, 219, 227
Picnic House	153

Pierce. Rev. William	305
Pierpont. Rev. Jonathan	287
Pillsbury Bluffs	351
Pinky	185-188, 191-192
Pirates	
see: Bellamy. Samuel Bull. Dixie Williams. Capt. Paul	
Planning Board	354
Pleasantdale	88, 118, 120, 263
Plough Patent	
see: Lygonia Patent	
Plush Mill	98
Plymouth Company	5-8, 12, 165
Point Village	113, 263, 266
see also: Willard	
Police Station	87-88
Pond Cove	33, 100, 153-155, 262-263, 270-271
Pond Cove Brook	34
Pond Cove House	153-154
Poor Farm	65, 97-98, 354-355
Popham. John	5
Portland, clipper ship	210
Portland Gale	226
Portland Head	47-48, 54, 223, 245
see also: Coast Watch Fort Williams	
Portland Head Light	130, 146, 224-230, 323
Portland Head. Battery at	
see: Fort Williams	
Portland Light Infantry	102
Portland Point	
see: Portland Head	
Portland Steam Packet Company	251
Post Office. Bowery Beach	113, 332
Post Office. Cape Cottage	160, 162, 332
Post Office. Cape Elizabeth	114
Post Office. Cape Elizabeth Depot	76
Post Office. Cape Elizabeth Ferry	87, 113
Post Office. Ferry Village	87, 113
Post Office. Pond Cove	332
Post Office. Pleasantdale	88
Post Office. South Portland	114
Post Office. Willard	113
Postal Service	54
Preble. Gen. Jedidiah	41
Presbyterians	38, 286-287, 289, 290
see also: Scots-Irish	
Price Control. Revolutionary War	47
Primary School. Pond Cove	273-274
see also: Grammer School. Pond Cove	
Privateers. Revolutionary War	47, 52
Privateers. War of 1812	171, 174-176
Province of Lygonia	21-22
Province of Maine	6-7, 16-17, 21, 23-25
Purchase. Thomas	19
Purse Seining	190-191
Purpoodock Club	344, 350-351
Purpooduck	27-36, 87, 114, 257-259, 284, 286, 288, 295
see also: Meeting House. Purpooduck	

Purpooduck Militia Company	44-46
Quakers	314
Queen Anne's War	31
Radio Station. U.S. Navy	242-243
Railroad Company. Cape Elizabeth	155-156
Railroad Company. Cape Elizabeth Shore	156
Railroad Company. Portland	156-157, 159, 161
Railroad Company. Portland, Saco and Portsmouth	68, 76
Randall. Joshua F.	217
Realty Company. Maine Coast	336-337
Realty Company. Portland	336
Realty Company. Suburban	334-335
Reed. Thomas B.	261
Reform School. State	264-265
Relief Station. Trundy's Reef	241-242
Religion	274-316
Revenue Cutter Service	240
Revolutionary War	45-50, 53, 168
see: Fort Hancock	
Nancy, schooner	
Reynolds. Edward C.	267
Ribero. Diego	1
Richmond, bark	13-15, 200-201
Richmond, ship	19, 201
Richmond. George	14, 200
Richmond's Island	1-4, 8-9, 28-29, 58, 74, 143, 155, 163, 193, 200-201, 236-237, 344
Richmond's Island Associates	155
Richmond's Island Plantation	10-21, 30, 165-167, 200-201, 276-277
Richmond's Island Roads	32, 193, 237
Richmond's Island Treasure	4-5, 74-76
Ridgeway	263, 270, 273
Rigby. Col. Alexander	20-23
Rigby Park	127-128
Ripley. Rev. Thomas B.	312
Riverside Cemetery	308-309, 354
Riverside Memorial Park	309
Road Maintainence	64
Robinson. Charles H.	269
Robinson. Francis	21
Robinson. Capt. John	167
Rolling Mill. Portland	88, 90-92, 102-103, 263
Roosevelt, steamer	219
Ross. John	137
Rum. Old Dart	175
Running Hill	263
St. John & Daniel Club	100
Salt Works	40
Samaritans. Ferry Village	113
Sand and Gravel Company. Portland	335
Sargent. Stephen	19, 201
Sawyer. Rev. Benjamin	298
Scarborough and Cape Elizabeth Fair	125-126
Schools	256-274
see also: Bayley. Robert	
Cushing. Loring	
Schools. Private	
see: Knights. S.C.	
Millett. S.C.	
School. Moving	257-260
School System. District	258-263, 271-273
Scots-Irish	32, 286-287
Scotland, brig	203
Sea Coast Company. Revolutionary War	46-47
Sea View House	154
Seal Cove	36, 141, 183, 199
see also: Bowery Beach	
Seaside Cemetery	64
Seaside Hall	100, 162
Sebago, steamer	212
Sebago Water	93, 112, 117-120, 337
Second Parish	
see: Falmouth. Second Parish of	
Secret Expedition	
see: Bagaduce Expedition	
Semeamis	2
Sentinel. Cape Elizabeth	104-105, 109, 111-112, 114, 117, 122-123
Seven Years War	38
Shallop	166
Ship Construction	205-208
Ship Cove	2, 139, 167, 201
see also: Fort Williams	
Shipbuilding Company. Portland	219
Shipwrecks	244-255
see also: **Annie C. Maguire**, bark	
Apollo, brig	
Australia, schooner	
Bay State, steamer	
Bohemian, steamer	
Charles, schooner	
D.W. Hammond, schooner	
Grand Turk, ship	
Isidore, bark	
Nancy, schooner	
Oakey L. Alexander, collier	
Shipyards	77, 205-208
see also: Brewer. Daniel	
Butler. Alford	
Butler. Cornelius B.	
Cahoon. James B.	
Dyer, Ezekiel	
Dyer. Joseph W.	
Dyer, Nathan	
Knight. Thomas E.	
Pickett. Benjamin W.	
Robinson. Capt. John	
Turner. George	
Shore Acres Land Company	341
Simonton. William	36-37, 167-168, 170, 201, 292, 295
Simonton's Cove	34, 37, 40, 50, 167-168, 183, 192, 251
Skunk Hill	
see: Thornton Heights	
Small Pox	48

Smith. Henry St. John	151
Smith. Francis O.J.	235, 238
Smith. Capt. John	2, 165
Smith. Rev. Thomas	34, 287-292
Smoking Tree	28
Snow. Rev. Benjamin P.	307
Snow Squall, clipper ship	213-215
Snowden. Rev. Samuel	309
Soldiers' and Sailors' Monument. Cape Elizabeth	114-115
Sons of America. Patriotic Order of the	101
South Congregational Church see: Meeting House, Spurwink	
South Portland	114, 118, 120, 122-123
South Portland. Town of	318-319
South Portland — Portland. Union of	318-319
Speedwell, ship	11
Sprague. Phineas W.	343-344, 349
Sprague Memorial Foundation. Phineas W.	350
Spring Point	27, 36, 47, 56
Spring Point Ledge	238
Spurwink	7, 17-18, 21, 27-34, 114, 257-258, 263, 270, 288, 295, 349
Spurwink Congregational Church see: Meeting House. Spurwink	
Spurwink Marshes	61, 93
Spurwink Militia Company	43
Spurwink River	7, 199
Squatters see: New Proprietors	
Squidrayset	3
Stamp Act	40
Stanford's Ledge	235
Stanwood. Franklin	150
Staples. Amelia D.	233, 247
Staples. Asbury	233
Staples. Charles W.	232-233, 247
Staples. Hiram	250
Staples. Michael	247
Stephenson.Albert	148-149
Stephenson. William H.	133, 148
Sterling. Robert T.	230
Stevens. John C.	151, 157
Stone Monument. Cape Elizabeth	230-231
Stone Sloops. Chebeague	235-236, 237
Stony Brook	149
Strout. "Billy"	229
Strout. Charles S.	228, 229
Strout. Joseph W.	227, 229-230, 251
Strout. Joshua F.	227-229, 251
Suburban Times	104
Sugar House. Portland	179
Summer Cottages	148-151, 154, 161-162
Sunnybank Cottage	151-152
Surplus Revenue	68
Tavern. Jane Woodbury's	50, 51
Taylor. Rev. Joshua	309
Taylor. Sam	125
Taylor's Reef	237
Temperance Reform Club	100

Temperance Watchmen Club	99
Temperance see also: Esty. Rev. Isaac Independent Order of Good Templars Washington Meeting	
Theatre. Cape	154, 157-160
Thomas Owen, brig	203
Thomas. William W.	114, 261, 349-350
Thompson. Fred	161
Thornton Heights	127, 350
Thorpe. Rev. John	278-280
Three Years War see: Governor Dummer's War	
Throat Distemper	290
Tide Mill. Knightville	92-93
Tiger, steam tug	210
Tories	47, 52
Tourists	129, 131-132, 138
see also: Canadian Tourists	
Town Hall. Cape Elizabeth	331
Town House. Cape Elizabeth (1837)	67-68, 95-96
Town House. Cape Elizabeth (1874)	96-97, 119, 266-267
Town House Corner	102, 114, 120
Town Manager	356
Treasure	74-76
Trelawny. Edward	276
Trelawny. John	22
Trelawny. Robert	8, 11-14, 16, 18, 20-23, 165-166, 200, 276
Trelawny. Samuel	22
Trelawny. Samuel P.	22
Trelawny and Goodyear Patent	8
Triumph, schooner	221-222
Trolley Lines	112, 155, 342
see also: Railroad Company. Cape Elizabeth Railroad Company, Cape Elizabeth Shore Railroad Co. Portland	
Trolley Park see: Cape Cottage Casino Theatre. Cape	
Trotting Park. Cape	79
Trundy. Capt. Horace G.	240-241
Trundy's Reef	189, 237-238, 241
Tucker. Richard	7-9, 13, 20-21
Turner. George W.	72, 107, 202
Turner's Island	68-69, 73, 88, 118, 120, 213, 215, 263, 266
Union Hall	102, 109, 112, 115, 123
Union Hearse Company	63-64
Vaill. Rev. Henry M.	307
Venerable Cunner Association and Propeller Club see: Cunner Club	
Veteran Soldiers' and Sailors' Association. Cape Elizabeth	333
Village Improvement Association. Cape Elizabeth	113
Vines. Richard	9, 12, 20-21

Walden. Capt. Green	149, 240, 249
Waldo. Samuel	39-40
Walker. Frederick	334, 343
Wallace, bark	212
War of 1812	57-58, 174-177
Warner, clipper ship	215
Washington B. Thomas, schooner	243
Washingtonian Meeting	100
Water Company. Portland	118
Water and Construction Company. Standish	119-120, 337
see also: Sebago Water	
Waterworth. Rev. John A.	308
Watts. Henry	24
Watts. John F.	225-226
Watt's Ledge	163, 237, 246
Webber. Samuel	284
Webster. Ebenezer, Jr.	304, 305
Weeks. Oliver	9
Welcome, ship	10
West India Trade	36-37, 166-168, 177-181
see also: Cushing. Col. Ezekiel Simonton. William Mariner. John	
Westbrook	73
Weymouth. Capt. George	5, 275
Whales	136
Whaling. Coastal	168
Wharf Point	37
Wheel Club. Portland	154
Wheelmen. Cape Elizabeth	113
White. John	34
White Sea, bark	210
Whitefield. Rev. George	290-291
Wildwood Club	162
Willard	116, 118, 120, 318
see also: Point Village	
Willard Beach	156
Willard Beach Casino	156-157
Willard. Capt. Benjamin J.	108, 188-189, 240
Willard. Capt. Simon	284
William III	25
Williams. James S.	226
Williams. Capt. Paul	32
Williams. Maj. Gen. Seth	324-325
Wind Mill. Colonial	40
Winter. John	9-10, 13-18, 20-23, 165-167, 200, 276-277
Winter. Mrs. John	13, 18
Winter. Sarah	13, 19
Winthrop. Gov. John	7, 20
Wireless Station. Cape Elizabeth	242-243
Witchcraft	278-279, 280-285
Wolves	41
Woodbury. Jane	
see: Tavern	
Woodbury. Joshua	33
York. Capt. Joseph H.	255
Yorkshire. County of	23-24
Zeb Cove	33, 221

www.ingramcontent.com/pod-product-compliance
Lightning Source LLC
Chambersburg PA
CBHW050832230426
43667CB00012B/1969